THE IMPERIAL GUIDE TO
FENG SHUI &
CHINESE ASTROLOGY

THE ONLY AUTHENTIC TRANSLATION
FROM THE ORIGINAL CHINESE

Thomas F. Aylward

WATKINS PUBLISHING

LONDON

Distributed in the USA and Canada by Sterling Publishing Co., Inc.
387 Park Avenue South, New York, NY 10016

This edition first published in the UK and USA 2007 by
Watkins Publishing, Sixth Floor, Castle House,
75–76 Wells Street, London W1T 3QH

1 3 5 7 9 10 8 6 4 2

Designed by Jerry Goldie
Typeset by Imagewrite

Printed and bound in Great Britain

Library of Congress Cataloging-in-Publication Data Available

ISBN 13: 978-1-84293-176-9
ISBN 10: 1-84293-176-8

www.watkinspublishing.com

For information about custom editions, special sales, premium and
corporate purchases, please contact Sterling Special Sales
Department at 800-805-5489 or specialsales@sterlingpub.com.

CONTENTS

Part II
The Imperially Authorized Treatise on Harmonizing Times and Distinguishing Directions

To my mentor, Professor Robert Eno of Indiana University, whose unsolicited call to a wavering graduate student in Taiwan convinced me to continue studying classical Chinese and in many ways changed the course of my life.

ACKNOWLEDGMENTS

I would like to begin my acknowledgments by thanking the person whose assistance contributed most to the effort that has resulted in this book – my wife, Kanokpan Lao-Araya. To be sure her love and encouragement sustained my spirits throughout the endeavor, but even more basic than this was the fact that she was gainfully employed and supported my involvement in a project that consumed my energies without promising any immediate financial recompense. I would also like to thank my son Francis and daughter Nora who both patiently accepted the circumstance of my being always at home but rarely their playmate. I will always cherish the three of you and am grateful for your support.

For reviewing and commenting on my introductory chapter, I would like to thank Professor Richard Smith of Rice University, Texas. Dr Smith generously and without hesitation agreed to assist me even though I was not a member of the formal academe – nor had I previously made his acquaintance. This selfless dedication to advancing research in spite of his own busy teaching and research commitments embodies the most praiseworthy characteristic of a scholar and teacher. Dr Smith's comments were numerous and invaluable and helped significantly to improve the accuracy of my Introduction.

My former classmate and friend Donald Durfee also volunteered to review the Introduction. Thanks to his professional editorial experience he was able to provide valuable insights on style and concision that helped me to tighten my prose and make the Introduction more easily understandable to the general reader. Don freely reviewed and commented on my manuscript while working as a full-time writer and editor and raising, with his wife, two young children. I am grateful for this contribution.

I owe many thanks to my sister and graphic designer, Tara Guild, who skillfully created all of the illustrations in this book. This task was especially daunting because the illustrations in the original were all labeled in Chinese, a language which she has never studied. Considering that she was also forced to create the illustrations by corresponding with me electronically half-way around the world, I am amazed by the quality of the results she produced.

Finally, I would like to express my deep appreciation to Michael Mann and

Penny Stopa at Watkins Publishing for their generous help and unflagging patience for a writer very new to the field of professional publishing. I am also extremely grateful to Shelagh Boyd who painstakingly edited my manuscript and saved me from making numerous errors in a subject area more novel to her than it is to me. Any errors remaining in the text are wholly my responsibility.

Hanoi, Vietnam
January 2006

Foreword

Much nonsense has been written about the Chinese practice known as *feng shui* (lit. wind and water; also translated 'geomancy,' 'siting' and so forth). But Mr Aylward's book, I am pleased to report, does not fall into this category. Quite the contrary, it provides an extremely valuable explanation of the sophisticated principles on which this pervasive (indeed transnational) social phenomenon is, and has long, been based. More than this, *The Imperial Guide to Feng Shui and Chinese Astrology* sheds useful light on a wide range of cosmologically grounded beliefs and practices that have been at the core of Chinese (also Japanese, Korean and Vietnamese) culture for hundreds, if not thousands, of years.

As Mr Aylward indicates in his carefully crafted Introduction, many of the ideas contained in the *Xieji bianfang shu* are either derived from, or very closely associated with, the ancient Chinese classic known as the *Yijing* or *Book of Changes*. It is no exaggeration to say that the *Changes* is the most significant single work in the entire Chinese cultural tradition. Having emerged in China about 3,000 years ago as an occult prognostication text, the *Yijing* eventually attained the status of a 'classic' in 136 BCE, and, as with the 'classics' of other major civilizations, East and West, the *Yijing* had a profound effect on Chinese culture throughout the imperial era (from 136 BCE to 1912 CE) in such diverse realms as language, philosophy, religion, art, literature, politics, social life, math, science and medicine.

Here is a description of the *Changes* by one of China's greatest intellectuals, Wang Fuzhi (1619–1692):

> [The *Yijing* is] the manifestation of the Heavenly Way, the
> unexpressed form of nature, and the showcase for sagely
> achievement. Yin and yang, movement and stillness, darkness
> and lightness, contraction and expansion – all are inherent in it.
> Spirit operates within it; the refined subtlety of ritual and music
> is stored in it; the great utility of humaneness and right behavior
> issues forth from it; and the calculation of order and disorder,
> good and bad fortune, life and death is in accordance with it.

The editors of the great eighteenth-century Chinese literary compilation known as the *Siku quanshu* (Complete Collection of the Four Treasuries) had this to say about the classic: 'The way of the *Changes* is broad and great. It encompasses everything, including astronomy, geography, music, military methods, the study of rhymes, numerical calculations, and even alchemy.'

So how, one might ask, does the *The Imperial Guide to Feng Shui and Chinese Astrology* shed light on the *Yijing* and its cultural legacy? If we examine carefully the sections of the *Xieji bianfang shu* that have been translated by Mr Aylward, we find full and illuminating discussions of virtually every major concept associated with the cryptic classic, from yin and yang, the Five Processes, the Eight Trigrams, and the Sixty-Four Hexagrams, to the Yellow River Chart, the Luo River Diagram, the Ten Heavenly Stems, the Twelve Earthly Branches, and the Twenty-Eight Lunar Lodges. Moreover, the *Xieji bianfang shu* reveals with remarkable clarity the way that these cosmic variables interact with one another and correlate with the seasons, the directions, musical notes, zodiacal signs and so forth.

For more than 2,000 years, Chinese scholars and professional diviners, including, of course, *fengshui* masters, have employed interpretive systems based on these variables to understand the nature of the phenomenal world and the patterns of change in the universe – past, present and future. These correlative systems, discussed at length in the *Xieji bianfang shu*, include Received Stems (*najia*), Received Notes (*nayin*), the Eight Palaces (*bagong*), and configurations of trigrams and hexagrams such as the Former Heaven (*xiantian*) and Latter Heaven (*houtian*) Sequences. Among the individuals associated with the creation or refinement of these systems are such famous and influential figures in Chinese history as Dong Zhongshu (c.179–c.104 BCE), Jing Fang (77–37 BCE), Guan Lu (c.210–256), Chen Tuan (d.989), Shao Yong (1011–77), Lai Zhide (1525–1604), Fang Yizhi (1611–1671), and Jiang Yong (1681–1762).

Listen to what Jiang has to say about cosmic correlations:

> The Yellow River Chart, the Luo River Diagram, trigrams and
> hexagrams, and individual lines all emanate from the same
> source, [they reflect] common trends, and are mutually
> interactive; hence, concepts such as *gougu* [a traditional system
> of triangulation] and *chengfang* ['mutiplication squares'] in
> mathematics, the five sounds and six notes [*wuyin liulü*] in
> music, the positions of the Seven Heavenly Bodies [*qiyao*] in
> astrology [*tianwen*], the Received Stem and Received Note
> systems of Five Processes Specialists, the resonant and pure
> consonants in phonetics, the Principles and Vital Breaths of the
> geomancers' compass, the *doushou* and *qimen* methods of the
> 'day-selection' experts, and even the foundations and principles
> of medicine –including the five movements and six 'breaths' of
> heaven and the veins of the human body – all emanate from the
> Yellow River Chart, the Luo River Diagram, trigrams,
> hexagrams, and lines.

Jiang goes on to argue that the degrees of the celestial sphere, the zodiacal signs,
and the Twenty-Four Seasonal Nodes had their origins in the Yellow River Chart
and the Luo River Diagram. So did mathematical harmonics and the pitch pipe,
which Jiang linked with standard units of length, capacity, weight and even
money.

With the fall of the Qing dynasty in 1912, such cosmologically grounded
ways of looking at the world lost favor among many Chinese intellectuals, in
part because they lost standing in the eyes of the 'modern' Republic. Yet they
still informed popular almanacs, popular divinatory practices and traditional Chinese medicine, as they do to this day. In fact, a recent survey
conducted by the Ethnology Research Institute of Taiwan's Academia Sinica
revealed that 83 per cent of the families in Taiwan have a copy of at least one
traditional-style almanac. Of the respondents, 69 per cent reported that
almanacs are 'very necessary' or 'necessary' to the conduct of their affairs and
only 19 per cent felt that they were 'not too necessary.' Although I know of
no comparable figures for contemporary Hong Kong, my guess is that the
percentage of almanacs owned, as well as the percentage of owners who find
them necessary in their daily lives, is at least as high. I suspect that one

might find similarly high levels of belief in *fengshui* in both environments.

Thus, *The Imperial Guide to Feng Shui and Chinese Astrology* not only provides us with a valuable window on the past, but it also allows us to understand more fully the remarkable tenacity of inherited beliefs and practices. I congratulate Mr Aylward on this achievement.

Richard J Smith
Rice University

PART I

TRANSLATOR'S INTRODUCTION

CHAPTER ONE

The Importance of Cosmology, Calendars, and Divination in Imperial China

The art of divination may not be unique to China, but it is difficult to imagine China without it. For more than 2,000 years this traditional art has been woven tightly into China's political and social fabric. Chinese emperors employed it when determining when to go to war or when to sue for peace. Ordinary Chinese relied on it when choosing when to plant and harvest, or schedule other important events such as weddings and funerals. Millions of people continue to practice this art to this day.

One of the most important forms of divination in China is a combination of astrology and geomancy, which I refer to as 'the art of scheduling and position-ing.' This art is predicated on the belief that the purpose of human existence is to act harmoniously with the flow of time and position oneself symmetrically within the stillness of space. A basic example of this is the knowledge that one should plant in spring and harvest in autumn and orient one's residence south-ward to absorb the warmth of the sun. According to the practitioners of this art, by studying the movements of the stars and planets and the patterns of the earth's physical features, we can discover when and where to act in all situations.

The Chinese state adopted the art of scheduling and positioning as imperial orthodoxy during the third century BCE. From the founding of the empire in 221 BCE until its collapse in 1911 CE, the state continuously employed professional diviners and sanctioned official texts about their art. There was a simple reason for the state's interest: the Chinese believed that the universe communicated its assessment of the emperor's performance through astral and terrestrial portents – portents that masters in the art of scheduling and positioning specialized in interpreting. Consequently, it was in the emperor's interest to carefully monitor the production of texts about this art and its tools, notably the calendar and the compass.

Throughout the imperial era, the state continually systematized and modified aspects of orthodoxy to serve imperial interests. Notably, the state incorporated astronomical advances from the West in the ninth and eighteenth centuries following the arrival in China of Indian Buddhists and European missionaries, respectively. These astronomical advances in turn influenced Chinese astrology. At the same time, however, popular cosmological theories and divinatory practices arose at the grass roots, which at times competed with and contradicted orthodox teachings. The state monitored these extra-orthodox traditions, incorporating elements that served its interests while banning others. As a result, the late-imperial version of orthodox cosmology and official divination were products of a long-running dialectic between official and popular proponents of those ideas and practices.

It was during the Qing dynasty (1644–1911 CE) that Emperor Qianlong (r.1736–1796 CE) had the last official word in this 2,000-year dialogue. In 1740 the emperor commissioned the *Treatise on Harmonizing Times and Distinguishing Directions* (hereafter the 'Treatise'), to reconcile disagreements among specialists concerning the correct methods for selecting times and orientations. By publishing this work, the emperor satisfied an important obligation: to rectify calendrical and geographic practices upon inheriting the mantle of state. Beyond this, the Treatise fit into a larger literary initiative that Emperor Qianlong had mandated, which sought to collect, assess, catalogue, and preserve every important book ever written in China.

The emperor assigned the work of compiling the treatise to scholar officials within the Bureau of Astronomy, a subunit of the powerful Board of Ritual. In compiling the Treatise, the officials began by summarizing the basic outlines of official cosmology. They also sought to incorporate every important document ever written on the art of scheduling and positioning and to pronounce authoritatively which methods were correct. The final text of the Treatise, therefore, came to be considered the official reference manual for imperial diviners and almanac makers. None of China's remaining six emperors would ever again attempt such a feat. The collapse of the Qing in 1911 CE marked the end of official state sponsorship of the art of scheduling and positioning and traditional cosmology in China. Consequently, the Treatise is widely regarded by both modern scholars and practitioners of the art of scheduling and positioning as the magnum opus of late-imperial Chinese cosmology.

The Chinese art of scheduling and positioning shaped the very core of traditional culture and philosophy. In contrast with the West, divination in China was considered neither supernatural nor superstitious. The information with which the art dealt was thought to derive from the natural universe itself and not from a transcendent power. Furthermore the art of scheduling and positioning played an integral part in state orthodoxy. Whenever the imperial bureaucracy did prohibit divinatory practices, such as the use of unofficial almanacs, the objective was not to stamp out superstition or heterodoxy. On the contrary, the throne was concerned about reserving for itself the right to engage in such sanctioned practices. The prohibited aspects of the art of scheduling and positioning were not inherently illicit; they were rather an imperial prerogative.

Throughout Chinese history the art of scheduling and positioning was not considered a mere dry court ritual, but had a place in virtually every aspect of life. Before consenting to an arranged marriage, parents would (and some still do) compare the eight characters of the bride's and groom's birth times to see if the two were well matched. Fortune-tellers were consulted for advice about illnesses both physical and mental. Farmers consulted almanacs to identify auspicious times for planting and harvesting. Generals sought similar advice about when to engage the enemy. The *Book of Changes* (*Yijing*), which supplied much of the source material for the art, was China's ultimate divination manual. It was a central text in the Confucian canon and was highly revered both as a book of philosophy and as an oracle. Many of China's elite consulted the *Book of Changes* on a daily basis. The language and imagery of this one book alone can be traced throughout Chinese literature and art. Considering the strength and prevalence of the traditional Chinese passion for divination, it is hardly surprising that the *Treatise on Harmonizing Times and Distinguishing Directions* should have assumed the great importance that it did.

This book is a translation of the imperial foreword and introductory chapters of the Treatise. The foreword summarizes the history of the art of scheduling and positioning and describes the importance of this tradition to the world of its compilers, the Chinese Empire of the eighteenth century. The first introductory chapter defines the foundational theories of cosmology and time-space divination and then summarizes the methods for selecting auspicious times. The second introductory chapter summarizes the methods for selecting auspicious positions and orientations. These chapters bridge the gap between general cosmological theories – such as yin/yang, Five Processes, and eight trigrams – and the specific divinatory practices of selecting times and orientations. Few works available in English address this important connection.

This translation covers only the first two chapters of the Treatise, which constitute around 15 per cent of the entire work. The first chapter discusses overarching cosmological principles as well as the specific principles governing the chronological, or heaven-focused, determinants of fortune. The second chapter describes the spatial, or earth-focused, determinants of fortune. The remainder of the Treatise consists of charts designed to help specialists appropriately place the gods and demons of times and orientations in the day charts of almanacs.

Overview of Chinese Cosmology

To fully understand the art of scheduling and positioning we must consider it within the context of traditional Chinese cosmology. Cosmology is a system of knowledge that describes the order of the universe in terms of its major constituent physical objects and temporal processes. It attempts to describe how the universe originated, how it is structured, and how it functions. Before the institution of the empire, during the classical period of Chinese philosophy, several different versions of cosmology existed. However, during China's first and second imperial dynasties, the Qin (221 BCE–206 BCE) and the Han (206 BCE–220 CE), the state recognized an official cosmology that was a synthesis of several earlier systems. From that time onward the official divinatory art of scheduling and positioning was inextricably linked to the theories of this orthodox cosmological synthesis.

The following is a summary of the most complete early cosmology, which appears in the mid-second-century BCE *Huainanzi*. In a time before time, all was chaos. Out of chaos evolved space and time. Space and time produced vital breath (*qi*). Vital breath separated; that which was clear and bright arose and first formed heaven, after which the congealing of that which was heavy and muddled formed earth. Heaven and earth produced yang and yin. Yang and yin produced the four seasons. The four seasons produced the myriad things (i.e. all things on earth). The hot vital breath of yang gathered to produce fire. The essence of fire became the sun. The cold vital breath of yin gathered to produce water. The essence of water became the moon. The remainder of the essences of sun and moon produced the stars. Heaven received the sun, moon, stars, and planets. Earth received rain, floods, dust, and dirt. After the formation of civilization, two mythical beings, Gong Gong and Zhuan Xu, battled one another to become emperor. In their fight they crashed into and shattered the Not-Circling Mountain, which was the northwest of the eight pillars that held heaven in its position above earth. Consequently, heaven tilted in the northwest as did the sun, moon, stars and planets. Also, earth sank in the southeast, towards which inclined waters and earth. A great flood ensued.

This cosmology consists of three phases: chaos, the formation of perfect cosmos, and the disruption of the perfect cosmic order. Historical time commences with this last phase and the act of disruption represents the cause of imperfection in our universe and, therefore, the quintessential problem of human existence. In practical terms the story of this mythical battle explains a major astronomical asymmetry, i.e. the tilting of the earth's axis. It is because of this tilt that the orbit of the sun through the fixed stars of the sky (the ecliptic) differs from the plane of the earth's equator projected onto the dome of stars (the celestial equator). We must assume that the ancient astronomers were considerably bothered by this asymmetrical non-coincidence of ecliptic and equator. They believed that it was proper for the sun to take the same path through the sky as that which was drawn by the earth's equator. The great cataclysmic flood of Chinese mythology is also attributed to the same event.

This catastrophe did not only have abstract astronomical significance. In fact, it is the very non-coincidence of ecliptic and equator that define the solstices and equinoxes and therefore the four seasons. The furthest point that the sun reaches below the equator is the winter solstice. The furthest point north is the summer solstice. The points at which the sun crosses the equator are the spring and autumn equinoxes. Ironically, the cosmology appears to indicate that the four seasons were formed prior to the great battle. The important thing to take from this story, however, is that the advocates of this cosmology clearly saw in this astronomical asymmetry a significant problem, which this myth sought to explain.

What the story fails to state explicitly, we can infer from Chinese mythology: human society existed before this cosmic battle. The contestant Zhuan Xu occupies a place in the roster of mythical Chinese emperors. He followed the inventors of the tools of civilization such as Shen Nong and Fu Xi, and was the third emperor after the legendary first claimant to the title, the renowned Huang Di or Yellow Emperor. After the death of Zhuan Xu's own successor, the mantle was transferred to Emperor Yao, the first of the Confucian sage emperors. Thus we see that a golden age of civilization was believed to have preceded the great battle. The destruction of the celestial northwest pillar had many ramifications. Throwing the earth's axis off kilter would obviously have created new challenges for astronomically based calendars. The flooding of the lands also demanded a herculean response from mankind. These were the challenges that confronted and were overcome by the legendary sage emperors Yao, Shun, and Yu: reforming the calendar and regulating floods. Their imperial actions re-established, for a time, the primordial, harmonious balance between heaven and earth, that is harmony of time and space.

From this Chinese story of genesis we can extract a schematic model of traditional cosmology. In the beginning all was chaos. From this chaos developed space and time, which constituted the two unique elements of the universe but which were inseparable. This pair generated a long series of correlates of themselves. Time produced clear and light vital breath, heaven, yang, fire, the sun and so forth. Space produced turbid and heavy vital breath, earth, yin, water, the moon, etc. The harmonious coexistence of yang and yin also produced seasons and the various objects, flora, and fauna of the world. Men existed in this ordered universe, but through man's fault, the perfect balance between heaven's harmonious time and earth's symmetrical space was in a very physical way disturbed but not completely destroyed.

Though certain themes in this Chinese myth resemble elements of Western cosmology, the contrasts are even more striking. We observe in the Chinese cosmology an emphasis on immanence as opposed to transcendence. There is no divine creator outside of the cosmic system. The universe it describes is organic. It grows of itself from a germ, and all of its parts are formed as if by cellular division or copulation. The act that creates man's dilemma affects not just man but everything in the cosmos. The flaw of the act was not that man disobeyed a transcendent, divine law and it did not result in man being expelled from paradise. Instead, the problem was that man disturbed a natural state of order of which he formed a part and in which he participated. The supreme entity in this cosmology is the universe itself. Man does not exist in isolation from the rest of the cosmos and therefore his action actually and physically harms heaven and earth. He is not expelled from paradise, but rather his act makes paradise imperfect. Both man and cosmos are forever after forced to live in the disorder that man created – a very environmentally conscious cosmology. Incidentally, this great calamity was wrought by males and the only woman who played a role in the cosmology was the goddess Nü Gua who eventually repaired the damage to the cosmic pillar caused by the two male combatants.

The *Huainanzi* cosmogony describes a process in which the indivisible, abstract concepts of space and time produce a concrete vital breath that is divisible. The vital breath bifurcates into heaven and earth, which in turn produce yang and yin. These processes of division followed by reproduction, or of reproduction followed by division, repeat themselves until the ordered cosmos is fully formed. In each stage of the process the cosmos reproduces itself in the form of ever finer microcosms. The more abstract and inseparable concepts of space and time are manifest more concretely as heaven and earth, and yin and yang. Yin and yang either copulate to produce a new microcosm that contains aspects of both parents or they separately replicate themselves. Whenever one individually produces something new, however, its counterpart also produces a new entity so that the two new products, considered together, form a balanced microcosm. An example of this is yang fire producing the sun, which is balanced by yin water producing the moon.

Each microcosm in the universe is either spatial (earth/yin) or temporal (heaven/yang), but in perfect symmetry each temporal microcosm is correlated with a spatial counterbalance. For example, yin and yang produce the four seasons (temporal): autumn and winter are yin; spring and summer are yang. In space these four seasons are correlated with the four directions. West and north, being yin, correlate with autumn and winter, respectively. East and south, being yang, correlate with spring and summer, respectively.

According to a metaphor of the *Huainanzi*, components of the various microcosms that are of the same cosmic class stimulate and respond to one another (*gan ying*) as the roots and branches of a plant. This connection is hierarchical. The roots correspond with the top of the hierarchy and the stems with the bottom. Heaven is the root of the yang, and earth the root of the yin aspects of each microcosm. Since all things of a kind are connected, an influence on a thing of one kind in one microcosm will affect all things of that kind in every other microcosm. However, influences on the roots tend to have a greater carry-on effect on the branches than vice versa. Within each microcosm there should be a balance between yin and yang. Therefore, the regular rhythms of heaven's times should balance with the symmetrical dimensions of earth's directions. If the moon were to gain ascendance over the sun, then this imbalance to the detriment of yang would negatively affect every manifestation of yang in the universe.

Correlating cosmos to the human body as a microcosm provided another way of interpreting each of the generations of microcosms produced during cosmic gestation. The head, being round and above, was correlated to heaven. The feet below were correlated to earth (imagining the two feet standing slightly apart and parallel to each other to form a square). The heart – for Chinese, the center of both thought and emotion – corresponded to the circumpolar stars, especially the Big Dipper. The eyes correlated to sun and moon, and so on. Some early stories of the cosmogony even describe the formation of the universe out of the body parts of a primordial giant – Pan Gu. Equipped with the body as a ubiquitous and elemental model whose organs were correlated to the parts of the universe, Chinese thinkers were able to work out correlations among every microcosm between the greater cosmos and the self.

At the core of these correlations we see that the same vital breath gives form to and animates both the cosmos and the body. In its dynamic aspect, this vital breath flows through the body like an invisible blood system. In the same way, heaven's vital breath flows in the movements of heavenly bodies. In the earth, it courses through the landscape like a network of underground rivers, sometimes nearing the surface, at other times diving deep below. Traditional Chinese medicine studies the ideal flow and irregular blockages of vital breath in the body. Daoist medical practices seek to coordinate the flow of vital breath in the individual human body with the vital breath of heavenly bodies. Chinese astrology studies the flow of vital breath in the movement of stars and planets and the art of *feng shui* examines the flow of vital breath in the earth's surface.

On the societal level, the body politic also constituted an important microcosm. The emperor correlated with the celestial pole – the axis of heaven. Moving outward in this celestial analogy, the empress and various close ministers corresponded with stars near the pole. The stars in the circumpolar region, that constantly remains above the horizon, formed the emperor's palace. The stars that lie along the celestial equator corresponded with the regions of the empire that lay in the four cardinal directions. In correlating the various micro-

cosms, ancient Chinese cosmologists did not forget the most important institution in Chinese culture, the family. Thus, father and mother were equated with
heaven and earth. As head of the family the father corresponded with the pole
of the heavens, emperor of the state, and heart of the body.

The correlation between cosmos and body extended the import of cosmology
from beyond the imperial palace to every human being. True, the emperor was
to society what the celestial pole was to the rest of the heavens. However, within
each human being the heart also stood as a perfect correlate to the axis of heaven.
Thus, on the celestial level of cosmos, the pole stars governed the movement
of the celestial dome. On the societal level, the emperor governed the people.
On the familial level, the father governed the family. On the personal level, the
human heart/mind governed the person. Consequently, the imperial obligation
to respect heaven's times and earth's directions extended to every other
human being.

Considering only the division of universe into yin and yang, the system might
not seem that difficult to comprehend, but the cosmologists applied several other
systems of categorization. Second in importance to yin and yang is the group
known as the Five Processes. The four directions and the center were correlated
with the Five Processes, and so symmetrically were the four seasons, plus a fifth
(see below). As the universe split into increasingly complex divisions, finer sets
of categories were generated. Beyond yin-yang and the Five Processes there were
groups of eight (trigrams), twelve (zodiacal constellations), twenty-four (solar
nodes and spatial directions), etc. Complicating matters almost infinitely
beyond this, the various groups of categories were also correlated with each
other in numerous ways.

Stepping back from this dizzying list of categories, we turn to the question
of man's position within the greater cosmos. The ancient cosmologists
believed that man occupied a pivotal position in the universe exactly between
the two great cosmic spheres of heaven and earth. Mankind was considered
the most important of the myriad things moving under the round umbrella of
heaven's times and resting above the square expanse of earth's space. The most
important of men was the emperor, known as the Son of Heaven. Within the
microcosm of human society, the emperor stood at the center. He corresponded with the celestial pole of heaven, the point in the sky which is
unmoved and around which revolves the rest of the stellar dome. Time was
defined with reference to the counterclockwise revolutions of the sun, moon,
and planets, and to the clockwise revolutions of the zodiacal signs and lunar

lodges. As the axis of all these motions, the celestial pole provided the ultimate reference point for all time measures. Interestingly enough, the axis of the earth did not lie in the center of the country that called itself the Middle Kingdom, i.e. China, but instead lay on Mount Kunlun somewhere in the west, northwest, or north.[1]

Traditionally, Chinese explained the relationship between the three realms of cosmos by analogy with the character for 'king' (*wang*), which contains three parallel horizontal lines connected by one central vertical line. The three horizontal lines were said to represent heaven, earth, and man, and the vertical line was analogized to the monarch. According to the political theory of the Mandate of Heaven, when the supreme ruler occupied his throne and behaved in accordance with the dictates of heaven, the universe would enjoy a state of harmony and the dynasty would flourish. By the same token, the emperor's failure to behave properly would throw the universe into disorder and bring about dynastic collapse. As the central plane between heaven and earth, mankind played a vital role in the cosmos. The function of man was to accord with and to participate in the cosmic balance between heaven's rhythmic motions and earth's symmetrical stillness. As the axis running through the realms of heaven, earth, and man, the emperor existed to effect order both within the microcosm of human society and among the three realms of macrocosm.

From Mythical to Historical Time

Emperors Yao, Shun, and Yu, the Confucian sage emperors, set the standard for all later emperors in respecting heaven's times and earth's directions. In the tales of their reigns recorded in the *Book of Documents* (*Shang shu*), we see that each emperor, upon ascending the throne, appointed ministers to rectify time measures and personally went or sent deputies out to survey the realm. The modern reader might consider these efforts rational ends that need not be questioned, but in order to understand the full meaning of these emperors' actions, we must consider how they intended to use this information.

From the beginning of Chinese history, regulating the calendar was considered to be one of the most important imperial acts.[2] In a vast agrarian society, proper maintenance of the calendar is of paramount importance since it ensures that crops are planted and harvested at the right times. Once the decentralized political structure of early China was replaced with a more centralized bureaucratic structure, a well-regulated calendar became even more important since it enabled the state to coordinate bureaucratic actions. From a religious perspective, an accurate calendar also enabled the state to schedule rituals at the proper times. Maintaining the calendar did a great deal to legitimize the state's power.

In addition to facilitating the agricultural, bureaucratic, and ritual functions of the Chinese government, calendars were intimately related to the practice of divination. We see evidence of this relationship in China's earliest written records, the oracle bones of the Shang dynasty (c.1500–c.1045 BCE). Some oracle bones bear inscriptions of questions posed to ancestral spirits about auspicious times for performing a certain act. The concern implicit in such questions presages what was to become a central tenet of the Confucian philosophy that was adopted as orthodoxy during the Han dynasty (206 BCE–220 CE). This concept can be rendered in English as 'timeliness,' and it refers to the virtue of being able to perform the correct action at the correct time.[3] Enabling individuals to realize the virtue of timeliness was one of the main functions of divination in China from the earliest times, as the oracle bone inscriptions attest. In order to help divine about timely behavior, fortune-tellers enlisted calendars as one of their primary tools.

Perhaps the most important application of calendrical and geographical knowledge was in the area of ritual practice. During the formation of orthodox cosmology several ritual texts were in circulation that described the behavior of the emperor that was appropriate for the twelve months of the year, e.g. the 'Monthly Ordinances' (Yue ling) chapter of the Record of Rites (Li ji). The main ideas of these texts are basically the same. The emperor possesses a hall of nine chambers arranged like a tic-tac-toe grid. For each month of the year, the emperor moves to occupy a new chamber. In some schemes three chambers are each used for two consecutive months, in others the final month of each season is spent in the central chamber. As he moves from chamber to chamber, the emperor adopts behavior appropriate to the Five Processes correlate of the month in question. Certain observances remain the same for all three months of one season, while other observances change monthly. The emperor adopts clothing, carriages, cereals, meats, sacrifices, demeanors, etc. in accordance with these ritual regulations.

In observing these monthly ordinances, the emperor emulates the clock-like motion of the handle of the Big Dipper which was one of the most important groups of stars in Chinese astrology. Each month, the handle of the Dipper points to one of twelve different directions on the earth's surface. Because the Dipper is one of the circumpolar constellations that never fall below the horizon in northern latitudes, it is associated with the axis of the sky and with the emperor as the axis of men. In moving from chamber to chamber and resting during each month in one chamber, the emperor follows harmoniously the temporal motions of heaven's constellations and remains at rest in symmetry with the spatial stillness of earth's directions. Heaven remains constantly in motion (yang) while earth is eternally still (yin). Between the two, the emperor alternately moves and remains at rest. By this combination of motion and stillness, the emperor actually conjoins and balances heaven's dynamic/time and earth's static/space. His ritual behavior is not merely an imitation of heaven and earth. It is a necessary condition for their harmonious coexistence.

The emperor's various monthly observances stimulate and respond not only to the cosmic forces of yin and yang, but also to the Five Processes, to the Twelve Earthly Branches (i.e. twelve directions), etc. According to these various categories, different emotional states and types of activities are appropriate for each of the four/five seasons and twelve months of the year. Spring is a time of sowing and, therefore, it is appropriate then to be kind and grant favors. By contrast, fall is a time of harvesting, so the emperor should be stern and execute punishments and conduct punitive military expeditions. It was fervently believed that performing an action that was in discord with the dictates of the season would harm the cosmic order and call down a negative reaction. This form of reasoning is sometimes described as 'sympathetic magic.'

According to Chinese cosmology, it is nature that indicates what makes a given time or orientation appropriate for a specific action. There is less emphasis on whether a given action is absolutely right or wrong, and more emphasis on what is the relatively appropriate time or place for an action. If an action is in harmony with the dictates of the various categories (yin/yang, Five Processes, etc.) that correspond to one point in the cycles of time, then the time is right. If that action will also occur in a position that is in symmetry with the applicable categories of space, then the orientation is also correct.

Underlying and animating this entire cosmic system is vital breath, or *qi*, which is conceived of as both energy and matter. Since it formed heaven and earth, yin and yang, and the rest of the universe, vital breath is the medium through which the correlated parts of each microcosm communicate their mutual stimulation and response. Vital breath constitutes both the material form and the animating principle of objects and events and so the correlation of things

13

in the universe includes both animate and inanimate objects. Consideration is given not only to living beings that move in time – motion in time represents yang and heaven; but also to inanimate objects that rest in space – stillness in space represents yin and earth. This way of viewing the universe is quite different from Western traditions.

Understanding the Chinese view of the relationship between animate and inanimate helps us to understand why it is not only timing of actions that matters, but also positioning and orientation in space. This also helps to explain why Chinese place such great emphasis on the timing of funerals and placement of graves. Vital breath pertains not only to the living but also to the dead (obviously the choice of 'vital' in translating this term sounds odd here but it does reflect a seeming contradiction in Chinese as well). The members of a family all share a great deal of the same vital breath. When a relative dies, his or her inanimate remains retain some of the same vital breath that continues to reside in his or her survivors. Therefore, the way we handle and inter a relative's remains will affect the vital breath of the deceased and by relation will also have an effect on our own vital breath and life.

Although both animate (yang, motion, time) and inanimate (yin, stillness, space) were important in the art of scheduling and positioning, time clearly took precedence over space. In the cosmology we have been discussing, vital breath was produced by space-and-time. The natures of space and time, of stillness and motion, were inherent throughout this vital breath. When vital breath itself bifurcated to form heaven and earth, it was heaven, the temporal aspect, that first completed its development. Being prior, heaven and, by extension, yang were considered superior to and dominant over earth and yin. In practice, this predominance of time over space manifests itself in the fact that the flow of time determines what direction will be auspicious or inauspicious. One could say that the movement of time causes a change in the lucky/unlucky charge of space.

We also know from the orthodox tradition that the process of vital-breath separation was never complete or absolute. Consequently, within heavenly vital breath there exists an aspect of earthly vital breath, and vice versa. Since the rest of the universe was formed by a continual replication of this process, all things contain within themselves some genetic material of their opposites. Furthermore, since things of a kind harmonize with each other, the yin aspect of heaven harmonizes with earth and the yang aspect of earth harmonizes with heaven. Therefore, although yang (time) takes precedence over yin (space), the two are in a sense genetically related and each must harmonize with the part of itself that inheres in its opposite.

It is the harmonious resonance among the various divisions of time and space that governs the art of scheduling and positioning. As we have seen, among the seasons of time, fall and winter are yin, but spring and summer are yang. In the time of a day, noon through midnight is yin, and midnight through noon is yang. In terms of space, west and north are yin while east and south are yang. To determine when and where to conduct an action, one considers how the action is classified and then matches its classification with an appropriate time and place. Granting rewards is a yang action and thus correlates with day, spring, and the direction east. Punishing crimes is a yin action and so correlates with night, fall, and the direction west. From this very generalized example, we see that it is the movements of time that determine which direction will be appropriate for any given action.

What made the art of scheduling and positioning far more complex than the example just given was both the variety of categories that had to be taken into consideration and the complexity of Chinese time measures. We have already mentioned the number of cosmic categories – yin/yang, Five Processes, eight trigrams, etc. – and these will be described in detail below. Many readers will have heard that the Western concept of time is linear but that Chinese conceive of time as cyclical. True though this is, the statement hardly reveals how complex the Chinese system is. Since early in the imperial period, Chinese employed four major cycles for reckoning time. Each cycle employed a sixty-unit sequence (the sexagenary cycle – *see below*), but the duration of the units in each cycle differed. The four cycles individually identified the year, month, day, and hour. The sexagenary cycle's terms were themselves comprised of one member each taken from two different cycles, one of ten units (Heavenly Stems) and one of twelve units (Earthly Branches). Each of the Heavenly Stems and Earthly Branches were categorized as either yin or yang. The stems and branches were also individually correlated with the Five Processes and other categories. In addition, the composite units of the sexagenary cycle also had their own correlates among the various cosmological categories.

In confronting this extremely complex divinatory system, the average Chinese could avail of two important resources. First there was the general rule that larger divisions took precedence over the smaller, which helped to simplify matters greatly. For example it was right to plant in spring directing worship to the east and to harvest in fall directing worship to the west, and everyone knew that it was generally auspicious to orient one's home to the south. Second was the fact that, when matters got trickier one could always resort to a handy almanac or consult a practitioner of the art of scheduling and positioning. The information provided, by almanac or specialist, enabled people to find minute exceptions to the general regulations by taking advantage of the daunting complexities inherent in the system. Thus, if it were necessary to cut down trees or punish criminals in the spring (actions appropriate to fall), a correct time and orientation could be found to allow such actions.

Specialists and almanacs were able to indicate exceptions to the general seasonal and directional rules by considering the finer cycles of time, i.e. month, day, and hour, and directions of space – divisions into eight, twelve, or twenty-four directions. These micro-time cycles and micro-directional divisions influence and modify the general conditions for scheduling and positioning that derive from the four seasons of the year and four cardinal directions. For the specialist to accurately determine what is proper, it is necessary to consider and reconcile all of the cosmic correlations among time cycles and divisions of space. The next section of this Introduction provides greater detail about the workings of the art.

CHAPTER TWO

Understanding the Art of Scheduling and Positioning

The art of scheduling and positioning described in the Treatise combines aspects of astrology and geomancy. This is born out in the title of the work, which in Chinese is *xie-ji bian-fang shu* (*shu* simply means book). The verbs *xie* and *bian*, which I have translated as 'to harmonize' and 'to distinguish,' indicate the act of first gathering together items that are scattered and then setting them in order, or in other words 'rectifying.' In this case, the things rectified are the divinatory traditions relating to the two nominal elements *ji* and *fang* or 'periods of time' and 'directions.' The imperial introduction and overall structure of the work demonstrate clearly that these terms refer to the arts of setting actions and objects in time and space so as to derive maximum benefit from the natural rhythms of the universe.

The type of astrology and *feng shui* described in the Treatise is remarkably formulaic. Any divinatory pronouncement based on the Treatise derives solely from the methodical application of rules that are explicitly defined in the text. This contrasts sharply with other divinatory systems both in China and the West that might be characterized as 'intuitive.' Intuitive divinatory systems base their recommendations on the enigmatic power of the diviner's mind. Although a concern with scheduling and positioning is evidenced in China as early as the Shang dynasty, astrology and *feng shui* did not assume the rule-based form exemplified by the Treatise until the Zhou dynasty (1045–221 BCE). The incipient forms of the art of scheduling and positioning were much more intuitive. Although certain Western astrological traditions may also be characterized as legalistic, the theory of time upon which they are based distinguishes them from the Chinese art of scheduling and positioning. Both traditions posit that predictions about the auspices of a time can be calculated methodically, but Western astrology assumes a continually and lineally progressing theory of time. As we have seen, Chinese cosmology assumes a flow of time that is more repetitive than it is progressive.

In the West, astrology is generally understood as the art of studying the movements of the sun, moon, and planets through the zodiacal signs in order to make predictions about the effects of these movements on human affairs. Although this accurately describes certain aspects of the Chinese art, readers should keep in mind that astrology in China entails significant additional elements that have no correlates in Western astrology. Geomancy refers to the art of divining by signs from the earth, a practice that does exist in the West but which is extremely obscure. Since the Chinese geomantic art of *feng shui* is becoming increasingly popular in the West, the term *feng shui* will be used rather than geomancy throughout this work.

The origins of Chinese astrology and *feng shui* lie buried in China's prehistoric lore. The practice of consulting ancestors and gods to select appropriate days for royal actions is documented in China's oldest written records – Shang dynasty (before 1000 BCE) oracle bone inscriptions. These inscriptions evidence the custom of divining lucky times, but the nature of this primitive form of divination is significantly different from the astrology described in the present work. Divining to select appropriate times during the Shang was left to the whim of the spiritual entity consulted and to the intuitive interpretation of the diviner. By contrast the fully formed system of time selection described in the Treatise is systematic, rule-based, and predictable.

The origins of this regularized system of Chinese astrology, and indeed of *feng shui*, roughly coincide with the birth of the Chinese Empire. The system contrasts somewhat with Western astrology, which might be said to emphasize the unique and ever-changing nature of the heavenly phenomena that determine a person's fate. Chinese astrology, however, tends to stress that the flow of cosmic forces through time produce a regular and predictable cycle of good and bad luck that people can know and to which we are morally obliged to attune ourselves. Elements of this understanding of the universe were formulated by Chinese philosophers during the latter half of the Zhou dynasty (1045–256 BCE) and were later adopted into official state orthodoxy during the Han (206 BCE–220 CE).

Although one might argue that the regular patterns observable in Shang dynasty burial sites suggest a nascent Chinese belief in the significance of positioning graves, prototypes of the late-imperial form of *feng shui* are not clearly documented before the Zhou dynasty. However, the important *feng shui* concept of *Taisui* or counter-Jupiter, which is described fully in the Treatise, is already documented in the *Huainanzi* (mid-second century BCE). The *Huainanzi* essentially states that it is considered lucky to have the direction of *Taisui* to one's back but unlucky to face *Taisui*. At the same time, it is considered lucky to be in the position that *Taisui* has just vacated but unlucky to be in the position towards which *Taisui* is progressing. This concept indicates that the movement of a heavenly body was understood to produce a force at one point on the surface of the earth that could be either beneficial or detrimental, depending on how one might be oriented toward the affected direction.

The methods of positioning or *feng shui* described in the Treatise determine the auspices of a space by examining its relationship to fluctuations in time. This approach is commonly referred to as the 'Compass school' of *feng shui*. It is important to remember, however, that there are significant other aspects of the art of *feng shui* that the Treatise does not address. Most books currently available in English deal with the 'Landform school' of *feng shui* which primarily examines the relationship between the unique physical features of an environment and a given structure. Since landforms and other *feng shui* principles are not the focus of the Treatise, I will not delve into those areas here.

The close organic relationship between Chinese astrology and *feng shui* is best exemplified by the concept of 'six harmonies,' which is the subject of a full section in Part I of the Treatise. In brief, this concept posits a powerful relationship between the zodiacal sign in the heavens in which the sun and moon converge (astrology) and one of twelve directions on the surface of the earth towards which the handle of the Big Dipper points (*feng shui*) each month. Understanding the six harmonies requires a bit of conceptual gymnastics and therefore a full description of its workings will be left for the appropriate section in the translation. However, the important thing to take from this is that the traditional Chinese understanding of the cosmos intuitively considered the dynamic existing between heaven and earth as though heaven and earth constituted two sides of one coin. Thus, astrology and *feng shui* can be understood as the brother-sister arts of interpreting the patterns formed by the regular and cyclical motion of the heavens over the supposedly still earth.

In the realms of astrology and *feng shui*, the spiritual emanations of heaven and earth manifest themselves as *shen* and *sha*, or gods and demons. These forces are normally referred to as heavenly gods (*tian shen*) and earthly demons (*di sha*), but this classification is rather deceiving because it implies that all of the heavenly spirits are good and that all of the earthly spirits are evil. A more accurate two-character name for these two spiritual entities, that was also used in the early literature, is *shen qi*. The first element of this pair is the same as the character *shen* of the former pair and means spirit, or more specifically in this instance a celestial spirit. The character *qi*, by contrast, refers to a terrestrial spirit. The term *shen qi* is occasionally expanded and rendered as heavenly spirits (*tian shen*) and earthly spirits (*di qi*).

To understand how these spiritual entities are perceived, it is necessary to consider both of the two pairs of names, which respectively provide the meanings of good and evil spirits and celestial and terrestrial spirits. This combined understanding produces four categories of spiritual entities, namely, heavenly gods, heavenly demons, earthly gods, and earthly demons. This is important to keep in mind because it runs somewhat counter to Western biases, which tend to associate gods of heaven with good, and spirits in the earth with the devil. Indeed, there is a similar bias in traditional Chinese conceptions of these entities, e.g. heavenly gods (*tian shen*) and earthly demons (*di sha*), but in their fullest development both heavenly and earthly spirits were believed to take both good and evil forms.

The importance of heavenly and earthly gods and demons cannot be underestimated, for they are among the most important elemental building blocks of Chinese astrology and *feng shui* as described in the Treatise. The history of the intellectual conception of these spiritual entities is not well understood. Many share the names of stars, constellations, and planets. Many of these stars were themselves named after mythological figures, structures in the imperial court, court officials, and imperial attributes or actions. Some of the gods and demons bear the names of more abstract Chinese cosmological concepts, such as 'The Great Convergence of Yin and Yang.'

These two conventions for naming the gods and demons reflect the two major components of Chinese astrology. One component of this astrological system bases predictions on supposed connections between actual heavenly bodies and time periods. These are essentially the gods and demons that are named after specific heavenly bodies or phenomena. The second component makes assertions based on conjunctions among various counting terms that Chinese use to record the flow of time, i.e. the sexagenary cycle, which is discussed in detail below. The sexagenary terms themselves have little or no connection to actual celestial bodies or phenomena.

This astrological system of gods and demons evolved as an offshoot of Chinese calendrical science. In prehistoric times, Chinese, like most other peoples, traced the flow of time by directly observing the movement of heavenly bodies. In doing this, they deduced that certain heavenly phenomena recurred rather consistently, producing mathematical rhythms. For example, over a number of years, the sun and the moon appear to converge in the same twelve zodiacal signs consistently and the planet Jupiter was perceived to move from one zodiacal sign to the next each year. Consequently, Chinese invented and began to use the terms of the sexagenary cycle as numerical counters to name units of time. Once these regular patterns had been recorded and named, astrologers began to use the sexagenary system in place of direct observation to predict and record the rhythms of time. Direct observation was never discarded, but rather came to be used primarily for astronomical and calendrical purposes.

The sexagenary cycle's time-counting terms performed an extremely important function in Chinese society. They allowed people to predict natural phenomena and respond to the rhythms of nature efficiently for the benefit of human society. Conversely, it was noted that ignoring the recommendations of the calendrical system brought calamity to people, e.g. crop failure. This was so because the calendrical counting terms were regarded as having their own innate power. The names and the patterns that they used to trace were believed to be manifestations of the power of nature itself. According to an ancient tradition, heaven hangs down from its dome stars in ordered patterns (*wen*), which formed the model for the written word. By studying these astronomical patterns, men discovered not only how to write, but indeed how to read the will of heaven. Thus, the counting terms were believed to be metaphysically existent entities. Once this level of conceptual abstraction was reached, Chinese began applying correlative analytical tools developed by early philosophers to the system of time counters.

This explanation may seem somewhat foreign and highly abstract, but in fact, there is a rough correlate of this type of thinking in Western culture, namely the dreaded date Friday the 13th. Opinions differ as to why, but the number 13 was believed to be unlucky and so the 13th of any month was considered a frightening day. Friday was also considered unlucky because it was the day of Jesus' crucifixion. Therefore, the conjunction of Friday and the 13th of a month was believed to be doubly unlucky. Although the underlying cosmology differs significantly, the Chinese astrological and *feng shui* concepts of gods and demons function in a similar way. However, the Chinese distinguished over 200 significant conjunctions in the measures of time. The counting systems that they used for time were also more complex, allowing for 60 different terms each for years, months, days, and hours as compared with a mere 24 hours in a day, 7 days in a week, 31 possible dates in a month, and 12 months in a year.

Although the compilers of the Treatise never define them so explicitly, the heavenly gods and demons are essentially lucky/unlucky times and the earthly gods and demons are auspicious/inauspicious orientations. The charge – lucky or unlucky – of a time or orientation also depends on the type of activity that is to be performed or the type of structure that is to be built. Therefore, a lucky heavenly god might benefit the performance of one act at a given time, while a different act performed at the same time might be hindered because of the influence of an unlucky demon. Similarly, it might be auspicious to orient one type of structure toward a given direction, while that same orientation might be inauspicious for another type of structure.

Heavenly gods (*tian shen*) and demons (*tian sha*) can thus be defined as predictable and regularly recurring forces that significantly promote or frustrate specific human actions. Conversely, earthly gods (*di shen*) and demons (*di sha*) can be defined as orientations in space that vary in accordance with conjunctions in the cycles of time and that significantly affect both specific human actions and physical constructions, e.g. homes and gravesites. These definitions indicate that the *feng shui* principle of orienting employed in the Treatise derives from the astrological principle of timing. It is also interesting to note that it could be lucky to orient a given structure toward a given direction at a certain time, but would be unlucky to choose the same orientation if the structure were built at another time, even though a structure, unlike an act, continues to occupy a place and face in the same direction throughout time.

These definitions of the gods and demons are also noteworthy for the items they omit, which are namely the 'who' and 'where' of astrology and *feng shui* calculations. Normally, when Chinese astrologers or *feng shui* masters calculate advice about actions or building projects, they factor in information about the person concerned and about the surroundings of the building in question. The Treatise, however, deals only with the general and universal principles of astrological timing and *feng shui* orienting, which is only one half of the complete predictive process. As such, believers in these arts would only have used the pronouncements of the Treatise independently to make decisions about relatively common day-to-day activities. This is not to say that the information in the Treatise would not be factored into assessments made about major decisions. It would. However, for matters of greater importance, the Treatise's general pronouncements about scheduling and positioning would have to be assessed in conjunction with information about the specific person concerned and the specific place in which a structure was to be built. Once the recommendations from both the general and specific sets of information had been reconciled, the mantic specialist could issue a final pronouncement.

In addition to the role that it played in shaping major decisions, this predictive system also influenced the way people carried out mundane day-to-day tasks. Confucian principles taught that individuals must strive to perfect their actions and speech to the minutest detail at all times. Perfecting behavior was defined as bringing one's actions into harmony with the natural order of the universe. Since the process of reconciling general pronouncements with specific information about individuals and sites was so complex and time consuming, laymen could not hope to make those calculations for all activities on a daily basis. Consequently, the Treatise proved an extremely valuable tool because its general pronouncements, once translated into the media of almanacs with daily recommendations, gave individuals a measure of confidence in making nearly every decision that affected their lives. To this day, Chinese who subscribe to these beliefs consult almanacs before they schedule such events as job interviews and Cesarean-section deliveries. Some individuals even consult almanacs for advice about when to get a haircut or have a suit tailored.

Critical consideration of the Treatise reveals some interesting observations about the relationship between orthodoxy and heterodoxy in traditional Chinese society. Examining differences across time and between different social groupings, we are able to see that the immense façade of a fiercely homogenous orthodoxy belies a rich tapestry of heterodox beliefs. Socially, the outward form of the system of gods and demons was generally accepted on all levels of Chinese society, but its inner workings were variously interpreted. Culturally, certain core elements of the system persisted throughout Chinese history, while diverse foreign traditions and domestic innovations were gradually grafted onto the core to flesh out the periphery.

The system of gods and demons of times and directions acted as a strong and highly flexible seam of social cohesion. To this day, Chinese almanacs are among the most commonly-found traditional texts in the homes of Chinese of varying social classes, both within China and among Chinese of the diaspora. Even Chinese Christians, who tend to be wary of traditions that might be interpreted as polytheistic, are not universally averse to keeping and using traditional-style almanacs in their homes. This system proved to be amenable to numerous different interpretations within Chinese society because of its ambiguous nature.

Although many of the gods and demons bear names that suggest concrete embodiments, the precise nature of the mathematical system by which their occurrence was calculated lends itself to quite a different interpretation. By introducing mathematical formulae that could predict the occurrence of these spiritual entities, the crafters of this system, to a certain extent, depersonalized and demystified the gods and demons and interpreted them as being subject to objective laws. Though the gods were still to be welcomed and the demons to be shunned, their appearance was no longer unpredictable or irrational. Thus, for a pragmatic Qing Confucian scholar in the emperor's employ, the system of gods and demons represented a complex discipline based on rational principles. Here it is interesting to note that Qing scholars classified the Treatise as a numerological work. Nevertheless, for the poor rural farmer, the awe-inspiring names of the various gods and demons still loomed in the forefront of his mind because he had no inkling of the mathematical formulae by which their appearance on the almanac was calculated. From this we see that the same gods and demons were respected by various strata of society, but their natures may have been differently conceived.

The great antiquity of the system also contributed to its nearly universal appeal. The origins of the gods and demons predate the advent of Buddhism to China. The roots of the system lay in the classical body of literature that was the common possession of both Confucianism and Daoism. Thus, neo-Confucians could see the system as a set of rational natural principles with which they were morally bound to conform. Daoists could accept the system as a tool for tracking the spiritual forces of nature – a tool that enabled them to properly schedule their ritual activities. Buddhists might view the gods and demons as emanations of karma. This flexibility of interpretation, together with the ambiguous nature of the gods and demons of times and directions, enabled the system to find a place in each of China's dominant religious and philosophical traditions. Therefore, the ideas embodied in the Treatise are among those that act as the common denominators of Chinese culture.

In addition to fostering social cohesion, the system of gods and demons served to define the core elements of Chinese cosmology. Throughout the commentary to the translation I have attempted to date each of the component elements of the Treatise's theoretical framework. This investigation reveals that the core elements of the system were already evident in the second century BCE. In fact, if one compares the Treatise's theoretical chapters to the cosmological chapters of the *Huainanzi*, one quickly realizes that the basic elements of the Qing dynasty system were almost perfectly summarized in that renowned Han dynasty text roughly nineteen centuries earlier.

As the uniformly accepted names of the gods belied divergent interpretations by different social groups, so the historical persistence of these core elements of the system masked a high degree of innovation and a continual process of evolution. This dynamic is attested to in Emperor Qianlong's personal intro-duction to the Treatise. In explaining why there was a need for the Treatise, the emperor describes in summary form the evolution of the system. He claims that in the earliest times the sages designed the system as a tool for bettering the lot of the people. In this primal form, the system was simple in the extreme and involved only the distinction of days as either hard (yang) or soft (yin). Over time, others added to and expanded the system, but these alter-ations eventually led to a confusion of the system as a whole. It was in consequence of this confused evolution that the emperor determined to sort out all of the errors, and commission this Treatise to define authoritatively and exhaustively the parameters of the system. Nevertheless, the rectification did not result in a reform to earlier simplicity but rather in a reconciling of dissonant traditions.

The emperor's discussion suggests a process by which a simple idea is developed and divided into ever finer constituent elements, which in turn must later be reintegrated to preserve the unity of the original idea. In this case, as astrologers and *feng shui* masters developed increasingly complex interpreta-tions of the basic elements of the system, certain contradictions became apparent. One school said a given time was auspicious, while another school said the same time was inauspicious. Whereas, a Western attempt at reforming this sort of fragmentation would be likely to result in a debate over the merits of either school's interpretations, in China the discrepancies were resolved differently. The Chinese reformers sought to synthesize the conflicting views by seeking out ever more complex explanations. In the case of conflicting interpretations of a conjunction among time counters, the solution often lay in identifying that one school was correct because the time in question was lucky for a given activity and that the opposing school was also correct because the same time was unlucky for a different activity.

The propensity of the Chinese intellectual tradition to resolve discrepancies by a process of syncretistic integration rather than through competitive selection explains why it is especially difficult to uncover evidence of external influence or internal dissent. Since the official state orthodoxy engaged in a constant process of ideological housekeeping, dissenting traditions were sapped of strength as their teachings were co-opted into the orthodoxy, while foreign innovations were retained but given a Chinese makeover.

Important foreign astronomical innovations that were adopted in China had little influence on the Chinese astrological tradition because astrology and astronomy were in a sense compartmentalized. In traditional China, two systems were employed to record time, one astronomical and another astrological. The truly astronomically-correct calendar was the one that attempted to reconcile solar and lunar months, the timing of the solstices and equinoxes, etc. It counted 12 months to a year each with 29 or 30 days and inserted additional months at regular intervals. This calendrical system underwent numerous significant changes throughout Chinese history. During the Tang dynasty, important astronomical advancements were brought to China from India as a great influx of Buddhist scriptures flowed into China. Similarly, during the Ming and Qing dynasties further astronomical advancements came into China together with other scientific innovations from Europe.

While these major changes were shaping the face of Chinese astronomy, the Chinese astrological arts were able to preserve their integrity primarily because they were defined with reference to a different time-recording system – the sexagenary stem-branch cycle. This system, which is described in detail below, counted years and days – and by extension months and hours – in continuous cycles of sixty units. Thus, in the sexagenary system, the beginning of a cycle of days did not correspond with the beginning of a month. The cycles simply repeated themselves independently ad infinitum. For the most part, the gods and demons of Chinese astrology and *feng shui* were defined in terms of these sexagenary units. Consequently, as the Chinese astronomical calendar was reformed and refined, the astrological system of counting days, months, years, and hours continued cycling almost unfazed. Although certain somewhat more astronomically-oriented astrological systems did come into vogue, for example during the Tang dynasty, none of these ever challenged the primacy of China's sexagenary-based astrological tradition.

CHAPTER THREE

Cosmological Forces and Their Rhythms

Yin and Yang

Although the Chinese terms yin and yang are found in most English diction-aries and are now familiar to many Westerners, a few words of introduction are perhaps warranted, since yin-yang thought plays a large part in the system of selecting lucky times and orientations. Yin and yang generally refer to two complementary and opposite forces or materials that constitute the universe. Originally the characters referred to the dark northern (yin) and sunny southern (yang) sides of a mountain. It is impossible to list all of their correlates, but in short, yin is associated with feminine, dark, heavy, motionless, passive, receptive, cold, the moon, the earth, the lower position, even numbers, etc. Yang, by contrast, represents masculine, light (as in bright), light (in weight), motion, active, providing, hot, the sun, heaven, the higher position, odd numbers, etc.

The concept of yin and yang has become very popular in the West partly because it is believed to represent a metaphysical view of the universe that gives equal importance to both male and female, making it quite attractive to advocates of gender equality. This balanced and non-pejorative understand-ing of yin and yang is evidenced in Chinese thought, but it is important to realize that Chinese thinkers have interpreted yin and yang in various different lights. For example, certain sections of the Daoist classic philosophical text the

Classic of the Way and Its Virtue (*Daode jing*) profess that yin is superior to yang and advocate embracing the yin. However, even when that work was compiled nearly 2,500 years ago, this advocacy of the yin was clearly put forth as an idea that was contrary to conventional thinking.

The conventional perception of yang/masculine superiority generally persisted throughout most of China's intellectual history and is evidenced in this Treatise. Although they are not mentioned in the Treatise as frequently as are the Five Processes and other concepts, yin and yang are foundational to Chinese cosmology. Therefore, it is important for the reader to keep in mind that the terms bear somewhat ambiguous connotations. At times the two forces are thought to advantageously complement one another, but at other times yang may take on the sense of good while yin appears to imply a force resembling evil.

The Five Processes

A preliminary understanding of the Five Processes is prerequisite to examining the text of the Treatise. The term 'Five Processes' is a translation of the two-character Chinese term *wuxing*. The component characters individually mean 'five' (*wu*) and 'a road,' 'a column,' 'to walk,' or 'movement,' etc. (*xing*). Early translators rendered the term as 'the five elements,' because explanations of the group bear some resemblances to Greek philosophical discussions of the four elements. However, the word 'element' can be very misleading because it suggests matter that exists in a static state and that is considered in isolation. By contrast, since the concept achieved its full development in the third century BCE, the Five Processes have been conceived of as existing in a dynamic flow, and each process is defined by its relative relation to the others.

The tendency to conceive of the processes as elements derives from the fact that the Chinese names of the individual processes refer to types of material – wood, fire, earth, metal, and water – which, being objects, are normally conceived of in a static state. Unfortunately, in identifying the individual processes, it is necessary to list them in a specific order relative to each other and thus to prejudice the reader toward one system of inter-relating the five. The sequence just given is known as the mutual production order. It is the order most commonly employed in the Treatise and has been preferred since very early times.

The earliest textual references describe the Five Processes as interrelating in cyclical sequences.[4] The two major cyclical sequences that have been used from ancient to modern times contrast dramatically. One holds that each process succeeds in the cycle by conquering its predecessor – the mutual conquest (*xiangke*) order. The other holds that each process gives birth to its successor – the mutual production (*xiangsheng*) order. A third sequence that also figures prominently in the Treatise has primarily numerological significance since it associates the processes with numbers arranged to form a magic square. The last is commonly referred to as the Great Plan (*Hong fan*) order since it first appears in a section of the *Book of Documents* (*Shang shu*) by that name.

The Great Plan sequence of the Five Processes

Although it is uncertain which developed first, the Great Plan sequence is the earliest documented. The text of the Great Plan is believed to have been written no later than approximately 400 BCE.[5] It describes a 'great plan' with nine divisions that the supreme god, Di, bestowed upon the sage emperor Yü. Di had withheld the plan from Yü's father because he had inadvisably dammed up the 'great waters' and consequently thrown the Five Processes into disarray – a bad thing. The Great Plan served to reorder the various relations that had been disturbed. The first of the nine divisions of the plan is none other than the Five Processes themselves. The description of this first division says:

> The first [division] is the Five Processes. One is called water.
> Two is called fire. Three is called wood. Four is called metal.
> Five is called earth. Water is said to wet downwardly. Fire is
> said to burn upwardly. Wood is said to be crooked and to be
> straight. Metal is said to comply and to constrain. Earth
> undergoes planting and harvesting. Wetting downwardly
> produces saltiness. Burning upwardly produces bitterness.
> Being crooked and being straight produces sourness.
> Complying and constraining produces peppery heat. Planting
> and harvesting produces sweetness.[6]

Since so little is said of the Five Processes in this earliest citation, it is tempting to read much into the text that is not explicitly expressed in the original. I have tried not to do so in the translation, but will rather suggest my interpretation here. The most significant element is what the passage says the processes do.

The original is rather ambiguous, but I would suggest that the example of earth can be used to interpret the others. Earth is said to receive planting and harvesting, which suggests the initial and final stages of the agricultural process. Similarly, the two character descriptions of what the other processes are said to do can be conceived of as beginnings and endings of processes. Thus, water can be thought of as soaking – its action – starting from the top and finishing when it reaches the bottom. Fire burns starting from the bottom and ending at the top. Wood would then be thought to proceed from crooked to straight, which is just what happens to wood when it is processed by a carpenter. Finally, metal proceeds from complying to constraining, since it first complies with being forged but later constrains other materials as a tool after it has been formed.

This interpretation reveals a great deal about how the Five Processes were considered to proceed individually, but the original passage is unfortunately silent on how the five interrelate. Later interpretations have focused on the numbers that the Great Plan assigns to the processes, for hints at how the passage might be trying to suggest that the processes interrelate. The Yellow River Chart and the Luo River Diagram expand upon the Great Plan's system of numbering to arrange the Five Processes on the five points of a plus sign (+) and in the boxes of a nine-segmented 'tic-tac-toe' square. By this arrangement, the graphics are able to visually depict the flow of the mutual production and mutual conquest orders. Richard J Smith says that late Zhou references hint to the existence of these two diagrams, but that they are not certainly documented until the Han period.[7]

The Great Plan sequence joins four of the Five Processes as two pairs of opposites and leaves the earth process at the end. Thus, water's opposition to fire is suggested both intuitively and by the fact that water moves down while fire moves up. Wood's opposition to metal is less intuitive. We will see later that metal is the process that conquers the wood process, just as water conquers the fire process. However, the only evidence in the Great Plan passage itself is perhaps the suggestion that metal, after being formed into a tool, is used to fashion wood and thus transforms wood from crooked to straight.

Assuming that water and fire refer to winter and summer, we see that the year begins with the cold of winter and culminates with heat and growth in midsummer. By the same token, wood correlates with the beginning of plant life in spring and metal signifies the end of plant life at the autumn harvest. Also, in the course of a day the sun begins its journey in the east and ends in the west.

The earth process appears at the end of the list since it is not a member of a pair of opposites nor is it the correlate of a season. Rather, the earth process is the medium upon which the other processes occur.[8]

The Mutual Conquest Sequence of the Five Processes

Reference to the mutual conquest sequence appears in part in the *Commentary of Zuo* (*Zuo zhuan*) to the *Spring and Autumn Annals* (*Chunqiu* – fourth century BCE) and in full in the *Spring and Autumn Annals of Mr Lü* (*Lüshi chunqiu* – third century BCE).[9] The sequence holds that water puts out fire, fire melts metal, metal cuts wood, wood digs earth (since wood and not metal tools were then used to work the land),[10] and earth dams water. As the text of the Treatise will show, this is generally considered a negative cycle, but it is seen to have utility since a conquering process can limit the negative effects of a subject process that is in excess. During the Qin and Han dynasties, the conquest sequence was used to describe the way that political dynasties succeeded one another, but by the first century BCE there was a shift towards interpreting dynastic succession in accordance with the mutual production sequence.[11]

It is helpful to note at this point that both the conquest and production sequences are sometimes written forwards and sometimes backwards, depending on whether the passive or active sense of conquest or production is employed. Thus, for the conquest sequence, it is sometimes said that water conquers fire, which conquers metal, which conquers wood, which conquers earth which conquers water (water, fire, metal, wood, earth). At other times, it is said that water is conquered by earth, which is conquered by wood, which is conquered by metal, which is conquered by fire, which is conquered by water (water, earth, wood, metal, fire). The latter, passive order, is normally used with the conquest sequence when discussing the succession of dynasties, since it proceeds chronologically from past to future. The important thing to remember is that although these orders appear to progress in opposite directions, they actually refer to the same sequence.

The Mutual Production Sequence of the Five Processes

Although it has been argued that the rulers of China justified their political ascent by reference to the conquest sequence before they ever employed the production sequence, the first reliable reference to the production sequence in the written record is arguably just as old as the conquest cycle. The calendrical chapters of the *Spring and Autumn Annals of Mr Lü* (*Lüshi chunqiu*) attest to the existence of the production cycle as early and the third century BCE, and it is probable that the concept existed even earlier than that.[12]

As mentioned above, the progression, from wood to fire to earth to metal to water, constitutes the mutual production or generation sequence. Wood is conceived as the fuel that makes possible the birth and life of fire. In burning things, fire produces ash which is assimilated with soil or dirt, so that fire is seen to produce earth. Earth was traditionally considered to be the womb in which metal was formed. Metal, when melted – and this correlation is the hardest for the modern reader to conceive – becomes liquid, which implies the creation of water. In many modern Asian languages, the word 'water' is still frequently used simply to indicate liquid. A later tradition argues that water is formed by condensing on cold metal. Finally, water was considered to be the material that gave birth to wood, thus completing the cycle in which each process gives birth to its immediate successor.

It has been suggested that the Five Processes developed from an earlier concept of a group of five known as the five materials or *wucai*. That group was believed to simply represent the most important materials required for the sustenance of human society and were comprised exactly of wood, fire, earth, metal and water. Together with grain, those five were also grouped under the rubric of the six stores or *liufu*.[13] If this hypothesis is accepted, it clearly demonstrates that the Five Processes were intimately related with the agricultural process.

In assimilating the Five Processes to an agricultural cycle, wood was considered the archetype of plant matter at the beginning of its life. Fire was thought to represent the flourishing and ripening of plants. Metal symbolized the scythe that harvested grain. Water represented the state of death and of stillness as well as the womb from which new plant life was generated. In this scheme, the earth process was conceived of as being central to the other four since it was the medium in which the entire agricultural process was made manifest. This would suggest that the mutual production sequence of the Five Processes developed out of the concept of the life cycle of cultivated grains.

The scheme just described also provided the conceptual framework for associating the Five Processes with the four seasons and the four directions, or five directions including the center. The four seasons and four directions represent mankind's most basic conceptions of time and space.[14] In traditional Chinese thought, the Five Processes are almost inconceivable without considering their relationship with the times of the seasons and the directions. Considering this, it becomes clear that the Five Processes were most basically conceived of as stages in the cycle of life. Wood represented the sun rising in the east and the budding of plant life in spring. Fire represented the direction south and summer – the hottest time of the year when plants flourished at the peak of lushness. Metal represented the setting sun in the west and autumn, the time of harvest. Water stood in the cold north and symbolized the storing of life in the death of a watery grave, as well as the place from which new life would arise the following year. Earth stood at the center and symbolized the primary medium upon which all four other agricultural stages took place and was thus not easily assimilated to a season.

The Correlation between the Mutual Conquest and Mutual Production Sequences

Wood	Fire	Earth	Metal	Water	PRODUCTION SEQUENCE
Metal	Wood	Earth	Water	Fire	CONQUEST SEQUENCE
Water	Fire	Wood	Metal	Earth	GREAT PLAN SEQUENCE

Once the production and conquest sequences had been fixed, it was only a matter of time before it was discovered that the two exhibited a remarkable mutual correlation.[15] Taking the production sequence as the standard – as it has been in China since early modern times – one observes that each process conquers the process that appears two places after itself in the production sequence. Also, each process is conquered by the process that appears two places prior to itself. Since the two sequences are symmetrically related, one will also observe that each process in the conquest sequence is produced by the process that appears two places after itself and produces the process that appears two places before itself.

In order to graphically represent this correlation, the two cycles are commonly depicted by the imagery of a five-pointed star within a pentagon. Normally the flow of the outer lines of the pentagon represents the production sequence and the flow of the inner lines in the star represent the conquest sequence. However, since the correlation is symmetrical, the identification of the lines can obviously be reversed.

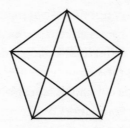

It is helpful to describe one example. Again, the production sequence is taken as the standard. Consider the earth process in the context of the entire production sequence:

Wood	Fire	Earth	Metal	Water

Listed in this way, it is easy to observe that the earth process is produced by the process that immediately precedes earth, i.e. fire. Earth produces the process that immediately succeeds earth, i.e. metal. Earth is conquered by the process that appears two places before earth, i.e. wood. Earth conquers the process that appears two places after earth, i.e. water. Thus:

Wood conquers Earth	Fire produces Earth	Earth	Metal is produced by Earth	Water is conquered by Earth

A C Graham suggests that the author of a passage from the *Huainanzi* was already aware of the correlation between the two sequences.[16] To quote the portion of that passage concerning Earth, as translated by John Major, 'When Earth is in its prime, Fire is old, Metal is about to be born, Wood is paralyzed, and Water is dead.'[17] This section of the *Huainanzi* reproduces a parallel statement for all of the Five Processes. The passage shows that, as earth is flourishing in its prime, the process fire, which had itself produced earth, is old, i.e. past its own prime. At the same time, the process metal, which earth produces, is about to be born; the process wood, which conquers earth, is paralyzed – because otherwise wood would conquer earth; and the process water, which earth conquers, is dead – because earth is in its prime and able to vanquish water.

Perhaps, we may speculate, it was the consolidation of this tightly woven system of relationships based upon the production sequence that led to the abandonment of the political theory of dynastic succession by the conquest sequence of the Five Processes mentioned above. Once the two sequences had been correlated in the way just described, it would be clear that any political power would have come to its position by succeeding its producer and not by conquering its predecessor.

Regardless of the order in which the sequences were established, what is perfectly clear is that the correlation of the two sequences, which takes production as primary and conquest as secondary, was firmly established in the realm of Chinese cosmology by the latter portion of the Han dynasty. This convention continued to govern the realm of traditional Chinese astrology and *feng shui* through to the writing of the Treatise as it still does today. Moreover, this correlation of the sequences gave numerological form to the idea of life cycles progressing through stages, which will be elaborated upon below.

The foregoing discussion raises the important practical question of what determined why one sequence – and not another – would be employed at any given time. To fully answer this question would require an exposition far beyond the scope of this Introduction and, in fact, the Treatise itself was to a certain extent created in order to answer that very question. This points to the great importance of the mantic specialist as the expert who was able to determine which of the complex sets of astrology and *feng shui* rules applied in any given circumstance. Nonetheless, a simple example should help the reader to understand the type of principles that guided the diviner in determining which sequence of Five Processes interrelationships applied.

Every moment in time and every direction on the compass obtain unique sets of 'coordinates' expressed as terms of the sexagenary cycle, described in detail below. The Heavenly Stems and Earthly Branches that make up the sexagenary cycle, in turn, are correlated with at least one of the Five Processes. One of the most basic techniques for assessing the auspiciousness of a point in time, for example, is for the diviner to study the relationship between the Five Processes correlates of the Heavenly Stems of the year, month, day, and hour in question. Thus, if the stem of the year was correlated with the wood process and the stem of the day was correlated with the fire process, then the sequence of interrelationship would be one of mutual production, since wood produces fire. This information would then have to be assessed to determine how that related to the activity in question. For example, if the emperor were seeking advice on whether to enter battle at that time, an act associated with the metal process, then the time might be considered inauspicious, since the fire process conquers the metal process. If by contrast, the emperor was contemplating building an earthen wall, then the time might be auspicious, since fire produces earth.

Series of Life Cycles

Only second in importance to the qualitative concepts of yin and yang and the Five Processes in the Treatise is the more quantitative concept of progressive life-cycle stages. As described above, it was perhaps the correlating of the production and conquest sequences of the Five Processes that, in fact, led to the development of the concept of stages in a cycle of life. The system of the *Huainanzi*, just discussed, divides the life cycle into five stages. The Treatise primarily refers to two other sets of life-cycle stages. The first divides the life cycle into three stages and the second employs twelve stages. When divided into three stages, a life cycle is normally considered to begin with birth (*sheng*, *changsheng*), progress to the stage of flourishing, maturity, or being in the prime (*wang*, *cheng*), and conclude with death, burial, or being stored away (*si*, *mu*, *ku*). The twelve-stage life cycle is obviously rather more complex and brings into the discussion the idea of pre-birth stages that follow upon death, which implies reincarnation. Consequently, discussion of the twelve individual stages will be presented below, at the introduction to the relevant section of the Treatise.

The most important point to remember with respect to life-cycle stages is that the Treatise almost always evaluates the nature of space and time with reference to the quality of a Five-Processes correlation firstly, and secondly, considers the quantitative aspect of the stage in which the given process is situated. In other words, it first asks what process governs the variable that is being assessed and, after that has been determined, it asks in which life-cycle stage is the applicable process located. Thus, the Five Processes together with the life-cycle stages provide the theoretical framework within which nearly all spatial and temporal valuations are made in the Treatise.

CHAPTER FOUR

The Counting Terms of Chinese Astrology and *Feng Shui*

According to the system of thought manifested in the Treatise, the progression of the metaphysical forces of yin and yang and the Five Processes through life-cycle stages determines how times – and by extension orientations – positively or negatively influence human behavior. Generally, the seasons of spring and summer are considered yang while autumn and winter are associated with yin. Also, the season of spring is associated with birth and the process wood, summer with flourishing and the process fire, autumn with death and the process metal, and winter with burial and the process water. Although these general associations are of great importance to astrology and *feng shui*, the divinatory arts seek to provide much more detailed and specific information. That objective is realized through the medium of the Chinese numerological system that has been used since ancient times to record the passage of time, i.e. the sexagenary cycle composed of the Heavenly Stems and Earthly Branches. These terms, in turn, are at times also correlated with the eight trigrams of China's classic *Book of Changes* (*Yijing*) enabling the Chinese astrologer and *feng shui* master to calculate chronological correlations of extreme complexity.

The Sexagenary Stem-Branch Cycle

For over 3,000 years, Chinese have recorded the passage of days by reference to a system designated imposingly in English as the sexagenary stem-branch cycle. The cycle consists of sixty unique pairs of terms, which are themselves comprised of one of Ten Heavenly Stems and one of Twelve Earthly Branches. The stems and branches are essentially two different sequences of numbers, each of the members of which is designated by one unique Chinese character. The Heavenly Stems are romanized as stem-*Jia*, stem-*Yi*, stem-*Bing*, stem-*Ding*, stem-*Wu*, stem-*Ji*, stem-*Geng*, stem-*Xin*, stem-*Ren*, and stem-*Gui*. The names of the Earthly Branches are branch-*Zi*, branch-*Chou*, branch-*Yin*, branch-*Mao*, branch-*Chen*, branch-*Si*, branch-*Wu*, branch-*Wei*, branch-*Shen*, branch-*You*, branch-*Xu*, and branch-*Hai*. Thus, the stems comprise a denary or 10-unit counting system and the branches form a duodenary or 12-unit counting system. (Stem-*Wu* and branch-*Wu* are written with the same romanization, but the Chinese characters are written differently.)

The sexagenary, or 60-unit, cycle is formed by sequentially and continuously pairing one Heavenly Stem with exactly one Earthly Branch until all possible combinations have been formed. Thus, after the ten stems have been paired with the first ten branches, the first stem is paired with the eleventh branch and then the second stem is paired with the twelfth branch. After that, all of the branches are exhausted, so the third stem is paired with the first branch, etc. In this way, each of the five odd-numbered stems is paired with each of the six odd-numbered branches, forming thirty pairs. At the same time, each of the five even-numbered stems is paired with each of the six even-numbered branches, forming an additional thirty pairs. According to Chinese belief, odd is correlated with yang and even with yin. Thus, in the sexagenary cycle, each pair is always either odd/yang or even/yin according to the number of the pair's component stem and branch. The complete set of sixty stem-branch pairs are set forth in their natural order in the tables below.

Although the sexagenary cycle was originally only used to count days, the system eventually came to be used to count years, months, and hours as well. Once applied in this way, an interesting symmetry appeared between the sexagenary designations of year and month and between those of the day and hour. As with most other calendars, the Chinese lunisolar year contains twelve months. The traditional Chinese day was comprised of twelve hours because the handle of the Big Dipper was perceived to indicate roughly the twelve

Jia	Yi	Bing	Ding	Wu	Ji	Geng	Xin	Ren	Gui
Zi	Chou	Yin	Mao	Chen	Si	Wu	Wei	Shen	You

Jia	Yi	Bing	Ding	Wu	Ji	Geng	Xin	Ren	Gui
Xu	Hai	Zi	Chou	Yin	Mao	Chen	Si	Wu	Wei

Jia	Yi	Bing	Ding	Wu	Ji	Geng	Xin	Ren	Gui
Shen	You	Xu	Hai	Zi	Chou	Yin	Mao	Chen	Si

Jia	Yi	Bing	Ding	Wu	Ji	Geng	Xin	Ren	Gui
Wu	Wei	Shen	You	Xu	Hai	Zi	Chou	Yin	Mao

Jia	Yi	Bing	Ding	Wu	Ji	Geng	Xin	Ren	Gui
Chen	Si	Wu	Wei	Shen	You	Xu	Hai	Zi	Chou

Jia	Yi	Bing	Ding	Wu	Ji	Geng	Xin	Ren	Gui
Yin	Mao	Chen	Si	Wu	Wei	Shen	You	Xu	Hai

different directions on the surface of the earth over the course of one day. Thus a traditional Chinese hour is equivalent to two modern hours. With exactly twelve months to each year and exactly twelve hours to each day, the respective months of each year and hours of each day are always designated by the same unit from the Twelve Earthly Branches.

The first month of each year is always a branch-*Yin* month, the second month is a branch-*Mao* month, the third month is a branch-*Chen* month, etc. An earlier calendar sequence actually had the first month of the year beginning with the winter solstice in the month designated by the first branch-*Zi*, but that system is now used only for astrological purposes. There are 'leap' or intercalary months in the Chinese system, but when inserted, those months take the same stem-branch pair of the month after which they are inserted and therefore the intercalary months do not upset the regular ordering of the months in the year. Similar to the months, the first hour of each day is always a branch-*Zi* hour, the second hour is a branch-*Chou* hour, the third hour is a branch-*Yin* hour, etc.

Because of the symmetry just described, the sexagenary cycles of months and hours run their courses completely within five years and five days, respectively. In ten years and in ten days, the cycle of months and hours repeat themselves completely a second time. This symmetrical relationship dictates that each of the sixty stem-branch combinations of months and hours will occur on only twelve of the sixty possible year and day stem-branch combinations. Since the months and hours do not concur with all of the sixty years and days, there are only 720 (i.e. 12 x 60, rather than 3,600 or 60 x 60) possible year/month and day/hour stem-branch combinations.[18]

Understanding the significant numbers and the myriad combinations of the sexagenary cycle is important because it sheds light on both the complexity and the numerical rhythms inherent in the system. Any hour in time is designated by a combination of four pairs of one stem and one branch representing the year, month, day, and hour. The interrelationship among those eight terms are what determine which heavenly or earthly god or demon might govern a given action or construction. The vast number of possible combinations reflects a cosmos of great complexity. The complexity of this system was sufficient to satisfy potential objections from skeptics because it was congruous with the human experience of a seemingly unpredictable cosmos. Nevertheless, the appearance of recurring patterns of symbolic numbers served to reassure those who sought solace in the system that the universe was not at all unpredictable, albeit complex and difficult to understand.

The Heavenly Stems and the Earthly Branches

The eight pairs of sexagenary terms that uniquely represent any year, month, day, and hour dictate which gods or demons, if any, will appear at a given time or in a specific direction. The values of the sexagenary terms are, in turn, based upon their correlations with the Five Processes and yin and yang. The correlations that pertain to the Ten Heavenly Stems are relatively straightforward. As mentioned above, the stems are alternately yang and yin according to their odd and even values. Consecutive pairs of the stems are taken to represent the yin and yang correlates of each of the Five Processes, beginning with stem-*Jia*, which is considered yang and is associated with the process wood. The correlations follow the mutual production order of the Five Processes. Thus, stem-*Yi* is yin wood, stem-*Bing* is yang fire, stem-*Ding* is yin fire, stem-*Wu* is yang earth, stem-*Ji* is yin earth, stem-*Geng* is yang metal, stem-*Xin* is yin metal, stem-*Ren* is yang water, and stem-*Gui* is yin water.

Three major systems are used to designate the Five-Processes correlations of the Twelve Earthly Branches. One system associates four sets of three branches with the processes of the cardinal directions – the process earth of the center is omitted. To visualize this system it is helpful to imagine the twelve branches taking the place of the numbers one through twelve on the face of a clock, as they sometimes do on Chinese clocks and watches. The branch-*Zi* stands at 12 o'clock, branch-*Chou* at 1 o'clock, etc. Thus, the branches of the direction north and the process water are 11, 12, and 1 o'clock or branch-*Hai*, branch-*Zi*, and branch-*Chou*. The branches of eastern wood are 2, 3, and 4 o'clock or branch-*Yin*, branch-*Mao*, and branch-*Chen*. The branches of southern fire are 5, 6, and 7 o'clock or branch-*Si*, branch-*Wu*, and branch-*Wei*. The branches of western metal are 8, 9, and 10 o'clock or branch-*Shen*, branch-*You*, and branch-*Xu*.

Although this clock analogy is helpful for imagining the directions of the branches, one must keep in mind that the Chinese hours are actually two-hour periods. Thus the twelve Chinese two-hour periods cover an entire day, with the branch-*Zi* 'hour' covering the period from 11 p.m. through 1 a.m. and with the branch-*Wu* 'hour' covering the two hours from 11 a.m. through 1 p.m. If one were to slow a normal clock to half speed, the rotation of the hour hand through the clock's 360 degrees would thus cover one traditional Chinese day of twelve two-hour periods. The memory of this time system is still evident in modern spoken Chinese, where the term 'before branch-*Wu*' (*shang Wu*) means 'morning' and 'after branch-*Wu*' (*xia Wu*) means 'afternoon.' Generally, the two-hour period of the branch-*Zi* is divided in half, with the first half of the period conceptually belonging to the last part of one day and with the second half belonging to the first part of the following day.

A second and derivative system of Five-Processes correlations for the Twelve Earthly Branches associates the last of each of the four sets of three branches with the process earth. Thus, branch-*Hai* (11 o'clock) and branch-*Zi* (12 o'clock) are water, while branch-*Chou* (1 o'clock) is earth. Branch-*Yin* (2 o'clock) and branch-*Mao* (3 o'clock) are wood, while branch-*Chen* (4 o'clock) is earth. Branch-*Si* (5 o'clock) and branch-*Wu* (6 o'clock) are fire, while branch-*Wei* (7 o'clock) is earth. Branch-*Shen* (8 o'clock) and branch-*You* (9 o'clock) are metal, while branch-*Xu* (10 o'clock) is earth. This system gives the process earth a place in the Five-Processes correlations of the twelve months. In that context, the beginnings of the months with branch-*Chen*, branch-*Wei*, branch-*Xu*, and branch-*Chou* are associated with the processes wood, fire, metal, and water, while the last part of those months are associated with the process earth. Thus, this derivative system of Five-Processes correlations for the twelve branches does not contradict the first, but is rather a refinement of the first system.

The third major system of Five-Processes correlations for the branches also differs from, but is not considered to negate or contradict, the other two. This system is known as the Triune Harmonies (*san he*). As with the last two examples, the triune-harmonies system is primarily concerned with the four cardinal processes, i.e. wood, fire, metal, and water – but not earth. However, further refinements of this system also provide a place for the earth process. The triune-harmonies system is based upon associations of the branches with life cycles of the processes.

Essentially, the branches of the four cardinal directions are thought to represent the full life forces of the processes, with branch-*Zi* (12 o'clock) representing flourishing water, branch-*Mao* (3 o'clock) representing wood, branch-*Wu* (6 o'clock) representing fire, and branch-*You* (9 o'clock) representing metal. The twelve branches are divided into equally separated groups of three. Assuming clockwise rotation, the branch that is four places before the cardinal branch is considered to represent the point of birth of that process and the branch that is four places after the cardinal branch represents the point of death or burial of the process. Thus, water is born in branch-*Shen* (8 o'clock), flourishes in branch-*Zi* (12 o'clock), and dies in branch-*Chen* (4 o'clock). Wood is born in branch-*Hai* (11 o'clock), flourishes in branch-*Mao* (3 o'clock), and dies in branch-*Wei* (7 o'clock). Fire is born in branch-*Yin* (2 o'clock), flourishes in branch-*Wu* (6 o'clock), and dies in branch-*Xu* (10 o'clock). Metal is born in branch-*Si* (5 o'clock), flourishes in branch-*You* (9 o'clock), and dies in branch-*Chou* (1 o'clock).

In addition to the individual Five-Processes correlations of the stems and branches just described, the sixty pairs of stems and branches that comprise the sexagenary cycle each possess unique Five-Processes correlations. These Five-Processes correlations of the pairs do not systematically derive from the correlations that pertain to either the component stems or branches. This system of Five-Processes correlations is referred to as the Received Notes system (*na yin*). Because the system is rather complex and is fully described in the Treatise, the details of those correlations will not be repeated here.

The Trigrams of the Book of Changes

The last major element in the system used to calculate auspicious times and orientations involves correlations between the stems and branches and the trigrams of the classic *Book of Changes* (*Yijing*). The *Book of Changes* is an ancient divinatory text, the backbone of which is a series of diagrams built up from eight graphs composed of three lines that may be either broken or solid, i.e. hard/yang or soft/yin. The eight graphs, known as trigrams, are combined in pairs to form an exhaustive set of sixty-four pairs, referred to as hexagrams. The names of the eight trigrams are trigram-*Qian* (metal), trigram-*Dui* (metal), trigram-*Li* (fire), trigram-*Zhen* (wood), trigram-*Kun* (earth), trigram-*Gen* (earth), trigram-*Kan* (water), and trigram-*Sun* (wood). The eight trigrams came to possess the Five-Processes correlations listed in parentheses, but those correlations play a relatively minor role in the Treatise.

More important than the trigrams' standard Five-Processes correlations is the system known as the 'Received Stem-*Jia* (*na Jia*),' which pairs the Ten Heavenly Stems with the eight trigrams. Since there are ten stems but only eight trigrams, trigram-*Qian* and trigram-*Kun* (containing all yang and all yin lines respectively) each take two Heavenly Stems. That pairing, which is elaborated upon in the Treatise is as follows: trigram-*Qian* (stem-*Jia* and stem-*Ren*), trigram-*Kun* (stem-*Yi* and stem-*Gui*), trigram-*Gen* (stem-*Bing*), trigram-*Dui* (stem-*Ding*), trigram-*Kan* (stem-*Wu*), trigram-*Li* (stem-*Ji*), trigram-*Zhen* (stem-*Geng*), and trigram-*Sun* (stem-*Xin*). The eight trigrams are also correlated with the four cardinal and four inter-cardinal directions in the system of twenty-four directions.[19]

CHAPTER FIVE

Astronomical Foundations of Chinese Astrology

Ancient Chinese astronomers did not conceive of the earth as being in motion. Instead, they perceived that within the heavens two sets of objects moved above a still earth. First, the stars of the night sky were conceived of as a dome or disk that rotated clockwise over the earth on an axis defined by the pole star (or, more generally, the Big Dipper). Second, the sun, the moon, and the five visible planets were believed to move counterclockwise over the earth – contrary to the motion of the stars – but also around the axis of the circumpolar region. The movement of the dome of stars was measured by reference to directions on the face of the earth. The movements of the sun, moon, and planets were traced against the backdrop of the dome of stars. Both the surface of the earth and the dome of the stars were divided into twelve equal parts, which were designated by the Twelve Earthly Branches.

To grasp this traditional Chinese understanding of the heavens, picture the solar system as a two-dimensional image viewed from above the earth's north pole. Consider only the sun, moon, earth, and the five visible planets (these were the major constituent elements of ancient Chinese astronomy). Earth, Jupiter, Mars, Venus, Saturn, and Mercury all trace counterclockwise orbits around the sun. The moon moves in a counterclockwise orbit around the earth. Earth rotates counterclockwise around its own axis. Next, imagine the visible stars as a sphere surrounding the solar system. This dome remains still as the planets orbit the sun and the moon orbits the earth. An extension of the earth's imaginary axis defines the North Star (Polaris) roughly at the center of the northern hemisphere of stars, although for the ancients this was not the axis. Ancient Chinese were correct in understanding that the five visible planets and the moon move against the background of the stellar dome in a counterclockwise motion. Since the earth orbits the sun in that same direction, from the earth's perspective, the sun appears to move counterclockwise around the earth against the background of the stellar dome.

Due to the earth's daily counterclockwise rotation around its axis and yearly counterclockwise orbit around the sun, the dome of the stars appears to revolve around the pole star in a clockwise motion. Since the earth revolves 360 degrees counterclockwise around its axis, the dome of stars appears to rotate 360 degrees clockwise each day. However, each day the earth also progresses one degree in its 360-degree counterclockwise orbit around the sun. This adds one degree to the apparent 360-degree daily clockwise rotation of the dome of stars, so the dome of stars actually appears to rotate 361 degrees daily. Consequently, over the course of an idealized 360-day year, the addition of one degree each day brings the dome of stars back to its original position at the end of each year.

The sun and the moon appear to be the two largest heavenly bodies in the sky. The position of the moon against the background of the stars can be directly observed most nights. The position of the sun among the stars can not be directly observed but must be extrapolated. The position of the sun at midday is roughly 180 degrees separated from the stars that are directly overhead at midnight. By extrapolating in this way, the ancient Chinese astronomer was able to know when the sun and moon were in the same position in relation to the dome of stars, even though this could not be directly observed. This phenomenon, known as a new moon, occurs when the moon moves in its orbit to a position between the sun and the earth. Consequently, from the earth's perspective, the sun and moon would appear to be in the same position among the stars if they could be seen.

The Chinese astronomer referred to the new moon as a convergence of the sun and moon. Since the sun and moon appear to converge relatively in the same twelve points against the dome of stars each year, it was possible to divide the dome into twelve equal sections, which were designated, among other names, by the Twelve Earthly Branches. These twelve Chinese zodiacal signs indicate the section of the sky where the sun and moon converge and so should not be confused with Western zodiacal constellations. When referring to the constellations of the stars, the Chinese employed a system of Twenty-eight Lunar Lodges.

In addition to serving as names for the twelve zodiacal signs, the Twelve Earthly Branches were used to describe twelve directions on the earth's surface. Branch-*Zi* corresponds to due north, branch-*Mao* to east, branch-*Wu* to south, and branch-*You* to west. Beyond these correspondences it is not accurate to use Western-compass directional terms such as northeast or north-northeast to designate the directions indicated by the remaining eight Earthly Branches. Western compasses are normally divided into four (90 degrees), eight (45 degrees), or sixteen (22.5 degrees) units, but the Chinese compass was generally divided into twelve (30 degrees) or twenty-four (15 degrees) units. The traditional Chinese divisions of twelve are better represented by reference to the numbers of a clock's face, similar to the way aviators sometimes describe their surrounding spectrum. In this way, north is 12 o'clock and branch-*Zi*. Thirty degrees east of north is 1 o'clock and the second branch – branch-*Chou*, etc. Traditionally Chinese placed the direction north at the bottom of compasses.

Employing the imagery of a clock face has the added advantage of revealing what must have been an amazingly symmetrical series of correspondences for the ancient Chinese astronomer. They discovered that in the middle of the branch-*Zi* hour (midnight) during the new moon (first day of the month) in the branch-*Zi* month (month of the winter solstice) the handle of the Big Dipper pointed to the branch-*Zi* direction (due north). In each succeeding Chinese two-hour period of that same day, the Dipper's handle would point to each of the corresponding directions, i.e. in the branch-*Chou* hour the handle would indicate 1 o'clock or the direction 30 degrees east of due north – the branch-*Chou* direction, etc.

Due to the gradual rotation of the stars throughout the course of the year, at the branch-*Zi* hour on the first day of each month, the handle of the Big Dipper would indicate the earthly branch of the direction that corresponded with the earthly branch of the respective month. The convergences of the sun and moon move counterclockwise through the twelve zodiacal signs, i.e. in reverse order through the Twelve Earthly Branches. At midnight on the first day of each month, the handle of the Big Dipper, however, pointed to a new direction in clockwise motion, i.e. in the order of the Twelve Earthly Branches of the directions.

This discovery must have strongly reinforced the ancient Chinese propensity to think in terms of cyclic change. Essentially, in the first hour of each year there was a pure correspondence between the beginnings of the year, the month, the day, and the directions. The year was originally believed to begin at the point of least sunlight during the winter solstice and to culminate with the peak of the sun's strength at the summer solstice. The month was believed to begin with the absence of moonlight during the new moon and to culminate with the full moon. The day was believed to begin at midnight and to culminate at noon. Finally, the directions were believed to begin at the bottom from the branch-*Zi* at 12 o'clock (north) and to culminate at the top with the branch-*Wu* direction at 6 o'clock (south). At a very early date the Chinese changed the beginning of the year to correspond with the month of the third earthly branch. Nevertheless, the original idea of the year beginning with the branch-*Zi* month was never forgotten and is still factored into certain astrological calculations.

The indications of the handle of the Big Dipper also determine the position of the Great Year (*Taisui*). The Great Year is often described as an imaginary heavenly body that moves contrary to the motion of the planet Jupiter. In fact, the Great Year is a visible phenomenon that refers to the direction to which the handle of the Big Dipper points when the new moon appears in the same zodiacal sign as the planet Jupiter.

As described above, the sun and moon 'converge' or appear within the same zodiacal sign twelve times each year. The planet Jupiter completes one orbit in slightly less than twelve years, meaning that it moves counterclockwise through roughly one zodiacal sign each year. This means that each year, one new moon appears in the zodiacal sign in which Jupiter is located. If one observes the handle of the Big Dipper during this rough alignment, it will be seen to indicate one of the twelve 'branch' directions on the earth's surface. Each succeeding year the indication of the Dipper's handle during the alignment will move clockwise to a new direction. The earthly branch of the direction indicated is none other than the earthly branch used to designate the year in question.[20]

These movements may be imagined as a calendrical clock with hour, day, month, and year arms. The second hand of a normal clock moves six degrees per second, the minute hand moves six degrees per minute, and the hour hand moves one degree every two minutes. The traditional Chinese hour is equivalent to two modern hours. Thus, there are twelve Chinese hours rather than twenty-four modern hours in a complete day and night. To reflect this, the calendrical clock's hour hand would have to move one degree every four minutes, rather than every two minutes. In other words, the clock's hour hand would have to move at half speed.

Traditionally the Chinese conceived of midnight as falling exactly half-way through the first of the twelve two-hour periods, which was the branch-*Zi* period.

The first modern hour of the branch-*Zi* period belonged to the last part of one day and the second modern hour belonged to the first part of the following day. On our imaginary half-speed clock, that would mean that the period from 11:30 to 12 o'clock would correspond to the first half of the branch-*Zi* period, i.e. 11:00 p.m. through 11:59 p.m. The second half of the branch-*Zi* period would fall between 12 o'clock and 12:30 on our half-speed clock and would correspond to 12:00 a.m. through 12:59 a.m. Consequently, one 360-degree revolution of the half-speed clock's hour hand would represent a full day and night.

To complete the calendrical clock, we would need to add a day hand, a month hand, and a year hand. For every revolution of the hour hand, the day hand would move twelve degrees, i.e. 360 degrees every 30 days. For every revolution of the hour hand, the month hand would move 1 degree, i.e. 360-degrees/360-day year. For every revolution of the day hand, the year hand would move one degree, i.e. 360-degrees/12 years. This imaginary clock divides the year into an ideal 360 days, as the Chinese did in some astrological reckonings.

The hour hand of this calendrical clock represents the 360-degree daily revolution of the earth, which creates the apparent clockwise rotation of the handle of the Big Dipper by 30 degrees every Chinese hour. The day hand represents the moon's ideal 30-day orbit around the earth. The month hand represents the earth's ideal 360-day orbit around the sun, which creates the apparent clockwise rotation of the handle of the Big Dipper by 30 degrees at the branch-*Zi* hour on each new moon. The year hand represents the planet Jupiter's ideal orbit by one degree/30-day month, which creates the apparent 30-degree/year clockwise rotation of the handle of the Big Dipper when the sun, the moon, and the planet Jupiter converge.

Although the reality of the Chinese calendar and the actual movements of heavenly bodies did not make these correspondences occur as perfectly as the ancient cosmologists would have liked, the scheme just described indicates the ideal that they deduced from their observations of the heavens. To the modern astronomer this world view must appear to twist scientifically observable, objective facts to serve a preconceived notion of the universe. However, to the ancient crafters of this system, the goal of observing the heavens was not simply to record natural phenomena disinterestedly, but rather to discern from the heavens the archetypal patterns that served to organize and give meaning to man's existence.

When compared with Western astrological traditions, the Chinese model stresses the great dome of stars more than it does the movements of the sun, moon, and planets. This is reflected in the Chinese notion that heaven and earth constitute a greater pair of opposites than sun and moon. Heaven, as the dome of stars, was considered the overarching reality within which the sun, moon, and planets carried out their motions above earth. The locations of the heavenly luminaries were observed and recorded primarily to evidence the movements of the great clock hand of the Big Dipper handle.

For its part, the handle of the Big Dipper visibly verified the regular cycles of heaven, which, as the active counterpart of earth, created the cycles of life and agriculture upon which man depended for sustenance. The Dipper was sometimes imagined as a celestial chariot in which the great god of heaven (*Taiyi*) rode through the course of the year. The Dipper also became a great magic symbol and is still used today by Daoist priests, who align ritual lamps in the shape of this asterism, or dance ritually along its pattern. A cult dedicated to the goddess Dou Mu, or Dipper Mother, is the focus of fervent worship among ethnic Chinese in Thailand and has over recent years been gaining popularity among ethnic Thais.

In China the goddess Dou Mu was assimilated to the Indian goddess Marici, who rides a chariot drawn by seven pigs corresponding to the seven stars of the Big Dipper. In Japan, Marici, known as Marishiten, serves as the patron goddess of bushido, the way of the martial arts. The Dipper was sometimes thought to have nine and sometimes seven stars. In China, the seven stars of the Dipper were often inscribed on sword blades and certain martial arts contain the powerful words 'seven stars' in their names. These martial associations of the Dipper reflect a very early tradition, which held that an army was doomed that progressed in the face of the Great Year (*Taisui*). Conversely, an army that stood with its back to Great Year was considered undefeatable.

CHAPTER SIX

Conclusion

The *Treatise on Harmonizing Times and Distinguishing Directions* is a concise and comprehensive summary of a cosmology that deeply influenced Chinese thought throughout the imperial period and continues to shape Chinese thought today. At the time the Treatise was promulgated, this cosmology was almost universally accepted in China and practitioners of astrology and *feng shui* were consulted by people of all creeds and social classes.

Today, although many Chinese disavow this ancient view of the world, astrology and *feng shui* are clearly alive and well in China, Taiwan, Hong Kong, and Singapore. Indeed, such traditional arts are even gaining popularity beyond the Chinese cultural sphere. Thus, the Treatise remains an important document today both because of the significant world view that it summarizes and because of the influence that it has on modern-day diviners who consult it to produce astrological almanacs and books on *feng shui*.

The dynamics of the universe described in the Treatise are especially fascinating to the modern mind because of the resemblance they bear to certain scientific ways of understanding the world. On first observation, the system of gods and demons appears rather archaic, not least because of the mystical terminology that it employs. Most scholars, and indeed the present author as well, refer to the subject of this Treatise as the art of selecting 'lucky' times and directions. A close inspection reveals that luck, as it is generally understood in the West, is not at all relevant to the system presented in the Treatise. Luck generally implies an unpredictable turn of events over which the individual has little or no control. However, few terms could be found that are more antithetical than luck to describe the system of gods and demons of times and directions.

As this introduction has indicated repeatedly, the cosmological outlook of the Treatise suggests a universe governed by regular and predictable fluctuations of energy. These cosmological forces can only act according to their rhythms and can not vary from these rhythms either for the benefit or to the detriment of humans. One could even argue that it is wrong to characterize such natural forces as either good or bad with regards to people, since that would imply, on the part of the gods or demons, a volition or will that they clearly lack. In fact, they are simply positive or negative. It is true that the spiritual forces are classified as either gods or demons, which suggests good and bad will. However, these categories only have meaning in reference to specific human activities. Thus, while the 'Destroyer of Earth' demon clearly marks an inauspicious time for building the walls of a house, the same entity actually marks a propitious time for breaking ground in a foundation. This spiritual force is merely one that promotes the destruction of earth and in some cases destruction, a negative force, can be advantageous to people.

The picture of traditional Chinese cosmology that this presents is quite similar to the way many scientific minds conceive of natural law. Both systems posit natural forces that exert themselves in the universe without apparent regard for human desire. People can know of these forces and can use both their productive and destructive energies to the advantage of humankind. At the same time, if we behave in a manner that puts us in the way of the destructive forces, harm will befall us. And just as the modern scientist argues that it is our calling to study and take advantage of natural law, so the compilers of the Treatise claim that it is one's duty to acquaint oneself with the system of timing and orienting so as to bring the self into harmony with the will of heaven.

The art of scheduling and positioning may be analogized to the skill of a surfer riding ocean waves. The cosmological forces of yin and yang and the Five Processes can be likened to the physical forces of current and surf that go to make up a wave. Although some surfers might disagree, most people would understand that the wave itself has no intent with respect to the surfer. The wave is simply the result of natural forces playing themselves out in the water. Nonetheless, the moment in which the surfer attempts to mount the wave and the angle at which she sets her board – her timing and positioning – will decide whether she catches the perfect ride, is left behind in the swells, or dangerously wipes out.

The wave is a single phenomenon, but its various segments are respectively more or less conducive to a good ride. In the same way, traditional Chinese cosmological forces are all part of an organic whole, but their different manifes-tations each lend themselves more or less to different activities. The skill of the surfer lies in knowing at what time and in what direction to catch a wave. The skill of the Chinese astrologer or *feng shui* master lies in knowing when and in what orientation to perform a given act or construct a building. Whether the reader chooses to digest the following translation with a mind to mastering Chinese astrology and *feng shui* or simply takes from it the pleasure that comes from marveling at the wonderful symmetry and complexity of traditional Chinese thought, please allow me to wish you good surfing.

PART II

THE IMPERIALLY AUTHORIZED TREATISE ON HARMONIZING TIMES AND DISTINGUISHING DIRECTIONS

Introduction

In ancient times Emperor Yao commanded his ministers Xi and He to deliver respectfully to the people the times of the seasons. Consequently, the people came to understand the appropriate periods for planting, ripening, reaping, and storing.[21] Later sages broadened and deepened this body of knowledge to such an extent that eventually hard (yang) days were deemed appropriate for conducting external affairs, while soft (yin) days were used for internal affairs. All of this is recorded in the classic canon. Throughout the reigns of hundreds of monarchs none of it was changed.

Over time the original understanding of days was altered and adepts of the mantic arts expounded explanations about the lucky, unlucky, cursed, and blessed nature of days that shocked and frightened the people.[22] In his commentary on the *Record of the Historian* (*Shiji*), the Han scholar Chu Shaosun explained that one school said a given time was lucky, while another school said the same time was unlucky; one school said a certain time was slightly lucky, while another said that time was utterly unlucky. Thus, this body of learning became thoroughly confused and its boundaries were completely lost. By the reign of Emperor Wu (r.141–87 BCE), numerous arguments were being put forth. Great men like Xun Yue (148–209 CE) and Wang Chong (27–ca.100 CE) reproved the system as irrational and rejected it without discussion.

Although heaven employs the sun and the moon to pace out the four seasons, men respectfully serve heaven by observing timeliness. Thus, monarchs and nobles respectfully accept as the way of heaven the actions of governing when light (order) prevails and retiring when darkness (chaos) prevails. Commoners and the masses respectfully accept as the way of heaven the actions

56

of working when the sun comes out and resting when the sun goes down. If this were not so, then there would be no day and night and dawn would not be followed by dusk. Any poet would ridicule such a supposition. This is something that everyone understands.

To address this great matter, a great cohort has been mobilized. These have harmonized the five periods[23] and differentiated the five directions to make both periods and directions accord with the natural character of heaven and earth. Not one inch nor fraction of an inch have they failed to analyze to the utmost. The final essence of and evidence for each principle has been traced back to its source. Stupid, restrictive, and erroneous explanations are all the fault of mantic artists. However, one cannot simply give up eating because one once choked on a bite of food.

The Bureau of Astronomy formerly published a work entitled the *Almanac for Selections* (*Xuanze tongshu*) in the twenty-second year (i.e.1683 CE) of Emperor Kangxi (r.1662–1722 CE). Although this book was written by the hands of professional astrologers, many errors appear in the text that in practice have created numerous contradictions. His Majesty, knowing that these deficiencies made the text unsuitable for use as an instructional tool, ordered the compilation of the *Investigation into the Origins of Astronomy and Time Periods* (*Xingli kaoyuan*). That book was printed and promulgated, but the editors' original text has yet to be revised, a task that will be left for another to do in the future.

Having considered this situation carefully and repeatedly, I consulted with my advisors and was told by them that the *Almanac* is full of errors and should be revised. Because of their requests, I have ordered my minister Yun Lù and others who have expertise in this field to clarify the principles but this time to do so without adding new materials for fear that this edition might later prove useless. Thus they were ordered to compile this text, which they have completed and which I am now promulgating. I hope that the errors contained herein will prove to be fewer than those found in earlier texts. However, one must keep in mind that some erroneous traditions have been in common use for so long that it would be inconvenient to the people to completely eliminate them.

I hereby bestow upon this book the name the *Treatise on Harmonizing Times and Distinguishing Directions*. 'Harmonizing times and distinguishing directions' indicates the act of paying respect to the time periods of heaven and directions of earth. In responding to the important situations that concern the true nature of heaven and earth, there are times for acting and refraining from action, for speaking and for remaining silent. This work explains which of those behaviors is lucky, unlucky, blessed, or cursed and thus shows clearly that which is not in accord with the Way. Regardless of whether one chooses to respectfully accord with these dictums, the lucky and unlucky, the blessing and the curse will ensue nonetheless.

This serves as the introduction.

The sixth year of Emperor Qianlong, the *wang* day of the 12th lunar month.

CHAPTER ONE

The Roots and the Springs – Part 1

Chapter One contains 36 sections. The 36 sections can be divided into four groups according to their conceptual contents, although these conceptual groupings are not explicitly described in the original. The first group, consisting of sections 3.1 through 3.10, discusses the Yellow River Chart, the Luo River Diagram and the Former and Latter Heaven arrangements of the eight trigrams. The two 'river' graphs primarily serve to depict the relation between the Five Processes and pairs of numbers as well as the respective production and conquest orderings of the Five Processes. Consequently, sections one through 10 primarily serve to define the correlations between the Five Processes and the eight trigrams.

The second conceptual grouping of sections from Chapter One consists of sections 11 through 26. These sections deal with the correlations between the Five Processes on the one hand and, on the other, the Ten Heavenly Stems, the Twelve Earthly Branches, the twelve zodiacal divisions of the heavens, the Twenty-Eight Lunar Lodge asterisms, and the periods of year, month, day, and hour. Essentially, these categories are constructs used in recording the passage of time by means of an astrological calendar. Therefore, this group of sections defines the correlations between the Five Processes and the stem-branch calendrical system.

The third group in Chapter One includes sections 27 through 32, which describe the Received Notes system. The Received Notes refer to a complex convention of correlating the Five Processes with successive pairs from the sexagenary cycle of stems and branches. The system is unique because the Five Processes are paired in an order that differs from those described in previous sections, i.e. mutual production, mutual conquest, etc. Therefore, the cycle of sixty is not merely an extension of the Five-Processes correlations that pertain to the component Heavenly Stem or Earthly Branch. The system also brings into the chapter Five-Processes correlations involving the twelve pitch-pipes and the pentatonic musical scale, which together form another series of sixty. The Received Notes system is recorded in traditional Chinese almanacs, but its primary function involves fate prediction and not the reckoning of time. Thus, these sections define the correlations between the Five Processes and the set of thirty Received Notes of the stem-branch sexagenary cycle.

The fourth group of sections in Chapter One, sections 33 through 36, describes the Received Stem-*Jia* system. This system establishes correlations between the eight trigrams and the Ten Heavenly Stems. An extension of this system also correlates the individual lines of the primary hexagrams with the Twelve Earthly Branches. Therefore, this system of correlations primarily serves to reconcile the trigrams and hexagrams of the *Book of Changes* (*Yijing*) with the stem-branch system, creating a bridge between the Five-Processes correlations of the two systems as discussed in the first and second groups of sections.

> The Chart and the Diagram[24] are the roots.
> The trigrams and their lines are the wellspring.
>
> Zhu Xi

Since the Yin Yang School has always followed these genuine principles, they serve as the background (lit. roots and spring) for the current study.

The Yellow River Chart

The renowned Confucian scholar Kong Anguo (fl.130 BCE) explains in his commentary to the *Book of Documents* that the Yellow River Chart was revealed to the sage emperor Fu Xi through patterns on the coat of a 'dragon' horse that emerged from the waters of the Yellow River. It was supposedly the sight of this pattern that inspired Fu Xi to create the eight trigrams of the *Book of Changes*. As will be seen later, the horse is the animal sign of the earthly branch-

Wu which corresponds to the yang direction south. (The Luo River Diagram was revealed on the shell of a turtle, which is the heraldic animal of the yin direction north among the four beasts of the cardinal directions.) The numbers of the Yellow River Chart are correlated with the Five Processes and the four cardinal directions plus center. Following the pairs of numbers clockwise produces the mutual production sequence, i.e. yang. The correlations of numbers and processes are identical in both Chart and Diagram, but the latter excludes the number ten.

In the Yellow River Chart, one and six, as water, reside in the north. Two and seven, as fire, reside in the south. Three and eight, as wood,

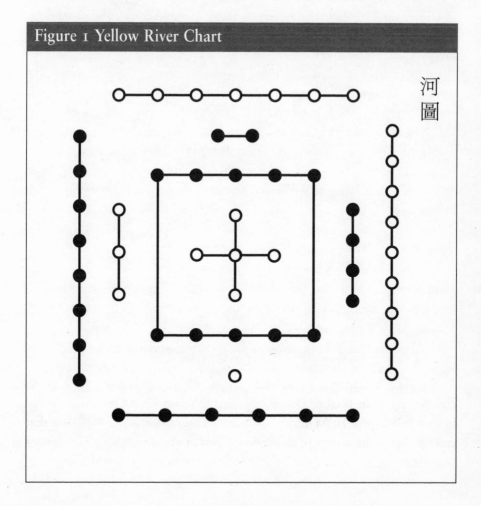

Figure 1 Yellow River Chart

河
圖

reside in the east. Four and nine, as metal, reside in the west. Five and ten, as earth, reside in the center. Northern water gives birth to eastern wood. Eastern wood gives birth to southern fire. Southern fire gives birth to central earth. Central earth gives birth to western metal. Western metal gives birth to northern water. This is the order in which the Five Processes mutually give birth to each other.

The Luo River Diagram

Kong Anguo describes a story of the Luo River Diagram's origin that sounds remarkably like that of the Yellow River Chart. The story posits that heaven inscribed the Luo River Diagram as marks on the back of a mysterious turtle, which was made to appear in the waters of the Luo River before the sage Emperor Yu, founder of the legendary Xia dynasty. From the numbers of the Diagram, Emperor Yu was able to devise the famous Great Plan of nine divisions discussed in the Introduction. Since the turtle is a symbol of water and the direction north, the Luo River Diagram has yin connotations. In the Luo River Diagram, the numbers are correlated with the Five Processes and tracing pairs of those numbers counterclockwise produces the mutual conquest sequence, i.e. yin. However, the Five Processes in this arrangement differ from their normal directional positions since those correspond only to the mutual production sequence.

In the Luo River Diagram, nine is at the head and one is at the tail (of the turtle). Three is on the left side and seven is on the right side. Two (right) and four (left) are the shoulders. Six (right) and eight (left) are the feet. Five occupies the center. One and six – water – conquer two and seven – fire. Two and seven – fire – conquer four and nine – metal. Four and nine – metal – conquer three and eight – wood. Three and eight – wood – conquer five – central earth. Five – central earth – conquers one and six – water. This is the mutual conquest order of the Five Processes.

Figure 2 Luo River Diagram

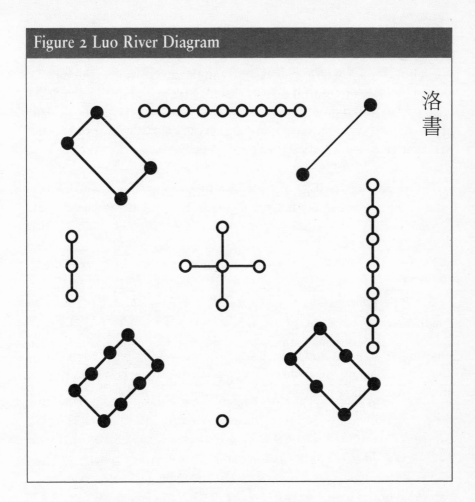

The Sequential Order of the Former Heaven Arrangement of the Eight Trigrams

The group of eight trigrams from the *Book of Changes* is often displayed in the shape of an octagon, with the bottom line of each trigram always in the interior of the octagon. Two major orders of arranging the trigrams predominate and are known respectively as the Former Heaven and Latter Heaven arrangements. The Former Heaven arrangement, to which this section refers, places each trigram directly across from its polar opposite. The opposite of a trigram is formed by changing each of its three lines to their opposite forms, i.e. broken lines (yin) are changed to solid lines (yang) and vice versa.

The positions of the lines are also important, with the bottom line being the most important, the middle line second, and the upper line being least important. Thus, this section designates trigram-*Qian*, trigram-*Dui*, trigram-*Li*, and trigram-*Zhen* as yang trigrams because in each of them the bottom line is solid (yang). Trigram-*Qian*, which contains three yang lines is placed in the uppermost position of the octagon, because, in Chinese thinking, up corresponds to the direction south and yang (contrary to the West, where up is considered north).

The remaining three yang trigrams are arranged counterclockwise from the position of trigram-*Qian*. Trigram-*Dui*, containing two yang lines in the bottom and middle positions, comes second after trigram-*Qian*. Third is trigram-*Li*, which like trigram-*Dui*, contains two yang lines, but with the second being in the least important top position. Fourth and final is trigram-*Zhen*, in which only the bottom line is yang. From this point, the numbers (5,6,7, & 8) of the yin trigrams, trigram-*Sun*, trigram-*Kan*, trigram-*Gen*, and trigram-*Kun* (yin because the bottom line of each is broken) proceed from that which is least yin, trigram-*Sun*, through to that which contains three yin lines, trigram-*Kun*.

This section also introduces Shao Yong (1011–1077 CE) who was one of the renowned 'five masters' of early Song Neo-Confucianism and a great enthusiast of numerology. Shao explains that trigram-*Qian* and trigram-*Dui* constitute the Greater Yang, because their bottom two lines are yang. By contrast, trigram-*Li* and trigram-*Zhen*, which are individually yang by virtue of their bottom yang lines, are called the Lesser Yin because they contain yin lines occupying the middle position, and middle and upper positions, respectively. A reversal of this logic also explains Greater Yin and Lesser Yang.

The important thing to remember about the sequence of the trigrams in this arrangement is that the trigrams are ordered from that which is most yang, trigram-*Qian*, to that which is least yang, i.e. most yin, trigram-*Kun*. Number one is paired with the most yang and number eight with the most yin.

The 'Appended Verbalizations' ('*Xici*') of the *Book of Changes* (*Yijing*) says:

'The Changes (*yi*) possess the Great Ultimate (*taiji*). This gives birth to Two Forms. Two Forms give birth to Four Images. Four Images give birth to the Eight Trigrams.'

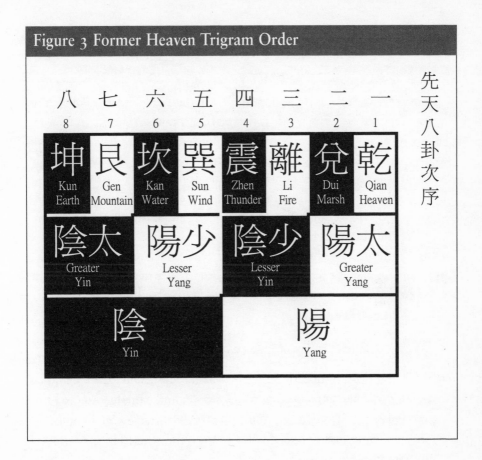

Figure 3 Former Heaven Trigram Order

Master Shao Yong said:

'Trigram-*Qian* is one. Trigram-*Dui* is two. Trigram-*Li* is three. Trigram-*Zhen* is four. Trigram-*Sun* is five. Trigram-*Kan* is six. Trigram-*Gen* is seven. Trigram-*Kun* is eight. Trigram-*Qian*, trigram-*Dui*, trigram-*Li*, and trigram-*Zhen* are yang.'[25] Trigram-*Sun*, trigram-*Kan*, trigram-*Gen*, and trigram-*Kun* are yin. Trigram-*Qian* and trigram-*Dui* are Greater Yang. Trigram-*Li* and trigram-*Zhen* are Lesser Yin. Trigram-*Sun* and trigram-*Kan* are Lesser Yang. Trigram-*Gen* and trigram-*Kun* are Greater Yin.

The Directional Positions of the Former Heaven Arrangement of the Eight Trigrams

The octagonal arrangement of the Former Heaven trigrams has been described in the preceding section. It is important for the reader to remember that Chinese place the direction south at the top of a compass. Therefore, the yang trigrams are all arranged starting from the pure yang trigram-*Qian* in the south, and the three remaining yang trigrams occupy everything east of south. The yin trigrams begin with trigram-*Kun* at due north and go on to occupy all positions west of north. This coincides with the general tendency of Chinese cosmology to associate south and east with yang, and north and west with yin.

This section also introduces another set of names that are occasionally used for the trigrams: Trigram-*Qian* is called Heaven. Trigram-*Kun* is called Earth. Trigram-*Gen* is called Mountain. Trigram-*Dui* is called Marsh. Trigram-*Zhen* is called Thunder. Trigram-*Sun* is called Wind. Trigram-*Li* is called Fire. Trigram-*Kan* is called Water.

The Explanation of the Trigrams (*Shuogua zhuan*) in the *Book of Changes* says:

'Heaven and Earth fix positions. Mountain and Marsh communicate vital breath. Thunder and Wind press upon and cover one another. Fire and Water do not issue forth one from the other. These are the mutual interactions of the Eight Trigrams.'

Shao Yong said:

'Trigram-*Qian* is in the south. Trigram-*Kun* is in the north. Trigram-*Li* is in the east. Trigram-*Kan* is in the west. Trigram-*Dui* resides in the southeast. Trigram-*Zhen* resides in the northeast. Trigram-*Sun* resides in the southwest. Trigram-*Gen* resides in the northwest. This is called the learning of the Former Heaven.'

Figure 4 Former Heaven Trigram Positions

The Sequential Order of the Latter Heaven Arrangement of the Eight Trigrams

Unlike the sequence of the Former Heaven trigrams, this section does not assign numbers from one through eight to the trigrams. Instead, it divides the eight into two groups, which are described as the male and female members of a family. Trigram-*Qian*, as pure yang, is called the father and trigram-*Kun*, pure yin, the mother. The other six trigrams are called the three sons and daughters. Again unlike the previous section, what distinguishes these trigrams as sons and daughters is not the yin or yang nature of the bottom line. Instead, the three

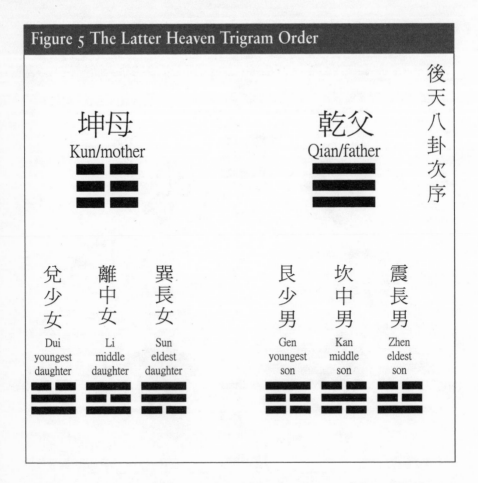

Figure 5 The Latter Heaven Trigram Order

坤母
Kun/mother

乾父
Qian/father

後天八卦次序

兌
少
女
Dui
youngest
daughter

離
中
女
Li
middle
daughter

巽
長
女
Sun
eldest
daughter

艮
少
男
Gen
youngest
son

坎
中
男
Kan
middle
son

震
長
男
Zhen
eldest
son

sons are the three trigrams that contain only one yang line and their respective birth order is determined by the location of that yang line. Trigram-*Zhen*, with one yang line on the bottom, is the eldest son. Trigram-*Kan*, with one yang line in the middle position, is the middle son. Trigram-*Gen*, with one yang line on the top, is the youngest son. The order of the daughters parallels this.

The Explanation of the Trigrams (*Shuogua zhuan*) in the *Book of Changes* says:

'Since trigram-*Qian* is Heaven it is referred to as Father. Since trigram-*Kun* is Earth it is referred to as Mother. Since trigram-*Zhen* sought first and obtained birth as a son, it is called Eldest Son. Since trigram-*Sun* sought first and obtained birth as a daughter, it is called

Eldest Daughter. Since trigram-*Kan* sought again and obtained birth as a son, it is called Middle Son. Since trigram-*Li* sought again and obtained birth as a daughter, it is called Middle Daughter. Since tri-gram-*Gen* sought thirdly and obtained birth as a son, it is called Youngest Son. Since trigram-*Dui* sought thirdly and obtained birth as a daughter, it is called Youngest Daughter.'

The Directional Positions of the Latter Heaven Arrangement of the Eight Trigrams

The quote from the *Book of Changes* given here explains the order of the trigrams around the octagon starting from trigram-*Zhen* at due east (south is up) and progressing clockwise to conclude with trigram-*Gen* in the northeast. The analogy is to a reverse progression through the emperor's palace grounds. It begins with trigram-*Zhen* as the most external position, from which the emperor departs the palace and progresses in through the palace to the most interior room in which the emperor privately assesses memorials.

Shao Yong's quote explains that trigram-*Qian*, as father, controls the three sons from the northwest and indeed all four 'male' trigrams in this arrange-ment are arrayed in line from northwest to due east. The females occupy southeast through due west.

The symmetry of the Latter Heaven Arrangement may be explained as follows: the trigram in the south (top) is transformed into the trigram in the north by reversing all three lines; the trigram in the southwest (top-right) is transformed into the trigram in the northeast by reversing the top (outermost) line; the trigram in the west (right) is transformed into the trigram in the east by reversing the middle line; the trigram in the northwest (bottom-right) is transformed into the trigram in the southeast by reversing the bottom (innermost) line.

The Explanation of the Trigrams (*Shuogua zhuan*) in the *Book of Changes* says:

'The Emperor proceeds out from trigram-*Zhen*, assembles in trigram-*Sun*, grants audiences in trigram-*Li*, dispatches orders in trigram-*Kun*, explains commands in trigram-*Dui*, plans war in trigram-*Qian*, arranges public works in trigram-*Kan*, and assesses memorials in trigram-*Gen*.'

Figure 6 The Latter Heaven Trigram Positions

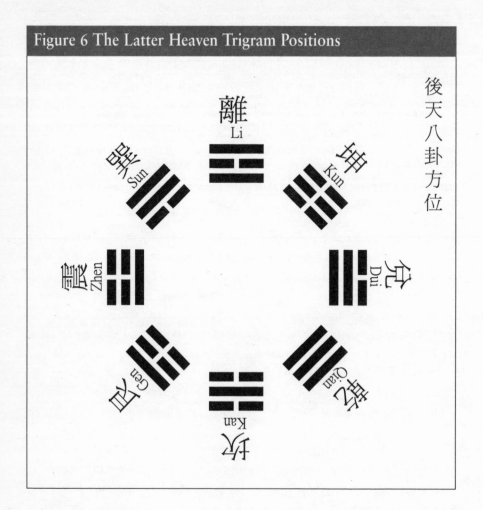

Shao Yong said:

'Trigram-*Qian* manages the three Sons from the northwest. Trigram-*Kun* manages the three daughters from the southwest.'[26] Trigram-*Qian*, trigram-*Kan*, trigram-*Gen*, and trigram-*Zhen* are yang. Trigram-*Sun*, trigram-*Li*, trigram-*Kun*, and trigram-*Dui* are yin.

Depiction of the Former Heaven Arrangement of the Trigrams Coupled with the Yellow River Chart

This scheme combines the Yellow River Chart with the Former Heaven trigrams. It explains the relationship between the two images by reference to the mutual production virtue of the Yellow River Chart, i.e. that the clockwise flow of the Five Processes in this arrangement has each producing its successor. When the pairs of numbers are depicted graphically in the Chart, odd numbers are unfilled (white) circles, representing yang, and even numbers are solid (black) circles, i.e. yin. Also, the larger number of each pair is depicted on the periphery and the smaller number is drawn nearest the center. On the left side 3 (odd/yang) and 8 (even/yin) stand for wood and east. On the top 2 (even/yin) and 7 (odd/yang) stand for fire and south. Thus in moving from left to the top, the yang number moves from the inside to the outside. In the same

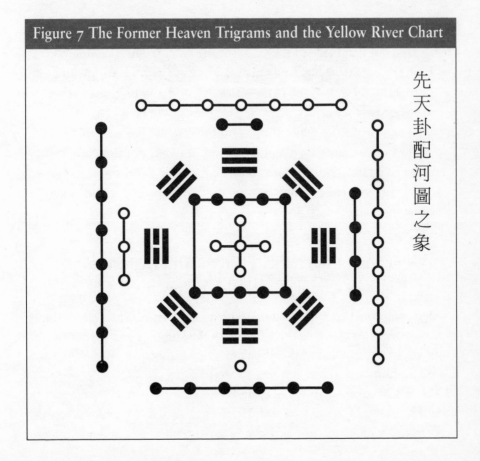

Figure 7 The Former Heaven Trigrams and the Yellow River Chart

先天卦配河圖之象

way, looking from right (west) to bottom (north), yin moves from the inside to the outside, symbolizing the growth of yin.

The passage explains that a similar pattern may be observed in the lines of the trigrams. From trigram-*Zhen*, which contains only one yang line on the bottom, to trigram-*Li* yang increases, since trigram-*Li* gains one yang line in the top position. From trigram-*Li* to trigram-*Dui*, yang is further strengthened, since trigram-*Dui* has two yang lines in the superior bottom and middle positions. Finally, from trigram-*Dui* to trigram-*Qian*, yang gains all three positions. The same rationale applies to the yin trigrams from trigram-*Sun* through trigram-*Kun*, with yin constantly increasing.

This shows that the images of the Yellow River Chart and the Former Heaven trigrams are seen to symbolize the increase of yang strength from spring in the east to the peak of yang during summer in the south. Thereafter, yin increases from fall in the west and peaks at winter in the north.

The 'Premier Appendix' (*Qimeng fulun*) of the *Book of Changes* says:

> 'At the left hand side of the Chart, yang is on the inside while yin is on the outside. Thus, yang grows while yin declines for the lines of trigram-*Zhen*, trigram-*Li*, trigram-*Dui*, and trigram-*Qian* as they are placed in the Former Heaven Arrangement. At its right hand side, yin is on the inside while yang is on the outside. Thus, yin grows while yang declines for the lines of trigram-*Sun*, trigram-*Kan*, trigram-*Gen*, and trigram-*Kun* as they are placed in the Former Heaven Arrangement. This, then, is what is used to depict the convergence of the two vital breaths.'

Depiction of the Latter Heaven Arrangement of the Trigrams Coupled with the Yellow River Chart

Having combined the Yellow River Chart with the Former Heaven trigrams, the compilers now combine the Chart with the Latter Heaven arrangement. However, in this instance, rather than analyzing component lines, the focus is on the trigrams' Five-Processes correlations.

The Yellow River Chart's water numbers, one and six, stand in the bottom (north) position adjacent to the Latter Heaven's placement of trigram-*Kan*, which is correlated with water. Similarly, the Chart's numbers two and seven, repre-

Figure 8 The Latter Heaven Trigrams and the Yellow River Chart

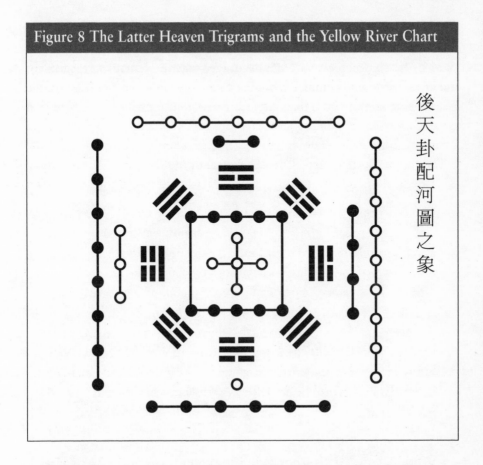

senting fire, appear in the top (south) position, adjacent to the Latter Heaven's positioning of trigram-*Li* – also associated with the fire process.

The remaining trigrams are grouped in pairs. Trigram-*Zhen* and trigram-*Sun*, representing wood, occupy the east and southeast positions in the Latter Heaven scheme and are thus adjacent to the Chart's numbers three and eight. Trigram-*Dui* and trigram-*Qian*, representing metal, occupy the west and northwest positions in the Latter Heaven scheme and are thus adjacent to the Chart's numbers four and nine.

Finally, trigram-*Kun* and trigram-*Gen* stand in the southwest and northeast positions in the Latter Heaven arrangement. These trigrams, associated with the earth process, are said to accompany the Yellow River Chart's central position of the numbers five and ten. The connection of these two trigrams to earth, standing across from each other as they do in the Latter Heaven arrangement explains the reference to the axis between branch-*Chou* and branch-*Wei*. In the Five Processes correlations of the Twelve Earthly Branches, branch-*Chou* and branch-*Wei* are associated with earth. As months, branch-*Chou* and branch-*Wei* constitute the last months of the winter and summer, respectively, and therefore mark the major break between the yin and yang portions of the year. In a sense, this axis is therefore, the basis of the curved S-shaped line that divides yin from yang in the famous *taiji* symbol.

The 'Premier Appendix' (*Qimeng fulun*) of the *Book of Changes* says:

> 'One and six of the Chart are water, which corresponds with the position of trigram-*Kan* in the Latter Heaven arrangement. Three and eight are wood, which corresponds with the position of trigram-*Zhen* and trigram-*Sun* in the Latter Heaven arrangement. Two and seven are fire, which corresponds with the position of trigram-*Li* in the Latter Heaven arrangement. Four and nine are metal, which corresponds with the position of trigram-*Dui* and trigram-*Qian* in the Latter Heaven arrangement. Five and ten are earth, which corresponds with the position of trigram-*Kun* and trigram-*Gen* in the Latter Heaven arrangement. This cycle flows through the four seasons and inclines at the axis line formed by branch-*Chou* and branch-*Wei*. This is what is used to depict the orderly progression of the five vital breaths.'

Numeration of the Former Heaven Arrangement of the Trigrams Coupled with the Luo River Diagram

This pairing of the Luo River Diagram's numbers with the Former Heaven trigram arrangement makes reference to the familial divisions into male and female sides together with birth orders first described in conjunction with the Latter Heaven sequence above. Essentially, in this combination of the two diagrams, the patriarchal trigram-*Qian* and the three sons are paired with the numbers 9, 8, 7, and 6 in descending order, while the matriarchal trigram-*Kun* and the three daughters are paired with the numbers 1, 2, 3, and 4 in ascending order. The odd and even values of the numbers in the first case appear to have no yin yang significance here. However, the compilers of the Treatise point out that another school does associate the trigrams with yin and yang according to the odd and even values of the numbers with which they are paired. In either case, both systems of correlating the Former Heaven trigrams with

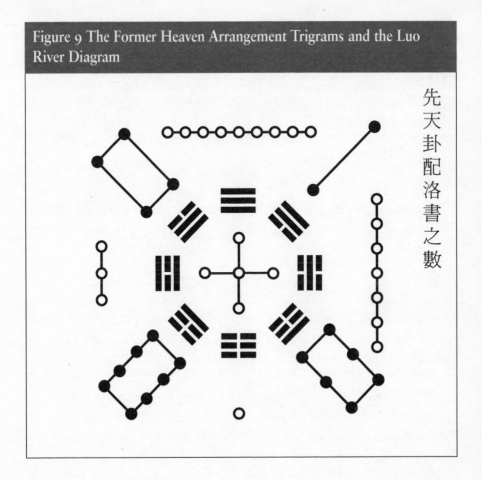

Figure 9 The Former Heaven Arrangement Trigrams and the Luo River Diagram

yin and yang differ from the scheme given when that arrangement was introduced above.

The 'Premier Appendix' (*Qimeng fulun*) of the *Book of Changes* says:

'Since the Luo River Diagram has nine numbers, the empty center is paired with five in order to match the numbers with the Eight Trigrams. Yang is above. Yin is below. Thus, nine is trigram-*Qian* and one is trigram-*Kun*. Thus, counting backwards from nine, trigram-*Zhen* is eight, trigram-*Kan* is seven, and trigram-*Gen* is six. This shows that trigram-*Qian* gives birth to the three yang. Also, counting forwards from one, trigram-*Sun* is two, trigram-*Li* is three, and trigram-*Dui* is four. This shows that trigram-*Kun* gives birth to the three yin. This manner of pairing the eight numbers with the Eight Trigrams is in accord with the positions of the Former Heaven arrangement.'

Compilers' Note: The Numerological School[27] pairs trigram-*Qian* with 9, trigram-*Kun* with 1, trigram-*Li* with 3, and trigram-*Kan* with 7. Since their numbers are odd, they are yang. Trigram-*Dui* is paired with 4, trigram-*Zhen* with 8, trigram-*Sun* with 2, and trigram-*Gen* with 6. Since their numbers are even, they are yin.

Numeration of the Latter Heaven Arrangement of the Trigrams Coupled with the Luo River Diagram

This section makes reference to the standard Five-Processes correlations of the eight trigrams, with one unique innovation. It parses trigram-*Gen* and trigram-*Kun*, the earth trigrams, into dry and wet earth, respectively. Presumably trigram-*Gen* is dry because its number in the Luo River Diagram, eight, is one less than the nine of the fire trigram-*Li*. Trigram-*Kun* is wet because its number, two, is one above the number one of the water trigram-*Kan*. The scheme is also unusual because it suggests that 'dry' earth (trigram-*Gen*) gives birth to metal, but that 'wet' earth (trigram-*Kun*) gives birth to wood. In the standard Five Processes mutual production cycle, earth gives birth to metal, but water gives birth to wood. In fact, wood's relationship to earth is actually destructive since wood conquers earth.

The compilers' note explains that the Latter Heaven arrangement of trigrams and the numbers of the Luo River Diagram are especially 'functional.' This assertion is given greater credence by virtue of attributing it to the venerable neo-Confucians Shao Yong and Zhu Xi. The implication is that these two schemes are more concerned with function than the Former Heaven arrangement and the Yellow River Chart. Function here means use or application and the compilers occasionally contrast the concept of function with body or physical form. Function is thus the dynamic aspect of a thing whereas its body or physical form refers to the static aspect of the same object. The conceptual constructs of substance (*ti*) and function (*yong*) were imported into Chinese thinking from Buddhism during the Tang dynasty. The important point is that due to their dynamic nature the Latter Heaven arrangement and the Luo River Diagram are better suited to application in the realm of astrology and *feng shui* than the Former Heaven arrangement and the Yellow River Chart.

Figure 10 The Latter Heaven Trigrams and the Luo River Diagram

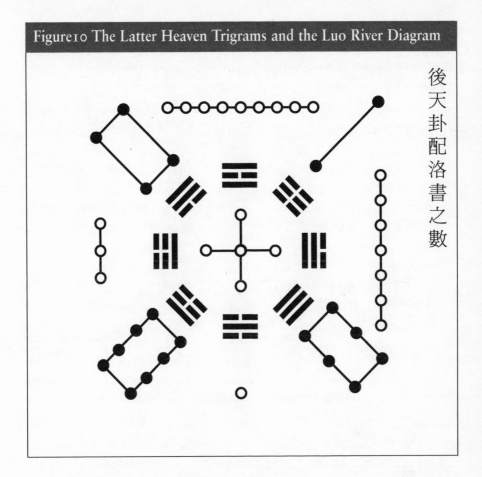

後天卦配洛書之數

The 'Premier Appendix' (*Qimeng fulun*) of the *Book of Changes* says:

'Since Fire is above and Water is below, nine is trigram-*Li* and one is trigram-*Kan*. Since Fire gives birth to Dry Earth, eight, being next in sequence to nine, is trigram-*Gen*. Since Dry Earth gives birth to Metal, seven and six, being next in sequence to eight, are trigram-*Dui* and trigram-*Qian*. Since Water gives birth to Wet Earth, two, being next in sequence to one, is trigram-*Kun*. Since Wet Earth gives birth to wood, three and four, being next in sequence to two, are trigram-*Zhen* and trigram-*Sun*. This manner of pairing the eight numbers with the Eight Trigrams is in accord with the positions of the Latter Heaven arrangement.'

Compilers' Note: Shao Yong regarded King Wen's arrangement of the Trigrams (i.e. the Latter Heaven arrangement) as the positions from which to enter into function and as the learning of the Latter Heaven. Zhu Xi regarded the Luo River Diagram as the function of numbers. The Numerological School's Flying Palace and Hanging Substitute (*fei gong diao ti*) all use the Latter Heaven arrangement of trigrams paired with the Luo River Diagram. This method uses the following sequence for the trigrams: trigram-*Kan* (1), trigram-*Kun* (2), trigram-*Zhen* (3), trigram-*Sun* (4), Middle (5), trigram-*Qian* (6), trigram-*Dui* (7), trigram-*Gen* (8), and trigram-*Li* (9). Liu Xin (c.46 BCE–23 CE) said, 'The eight trigrams and the nine emblems face one another as exterior and interior.' Zhang Heng (78–139 CE) said, 'In layering (i.e. 'distinguishing') them, the sage uses the divination by milfoil (i.e. the trigrams), while in blending (i.e. 'harmonizing') them, he uses the nine palaces (i.e. the nine numbers of the Luo River Diagram). From all of this evidence, we know that the origins of this system are in the distant past.'

The Heavenly Stem-*Jia* Periods

This section[28] demonstrates that the use of the term 'stem-*Jia*' in the title was meant to refer to the entire system of stems and branches. This reference to the entire system by only the first of the Ten Heavenly Stems is a common convention and appears repeatedly throughout the Treatise. The section lists alternate names for the Heavenly Stems and Earthly Branches used to designate months and years. The alternate names for the stems of the months and years are called monthly yang and yearly yang. Though the Treatise doesn't use the term, the 'names' of the months and years, i.e. alternate names for their Earthly Branches, are sometimes known as the monthly yin and yearly yin. Thus, the Heavenly Stems are yang and Earthly Branches are yin.

From this point forward, the Treatise begins to quote large sections from the *Investigation into the Origins of Astronomy and Time Periods* (*Xingli kaoyuan* 1713 CE). At some points, these borrowings are noted but not consistently. In any case, many of these passages are themselves quotes from other sources, as is the case here. The dates traditionally given for the *Rites of the Zhou* (*Zhou li*) and the *Erya* are questionable, but those of the commentator

Zheng Xuan (127–200 CE), whom we shall see again, are known with certainty. The alternate names given for the stems and branches are quite ancient and are probably of non-Chinese origin. The meanings of the alternate names are unclear and in any case have little bearing on the Treatise as a whole. Therefore, I have not translated them.

The *Rites of the Zhou* (*Zhou li*) contains a reference to the names of the ten days, the twelve zodiac signs (*chen*), the twelve months, the twelve years, and the twenty-eight asterisms. Zheng Xuan annotates that reference, saying:

> 'The "days" refers to the stem-*Jia* through the stem-*Gui*. The "zodiac signs" refers to the branch-*Zi* through the branch-*Hai*. The "months" refers to *Ju* through *Tu*. The "years" refers to *Shitige* through *Shifenruo*. The "asterisms" refers to Horn (*jiao*) through Chariot (*zhen*).'

The *Erya* says:

> 'The monthly yang, when in stem-*Jia*, is called *Bi* ("a net"). In stem-*Yi*, it is called *Ju* ("an orange"). In stem-*Bing*, it is called *Xiu* ("refined"). In stem-*Ding*, it is called *Yu* ("cage"). In stem-*Wu*, it is called *Li* ("grindstone"). In stem-*Ji*, it is called *Ze* ("rule"). In stem-*Geng*, it is called *Zhi* ("blocked"). In stem-*Xin*, it is called *Sai* ("to stuff"). In stem-*Ren*, it is called *Zhong* ("end"). In stem-*Gui*, it is called *Ji* ("extreme").
>
> 'The names of the months are as follows: the first month is *Ju* ("woman, take" branch-*Yin*); the second is *Ru* ("like" branch-*Mao*), the third is *Bing* ("bright" branch-*Chen*), the fourth is *Yu* ("residence" branch-*Si*), the fifth is *Gao* ("pool" branch-*Wu*), the sixth is *Qie* ("altar" branch-*Wei*), the seventh is *Xiang* ("appearance" branch-*Shen*), the eighth is *Zhuang* ("stout" branch-*You*), the ninth is *Yuan* ("prime" branch-*Xu*), the tenth is Yang ("yang" of "yin yang" branch-*Hai*), the eleventh is *Gu* ("offence" branch-*Zi*); the twelfth is *Tu* ("road" branch-*Chou*).
>
> 'The yearly yang, when the Great Year is in stem-*Jia*, is called *E'peng*. In stem-*Yi*, it is called *Zhenmeng*. In stem-*Bing*, it is called *Rouzhao*. In stem-*Ding*, it is called *Qiangyu*. In stem-*Wu*, it is called

Zhaoyong. In stem-*Ji*, it is called *Tuwei*. In stem-*Geng*, it is called *Shangzhang*. In stem-*Xin*, it is called *Zhongguang*. In stem-*Ren*, it is called *Xuanyi*. In stem-*Gui*, it is called *Zhaoyang*.

'The names of the years are as follows: when the Great Year (*Taisui*) is in the zodiac sign of the branch-*Yin*, it is called *Shitige*. In the branch-*Mao*, it is called *Dan'e*.[29] In the branch-*Chen*, it is called *Zhixu*. In the branch-*Si*, it is called *Dahuangluo*. In branch-*Wu*, it is called *Dunzang*. In the branch-*Wei*, it is called *Xiexia*. In the branch-*Shen*, it is called *Tuntan*. In the branch-*You*, it is called *Zuo'o*. In the branch-*Xu*, it is called *Yanmao*. In the branch-*Hai*, it is called *Dayuanxian*. In the branch-*Zi*, it is called *Kundun*. In the branch-*Chou*, it is called *Chifenruo*.'

The Ten Stems, the Twelve Branches, the Twelve Pitch Pipes, and the Twenty-Eight Houses

The majority of this section is a quote from the first-century-CE *Record of the Historian* (*Shiji*), which lists the Twenty-Eight Lunar Lodges[30] together with the correlated eight winds, twelve months of the year, Twelve Earthly Branches, Twelve Pitch Pipes, and Ten Heavenly Stems. The main point of that text and, by extension, the justification for the compilers including it in the current work, was to describe the connection between these groups of cycles and the flux of yin and yang throughout the course of the year. The passage begins with the 'Not Circling' wind in the northwest, between the ninth and tenth months, which represented the peak of yin and death. From there it describes the birth of yang and the life-cycle of yang throughout the course of the year and through the Twenty-Eight Lunar Lodges.

The anchor of the passage is the set of lunar lodges. These correspond to minor constellations, or asterisms, in front of which the sun and moon appear to proceed around the earth. They are termed 'lunar' because similar groups of constellations have been used in several cultures to trace the progression of the moon through the stars over the course of a month, i.e. with the moon 'lodging' in a different asterism each night, which alas it does not. To reflect the conventional conception of the yin-yang cycle, the passage proceeds through the lodges clockwise, as the seasons and directions move, rather than counterclockwise, as the moon actually progresses through the lodges.

The placement of the various other groups among the lodges appears somewhat jumbled in the passage. Furthermore, the names of ten of the lodges given here differ from the standard listing. The important thing to take from this passage is the way it correlates stars, months, seasons, and directions. As such, the passage gives an early prototype of the twenty-four mountains system, which is described fully below. Cai Yong[31] (133–192 CE) was a Confucian scholar and civil servant in the employment of the Han Emperor Lingdi (r.168–189 CE).

The *Study of Calendrics* (*Xingli kaoyuan*) says:[32]

'In his *Independent Conclusions* (*Duduan*) Cai Yong says:

"The Heavenly Stems are trunks. They have the ten names, stem-*Jia*, stem-*Yi*, stem-*Bing*, stem-*Ding*, stem-*Wu*, stem-*Ji*, stem-*Geng*, stem-*Xin*, stem-*Ren*, and stem-*Gui*. The Earthly Branches are limbs. They have the twelve names, branch-*Zi*, branch-*Chou*, branch-*Yin*, branch-*Mao*, branch-*Chen*, branch-*Si*, branch-*Wu*, branch-*Wei*, branch-*Shen*, branch-*You*, branch-*Xu*, and branch-*Hai*."

'In the "Monthly Ordinances" ("*Yue ling*") chapter of the *Book of Rites* (*Liji*), the days pertaining to the spring months are stem-*Jia* and stem-*Yi*. The days pertaining to the summer months are stem-*Bing* and stem-*Ding*. The days pertaining to central earth are stem-*Wu* and stem-*Ji*. The days pertaining to the fall months are stem-*Geng* and stem-*Xin*. The days pertaining to the winter months are stem-*Ren* and stem-*Gui*.'

The 'Regulation Book' ('*Lüshu*') of the *Record of the Historian* (*Shiji*) says:[33]

'The seven uprights, the Twenty-Eight Houses, and the regulation Pitch Pipe periods are what heaven uses to connect the Five Processes. The vital breath of the eight uprights is what heaven uses to mature and bring to fruition the myriad things. The "houses" are where the sun and moon are housed. "Housing," here, refers to the housing of vital breath.

'The Not-Circling Wind[34] resides in the northwest and governs the taking of life. The Eastern Wall lodge resides to the east of the

Not-Circling Wind and governs the summoning of living vital breath. To the east of this is the Encampment lodge. The Encampment governs the conception of and giving birth to yang vital breath. To the east of this is the Dangerous Height lodge. The "dangerous height," here, refers to a high wall that is at risk of being razed to the ground. This indicates that the yang vital force is at danger [because it is infantile]. This is the tenth month. Among the Pitch Pipes, this corresponds to the Responsive Bell. This indicates that the yang vital breath is responding and need not be attended to. Among the twelve sons (Earthly Branches), this is branch-*Hai*. The character "*hai*," in this context, means "ordained." That is to say that the yang vital-breath is buried below as it ought to be.

'The Vast Darkness Wind resides in the north. This name indicates that the yang is below. The yin is dark, while the yang is vast and great. Therefore, it is called the Vast Darkness. To the east of this is the Void lodge. The 'void,' which is equally capable of being existent (*shi*) or of being void (*xu*), indicates that yang vital breath (assumed to be existent, *shi*, as opposed to yin, which would be void, *xu*) in the winter is buried in a void. When the sun reaches the winter solstice, one yin descends and buries itself while one yang rises and unfolds itself. Therefore, this lodge is called the Void. To the east of this is the Maiden in Waiting. This indicates that the myriad things are in the process of exchanging positions. The vital breaths of yin and yang have not yet separated, but are still pressing upon each other like [the white and yolk] of an egg. Therefore, this lodge is called the Maiden in Waiting. This is the eleventh month. Among the Pitch Pipes, this corresponds to the Yellow Bell. Yellow Bell implies that the yang vital breath follows along the Yellow Spring and proceeds out. Among the twelve sons (Earthly Branches), this is branch-*Zi*. Branch-*Zi*, in this context, means "nurture." That is to say that the myriad things are being nurtured below. Among the ten mothers (Heavenly Stems), this is stem-*Ren* and stem-*Gui*. The character *ren* indicates "cultivating" because the yang vital breath cultivates the myriad things below. The character *gui* indicates "measuring" because the myriad things can be weighed and measured.

'To the east is the Pulling Ox lodge. The "pulling" indicates that the yang vital breath pulls the myriad things along and leads them out. The "ox" means "pushing forth," which refers to the fact that the ground, though frozen, can push forth and give birth. In the same way, an ox is capable of plowing, planting, and growing the myriad things. To the east of this is the Establishing Stars lodge. The Establishing Stars "establish" various forms of life. This is the twelfth month. Among the Pitch Pipes, it is the Great Regulator (*Da Lü*). Among the twelve sons (Earthly Branches), Great Regulator is branch-*Chou*. The character "*chou*", in this context, means a knot, indicating that the yang vital breath is above and has not yet descended; the myriad things are cramped and knotted together and have not yet issued forth.

'The Ordering Wind resides in the northeast. It governs the sending forth of the myriad things. The meaning of "ordering" in this context is that the wind sets the myriad things in order and sends them forth. This is why it is called the Ordering Wind. To the south is the Winnowing Basket (*Ji*) lodge. The name "Winnowing Basket" indicates that the myriad things are rooted. This is why it is called the Winnowing Basket. This is the first month. Among the Pitch Pipes, it is the Magnificent Gatherer. The name "Magnificent Gatherer" indicates that the myriad things are born together in a cluster. Therefore, it is called the Magnificent Gatherer. Among the twelve sons (Earthly Branches), it is branch-*Yin*. The character '*yin*' indicates that the myriad things are "wriggly" (homophonous with "*yin*") when they begin to be born. Therefore, it is called branch-*Yin*.

'To the south is the Tail lodge. The name "tail" indicates that the myriad things are in the shape of tails when they begin to be born. To the south is the Heart lodge, which is to suggest that the myriad things have vibrant "hearts" when they begin to be born. To the south is the Room lodge. The name "room" indicates that this forms the gates and doors of the myriad things. When they arrive at the gates, they proceed out.

'The Brilliant Abundance Wind resides in the east. The name "Brilliant Abundance" indicates that the bright mass of things completely proceed out. This is the second month. Among the Pitch Pipes, it is the

Interval Bell. The name "interval" indicates that the yin and yang are intermingled. Among the twelve sons (Earthly Branches), it is branch-Mao. The character "*mao*" in this context means "verdant," indicating that the myriad things grow verdantly at this time. Among the ten mothers, this is stem-*Jia* and stem-*Yi*. The reference to "*jia*," or shell, indicates that the myriad things make the ritual prognostication on the tortoise shell and proceed out [in the royal manner]. The term "*Yi*" is homophonous with the word for "crashing," indicating that the myriad things are born in a crashing mass.

'To the south is the Root lodge. The name "root" indicates that the myriad things have all arrived. To the south of this is the Pride (lit. "neck") lodge. The name of this lodge indicates that the myriad things proudly make their appearance. To the south of this is the Horn lodge, which name indicates that the myriad things all sprout small branches like horns. This is the third month. Among the Pitch Pipes, it is Virginal Purity. The name indicates that the myriad things are all purely born. Among the twelve sons (Earthly Branches), it is branch-Chen. The character "*chen*" is homomorphous with a character that means arousal, indicating that the myriad things are all aroused.

'The Clear Brilliance wind resides in the southeast. From its corner it governs the winds blowing on the myriad things. To the west of this is the Chariot Bumper lodge. This name suggests that the myriad things are growing large and crashing forth like a bumper. To the west of this is the Wings lodge. This name indicates that the myriad things have assistants [i.e. its wings are a bird's assistants]. This is the fourth month. Among the Pitch Pipes, this corresponds to the Median Regulator. The name "median regulator" suggests that the myriad things exhaustively set forth in order together, proceeding to the west. Among the twelve sons (Earthly Branches), it is branch-Si. The character "*si*," which is the same graph as "*ji*," or "already" suggests that the yang vital energy is already exhausted.

'To the west of this is the Seven Stars lodge.[35] The name of this lodge derives from the fact that the numbers of yang are completed with seven. Thus, this is called the Seven Stars. To the west of this is the Extension lodge. The name of this lodge highlights the fact that the myriad things have reached their maximum extension. To the west of this is the Downpour lodge.[36] The name of this lodge indicates that the myriad things are in decline and thus yang vital breath is pouring downwards. Thus, it is called downpour. This is the fifth month. Among the Pitch Pipes, it corresponds to Luxuriance and Guests. It bears this name because the yin vital breath is youthful and is thus called luxuriant while the paralyzed yang is no longer in power and is thus like a guest.

'The Midday Sunlight Wind resides in the south. This name indicates that the yang vital breath has reached its peak limit and is thus called the Midday Sunlight Wind.[37] Among the twelve sons (Earthly Branches), it is branch-*Wu*. The term "*wu*" indicates that the yin and yang are exchanging and is thus called branch-*Wu*.[38] Among the ten mothers, it is stem-*Bing* and stem-*Ding*. The name *Bing* indicates that the way of yang shines brightly.[39] The name *Ding* indicates that the myriad things are stout and vigorous.[40]

'To the west of this is the Bow lodge. This indicates that the myriad things descend clamorously and approach death [i.e. bending down like a bow]. To the west of this is the Wolf lodge. This indicates that the myriad things can be weighed and measured; [this is to] cut apart the myriad things and is thus called the Wolf.[41]

'The Cool Wind resides in the southwest corner and governs earth. The earth deeply pulls in the vital breath of the myriad things.[42] This is the sixth month. Among the Pitch Pipes, it is the Forest Bell. The name "Forest Bell" indicates that the myriad things are nearing death and their vital breath is heavy [lit. numerous like the crowded trees of a forest].[43] Among the twelve sons (Earthly Branches), it is branch-*Wei*. The character "*wei*" indicates that the myriad things are ripened and are nutritious [since the branch-*Wei* is homophonous and homographic with the word for flavor].

'To the north of this is the Punishment lodge. The name of this lodge indicates that the myriad things have been apprehended and can be punished.[44] To the north of this is the Triad lodge. The name "triad" indicates that the myriad things may be tried or investigated [since the graph for "triad" has another meaning, which is "to censure or try."] This is the seventh month. Among the Pitch Pipes, it is Capital Punishment. This name indicates that the yin vital breath kills the myriad things. Among the twelve sons (Earthly Branches), it is branch-*Shen*. The character "*shen*," which means "to extend," indicates that yin is in power and extends [its] killing [action] to the myriad things.

'To the north of this is the Marsh lodge.[45] The name, [with a character that is graphically similar to another that means "to contact" or "to ram"], indicates that the myriad things all meet with death. To the north of this is the Remaining lodge. The name of this lodge indicates that the yang vital breath remains in place.[46] This is the eighth month. Among the Pitch Pipes, it is Southern Regulator. The name indicates that, in its progression, yang vital breath has entered the grave. Among the twelve sons (Earthly Branches), it is branch-*You*. The character "*you*" here indicates the great age of the myriad things.[47]

'The Gate of Heaven Wind resides in the west. The first character in the name of this wind – *chang* – means 'to lead,' while the second character – *he* – means "to bury." The name of this wind, therefore, indicates that in the way of the yang vital breath, the myriad things are submerged, or buried, in the Yellow Spring. Among the ten mothers, this is stem-*Geng* and stem-*Xin*. *Geng* means "to transform," indicating that the yin vital breath transforms the myriad things. *Xin* means "laborious," indicating that the myriad things experience great difficulty in [holding on to] life. To the north of this is the Stomach lodge.[48] The name indicates that the myriad things approach burial and are all cramped together [like intestines]. To the north of this is the Gathering lodge. This name indicates that the myriad things are all gathered within. To the north of this is the Stride lodge. This governs the fatal poisoning and subsequent burying of the myriad things. This is the ninth month. Among the Pitch Pipes, it is Lacking Issuance. This indicates that the yin vital breath has risen to power and the yang vital breath has no more surplus. Therefore, it is called Lacking Issuance. Among the twelve sons (Earthly Branches), it is branch-*Xu*. This indicates that the myriad things have all been exhausted and is therefore called branch-*Xu* (the graph of the character "*xu*"is a great axe, indicating cutting/killing).'

The Four Sequences

This section outlines the correlation between four of the Five Processes and the Twelve Earthly Branches. The authors imply that the branches here refer to the names of the zodiacal signs. Presumably this would explain why the process earth does not figure in the account since the zodiacal signs are part of the heavens.

Branch-*Yin*, branch-*Mao*, and branch-*Chen* are wood.

Branch-*Si*, branch-*Wu*, and branch-*Wei* are fire.

Branch-*Shen*, branch-*You*, and branch-*Xu* are metal.

Branch-*Hai*, branch-*Zi*, and branch-*Chou* are water.

The above indicates that spring, summer, fall, winter, and the five vital breaths accord with the commands of the stars (i.e. of the zodiacal signs).

The Six Zodiac Divisions

This section lists the yin-yang correlations of the Twelve Earthly Branches, with the odd-numbered branches as yang and the even-numbered branches as yin. It suggests that the four yang trigrams receive the six yang branches, etc., but the implication of this is unclear.

Branch-*Zi*, branch-*Yin*, branch-*Chen*, branch-*Wu*, branch-*Shen*, and branch-*Xu* are yang.

Branch-*Chou*, branch-*Mao*, branch-*Si*, branch-*Wei*, branch-*You*, and branch-*Hai* are yin.

The above has yang following yang and yin following yin. The four yang trigrams receive the six yang zodiacal signs and the four yin trigrams receive the six yin zodiacal signs.

The Twelve Months Summon Hexagrams

This rather repetitive section is of great import because it presents the classical foundation of the indications of the handle of the Big Dipper. Throughout the twelve months of the year the sun and moon move to the left, i.e. counterclockwise, converging consecutively in the twelve zodiacal signs. At the same time, the handle of the Big Dipper moves to the right, i.e. clockwise, consecutively pointing out the twelve directions of the earth's surface. Instead of using the names of the twelve branches for the twelve zodiacal signs in which the sun and moon converge, Zheng Xuan (127–200 CE) here uses alternate names. He also refers to the twelve months, by a common Chinese convention, as the first, middle, or last month of the respective season. Zheng Xuan's commentary here was made in relation to the Monthly Ordinances chapter of the *Book of Rites* (*Liji*), which is a work of the Han period. This section also associates hexagrams with each of the twelve months of the year. The months progress from being completely yang in the first month of summer, i.e. the fourth lunar month, to being completely yin in the first month of winter, i.e. tenth lunar month. Thereafter, each month becomes progressively yang again. Remember that the lines of hexagrams are read from the bottom to the top, or in the circular diagram, from the exterior of the circle to the interior.

The *Study of Calendrics* (*Xingli kaoyuan*) says:[49]

'The first month, the establishing of the branch-*Yin*, and the Peace hexagram (*Tai* #11).

"Zheng Xuan's annotation to the first month of spring in the 'Monthly Ordinances' ('*Yue ling*'), says:

'In the first month of spring, the sun and moon converge in the Seeking (*juzi*) constellation and the Dipper establishes the direction of the branch-*Yin*. The first month is the month of three yang and the Peace hexagram is the hexagram of three yang. Therefore, the Peace hexagram accompanies the first month.

'The second month, the establishing of the branch-*Mao*, and the Power of the Great hexagram (*Dazhuang* #34).

"Zheng Xuan's annotation to the second month of spring in the

Figure 11 The Twelve Months Summon Hexagrams

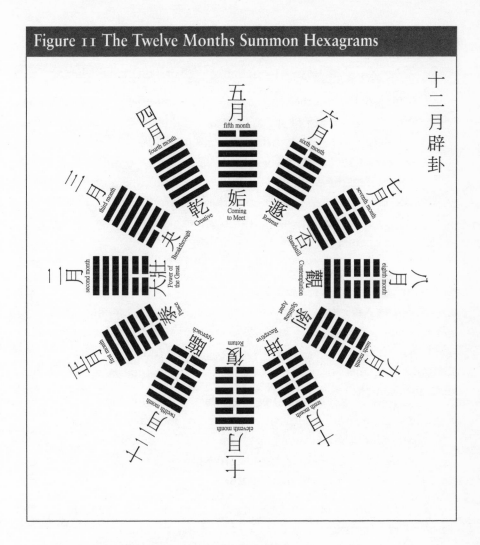

'Monthly Ordinances' ('*Yue ling*'), says:

'In the middle month of spring, the sun and moon converge in the Descending and Gathering (*jianglou*) constellation and the Dipper establishes the direction of the branch-*Mao*. The second month is the month of four yang and the Power of the Great hexagram is the hexagram of four yang. Therefore, the Power of the Great hexagram accompanies the second month.

'The third month, the establishing of the branch-*Chen*, and the Breakthrough hexagram (*Guai* #43).'

"Zheng Xuan's annotation to the third month of spring in the 'Monthly Ordinances' ('*Yue ling*'), says:

> 'In the last month of spring, the sun and moon converge in the Great Bridge (*daliang*) constellation and the Dipper establishes the direction of the branch-*Chen*. The third month is the month of five yang and the Breakthrough hexagram is the hexagram of five yang. Therefore, the Breakthrough hexagram accompanies the third month.

'The fourth month, the establishing of the branch-*Si*, and the Creative hexagram (*Qian* #1).'

"Zheng Xuan's annotation to the first month of summer in the 'Monthly Ordinances' ('*Yue ling*'), says:

> 'In the first month of summer, the sun and moon converge in the Genuine Grandeur (*shichen*) constellation and the Dipper establishes the direction of the branch-*Si*. The fourth month is the month of pure yang and the Creative hexagram is the hexagram of pure yang. Therefore, the Creative hexagram accompanies the fourth month.

'The fifth month, the establishing of branch-*Wu*, and the Coming to Meet hexagram (*Gou* #44).'

"Zheng Xuan's annotation to the middle month of summer in the 'Monthly Ordinances' ('*Yue ling*'), says:

> 'In the middle month of summer, the sun and moon converge in the Quail's Head (*chunshou*) constellation and the Dipper establishes the direction of branch-*Wu*. At the summer solstice, there is one yin and the Coming to Meet hexagram is the hexagram of one yin. Therefore, the Coming to Meet hexagram accompanies the fifth month.

'The sixth month, the establishing of the branch-*Wei*, and the Retreat hexagram (*Dun* #33).'

"Zheng Xuan's annotation to the last month of summer in the 'Monthly Ordinances' ('*Yue ling*'), says:

'In the last month of summer, the sun and moon converge in the Quail's Fire (*chunhuo*) constellation and the Dipper establishes the direction of the branch-*Wei*. The sixth month is the month of two yin and the Retreat hexagram is the hexagram of two yin. Therefore, the Retreat hexagram accompanies the sixth month.

'The seventh month, the establishing of the branch-*Shen*, and the Standstill hexagram (*Pi* #12).'

"Zheng Xuan's annotation to the first month of fall in the 'Monthly Ordinances' ('*Yue ling*'), says:

'In the first month of fall, the sun and moon converge in the Quail's Tail (*chunwei*) constellation and the Dipper establishes the direction of the branch-*Shen*. The seventh month is the month of three yin and the Standstill hexagram is the hexagram of three yin. Therefore, the Standstill hexagram accompanies the seventh month.

'The eighth month, the establishing of the branch-*You*, and the Contemplation hexagram (*Guan* #20).'

"Zheng Xuan's annotation to the middle month of fall in the 'Monthly Ordinances' ('*Yue ling*'), says:

'In the middle month of fall, the sun and moon converge in the Longevity Stars (*shouxing*) constellation and the Dipper establishes the direction of the branch-*You*. The eighth month is the month of four yin and the Contemplation hexagram is the hexagram of four yin. Therefore, the Contemplation hexagram accompanies the eighth month.

'The ninth month, the establishing of the branch-*Xu*, and the Splitting Apart hexagram (*Bo* #23).'

"Zheng Xuan's annotation to the last month of fall in the 'Monthly Ordinances' ('*Yue ling*'), says:

> 'In the last month of fall, the sun and moon converge in the Great Fire (*dahuo*) constellation and the Dipper establishes the direction of the branch-*Xu*. The ninth month is the month of five yin and the Splitting Apart hexagram is the hexagram of five yin. Therefore, the Splitting Apart hexagram accompanies the ninth month.

'The tenth month, the establishing of the branch-*Hai*, and the Receptive hexagram (*Kun* #2).'

"Zheng Xuan's annotation to the first month of winter in the 'Monthly Ordinances' ('*Yue ling*'), says:

> 'In the first month of winter, the sun and moon converge in the Splitting Wood (*ximu*) constellation and the Dipper establishes the direction of the branch-*Hai*. The tenth month is the month of pure yin and the Receptive hexagram is the hexagram of pure yin. Therefore, the Receptive hexagram accompanies the tenth month.

'The eleventh month, the establishing of the branch-*Zi*, and the Return hexagram (*Fu* #24).'

"Zheng Xuan's annotation to the middle month of winter in the 'Monthly Ordinances' ('*Yue ling*'), says:

> 'In the middle month of winter, the sun and moon converge in the Stellar Period (*xingji*) constellation and the Dipper establishes the direction of the branch-*Zi*. At the winter solstice, one yang begins to be born and the Return hexagram is the hexagram of one yang. Therefore, the Return hexagram accompanies the eleventh month.

'The twelfth month, the establishing of the branch-*Chou*, and the Approach hexagram (*Lin* #19).'

"Zheng Xuan's annotation to the last month of winter in the 'Monthly Ordinances' ('*Yue ling*'), says:

> In the last month of winter, the sun and moon converge in the Dark Hole (*xuanxiao*) constellation and the Dipper establishes the direction of the branch-*Chou*. The twelfth month is the month of two yang and the Approach hexagram is the hexagram of two yang. Therefore, the Approach hexagram accompanies the twelfth month.'"

The *Study of Calendrics* (*Xingli kaoyuan*)[50] quotes the '*Book of the Department of Astronomy*' (*Tianguan shu*) from the *Record of the Historian* (*Shiji*) as saying, 'The handle of the Dipper indicates [the relevant direction] at sundown, the mouth of the bowl does so at midnight, and the front lip of the bowl does so at sunrise.'[51] The *Study of Calendrics* (*Xingli kaoyuan*) then goes on to quote the *Pivot of the Dipper* (*Chunqiu yundou shu*) as saying:

'The first star [in the Dipper] is Celestial Pivot. The second is Jade Emblem. The third is Oblong Pearl. The fourth is Scepter. The fifth is Battering Ram. The sixth is Opening Yang. The seventh is Wavering Light. The first through the fourth are the bowl and the fifth through the seventh are the handle. Together, these comprise the Dipper. Thus, at dusk [6 p.m.] on the first month, the handle of the Dipper points to the direction of the branch-*Yin*. At midnight, the mouth of the ladle points to the direction of the branch-*Yin*. At dawn [6a.m.], the lip of the ladle points to the direction of the branch-*Yin*.

'The palace [i.e. zodiacal sign] in which the sun and moon converge is referred to as the Lunar Compliance. The Seeking (*juzi*) constellation is the branch-*Hai*. The Descending and Gathering (*jianglou*) constellation is the branch-*Xu*. The Great Bridge (*daliang*) constellation is the branch-*You*. The Genuine Grandeur (*shichen*) constellation is the branch-*Shen*. The Quail's Head (*chunshou*) constellation is the branch-*Wei*. The Quail's Fire (*chunhuo*) constellation is branch-*Wu*. The Quail's Tail (*chunwei*) constellation is the branch-*Si*. The Longevity Stars (*shouxing*) constellation is the branch-*Chen*. The Great Fire (*dahuo*) constellation is the branch-*Mao*. The Splitting Wood (*ximu*) constellation is the branch-*Yin*. The Stellar Period (*xingji*) constellation is the branch-*Chou*. The Dark Hole (*xuanxiao*) constellation is the branch-*Zi*.

'Branch-*Zi* is called Divine Lord. Branch-*Chou* is called Great Luck. Branch-*Yin* is called Meritorious Minister. Branch-*Mao* is called Great Hub. Branch-*Chen* is called Celestial Dipper. Branch-*Si* is called Great Monad. Branch-*Wu* is called Victorious Light. Branch-*Wei* is called Lesser Luck. Branch-*Shen* is called Transmission. Branch-*You* is called Dipper's Assistant. Branch-*Xu* is called River Dipper. Branch-*Hai* is called Light of the Sacrificial Cup.

'In employing the way of heaven and revolving to the left, the Lunar Establishment [i.e. the branch/direction that the handle of the Dipper indicates each month] serves as the Heavenly Door-Bolt. In accepting the command of the way of earth and rotating to the right, the Lunar Compliance [i.e. the branch/zodiacal-sign in which the sun and moon converge] serves as the Earthly Chariot-Axle.'

The preceding paragraph displays a rich and tightly woven parallelism, to which the English rendering hardly does justice. The first sentence consists of terms that imply active commanding, while the second sentence contains terms that suggest the servile reception of commands. The door-bolt imagery suggests an object which holds the key to rotation but is not itself rotated, while the chariot-axle is an object that is passively rotated. The Heavenly Door-Bolt, also known as the Heavenly Gate, is the star Zeta Tauri, which lies near the border between the lunar lodges Net (*Bi*) and Beak *(Zi)*, i.e. constellations of branch-*You* (Taurus) and branch-*Shen* (Gemini). This star[52] is perhaps significant since it stands at the point where the rough swath of the Milky Way bisects the ecliptic.

The references to right and left here appear to assume that the viewer observes the sky facing north, even though Chinese maps are normally oriented to the south. This would make sense because the pole star and Dipper can only be observed by facing north. When one does so, the Dipper, which is above the northern horizon part of the year will appear to enter the sky from the east (right) and proceed to south then west (left). Thus the Lunar Establishment moves to the left. The sun and moon converge in the zodiacal signs in reverse, i.e. from west (left) to east (right).

Diagram of the Twelve Zodiacal Signs and the Twenty-Eight Lunar Lodges

The author of the text cited here, *Collected Writings on Measuring the Ocean with a Shell* (*Lihai ji*), was a Ming dynasty Confucian scholar named Wang Kui (late fourteenth century), who was apparently a follower of the numerological-minded Song scholar Shao Yong. Although Wang argues that the animal signs of the twelve zodiacal mansions are of great antiquity, the evidence he presents is less than convincing. It is safe to say that the animal signs were in use during the Song dynasty. The explanations of the origins of the animal signs for both the twelve zodiacal signs and for the Twenty-Eight Lunar Lodges are pure conjecture. Some of the animals are real and some are mythical. Unlike the animal signs of the zodiac, the symbols of the lunar lodges are rarely used in Chinese astrology. The names of the lunar lodges presented above were not the standard set, but those given here are.

The *Collected Writings on Measuring the Ocean with a Shell* (*Lihai ji*) says:

'The twelve emblematic animals of the zodiac are as follows: Branch-*Zi* is the extreme of yin. It is concealed in darkness. Since it covers its own tracks, the rat is taken to symbolize branch-*Zi*. Branch-*Wu* is the extreme of yang. It is clearly-manifest, strong, and vigorous. Since it gallops with great speed, the horse is taken to symbolize branch-*Wu*.

'Branch-*Chou* is yin looking down with caring love. Since it looks down and lovingly licks its calf, the ox is taken to symbolize branch-*Chou*. Branch-*Wei* is yang looking up and upholding propriety. Since the young goat [respectfully] kneels down to suckle from its mother, the goat is taken to symbolize branch-*Wei*.

'Branch-*Yin* is three yang. When yang nears victory, it becomes

95

Figure 12 Diagram of the Twelve Zodiacal Signs and the Twenty-Eight Lunar Lodges

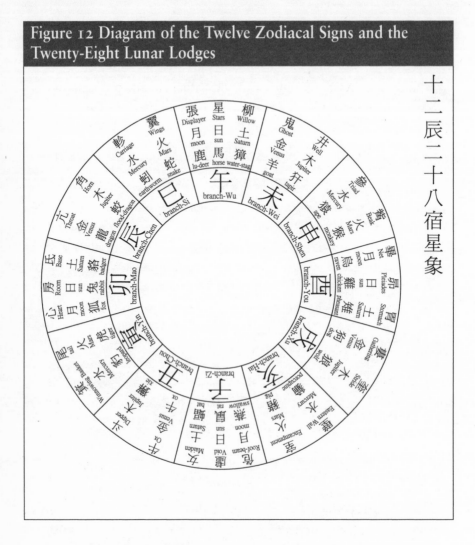

fierce. Therefore, the tiger is taken to symbolize branch-*Yin*. Branch-*Shen* is three yin. When yin achieves victory, its nature is crafty. Therefore, the monkey is taken to symbolize branch-*Shen*.

'Branch-*Mao* and branch-*You* are respectively the gates of the sun and the moon. Each of these emblems thus serves as a door hinge. Rabbits lick their virile fur and become pregnant. They feel but do not intertwine. Chickens join their legs together but do not produce offspring. They intertwine but do not feel.

'In branch-*Chen* and branch-*Si*, yang arises and transforms. The dragon is superior at this and the snake is second to the dragon. Therefore, since they are animals that transform, the dragon and the snake, respectively, symbolize branch-*Chen* and branch-*Si*.

'In branch-*Xu* and branch-*Hai*, yin gathers in and protects. The dog is superior at this and the pig is second to the dog. Therefore, since they are animals that subdue and remain calm, the dog and the pig, respectively, symbolize branch-*Xu* and branch-*Hai*.

'It is incorrect to assert that an incomplete set of animals are taken as symbols. Clearly, one could not believe that this system is meaningless since it specifically puts forth twelve animals out of a myriad number of possible beasts.'

The *Study of Calendrics (Xingli kaoyuan)* says:[53]

'The twelve beasts of the zodiac derive from an ancient tradition, the origin of which is no longer traceable. The symbols are: branch-*Zi* – Rat; branch-*Chou* – Ox; branch-*Yin* – Tiger; branch-*Mao* – Rabbit; branch-*Chen* – Dragon; branch-*Si* – Snake; branch-*Wu* – Horse; branch-*Wei* – Goat; branch-*Shen* – Monkey; branch-*You* – Chicken; branch-*Xu* – Dog; and branch-*Hai* – Pig.

'Although the tradition does not appear in the classics, an examination of Chinese literature reveals that the tradition predates the Song dynasty [to which period some have attributed it]. The *Biography of Yu Maoying (Yu Maoying zhuan)* speaks of, "eating in the branch-*Mao* place." The *Further Writings of Ji Zhangguan (Ji Zhangguan waiwen)* says that "in procuring things, the tiger enters and exits from the direction of branch-*Yin*." This evidence of the system was thus present even during the Tang dynasty.

'The *Biography of Guan Lu (Guan Lu zhuan)* examines a prognostication concerning "the eastern direction, the first day of the lunar month, and the dragon and snake" and declares that it implies "changing, transforming, mutually pushing and meeting in branch-*Chen* and branch-*Si*." The *Zhao zhou* says that, "the Overseer of the Horses manages the direction of branch-*Wu*." From these two references, we thus know that the tradition dates at least to the Han and Jin dynasties.[54]

'Looking even further into the past, we find that the fortune-teller Chen Jingzhong, when singing the praises of the state that boasted the surname Jiang and explaining the *Spring and Autumn Annals* (*Chunqiu*), said, "Six and four accompany the heavenly stem-*Xin* and the earthly branch-*Wei*. The stem-*Xin* is trigram-*Sun*, which corresponds to the eldest daughter and branch-*Wei* is the goat. The character 'goat' written above the character 'female' produces the character 'Jiang'." This shows that the system already existed during the Zhou dynasty.

'A relatively modern convention assigns animal images to the Twenty-Eight Lunar Lodges on the basis of each lodge's association with one of the twelve zodiacal signs. Thus, because branch-*Zi*, branch-*Wu*, branch-*Mao* and branch-*You* are the signs of the cardinal directions, each of them takes three lunar lodges.

'Of the three lodges, Maiden, Void, and Roof-Beam associated with the zodiacal sign of branch-*Zi*, Void resides in the center and therefore retains the original image of branch-*Zi*, i.e. the Rat. Maiden's sign is a bat and Roof-Beam's is a swallow. The animal signs of these two lodges are thus derived from the similarity in appearance of these animals to the rat.

'Of the three lodges, Base, Room, and Heart, associated with the zodiacal sign of branch-*Mao*, Room resides in the center and therefore retains the original image of branch-*Mao*, i.e. the Rabbit. Base's sign is a badger and Heart's is a fox. The animal signs of these two lodges are thus derived from the similarity in appearance of these animals to the rabbit.

'Of the three lodges, Willow, Stars, and Displayer associated with the zodiacal sign of branch-*Wu*, Stars resides in the center and therefore retains the original image of branch-*Wu*, i.e. the Horse. Willow's sign is a water stag and Displayer's is a lu-deer. The animal signs of these two lodges are thus derived from the similarity in appearance of these animals to the horse.

'Of the three lodges, Stomach, Pleiades, and Net associated with the zodiacal sign of branch-*You*, Pleiades resides in the center and therefore retains the original image of branch-*You*, i.e. the Chicken. Stomach's sign is a pheasant and Net's is a raven. The animal signs of these two lodges are thus derived from the similarity in appearance of these animals to the chicken.

'The remaining eight zodiacal signs (branch-*Yin*, branch-*Shen*, branch-*Si*, branch-*Hai*, branch-*Chen*, branch-*Xu*, branch-*Chou*, and branch-*Wei*) each govern two lodges and the lodge closest to the center of the sign is taken to be the most important.

'In the sign of branch-*Chen*, the Throat lodge is closest to the center. Therefore, it takes the original image of the dragon. Horn resides to its side. Thus, the flood-dragon, being similar in form to the dragon, is taken to accompany Horn.

'In the sign of branch-*Yin*, Tail is closest to the center. Therefore, it takes the original image of the tiger. Winnowing Basket resides to its side. Thus, the leopard, being similar in form to the tiger, is taken to accompany Winnowing Basket.

'In the sign of branch-*Chou*, the Ox lodge is closest to the center. Therefore, it takes the original image of the ox. Dipper resides to its side. Thus, the *xie*, being similar in form to the ox, is taken to accompany the Dipper.

'In the sign of branch-*Hai*, the Encampment is closest to the center. Therefore, it takes the original image of the pig. Eastern Wall resides to its side. Thus, the porcupine, being similar in form to the pig, is taken to accompany the Eastern Wall.

'In the sign of branch-*Xu*, Gathering is closest to the center. Therefore, it takes the original image of the dog. Stride resides to its side. Thus, the wolf, being similar in form to the dog, is taken to accompany Stride.

'In the sign of branch-*Shen*, Beak is closest to the center. Therefore, it takes the original image of the monkey. Triad resides to its side. Thus, the ape, being similar in form to the monkey, is taken to accompany Triad.

'In the sign of branch-*Wei*, Ghost is closest to the center. Therefore, it takes the original image of the goat. Well resides to its side. Thus, the tapir, being similar in form to the goat, is taken to accompany Well.

'In the sign of branch-*Si*, Wings is closest to the center. Therefore, it takes the original image of the snake. Carriage resides to its side. Thus, the earthworm, being similar in form to the snake, is taken to accompany Carriage.'

The Twenty-Eight Lodges Paired with the Days

The compilers describe here a system that pairs the sixty days of the sexagenary cycle with the Twenty-Eight Lunar Lodges. There are 420 possible combinations of the two sets because that is the least common multiple of 60 and 28. In combining this way, the sixty-day cycle repeats itself fully seven times. For all this explanation, the compilers point out that, although it is retained in calendars, the system is hardly ever used.

The authors also refer to a system of pairing the Twenty-Eight Lodges with the seven major heavenly bodies, i.e. the sun, moon, and five visible planets. This produces four seven-day weeks to one cycle of the Twenty-Eight Lodges. Although the authors point out that this system is only rarely used in China, it is, interestingly enough, still used in Japan to name the seven modern week days: sun for Sunday, moon for Monday, Mars/fire for Tuesday, Mercury/water for Wednesday, Jupiter/wood for Thursday, Venus/metal for Friday, and Saturn/earth for Saturday. This pattern, incidentally, introduces yet another sequence of the Five Processes – fire, water, wood, metal, earth – that does not appear to be otherwise used by Chinese cosmologists.

The *Study of Calendrics (Xingli kaoyuan)* says:[55]

'There are sixty days and Twenty-Eight Lodges. Four hundred and twenty days constitute one cycle. The 420 days exhaust the possible pairings of the sixty days with the Twenty-Eight Lodges. Therefore, there are seven beginnings [of the sixty-day cycle]. This is explained as follows: in the first beginning, the day stem-*Jia*/branch-*Zi* is paired with the Void lodge. The image of branch-*Zi* is the rat and the day of the Void lodge is also the rat. In the second beginning, stem-*Jia*/branch-*Zi* arises in the Stride lodge. In the third beginning, it arises in the Net lodge. In the fourth beginning, it arises in the Ghost lodge. In the fifth beginning, it arises in the Wings lodge. In the sixth beginning, it arises in the Base lodge. In the seventh beginning, it arises in the Winnowing Basket lodge. Once the cycle of sixty days that is initiated at the seventh beginning has been exhausted, the stem-*Jia*/branch-*Zi* day again arises in the Void lodge. Having been completed, the greater cycle starts again. The exact year, month, and day on which the first beginning arose cannot be determined.'

Compilers' Note: The sun, moon and planets pass one another confusedly and at different speeds as they follow their respective paths through the Twenty-Eight Lodges. If one investigates into the origin of this calendar that is based on the movements of the heavenly bodies as they lag, pass, fall behind, or take the lead, it must have originally started on a stem-*Jia*/branch-*Zi* year, month, day, and hour with the sun in the Void lodge, the moon in the Roof-Beam lodge, and the arrayed respectively in the lodges Encampment (Mars/fire), Eastern Wall (Mercury/water), Stride (Jupiter/wood), Gathering (Venus/metal), and Stomach (Saturn/earth).

After a short while the moon moved beyond the degree in which it should have been located [according to the system – because the moon moves the fastest at 13 degrees per day]. If this is so, then how could the seven heavenly bodies next proceed to their consecutive positions in the lunar lodges from the Pleiades lodge to the Ghost lodge. Not one among them behaves as the system claims it should. In ten thousand instances, not one of the heavenly bodies proceeds according to this orderly principle.

If one examines all of the documents from China's past for evidence of this system, none of them explains the pairing of the Twenty-Eight Lunar Lodges with the seven upright ones, [i.e. sun, moon, and five planets]. One only finds an explanation of the system upon examining the canon of astrology [lit. good and bad heavenly bodies and lucky and unlucky days and hours] from countries west of China. It is likely that, since other countries do not know the names of the Ten Heavenly Stems and Twelve Earthly Branches, they use the Twenty-Eight Lodges to record the days. Thus, they pair the Seven Heavenly Bodies with the Twenty-Eight Lodges just as Chinese pair the Heavenly Stems with the Earthly Branches. The Western method is not meant to imply that the Seven Heavenly Bodies are each exactly located in the said lodge [but rather is simply a convention for recording the days].

This system treats the heavenly bodies and lodges that pertain to a person's birthday as his or her true fate and refers to this as the fate lodge. It also takes the heavenly bodies and lodges that are encountered in relation to any activity and uses these to determine the fated good or bad luck of that endeavor. In doing this, the system considers the relative natures of the constellations and heavenly bodies and examines how these interact with the relative quality (lit. hardness or softness) of the said activity. This system is thus similar to the Chinese *jianchu* system of fate calculation.

The lunar lodges are associated with the heavenly bodies in this manner: the lodges Void, Pleiades, Stars, and Room belong to the sun. The lodges Roof, Net, Extension, and Heart belong to the moon. The lodges Encampment, Beak, Wings, and Tail belong to Mars (the Fire Star). The lodges Wall, Triad, Chariot, and Winnowing Basket belong to Mercury (the Water Star). The lodges Stride, Well, Horn, and Dipper belong to Jupiter (the Wood Star). The lodges Gathering, Ghost, Neck, and Ox belong to Venus (the Metal Star). The lodges Stomach, Willow, Base, and Maiden belong to Saturn (the Earth Star).

The names of the convergences of heavenly bodies with lunar lodges derive from foreign languages. For example, when the sun is in *Huihu* ('returning hawk') it is called *Mi* ('honey'). In *Bosi*, it is called *Yaosenwu*. In *Tianlan*, it is called *Anidiye*. These appellations are again explained as being the equivalent of the Chinese names of the days, i.e. stem-*Jia*/branch-*Zi*, etc. The remaining examples are similar to those just given. After seven beginnings, the system starts again, which is perfectly appropriate for this system. The documentary evidence also explains that this system was used in order to facilitate communication between China and the countries of the West.

Compilers' Note: Each year the makers of calendars note these pairings in red ink under the sixty stem-*Jia*/branch-*Zi* pairings in almanacs, but they have no use. Among the numerous methods for calculating the good and evil spirits of time, only two – *Fuduan* and *Anjin* – are determined with reference to this system. The remainder [of lucky and unlucky star spirits] is in no way related to this system. However, since other nations use this system for their calendars, Chinese calendar-makers continue to include it in their works. In this way, it enables outsiders to know what stem-branch pair applies to a given day and, therefore, the inclusion of the lodges in modern calendars is very useful and must not be dispensed.

The Five Processes

Although titled simply The Five Processes, this section primarily focuses on reconciling the timing of the earth process among the seasons and its spacing among the directions. The correlation of the earth process with the central direction was a very early and perhaps a self-evident convention. However, this presented a problem when correlating seasonal times, of which there are only four, with directions. One mid-third-century-BCE text, the *Spring and Autumn Annals of Master Lü*, placed earth among the circumferential directions in the southwest on the grounds that earth fell between fire (south/summer) and metal (west/fall) in the mutual production sequence of the Five Processes. The late-first-century-CE *Recensions from the White Tiger Observatory*, by contrast, places earth between each of the seasons and thus at each of the inter-cardinal directions, i.e. SW, NW, NE, SE.

To explain the ambiguity concerning the central versus peripheral placement of the earth process, the compilers point to the dual nature of earth. On the one hand, earth (the world), as the correlate of heaven, is vital breath, i.e. spirit. On the other hand earth (soil), as one of the Five Processes, is matter. As the correlate of heaven, earth (the world) occupies the center and is still, in contrast to heaven, which is around earth and in motion. As one of the processes, earth (soil) with the other processes occupies the periphery and is dynamic since the processes are by definition in motion.

To balance matters, Chinese astrologers developed the convention of allocating the last eighteen days of each season to the earth process, which by correlation meant the directions southwest, northwest, northeast, and southeast. This convention assumed an ideal 360-day year. As such, earth would govern four times eighteen, or seventy-two days, during the four seasonal changes, while the other four processes would each govern seventy-two consecutive days from the onset of the respective season. Note that this does not occur in practice since the Chinese calendar does not employ a 360-day year.

The compilers further explain this parsing of the seasons and directions with reference to the trigrams in the Latter Heaven arrangement. They explain that trigram-*Kun* and trigram-*Gen*, which form a southwest–northeast axis, represent the physical body of earth because those two trigrams are associated with the earth process. One must assume that in doing so, they are associating trigram-*Kun* in the southwest with the branch-*Wei*, which is also associated with the southwest and the last month of summer. Similarly trigram-*Gen* must

103

represent the branch-*Chou*, which is associated with northeast and the last month of winter. To complete this scheme, the compliers explain that the northwest–southeast axis, which designates the transitions between fall/winter and spring/summer, represents the spiritual function of earth. This axis is associated with the non-earth trigram-*Qian* and trigram-*Sun*, which must correlate with the branch-*Xu* and branch-*Chen*. This latter axis, the compilers correlate with the doors of the Dipper, which appears to be an alternate name for the Gates of Heaven and Doors of Earth (*see below*). Thus, the compilers contrast earth's physical body – the southwest–northeast axis – with earth's spiritual function – the northwest–southeast axis.

The *Study of Calendrics* (*Xingli kaoyuan*) says:[56]

'Among the six classics, the *Book of Documents* (*Shang shu*) contains the first references to the Five Processes. The 'Great Plan' ('*Hong fan*') section says, "One is water. Two is fire. Three is wood. Four is metal. Five is earth."[57] 'The Plan of Yu the Great' ('Da Yu mo') section says, "Water, fire, metal, wood, earth, and grain alone support life."[58] Their origin derives from the numbers of the Yellow River Chart and the Luo River Diagram, wherein one and six are water, two and seven are fire, three and eight are wood, four and nine are metal, and five and ten are earth. In the Chart, rotating to the left [i.e. clockwise] is mutual production [i.e. 1/6 water produces 3/8 wood, which produces 2/7 fire, which produces 5/10 earth, which produces 4/9 metal, which produces 1/6 water]. In the Diagram, revolving to the right [i.e. counterclockwise] is mutual conquest [i.e. 1/6 water conquers 2/7 fire conquers 4/9 metal conquers 3/8 wood conquers 5 earth conquers 1/6 water].

'In the Chart and the Diagram, earth is associated with the numbers five and ten of the central palace. It lacks a fixed position (relative to the four seasonal times); it lacks a specialized physical embodiment (relative to the four seasonal directions). Only in the *Spring and Autumn Annals of Master Lü* (*Lüshi chunqiu*) do we first see earth linked with the last month of summer in accordance with [earth's position in] the mutual production sequence [of the Five Processes]. In the *Recensions from the White Tiger Observatory* (*Baihu tongyi*) we again see earth linked with a division of time. In this instance earth prospers in the last month of each of the four seasons, i.e. the months of branch-*Chen*, branch-*Xu*, branch-*Chou*, and branch-*Wei*. In King Wen's 'Latter Heaven' arrangement of the trigrams, the two earth trigrams, trigram-*Kun* and trigram-*Gen*, stand alone in the interstices of summer-fall and winter-spring because fire (summer) must first obtain earth before it can create metal (fall) and water (winter) must first obtain earth before it can create wood (spring).'

Compilers' Note: The word 'processes' refers to [the Five Processes' action of] 'proceeding' upon the earth. Their matter proceeds on the earth. Their vital breath penetrates to heaven. Because they number five, they are referred to as the Five Processes.

The earth (*di* – world) is earth (*tu* – soil). When speaking of it as the counterpart of heaven, we refer to it as earth (*di*). When speaking of its matter, we refer to it as unmoving earth (*gutu*). The word 'unmoving' is used to indicate that it is the lord of the four other processes. As a lord, it does not specialize its activities [like the seasons hot-cold-wet-dry] nor does it permanently fix its abode [like the directions north, south, east, west].

Now fire (summer) conquers metal (fall), but fall (metal) follows upon the summer (fire) months. Thus, it is said that, there being four directions, there must also be a center and this center is unmoving earth. This central, unmoving earth is capable of inheriting the mantle of fire's old age (the end of summer) and of producing metal (fall).

In succeeding each other throughout the seasons, the four cardinal processes each govern more of their respective seasons, while earth governs less. Thus, it is said that the final month of each of the four seasons is unmoving earth, i.e. branch-*Chen* (3rd month), branch-*Xu* (9th month), branch-*Chou* (12th month), and branch-*Wei* (6th month). In each of those final months, the first twelve days are said to belong to the process of the respective season. Earth then governs the last eighteen days of those months. Thus each of the Five Processes governs seventy-two days of the year.

Trigram-*Kun* and trigram-*Gen*, two earth[-times] residing at the interstices of the four vital breaths, serve as the true body of earth. The Latter Heaven diagram illustrates this. Trigram-*Qian* and trigram-*Sun*, two [earth-]directions occupying the doors of the Dipper, show the divine function of earth. The discussion of the 'movement of the vital breaths' in the *Plain Inquiry* (*Suwen*) explains this. Thus, the earth's lordship over the four other processes can be discerned. In these cases there are concrete images that can be used to illustrate the truth of their statements. If there were no such images then there would be nothing to distinguish from the earth process any of the other eight Earthly Branches, i.e. branch-*Yin*, branch-*Shen*, branch-*Si*, branch-*Hai*, branch-*Zi*, branch-*Wu*, branch-*Mao*, and branch-*You*. How could that be so? Thus, if it were not for earth, then water, fire, metal and wood would not have anything on which to proceed; that on which they proceed is in each case earth.

The Governing Periods of the Five Processes

As with the last section, we see here an outline of the method for assigning four parts of the year to the governance of the earth process. There is a difference between the methods described in the two sections. The one described here is the method that appears to be used by Chinese calendar-makers today. Regardless of which method one might use, neither could produce the exact figure of 72 days per process because, as mentioned above, there are 354 and not 360 days to a year, that is six months of 29 days and six months of 30 days. The method of the last section claimed that earth governed the last 18 days of the final months of each season, while the process of the relevant season governed the first 12 days. That method would slightly cheat the earth of its 72 days per year. The method described in this section counts not from the onset of a month but rather from one of the 24 seasonal 'nodes,' which were originally solar markers based on a 360-day year. Thus, the earth process takes the 18 days preceding the 'establishment' of each season. In this way, earth would always govern 72 days per year. In modern Chinese calendars, the solar nodes are adjusted to coincide with a normal solar year of 365.25 days. Consequently, earth always gets its 72 days, but the other seasons end up getting a little more because of the 5.25 extra days.

Figure 13 The Governing Periods of the Five Processes

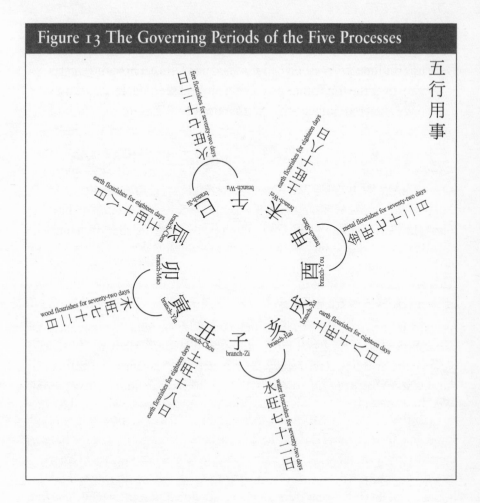

The *Study of Calendrics (Xingli kaoyuan)* says:[59]

'The *Classic of the Divine Pivot (Shenshu jing)* says:

"There is a fixed time in which each of the Five Processes flourishes. Only earth resides without a fixed position. Thus, it flourishes for a period of eighteen days before the establishment of each of the four seasons."

'The *Period Regulations (Li li)* says:

"From the establishment of spring, wood; from the establishment of summer, fire; from the establishment of fall, metal; and from the establishment of winter, water – each flourishes for seventy-two days. The process of earth, in turn, flourishes for the eighteen days that immediately precede each of the four seasonal establishments, which when summed provides earth with seventy-two days as well. Thus altogether, there are three hundred and sixty days and the year is complete therein."'

The Birth and Flourishing of the Five Processes

This section explains the twelve-stage life cycle[60] mentioned briefly in the Introduction. As the compilers themselves point out, this cycle is one of the most important concepts in Chinese astrology and *feng shui*. It would be impossible to calculate the appearance of most of the gods and demons of times and orientations without some reference to this system. I am forced to say 'some' reference because many of the astrological formulae are based upon only three of the twelve stages from this cycle, namely, birth, flourishing, and burial. In fact, it is probable that the twelve-stage cycle is only a later elaboration of the unquestionably early birth/flourishing/burial trio, known as the Triune Harmonies (*san he*). The Triune Harmonies, which are discussed further below, are mentioned in the *Huainanzi*, but the antiquity of the twelve-stage cycle is unclear.

Essentially, this system posits that the Five Processes progress through stages in a life cycle marked by the Twelve Earthly Branches. On the basis of the order in which the stages are presented here, we can divide the twelve stages into three conceptual categories. The first through the fourth stages mark the beginning of life and ascent through young adulthood (ascent stages). The fifth through the eighth stages mark the peak of life and descent through death (descent stages). The ninth through the twelfth stages represent what happens to the process after death, which is to say burial and coming to being once again in the 'womb' prior to birth (dormancy stages). The first stages of these three groupings are the Triune Harmonies, i.e. birth, flourishing, and burial. It is interesting to note that the last two phases, i.e. conception and development (in the womb), are conceptually grouped as a part of the life that has just ended, rather than, as moderns might assume, being a part of the coming life.

With reference to the Ten Heavenly Stems, the five yang/positive stems progress through the stages in the order of the Earthly Branches, while the five yin/negative stems move through the branches in reverse order i.e. counterclockwise. The point of departure between these two opposing cycles is the division between the ascent/descent stages and the dormancy stages. Thus, as the authors say, where yang is born, i.e. begins ascent, yin dies, i.e. enters dormancy and conversely, where yin is born, yang dies and enters dormancy. The two cycles converge at the division between the ascent and descent stages. Thus, where yang finishes its ascent, yin peaks and begins its descent, and vice versa. One will observe from the chart below that this means the yin and yang versions of any process are in the dormancy stages simultaneously, while their ascent and descent stages are reversed.

Ascent				Descent				Dormancy			
1	2	3	4	5	6	7	8	9	10	11	12
Descent				Ascent				Dormancy			
8	7	6	5	4	3	2	1	12	11	10	9

Although the compilers do not make a point of this, one will notice that the stages could also readily be divided into two halves, with stages eleven through four representing the waxing of life and stages five through ten representing the waning of life.

The compilers also discuss the placement of the earth process in this scheme. Earth is said to be 'born' in branch-*Shen* and to be 'dependently born' in branch-*Yin*. They explain the birth of earth in branch-*Shen* by reference to the correlation between branch-*Shen* and trigram-*Kun*, which is the ultimate earth trigram. Nonetheless, although earth's birth in branch-*Yin* is designated 'dependent,' that correlation appears to be the one used in the original diagram. Therefore, we see that the earth process is essentially treated exactly as is the fire process – born in branch-*Yin*, flourishing in branch-*Wu* and being buried in branch-*Xu*. The connection of earth with both branch-*Yin* and branch-*Shen* harks back to the axial connection of the earth process with the directions southwest (branch-*Shen*) and northeast (branch-*Yin*).

The *Study of Calendrics* (*Xingli kaoyuan*) says:[61]

> 'Wood is born in branch-*Hai*. Fire is born in branch-*Yin*. Metal is born in branch-*Si*. Water is born in branch-*Shen*. Earth is also born in branch-*Shen* and is dependently born in branch-*Yin*. Each proceeds clockwise in its periods or phases through the twelve zodiac signs from being born, to being ritually bathed, to donning cap and

sash, to approaching official appointment, to imperially flourishing, to declining, to sickening, to dying, to being buried, to terminating, to being conceived, and to being nourished in the womb. Thus, the way of heaven is continually giving birth in an unending cycle so that as the direction of wood is flourishing, fire has already been born. Also, as the direction of fire is flourishing, metal has already been born. Again, as the direction of metal is flourishing, water has already been born. Finally, as the direction of water is flourishing, wood has already been born.

'From birth each proceeds with the natural flow. The immature must grow to maturity. The accomplished must decline. Each ends and begins again. In this way, they continually cycle unceasingly. This is the way in which the four seasons overlap one another; it is the way by which the five vital breaths proceed with the natural flow.

'The assertion that earth is born in branch-*Shen* and is dependently born in branch-*Yin* is based upon the respective positions of trigram-*Kun* and trigram-*Gen* in the Latter Heaven arrangement of trigrams. "In trigram-*Kun*," says the *Book of Changes* (*Yijing*) "the myriad things all receive their due nourishment." "In trigram-*Gen*" it says, "is the final end and absolute beginning of the myriad things."'

Compilers' Note: In the *Study of Calendrics* (*Xingli kaoyuan*), the explanation of the meaning of the Five Processes' birth is very lucid. However, it only begins to explain how earth is born in branch-*Yin* and branch-*Shen*, without going into details. According to the current investigation, both water and earth are born in the zodiac sign branch-*Shen* because branch-*Shen* is associated with trigram-*Kun*, which in turn is associated with the earth (*di* the world) and water is the substance in which earth (*tu* soil) congeals.

The argument for earth's dependent birth in branch-*Yin* derives from the fact that branch-*Yin* is the first month of Spring. In the first month of spring, the vital breath of heaven descends and the vital breath of earth ascends. It is by this that heaven and the earth unite and harmonize and it is by this that plants and trees bud and grow.

The Great Plan School (*Hong fan jia*) alone regards the birth of earth in branch-*Shen* as the form (lit. 'body') of the Five Processes. The various yin-yang selection schools all regard the birth of earth in branch-*Yin* as the function (lit. 'use') of the Five Processes.

Being born in branch-*Yin* and approaching official appointment in branch-*Si*, earth achieves prosperity after metal has already been born. This ordering places earth and metal in their proper sequence with wood, fire, and water. Thus, taking earth as being born in branch-*Yin* is in accordance with the mutual production order of the Five Processes. This clearly proceeds from the same natural principle as the 'Monthly Ordinances' ('*Yue ling*' chapter of the *Liji or Book of Rites*). The 'Monthly Ordinances' places the flourishing of earth at the interstice between summer and fall in accordance with the mutual production order of the four seasons. This is not an arbitrary explanation.

In addition to this there is also the tradition concerning yang dying where yin is born and yang proceeding with the flow while yin moves against the flow. According to this tradition, the first heavenly stem-*Jia* (1/10), which is (yang) wood, dies in the earthly branch-*Wu* (6/12) and in this same position the second heavenly stem-*Yi* (2/10), which is (yin) wood, is born. Stem-*Bing* (3/10), yang fire, and stem-*Wu* (5/10), yang earth, die in the earthly branch-*You* (9/12), wherein stem-*Ding* (4/10), yin fire, and stem-*Ji* (6/10), yin earth, are born. The stem-*Geng* (7/10), yang metal, dies in the earthly branch-*Zi* (1/12), wherein the stem-*Xin* (8/10), yin metal is born. The stem-*Ren* (9/10), yang water, dies in the earthly branch-*Mao* (3/12), wherein the stem-*Xin* (10/10), yin water is born.

From birth to ritual bathing and onward through the rest of the twelve positions, they always rotate in opposite directions.

Where yang dies (8th stage), its yin counterpart is born (1st stage) and where yin dies (8th stage), its yang counterpart is born (1st stage).

This constitutes the divergence of the two vital breaths [yin and yang].

Where a yang element approaches official appointment (4th stage), its yin counterpart imperially flourishes (5th stage). Where a yin element approaches official appointment (4th stage), its yang counterpart imperially flourishes (5th stage).

This constitutes the convergence of the four seasons.

Proceeding with the flow and moving against the flow; diverging and converging – these form a miraculous pattern.

If one speaks of the ten stems, then there is the diverging of yin and yang.

If one speaks of the Five Processes, then yang moves consecutively and yin moves counter-consecutively (i.e. convergence of yin and yang).

These are the natural truths of heaven and earth. Those who speak of numerology all treat this concept as foundational. Good fortune and bad fortune, benevolent spirits and malevolent spirits all arise from it.

The Stems, Branches, and the Five Processes

This section specifies the Five-Processes correlations of the Ten Heavenly Stems and Twelve Earthly Branches. The standard correlations are outlined first, followed by a unique system of correlating processes with branches attributed to the 'Five Planets School.' In Chinese the same graph is used to represent both the words 'star' and 'planet,' but since this is prefixed by the number five we know that they are here referring to the five planets that are visible to the naked human eye, namely, Mars, Mercury, Jupiter, Venus, and Saturn. This is further suggested by the fact that the branch-*Wu* and branch-*Wei* are not correlated with any of the Five Processes, but rather with the sun and moon, which Chinese astronomers considered to be the two other major 'moving' heavenly bodies. We know, therefore, that we are dealing here with a somewhat more astronomically-minded school of thought.

As we have seen before, the five planets are correlated with the Five Processes and the Five Planets School associates these with five pairs of the Twelve Earthly Branches. Thus we find Mars/fire correlated with the branch-*Mao* and branch-*Xu*; Mercury/water with branch-*Si* and branch-*Shen*; Jupiter/wood with branch-*Yin* and branch-*Hai*; Venus/metal with branch-*Chen* and branch-*You*; and Saturn/earth with branch-*Zi* and branch-*Chou*. The sun, then, takes branch-*Wu* and the moon branch-*Wei*. This effectively provides us with yet another sequence for the Five Processes: earth, wood, fire, metal, and water. Essentially, this is the mutual production sequence, but here earth, which should stand between fire and metal, is placed at the beginning of the sequence. Some traditional thinkers argued that this scheme could be explained as follows: Branch-*Wu* and branch-*Wei*, as sun and moon, represent heaven. Branch-*Zi* and branch-*Chou*, as Saturn/the earth process, represent the earth as in the world/counterpart to heaven. Thus, branch-*Wu* and branch-*Wei*, represent up, branch-*Zi* and branch-*Chou* represent down, and the four other pairs of stems represent the four seasons and four cardinal directions, following the mutual production order.

This scheme of pairing the twelve branches is exactly the same as the six harmonies, which is discussed below. Since the six harmonies arrangement was apparently based on an observable astronomical phenomenon, we must assume that the Five Planets School's correlations of processes and branches was originally inspired by the six harmonies. The explanation about heaven and earth sandwiching the other four processes fits well with traditional Chinese cosmology, but one can't help but wonder why the five planets and their processes are correlated in this specific way with the twelve zodiacal signs. The scheme is reminiscent of the correlation between the seven heavenly bodies and the days of the week discussed above, but the order of the processes/planets differs.

Figure 14 The Stems, Branches, and the Five Processes

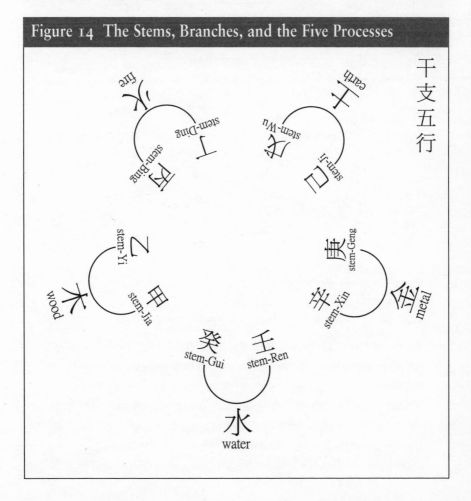

Figure 15 The Stems, Branches, and the Five Processes

The *Study of Calendrics* (*Xingli kaoyuan*) says:[62]

'As for the Heavenly Stems, stem-*Jia* and stem-*Yi* are wood; stem-*Bing* and stem-*Ding* are fire; stem-*Wu* and stem-*Ji* are earth; stem-*Geng* and stem-*Xin* are metal; and stem-*Ren* and stem-*Gui* are water.

'Among the Earthly Branches, branch-*Yin*, branch-*Mao*, and branch-*Chen* are of the class of wood and accompany the direction east. Branch-*Si*, branch-*Wu*, and branch-*Wei* are of the class of fire and accompany the direction south. Branch-*Shen*, branch-*You*, and branch-

Figure 16 The Stems, Branches, and the Five Processes

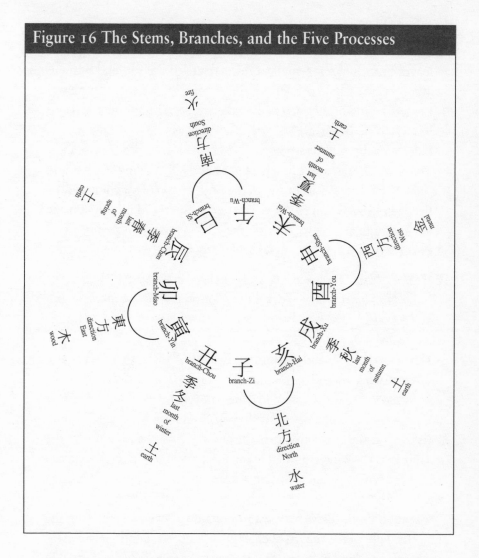

Xu are of the class of metal and accompany the direction west. Branch-*Hai*, branch-*Zi*, and branch-*Chou* are of the class of water and accompany the direction north. Earth, in turn, flourishes dependently within branch-*Chen*, branch-*Xu*, branch-*Chou*, and branch-*Wei* and accompanies the last month of each of the four seasons.

'The Five Planets School,[63] "also regards branch-*Yin* and branch-*Hai* as belonging to the class of wood. They regard branch-*Mao* and branch-*Xu* as belonging to the class of fire. They regard branch-*Chen* and branch-*You* as belonging to the class of metal. [They regard branch-

Si and branch-*Shen* as belonging to the class of water.] They regard branch-*Zi* and branch-*Chou* as belonging to the class of earth. This leaves branch-*Wu* serving as the correlate of the sun and branch-*Wei* serving as the correlate of the moon.[64] Since they are below, branch-*Zi* and branch-*Chou* are taken to be earth. Branch-*Wu* and branch-*Wei*, being above, are regarded as the sun and moon. Branch-*Yin*, branch-*Mao*, branch-*Chen*, branch-*Si*, branch-*Shen*, branch-*You*, branch-*Xu*, and branch-*Hai* are thus divided on the left and right-hand sides. In accord with the progression of the four seasons between heaven and earth, they are thus matched in pairs on the left and right and these pairs are then distinguished in keeping with the order of wood, fire, metal and water.'"[65]

Compilers' Note: The preceding is all contained in the *Study of Calendrics* (*Xingli kaoyuan*). That work's description of the five planets and Five Processes, however, is only introductory and is not a complete exposition.

Heaven is the sun and the moon. The five planets, themselves, are the excess of the sun and the moon.[66] The earthly branch-*Wu* and branch-*Wei* are associated with trigram-*Li* (yang-yin-yang). The earthly branch-*Zi* and branch-*Chou* are associated with trigram-*Kan* (yin-yang-yin). Trigram-*Li* is the sun and trigram-*Kan* is the moon. Thus, the reason why the earthly branch-*Wu* is regarded in this system as the sun is self-evident. However, why is it that the earthly branch-*Zi* is not regarded here as the moon?

The moon is the essence of water hung up above and receiving the reflected light of the sun. As such, it does not correspond to the northern position of the earthly branch-*Zi* [since the branch-*Zi* and its correlated direction north are considered 'below']. The vital breaths of branch-*Zi* and branch-*Chou* stand opposite that which is above and thus opposite the direction of the sun. This clearly demonstrates that [the moon] is in the position of branch-*Wei*.

Earth (world) consists of the process of water and the process of earth (soil). The earthly branch-*Zi* belongs to the process of water and the earthly branch-*Chou* belongs to the process of earth. Branch-*Chou* is also the requisite earth branch among the three water-affiliated branches [since each of the four groups of three branches has one branch affiliated with earth]. Thus, there is no doubt that these two branches constitute the physical body of the earth.

Earth (world) is of the process of earth (soil). Therefore, branch-*Zi* and branch-*Chou* are of the process of earth.

Heaven is positioned above. Earth is positioned below. Proceeding in between the two, there must be wood, fire, metal, and water.

Branch-*Zi* and branch-*Chou* are of the processes water and earth. At the border where water and earth meet, wood must be born. The branch-*Hai* and branch-*Yin* are, therefore, regarded as being of the process of wood. In one wood is born [i.e. branch-*Hai*] and in the other wood assumes office [i.e. approaches official appointment in branch-*Yin*].

Where wood is accomplished, fire already proceeds out. Fire is born in branch-*Yin* and wood flourishes in branch-*Mao*. Having flourished, wood must be replaced. Having been replaced, wood must return to its roots. Therefore, branch-*Mao* and branch-*Xu* are held to be of the process of fire.

If branch-*Mao* and branch-*Xu* are fire, then branch-*Xu* must function as the vital breath of Auburn Heaven [auburn=yellow=earth]. The place where stem-*Wu* first comes to reside in the vital breath of Auburn Heaven is branch-*Chen*. The branch-*Chen* is also the stem-*Wu*. Where earth flourishes, it must give birth to metal. Therefore, the earthly branch-*Chen* and branch-*You* are taken to be of the process of metal. The branch-*You* is the place of the process metal's imperial flourishing.

The branch-*You* occupies the ultimate point of metal flourishing, but before metal arrived at this extreme, water was already born in branch-*Shen*. The palace opposite branch-*Shen* is branch-*Si*. Branch-*Si* is the mother of the process metal.[67] The process water must take the earthly branch-*Shen* and branch-*Si* because branch-*Shen* and branch-*Si* are adjacent to the highest positions of the branch-*Wu* and branch-*Wei*, which lack water.

If one holds forth the mother, then the son will return. The process of water, unable to reside in earth, stands on its own. The positions of branch-*Zi* and branch-*Chou* represent water when it is together with earth. This represents the fate of the process earth and not the fate of the process water. Water can stand apart from earth and still be called water only if water receives the vital breath of its mother [i.e. metal/branch-*Shen*]. Therefore, the branch-*Shen* and branch-*Si* are correlated with the process of water. Water is the wellspring from which are born the myriad things.

It is on this basis that the water process is thought to reside on the flanks of the sun and moon. Next comes metal, which is followed by fire, which is followed by wood, which is followed by earth. This is the order of the five woofs, or latitudinal lines. Water is closest to the sun, followed by metal, followed by fire, followed by wood, followed by earth. This is the natural order of the flanking of heaven. Water and earth give birth to wood, which in turn gives birth upwardly to create fire. Earth again gives birth upwardly to create metal. And finally earth again gives birth upwardly to create water. This is akin to the way the lines of the trigrams move from lower positions to higher. This is the natural order of progression upon the earth. Thus, the five planets and the Five Processes each have concrete principles and are not merely the forced imaginings of men.

The Triune Harmonies

Considering that the concept of the Triune Harmonies[68] is one of the most important elements of traditional Chinese astrology and *feng shui*, the compilers description below is relatively brief. Perhaps they chose to economize on text here because they considered the Triune Harmonies to be a subset of the twelve-stage life cycle discussed above. Nonetheless, as stated in the commentary on that section, it is most likely that the Triune Harmonies concept was the earliest aspect of the twelve-stage cycle.

The Triune Harmonies system correlates the Twelve Earthly Branches with the Five Processes. In this respect, the concept resembles the standard system of correlating the branches with processes described above. In the standard system, the three northern branches (branch-*Hai*, branch-*Zi*, branch-*Chou*) are water, the three eastern branches (branch-*Yin*, branch-*Mao*, branch-*Chen*) are wood, and so forth. Like that system, the Triune Harmonies confidently correlates the four cardinal processes of water, wood, fire, and metal, but both systems seem to have conflicting conventions for correlating the earth process with branches. The difference between the two systems is spatial versus temporal. The standard correlations allocate the three branches of a given direction to the process associated with that direction. The Triune Harmonies, however, presumes the twelve-stage life cycle and assigns phases in the life of a process to each of three Earthly Branches. Although there appear to have been some discrepancies about naming the respective stages (mature versus flourish, die versus bury), the earliest systems are essentially in agreement that one stage represents initiation of life, the next life's climax, and the last life's conclusion. Rather than being consecutive branches, the Triune Harmonies are evenly distributed at three four-unit intervals among the Twelve Earthly Branches. This suggests that the processes were somehow thought to live out their existence throughout all twelve branches.

As with the standard 'directional' correlations with processes, Chinese thinkers appear to have disagreed about how to cope with the earth-process/earthly-branch correlations, because the earth process was associated with the center while the branches represented peripheral loci. Apparently assuming the preeminence of the mutual production sequence of the processes, all agreed that earth must somehow correlate with branches between those of fire and metal. The standard convention in late-imperial China was to correlate earth with the same stages and branches as the fire process, but the compilers point out that the *Huainanzi* took a different approach. While the *Huainanzi* did associate earth with the same branches as fire, the stages differed in order. Fire reached maturity in branch-*Wu*, where earth was born. Fire died in branch-*Xu*, where earth reached maturity. Fire was born in branch-*Yin*, where earth died.

The translation 'Triune Harmonies' sounds somewhat awkward, but is used to distinguish this concept from two other 'harmonies' in the Treatise. There are three 'harmonies' in the Treatise: the Triune Harmonies (*san he*), the five harmonies (*wu he*), and the six harmonies (*liu he*). The latter two refer to five pairs of Heavenly Stems and six pairs of Earthly Branches. As such, those two systems must be distinguished from this system, which refers to four or five trios of branches, even though the Chinese terms do not in themselves make this distinction.

Interesting though they may be, the sets of forty-five days referred to in the *Huainanzi* passage are not to my knowledge employed by any prominent astrological or *feng shui* school. For more on these, see Major's translation and commentary.

Branch-*Shen*, branch-*Zi*, and branch-*Chen* harmonize as the office of water.

Branch-*Hai*, branch-*Mao*, and branch-*Wei* harmonize as the office of wood.

Branch-*Yin*, branch-*Wu*, and branch-*Xu* harmonize as the office of fire.

Branch-*Si*, branch-*You*, and branch-*Chou* harmonize as the office of metal.

Figure 17 The Triune Harmonie

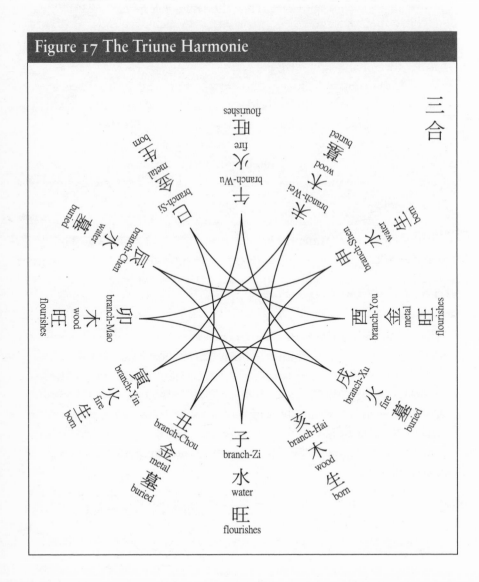

The *Study of Calendrics (Xingli kaoyuan)* says:[69]

'The Trinities take the three life phases of birth, flourishing, and burial to constitute a unitary office. Water is born in branch-*Shen*, flourishes in branch-*Zi*, and is buried in branch-*Chen*. Therefore, branch-*Shen*, branch-*Zi*, and branch-*Chen* harmonize as the office of water. Wood is born in branch-*Hai*, flourishes in branch-*Mao* and is buried in branch-*Wei*. Therefore, branch-*Hai*, branch-*Mao*, and branch-*Wei* harmonize as the office of wood. Fire is born in branch-*Yin*, flourishes in branch-*Wu*, and is buried in branch-*Xu*. Therefore, branch-*Yin*, branch-*Wu*, and branch-*Xu* harmonize as the office of fire. Metal is born in branch-*Si*, flourishes in branch-*You*, and is buried in branch-*Chou*. Therefore, branch-*Si*, branch-*You*, and branch-*Chou* harmonize as the office of metal.'

Compilers' Note: The *Huainanzi* says:
'Wood is born in branch-*Hai*, reaches maturity in branch-*Mao*, and dies in branch-*Wei*. These three zodiac signs are all wood. Fire is born in branch-*Yin*, reaches maturity in branch-*Wu*, and dies in branch-*Xu*. These three zodiac signs are all fire. Earth is born in branch-*Wu*, reaches maturity in branch-*Xu*, and dies in branch-*Yin*. These three zodiac signs are all earth. Metal is born in branch-*Si*, flourishes[70] in branch-*You*, and dies in branch-*Chou*. These three zodiac signs are all metal. Water is born in branch-*Shen*, reaches maturity in branch-*Zi*, and dies in branch-*Chen*. These three zodiac signs are all water. Therefore, there are [altogether] five victories (i.e. one for each of the Five Processes). Birth is the first [phase]. Reaching maturity is the fifth. Conclusion is the ninth. Five [processes multiplied by] nine [phases equals] forty-five. Thus, after forty-five days the god migrates one place. One must employ three migrations in addition to [the first] five [i.e. each of the Five Processes takes one 45-day period, 5 X 45 = 225, 360 – 225 = 135, 135 ÷ 45 = 3]. Therefore, after eight migrations, the year is completed.'[71]

Further Compilers' Note: When the Yin Yang School speaks of the trinities, they only refer to those of water, fire, wood, and metal, without mentioning that of earth. This being as it is, in speaking of texts affiliated with the Yin Yang School, the *Huainanzi* can certainly be considered one of the older examples. Although the tradition concerning the trinities might not have originated in the *Huainanzi*, it is clear that the concept of an earth trinity did not persist after the *Huainanzi*. Why this occurred is unclear. What is certain is that later generations made no distinction between the trinities of earth and fire, while the *Huainanzi* said earth was born in branch-*Wu*, reached maturity in branch-*Xu*, and died in branch-*Yin* (fire of course being born in branch-*Yin*, reaching maturity in branch-*Wu*, and dying in branch-*Xu*). No other texts contain this distinction made in the *Huainanzi*. Although the *Huainanzi* tradition is no longer used, we have presented this exposition in order to treat of the subject exhaustively.

The Six Harmonies

The six harmonies is another of the most quintessential concepts of Chinese astrology and *feng shui*. In terms of observable, astronomical phenomena, the six harmonies was thought to reflect the symmetrical and opposing movements of the stars of the heavens and the convergences of the sun and moon (i.e. new moon). Ancient Chinese astronomers observed that the convergences of the sun and moon appeared to occur in counterclockwise progression through the earthly-branch zodiacal signs. Conversely, the handle of the Big Dipper rotated clockwise, and at the same pace, as it pointed out the earthly-branch directions of the earth's surface. These two equal but opposing cycles crossed paths half-way between branch-*Zi* and branch-*Chou* and again half-way between branch-*Wu* and branch-*Wei*. Thus, when the sun and moon converged in the zodiacal sign of branch-*Zi*, the handle of the Big Dipper pointed to the direction of the branch-*Chou*. Conversely, when the sun and moon converged in the zodiacal sign of branch-*Chou*, the handle of the Big Dipper pointed to the direction of the branch-*Zi*.

Since these two cycles moved both at the same speed and in opposite directions, the luni-solar convergence always occurs in the earthly branch directly opposite to the branch that the Dipper handle indicates, and vice versa. On a clock face, this would mean that 12 and 1 form a pair (branch-*Zi* and branch-*Chou*), 11 and 2 form a pair (branch-*Hai* and branch-*Yin*), 10 and 3 form a pair (branch-*Xu* and branch-*Mao*), etc. The two cycles converge and then diverge again at 12:30 and again at 6:30.

The authors refer to the two cycles as the 'Lunar Establishment' and the 'Lunar Compliance.' The Lunar Establishment (*yue jian*) is a spatial concept because it refers to the direction on the earth's surface that the handle of the Dipper indicates during the convergence of the sun and moon (new moon). The Lunar Compliance (*yue jiang*), by contrast, is a temporal concept that refers to the zodiacal sign in which the sun and moon converge. It is called compliance because the moon is thought to comply with the sun, which is the moon's superior. The texts quoted by the compilers are rather late, but the concept of six harmonies was already latent in Zheng Xuan's commentary on the 'Monthly Ordinances' ('*Yue ling*') chapter of the *Book of Rites* (*Liji*). It should be noted here that the *Huainanzi* contains a six harmonies system that is quite different from the current version. In that apparently earlier system, the earthly-branch designations of the months were linked diametrically across an imaginary circle, so that the middle month of winter (branch-*Zi*) was linked to the middle month of summer (branch-*Wu*), the last month of winter (branch-*Chou*) was linked with the last month of summer (branch-*Wei*), etc.

Branch-*Zi* harmonizes[72] with branch-*Chou*. Branch-*Yin* harmonizes with branch-*Hai*. Branch-*Mao* harmonizes with branch-*Xu*. Branch-*Chen* harmonizes with branch-*You*. Branch-*Si* harmonizes with branch-*Shen*. Branch-*Wu* harmonizes with branch-*Wei*.

The *Collected Writings on Measuring the Ocean with a Shell* (*Lihai ji*) says:

'According to the Yin Yang School, the Earthly Branches form six harmonies.

'When the sun and the moon converge in the zodiacal sign of branch-*Zi*, the Dipper's handle points to (lit. the Dipper establishes) the branch-*Chou* direction (30° NE – 1 o'clock). When the sun and the moon converge in the zodiacal sign of branch-*Chou*, the Dipper's handle points to the branch-*Zi* direction (0° N – 12 o'clock). Therefore, branch-*Zi* and branch-*Chou* harmonize with each other.

'When the sun and the moon converge in the zodiacal sign of branch-*Yin*, the Dipper's handle points to the branch-*Hai* direction (330° NW – 11 o'clock). When the sun and the moon converge in the zodiacal sign of branch-*Hai*, the Dipper's handle points to the branch-*Yin* direction (60° NE – 2 o'clock). Therefore, branch-*Yin* and branch-*Hai* harmonize with each other.

'When the sun and the moon converge in the zodiacal sign of branch-*Mao*, the Dipper's handle points to the branch-*Xu* direction (300° NW – 10 o'clock). When the sun and the moon converge in the zodiacal sign of branch-*Xu*, the Dipper's handle points to the branch-*Mao* direction (90° E – 3 o'clock). Therefore, branch-*Mao* and branch-*Xu* harmonize with each other.

Figure 18 The Six Harmonies

'When the sun and the moon converge in the zodiacal sign of branch-*Chen*, the Dipper's handle points to the branch-*You* direction (270° W – 9 o'clock). When the sun and the moon converge in the zodiacal sign of branch-*You*, the Dipper's handle points to the branch-*Chen* direction (120° SE – 4 o'clock). Therefore, branch-*Chen* and branch-*You* harmonize with each other.

'When the sun and the moon converge in the zodiacal sign of branch-*Si*, the Dipper's handle points to the branch-*Shen* direction (240° SW – 8 o'clock). When the sun and the moon converge in the zodiacal sign of branch-*Shen*, the Dipper's handle points to the branch-*Si* direction (150° SE – 5 o'clock). Therefore, branch-*Si* and branch-*Shen* harmonize with each other.

'When the sun and the moon converge in the zodiacal sign of branch-*Wu*, the Dipper's handle points to the branch-*Wei* direction (210° SW – 7 o'clock). When the sun and the moon converge in the zodiacal sign of branch-*Wei*, the Dipper's handle points to the branch-*Wu* direction (180° S – 6 o'clock). Therefore, branch-*Wu* and branch-*Wei* harmonize with each other.'

The *Study of Calendrics* (*Xingli kaoyuan*) says:[73]

'The Six Harmonies means that the Lunar Establishment and the Lunar Compliance are considered to harmonize with one another. Thus, in the first month, the Lunar Establishment indicates the branch-*Yin* direction and the Lunar Compliance occurs in the zodiacal sign of branch-*Hai*. Consequently, branch-*Yin* and branch-*Hai* harmonize. In the second month, the Lunar Establishment indicates the direction of branch-*Mao* and the Lunar Compliance occurs in the zodiacal sign of branch-*Xu*. Consequently, branch-*Mao* and branch-*Xu* harmonize. The Lunar Establishment [following the path of heaven][74] revolves to the left[75] [i.e. clockwise against the earth's branch directions] while the Lunar Compliance [following the movement of the sun] rotates to the right [i.e. counterclockwise against heaven's branch zodiacal signs]. Moving with the flow and moving against the flow, respectively, the relevant branches of the Lunar Establishment and Lunar Compliance face one another. Therefore, they constitute the

Compilers' Note: The Lunar Compliance is determined with reference to the sun. The moon does not have light, but reflects the light of the sun. The moon moves with the sun and by their uniting (lit. harmonizing), they provide the means for breaking the year into periods. Thus, the sun is that with which the moon complies and therefore their meeting is called the Lunar Compliance. This term does not indicate that there is some star spirit other than the one constituted by the meeting of the sun and moon. This follows the sun's passage to the right [i.e. counterclockwise] through the sky. When the convergence occurs in branch-*Hai*, it is called the Seeking (*juzi*) constellation. When it occurs in branch-*Xu*, it is called the Descending and Gathering (*jianglou*) constellation. In branch-*You*, it is the Great Bridge (*daliang*) constellation. In branch-*Shen*, it is the Genuine Grandeur (*shichen*) constellation. In branch-*Wei*, it is the Quail's Head (*chunshou*) constellation. In branch-*Wu*, it is the Quail's Fire (*chunhuo*) constellation. In branch-*Si*, it is the Quail's Tail (*chunwei*) constellation. In branch-*Chen*, it is the Longevity Stars (*shouxing*) constellation. In branch-*Mao*, it is the Great Fire (*dahuo*) constellation. In branch-*Yin*, it is the Splitting Wood (*ximu*) constellation. In branch-*Chou*, it is the Stellar Period (*xingji*) constellation. In branch-*Zi*, it is the Dark Hole (*xuanxiao*) constellation. This construct was mentioned already in the *Zuo Commentary* to the *Spring and Autumn Annals* (*Chunqiu Zuozhuan*). To this day, the passage of the Lunar Compliance through the degrees of the palaces (zodiacal signs) has been recorded in public documents.

The Five Hidden Rats

The system[76] described in this section is commonly employed by astrologers to determine an individual's sexagenary cycle designation for the hour of birth. Essentially, the system describes the symmetry between sexagenary combinations of days and hours. On the basis of the observed symmetry, the system provides a formula for conveniently determining the stem-branch pair of a given hour if one already knows the stem-branch pair of the day in question. The same logic also underlies the system of the five hidden tigers described in the following section. Aside from serving as an astrologer's rule of thumb, this logic provides the inspiration behind the five harmonies' transformations of the vital breaths, which is described two sections below. The five harmonies system plays a very important role in the arts of astrology and *feng shui* and is much more than a simple rule of thumb.

A traditional Chinese day is composed of twelve two-hour periods. Each of the two-hour periods is designated by one of the sixty stem-branch pairs. There are Twelve Earthly Branches. Consequently, each of the twelve two-hour periods of a day is always designated by the same earthly branch. In other words, the first two-hour period is always the branch-*Zi* hour, the second two-hour period is the branch-*Chou* hour, etc. The stem designation of the hour, however, does change. In combining to form the sexagenary cycle, the five odd stems combine with the six odd branches and the five even stems combine with the six even branches. Therefore, the branch-*Zi* hour produces only five unique stem-branch pairings, i.e. stem-*Jia*/branch-*Zi*, stem-*Bing*/branch-*Zi*, stem-*Wu*/branch-*Zi*, stem-*Geng*/branch-*Zi*, and stem-*Ren*/branch-*Zi*. Since the symbolic animal of the branch-*Zi* is the rat, these five stem-branch hour pairs are referred to as the five rats.

Traditional Chinese days are also designated by one of the sixty stem-branch pairs. Since there are exactly twelve two-hour periods in one day, the complete cycle of hourly stem-branch pairings exhausts itself in exactly five days, i.e. five days times twelve hours equals sixty. If one considers the stem-branch pairings used to designate the days, one will observe that there are only Ten Heavenly Stems. Therefore, the days with the first (stem-*Jia*) and sixth (stem-*Ji*) stems will always begin with the stem-*Jia*/branch-*Zi* hour. Similarly, the days with the second (stem-*Yi*) and seventh (stem-*Geng*) stems will always begin with the stem-*Bing*/branch-*Zi* hour. After the sixty unique stem-branch pairings of days, the cycle of hours will thus begin again on a stem-branch stem-*Jia*/branch-*Zi* hour with a stem-branch stem-*Jia*/branch-*Zi* day. Therefore, there are only 720 possible combinations of stem-branch pairs for both hours and days. However, if one knows the stem of the day in question, one can use this system to determine the first hour and thereafter calculate the stem-branch pair for any hour in that day.

> Stem-*Jia* and stem-*Ji* days begin with the stem-branch hour stem-*Jia*/branch-*Zi*. Stem-*Yi* and stem-*Geng* days begin with the stem-branch hour stem-*Bing*/branch-*Zi*. Stem-*Bing* and stem-*Xin* days begin with the stem-branch hour stem-*Wu*/branch-*Zi*. Stem-

Figure 19 The Five Hidden Rats

Ding and stem-*Ren* days begin with the stem-branch hour stem-*Geng*/branch-*Zi*. Stem-*Wu* and stem-*Gui* days begin with the stem-branch hour stem-*Ren*/branch-*Zi*.

The *Study of Calendrics* (*Xingli kaoyuan*) says:[77]

'The stem-branch stem-*Jia*/branch-*Zi* day begins with the stem-branch stem-*Jia*/branch-*Zi* hour. Counting from stem-*Jia*/branch-*Zi* in order to the next day, then the branch-*Zi* hour obtains the stem-branch pair stem-*Bing*/branch-*Zi*. Therefore, the stem-*Yi* day begins with stem-branch pair stem-*Bing*/branch-*Zi* hour. From stem-*Jia* to stem-*Ji*, five days pass (i.e. stem-*Jia*/branch-*Zi*, stem-*Yi*/branch-*Chou*, stem-*Bing*/branch-*Yin*, stem-*Ding*/branch-*Mao*, and stem-*Wu*/branch-*Chen*) and altogether sixty [two] hour periods. Therein, the stem-branch pairs (lit. 'the blossoms of stem-*Jia*') are complete and they begin again. Therefore, the branch-*Zi* hour of the stem-*Ji* day is also the stem-branch stem-*Jia*/branch-*Zi* hour.'

The Five Hidden Tigers

Similar to the system just described, the hidden tigers concept is based on the fact that there are twelve months in a year and the first month always takes the earthly branch-*Yin*. The emblematic animal of branch-*Yin* is the tiger. Therefore, the five tigers are stem-*Jia*/branch-*Yin*, stem-*Bing*/branch-*Yin*, stem-*Wu*/branch-*Yin*, stem-*Geng*/branch-*Yin*, and stem-*Ren*/branch-*Yin*. If one knows the Heavenly Stem of the year in question, one will know which of these months the year begins with, and can thereby determine the stem-branch combination of any month in that year. As with the hidden rats, the symmetry of the pairings produces exactly 720 unique combinations of year and month stem-branch pairs.

Stem-*Jia* and stem-*Ji* years begin with the stem-*Bing*/branch-*Yin* month. Stem-*Yi* and stem-*Geng* years begin with the stem-*Wu*/branch-*Yin* month. Stem-*Bing* and stem-*Xin* years begin with the stem-*Geng*/branch-*Yin* month. Stem-*Ding* and stem-*Ren* years begin with the stem-*Ren*/branch-*Yin* month. Stem-*Wu* and stem-*Gui* years begin with the stem-*Jia*/branch-*Yin* month.

The *Study of Calendrics* (*Xingli kaoyuan*) says:[78]
'In great antiquity, the system of calendar recording must have originated on a stem-*Jia*/branch-*Zi* year, month, day, and hour. This means that the recording must have begun at the winter solstice during the eleventh month, i.e. stem-*Jia*/branch-*Zi* month, of a stem-*Jia*/branch-*Zi* year. Since in the first month the Lunar Establishment indicates branch-*Yin*, that month must obtain the stem-branch pair stem-*Bing*/branch-*Yin*. The second month is stem-*Ding*/branch-*Mao*. Counting

Figure 20 The Five Hidden Tigers

in this order along to the next year, the first month obtains the stem-branch pair stem-*Wu*/branch-*Yin*. Therefore, in stem-*Yi* years, the stem-branch pairings of the month arise from stem-*Wu*/branch-*Yin*. From stem-*Jia* to stem-*Ji*, five years pass and thus a full sixty months. Therein, the stem-branch pairs are complete and they begin again. Therefore, the first month of the stem-*Ji* year is also stem-*Bing*/branch-*Yin*.

The Five Harmonies' Transformations of the Vital Breaths

Simply stated, the 'five harmonies' transformations of the vital breaths' refers to the fact that five unique pairs of years consistently produce the same Five-Processes correlates for the third and fourth lunar months. For example, in years with the heavenly stem-*Jia* or stem-*Ji*, the third and fourth lunar months are always correlated with the earth process. The Five-Processes correlates of lunar months are determined by the months' Heavenly Stems. In stem-*Jia* and stem-*Ji* years, the third lunar month is always stem-*Wu*/branch-*Chen* and the fourth lunar month is always stem-*Ji*/branch-*Si*. Stem-*Wu* and stem-*Ji* are correlated with the earth process. Therefore, it is said that years with stem-*Jia* and stem-*Ji* harmonize to create the vital breath of the earth process.

If we arrange the Heavenly Stems in a circle, we will notice that the stems that harmonize stand diametrically opposite each other, i.e. stem-*Jia* and stem-*Ji* (1st & 6th), stem-*Yi* and stem-*Geng* (2nd & 7th), stem-*Bing* and stem-*Xin* (3rd & 8th), stem-*Ding* and stem-*Ren* (4th & 9th), and stem-*Wu* and stem-*Gui* (5th & 10th). The compilers analogize this method of pairing numbers to the methods of the Yellow River Chart and the Luo River Diagram. The observation that years with these pairs of Heavenly Stems consistently produce months with the same stems is merely an extension of the 'Hidden Tigers' formula described above. What is new in this construct is the emphasis that it places on the Five Processes correlates of the third and fourth lunar months.

To understand why such importance is placed on these particular months, we must consider the astronomical significance of the months' Earthly Branches, i.e. third month branch-*Chen* and fourth month branch-*Si*. In terms of Chinese astrology and *feng shui*, the earthly branch pertaining to a lunar month is the earthly branch of the direction on the earth's surface indicated by the handle of the Big Dipper when the sun and moon 'converge' (new moon). Remember that, if we lie on our backs looking up at the sky, the Dipper's handle will appear to rotate counterclockwise, but in this scheme we are considering the earth's surface. In this respect, the handle of the Dipper points north, then east, then south, then west. The twelve directional indications of the handle are assigned to the terrestrial compass and to the names of the twelve months.

In addition to designating directions, we will recall that the branches are used to designate the twelve zodiacal constellations. In naming these, however, the ancient Chinese astronomer conceptually projected the images of the zodiacal constellations onto the earth's surface. Thus, if outlines of the Western equivalents of the Chinese zodiacal constellations were inscribed next to each of the Earthly Branches, they would have to be drawn in mirror image. The same can be said for ancient Chinese depictions of the Big Dipper, which were drawn not as if the observer were looking at the sky, but rather as if he were looking through the Big Dipper onto the earth's surface. This explains why the Chinese zodiacal constellations are named after Earthly Branches in what appears to be reverse order. When the constellations are projected as mirror images onto the earth's surface, they are in fact named in order, i.e. clockwise. When the constellations come into view across the night sky, however, we see them in reverse or counterclockwise order, i.e. first Pisces (branch-*Hai*), followed by Aries (branch-*Xu*), then Taurus (branch-*You*), etc.

Considering the above, an interesting correspondence appears if one rotates the mirror-image ring of zodiacal constellations to the positions that they occupy relative to the earth's twelve directions at the end of the third and beginning of the fourth lunar months. At that time, the zodiacal constellations occupy positions that almost perfectly correlate to the twelve earthly directions. In other words, the constellation Aquarius (branch-*Zi*) will be above the horizon due north, Leo (branch-*Wu*) will be in the zenith of the sky and apparently due south, etc. In this way, the branch-*Chen* constellation (Libra) will be above the branch-*Chen* direction and the branch-*Si* constellation (Virgo) will be above the branch-*Si* direction. If one were to draw a line from the boundary of Libra (branch-*Chen*) and Virgo (branch-*Si*) to the boundary between Aries (branch-*Xu*) and Pisces (branch-*Hai*), that line would almost perfectly bisect the North Star (Polaris) and the star at the tip of the handle of the Big Dipper (Greek – Eta Ursa Majoris; Arabic – Alkaid; Chinese – Yao Guang). On the basis of this correspondence, the ancient Chinese astronomer must have been using the two stars just mentioned to determine the indications of the handle of the Big Dipper. At present, the alignments just described appear to occur at approximately 8:30 p.m. of the date in question.

The above reveals the astronomical explanation of the apparently mysterious term 'Gates of Heaven and Doors of Earth.' The Doors of Earth must refer to the alignment of zodiacal constellations and earthly directions just described and that alignment must correspond to the direction southeast and to the 'Beginning of Summer' solar node on or about 5 May (i.e. end of third or branch-*Chen* and beginning of fourth or branch-*Si* lunar months). At that time, heaven's times, as zodiacal constellations, come temporarily into alignment with earth's directions and then diverge once again. This explains why the Five-Processes correlates of the months' Heavenly Stems were considered so important. This was a time of alignment and transformation and the Heavenly Stems of the months in question governed the Five Processes polarity of that time. Six months after the 'Beginning of Summer' the diametrical line bisecting Polaris and Eta Ursa Majoris would again align with the directions southeast and northwest, but this time rotated 180 degrees. This second alignment corresponds to the 'Gates of Heaven,' which is the direction northwest and the 'Beginning of Winter' solar node (7 November). It should also be noted here that the division between the branch-*Chen* and branch-*Si* constellations marks the traditional point of dividing the circle of Twenty-Eight Lunar Lodges, the first being the Horn lodge in the branch-*Chen* and the twenty-eighth being the Chariot lodge in the branch-*Si*.

The timing of these convergences could hardly have seemed more significant to the ancient Chinese astronomer, for they occur almost precisely at the halfway points between spring and summer and between fall and winter. As such, the convergences served to define the boundaries between those two pairs of seasons. This boundary was based on the solar-node system rather than on luni-solar months. It was, therefore, thought to occur only roughly between the branch-*Chen* and branch-*Si* months, rather than occurring exactly on the last day of the branch-*Chen* or first day of the branch-*Si* month. The 'Beginning of Summer,' as a solar node, was defined with reference to the solstices and equinoxes. It therefore falls sometimes at the end of the branch-*Chen* month and sometimes at the beginning of the branch-*Si* month. If we consider the Five-Processes correlations of the months, we will recall that the eighteen days preceding the 'Beginning of Summer' were dedicated to the earth process. That earth-process period is normally referred to as the end of the branch-*Chen* month, but since it is actually keyed to a solar node, it often spans both the branch-*Chen* and branch-*Si* months.

To understand the complex nexus of associations described here, we must keep in mind the significance of the transitions from branch-*Chen* to branch-*Si* and from stem-*Wu* to stem-*Ji*. As we have seen, the transition from the branch-*Chen* month to the branch-*Si* month marks the first seasonal change of the year – spring to summer – and is also the first part of the year governed by the earth process. In terms of animal symbolism, branch-*Chen* is the dragon and branch-*Si* is the snake. These two animals uniquely symbolize change.

In terms of directional correlations, the diametrical line from branch-*Chen*/branch-*Si* to branch-*Xu*/branch-*Hai* is the diagonal from southeast to northwest. This line does not only represent the alignment of the zodiacal constellations and earthly directions. It is also perhaps the most important diametrical boundary of ancient Chinese cosmology. Chinese myths explain that this important boundary was created as the result of a cataclysmic battle between Gong Gong and Zhuan Xu. It was believed that originally the dome of the sky was perfectly centered directly overhead and was balanced on four celestial pillars in the northeast, southeast, southwest, and northwest (i.e. the celestial equator and the ecliptic coincided). However, during the divine battle, the two gods crashed into and shattered the northwestern celestial pillar – the Not-Circling Mountain. Consequently, the dome of the sky shifted to the northwest and the earth sank towards the southeast, thus starting the 'Great Flood' of Chinese mythology. This conveniently corresponded with the early Chinese understanding of their national topography which saw mountains in the northwest and oceans to the southeast.[79] This diametrical line is also symbolized by the curved boundary between yin and yang in the famous Diagram of the Great Ultimate (*taiji tu*).

In addition to the line bisecting the Earthly Branches, the 'Five Processes transformations of the vital breaths' also stresses the importance of heavenly stem-*Wu* and stem-*Ji*, which are normally correlated with the center and the earth process. These stems are normally thought to lack a unique time among the four seasons and space among the four directions. As the fifth and the sixth, they stand in the middle of the sequence of Ten Heavenly Stems. In the Hidden Rats and Hidden Tigers systems discussed above, the sixty stem-branch pairs of hours and months are exhausted after five days and five years, respectively, resume on the sixth day and sixth year, and complete a second cycle on the tenth day and tenth year. Thus, although the stems are sometimes divided in half according to their odd (yang) and even (yin) numbering, this scheme divides the ten in half from one to five and from six to ten. In the sixty stem-branch cycle of days, the days with the first five stems govern one complete cycle of sixty hours and the days with the last five stems govern a second cycle. The same is true for the stems of the years in relation to the sexagenary cycle of months.

The earliest text cited in this exposition is the *Plain Inquiry of the Yellow Emperor* (*Huangdi suwen*), which pretends to great antiquity, but dates to perhaps the late Han period. The text claims to represent questions made by the mythical Yellow Emperor to one of his chief ministers, the medical doctor Qi Bo. Though one might assume that this medical treatise would be of little relevance to Chinese cosmology, the philosophical underpinnings of Chinese medicine and metaphysics are closely linked. The compilers of the present Treatise also quote the Tang dynasty commentator on the *Plain Inquiry* (*Suwen*, abbreviated title), Wang Bing, as well as the Song dynasty editor of the text, a well-known scholar named Shen Gua (1031–1095 CE). In Wang Bing's explanation of the transformations, he argues the correctness of the Hidden Stem-*Jia* (*dunjia*) School, which, in contrast to other numerological schools,

Figure 21 The Five Harmonies' Transformations of the Vital Breaths

135

associates the stem-*Wu* with the division between branch-*Chen* and branch-*Si* and associates the stem-*Ji* with the division between the branch-*Xu* and branch-*Hai*.

Stem-*Jia* and stem-*Ji* harmonize. Stem-*Yi* and stem-*Geng* harmonize. Stem-*Bing* and stem-*Xin* harmonize. Stem-*Ding* and stem-*Ren* harmonize. Stem-*Wu* and stem-*Gui* harmonize.

Stem-*Jia* and stem-*Ji* transform and create earth. Stem-*Yi* and stem-*Geng* transform and create metal. Stem-*Bing* and stem-*Xin* transform and create water. Stem-*Ding* and stem-*Ren* transform and create wood. Stem-*Wu* and stem-*Gui* transform and create fire.

The *Study of Calendrics* (*Xingli kaoyuan*) says:[80]

'The five harmonies indicate that the five pairs of positions that face each other each constitute a harmony. In the Yellow River Chart, the pairs one and six, two and seven, three and eight, four and nine, and five and ten each constitute harmonies. If one correlates this to the order of the ten stems, then, one being stem-*Jia* and six being stem-*Ji*, stem-*Jia* and stem-*Ji* harmonize. Two is stem-*Yi* and seven is stem-*Geng*. Therefore, stem-*Yi* and stem-*Geng* harmonize. Three is stem-*Bing* and eight is stem-*Xin*. Therefore, stem-*Bing* and stem-*Xin* harmonize. Four is stem-*Ding* and nine is stem-*Ren*. Therefore, stem-*Ding* and stem-*Ren* harmonize. Five is stem-*Wu* and ten is stem-*Gui*. Therefore, stem-*Wu* and stem-*Gui* harmonize.'[81]

The [stem of the] year gives rise to the [stem of the] month and the [stem of the] day gives rise to the [stem of the] hour. After passing five [years/days], the cycle of the stem-branch pairs [of months/hours] is completed and begins again. This is another meaning of the term 'five harmonies.'

Compilers' Note: Shen Gua held that the most lucid discussion of the principle of the transformation of the vital breaths appears in the *Plain Inquiry of the Yellow Emperor* (*Huangdi suwen*). The *Plain Inquiry* (*Suwen*) mentions 'five movements and six vital breaths.' The five movements are as follows: stem-*Jia* and stem-*Ji* constitute the earth movement; stem-*Yi* and stem-*Geng* constitute the metal movement;

stem-*Bing* and stem-*Xin* constitute the water movement; stem-*Ding* and stem-*Ren* constitute the wood movement; stem-*Wu* and stem-*Gui* constitute the fire movement.

The Yellow Emperor asked Qi Bo where the five movements originated. Qi Bo explained the great beginning of heaven's primordial arranging of patterns[82] saying, 'It began in the division between stem-*Wu* and stem-*Ji*. This "division between stem-*Wu* and stem-*Ji*" is none other than a diametrical line drawn from the space between the adjacent lunar lodges Stride and Eastern Wall to the space between the opposite pair of adjacent lunar lodges Horn and Chariot. The divisions of Stride/Eastern Wall and of Horn/Chariot are respectively the Gates of Heaven and the Doors of Earth.'

Wang Bing commented on the above passage, explaining, 'In the Hidden Stem-*Jia* system the six [stem-branch pairs with] stem-*Wu* are the Gates of Heaven and the six [stem-branch pairs with] stem-*Ji* are the Doors of Earth. The Gates of Heaven are formed in the interstice of the zodiacal signs branch-*Xu* and branch-*Hai*, at the division between the lunar lodges Stride and Eastern Wall. The Doors of the Earth are formed in the interstice of the zodiacal signs branch-*Chen* and branch-*Si*, at the division between the lunar lodges Horn and Chariot. Yin and yang both begin in branch-*Chen*. Saying that the five movements arise in Horn and Chariot is equivalent to saying that the five movements begin in branch-*Chen*.'

In years with heavenly stem-*Jia* and stem-*Ji*, the vital breath of Auburn Heaven's stem-*Wu* and stem-*Ji* cross the lodges Horn and Chariot. Horn belongs to the class of branch-*Chen* and Chariot belongs to the class of branch-*Si*. These years thus obtain the stem-branch pairs stem-*Wu*/branch-*Chen* and stem-*Ji*/branch-*Si* [for the third and fourth months, which represent the Doors of the Earth]. Both stems are of the process of earth. Therefore, these constitute the movement of earth.

In years with heavenly stem-*Yi* and stem-*Geng*, the vital breath of Ivory Heaven's stem-*Geng* and stem-*Xin* cross the lodges Horn and Chariot. These years thus obtain the stem-branch pairs stem-*Geng*/branch-*Chen* and stem-*Xin*/branch-*Si* [for the third and fourth months]. Both stems are of the process of metal. Therefore, these constitute the movement of metal.

In years with heavenly stem-*Bing* and stem-*Xin*, the vital breath of Primordial [Black] Heaven's stem-*Ren* and stem-*Gui* cross the lodges Horn and Chariot. These years thus obtain the stem-branch pairs stem-*Ren*/branch-*Chen* and stem-*Gui*/branch-*Si* [for the third and fourth months]. Both stems are of the process of water. Therefore, these constitute the movement of water.

In years with heavenly stem-*Ding* and stem-*Ren*, the vital breath of Verdant Heaven's stem-*Jia* and stem-*Yi* cross the lodges Horn and Chariot. These years thus obtain the stem-branch pairs stem-*Jia*/branch-*Chen* and stem-*Yi*/branch-*Si* [for the third and fourth months]. Both stems are of the process of wood. Therefore, these constitute the movement of wood.

In years with heavenly stem-*Wu* and stem-*Gui*, the vital breath of Vermillion Heaven's stem-*Bing* and stem-*Ding* cross the lodges Horn and Chariot. These years thus obtain the stem-branch pairs stem-*Bing*/branch-*Chen* and stem-*Ding*/branch-*Si* [for the third and fourth months]. Both stems are of the process of fire. Therefore, these constitute the movement of fire.

The movements look upon the Horn lodge and the Chariot lodge. Thus, the vital breaths are the Stride lodge and the Eastern Wall lodge. Together, the vital breaths and the movements constantly serve as the Gates of Heaven and the Doors of Earth.

When stem-*Wu* and stem-*Ji* are in Horn and Chariot, stem-*Jia* and stem-*Yi* are in Stride and Wall. Thus, in stem-*Jia* and stem-*Ji* years these must be stem-*Jia*/branch-*Xu* and stem-*Yi*/branch-*Hai*.[83] This is why the *Plain Inquiry* (*Suwen*) says, 'When the process earth is positioned at the bottom, the vital breath of wind (i.e. wood) mounts above it.'

When stem-*Geng* and stem-*Xin* are in Horn and Chariot, stem-*Bing* and stem-*Ding* are in Stride and Wall. Thus, in stem-*Yi* and stem-*Geng* years these must be stem-*Bing*/branch-*Xu* and stem-*Ding*/branch-*Hai*. This is why the *Plain Inquiry* (*Suwen*) says, 'When the process metal is positioned at the bottom, the vital breath of fire mounts above it.'

When stem-*Ren* and stem-*Gui* are in Horn and Chariot, stem-*Wu* and stem-*Ji* are in Stride and Wall. Thus, in stem-*Bing* and stem-*Xin* years these must be stem-*Wu*/branch-*Xu* and stem-*Ji*/branch-*Hai*. This is why the *Plain Inquiry* (*Suwen*) says, 'When the process water is positioned at the bottom, the vital breath of earth mounts above it.'

When stem-*Jia* and stem-*Yi* are in Horn and Chariot, stem-*Geng* and stem-*Xin* are in Stride and Wall. Thus, in stem-*Ding* and stem-*Ren* years these must be stem-*Geng*/branch-*Xu* and stem-*Xin*/branch-*Hai*. This is why the *Plain Inquiry* (*Suwen*) says, 'When wind [the process wood] is positioned at the bottom, the vital breath of metal mounts above it.'

When stem-*Bing* and stem-*Ding* are in Horn and Chariot, stem-*Ren* and stem-*Gui* are in Stride and Wall. Thus, in stem-*Wu* and stem-*Gui* years these must be stem-*Ren*/branch-*Xu* and stem-*Gui*/branch-*Hai*. This is why the *Plain Inquiry* (*Suwen*) says, 'Facing the process of fire at the bottom, the vital breath of water mounts above it.'

The Five Processes School (*wuxing jia*) holds that the stem-*Wu* is dependent on the branch-*Si* and that the stem-*Ji* is dependent on branch-*Wu*. The Six Stem-*Ren* School (*liuren jia*) holds that the stem-*Wu* is dependent on the branch-*Si* and that the stem-*Ji* is dependent on the branch-*Wei*. Only the *Plain Inquiry* (*Suwen*) holds that the stem-*Wu* is dependent on the branch-*Xu* and that the stem-*Ji* is dependent upon the branch-*Chen*.

The Hidden Stem-*Jia* (*dun Jia*) holds that the six [stem-branch pairs that begin with] stem-*Wu* are the Gates of Heaven and that the six [stem-branch pairs that begin with] stem-*Ji* are the Doors of Earth. This is in accord with the statements in the *Plain Inquiry* (*Suwen*).

Water and earth mutually follow each other.

Water is the offspring of metal. Consequently, yang earth [i.e. the stem-*Wu*] resides in the final stage[84] of the process of metal,[85] which is taken to be the beginning of branch-*Hai*.[86]

Water is the mother of wood. Branch-*Si* is the ancestor of metal. Consequently, yin earth [i.e. the stem-*Ji*] resides[87] in the burial stage of the process of water,[88] which is taken to be the beginning of branch-*Si*.

Therefore, being referred to as the Gates of Heaven and Doors of Earth, they are the place from which myriad things proceed out.

The saying of the Star School (*xing jia*) [Five Planets School] that goes 'upon encountering the dragon [i.e. branch-*Chen*], they transform' also originates from this. This then is the origin of the ten stems' transformations of the vital breaths.

139

The Received Notes

This and the following five sections of the Treatise are dedicated to a rather complex system that bears the deceptively simple name 'Received Notes' (*na yin*). The Received Notes system assigns Five-Processes correlates to each of the sixty stem-branch pairs according to a methodical formula. These Five-Processes correlates are based solely on the Received Notes formula and cannot be otherwise extrapolated from the pairs' component stems or branches.

The formula states that each pair, beginning with the pair stem-*Jia*/branch-*Zi*, takes the neighboring pair of its own kind as a spouse and then gives birth to an offspring eight pairs after itself; this continues for three 'generations,' after which the fourth generation takes the correlate of the following process; the order of the processes assigned is metal, fire, wood, water, earth; after five groups of three pairs are thus assigned Five-Processes correlates, the system resumes again from the pair stem-*Jia*/branch-*Wu* and exhausts the final thirty stem-branch pairs. The concept of taking like as a spouse means that the pair stem-*Jia*/branch-*Zi* stands next to the pair stem-*Yi*/branch-*Chou*; the yang stem-*Jia* and the yin stem-*Yi* are both correlated with the wood process; therefore, the yin (even/female) pair stem-*Yi*/branch-*Chou* is the wife of the yang (odd/male) pair stem-*Jia*/branch-*Zi*; when the shifts of eight pairs exceed pair number sixty, the sequence is assumed to cycle back to pair number one, i.e. pair #57 plus 8 pairs equals pair #5.

Shen Gua said, 'The sixty "stem-branch pairs" [lit. stem-*Jia*/branch-*Zi*] possess Received Notes. This is a great mystery.[89] The number sixty derives from the following. There is a method by which the Pitch Pipes are rotated so that each pipe produces the Palace Note [*gong*]. According to this method, each pipe contains Five Notes and the Twelve Pipes, therefore, receive sixty notes.

'The vital breaths originate in the east and proceed towards the right. The notes arise in the west and proceed towards the left. Facing one another from their respective places, yin and yang give birth to the transformations. The vital breaths are said to originate in the east because the four seasons originate from wood [spring] and proceed to the right; wood turns to fire, fire turns to earth, earth turns to metal, and metal turns to water. The notes are said to arise in the west because the Five Notes begin with metal and revolve to the left; metal turns to fire, fire turns to wood, wood turns to water, and water turns to earth.'

The Received Notes system uses the same method as the Received Stem-*Jia* (*na Jia*) system of the *Book of Changes* (*Yijing*). In the Received Stem-*Jia* system, trigram-*Qian* receives stem-*Jia* and trigram-*Kun* receives stem-*Gui*. The Received Stem-*Jia* system, therefore, begins with trigram-*Qian* and ends with trigram-*Kun*. The Received Notes system begins with the metal process, which is correlated with trigram-*Qian*, and ends with the earth process, which is correlated with trigram-*Kun*.

'The Received Notes method is as follows. According to the "mutual production" method of the yin and yang Pitch Pipes, each pipe takes another of its own kind as a wife, shifts eight places, and gives birth to a son. According to the "three beginnings" periods of the Hidden Stem-*Jia* (*dun Jia*) school, the three thirds of each of the Five Processes are arranged in the order: middle-first-last.

The pair stem-*Jia*/branch-*Zi* is the middle third of the metal process.'

Stem-*Jia*/branch-*Zi* is the Exchange Note [*shang*–metal] of the Yellow Bell[90] [branch-*Zi*] pitch pipe.

'The pair stem-*Jia*/branch-*Zi* takes as its wife the adjacent pair stem-*Yi*/branch-*Chou*.'

Stem-*Yi*/branch-*Chou* is the Exchange Note [*shang*–metal] of the Great Regulator [branch-*Chou*] pitch pipe. 'Adjacent' means that the stems are of a pair, like stem-*Jia* and stem-*Yi* [both wood] or stem-*Bing* and stem-*Ding* [both fire].[91] The instances below follow this pattern.

'Shifting eight places, these pairs downwardly give birth to the pair stem-*Ren*/branch-*Shen*, which is the first third of the metal process.'

Stem-*Ren*/branch-*Shen* is the Exchange Note [*shang*–metal] of the Tranquil Pattern [branch-*Shen*] pitch pipe. 'Shifting eight' refers to the Great Regulator [branch-*Chou*] pitch pipe giving birth downwardly to the Tranquil Pattern [branch-*Shen*] pitch pipe. The instances below follow this pattern.

> 'The pair stem-*Ren*/branch-*Shen* takes as its wife the adjacent pair stem-*Gui*/branch-*You*.'

Stem-*Gui*/branch-*You* is the Exchange Note [*shang*–metal] of the Southern Regulator [branch-*You*] pitch pipe.

> 'Shifting eight places, these pairs upwardly give birth to the pair stem-*Geng*/branch-*Chen*, which is the last third of the metal process.'

Stem-*Geng*/branch-*Chen* is the Exchange Note [*shang*–metal] of the Maiden Purity [branch-*Chen*] pitch pipe. With this, the three beginnings of the metal process are concluded. If one only considers the yang zodiacal signs [*chen*, i.e. Earthly Branches], then according to the Hidden Stem-*Jia* School, these proceed with the flow from middle third [stem-*Jia*/branch-*Zi*, water flourishes in branch-*Zi*], to first third [stem-*Ren*/branch-*Shen*, water is born in branch-*Shen*], to last third [stem-*Geng*/branch-*Chen*, water is buried in branch-*Chen*]. However, if one also considers the wives [i.e. stem-*Yi*/branch-*Chou*, stem-*Gui*/branch-*You*, and stem-*Xin*/branch-*Si*], then it runs against the natural flow, which would be from first to middle to last [metal dies in branch-*Chou*, flourishes in branch-*You*, and is born in branch-*Si*].

> 'The pair stem-*Geng*/branch-*Chen* takes as its wife the adjacent pair stem-*Xin*/branch-*Si*.'

Stem-*Xin*/branch-*Si* is the Exchange Note [*shang*–metal] of the Median Regulator [branch-*Si*] pitch pipe.

> 'Shifting eight places, these pairs downwardly give birth to the pair stem-*Wu*/branch-*Zi*, which is the middle third of the fire process.'

Stem-*Wu*/branch-*Zi* is the Summoning Note [*zhi*–fire] of the Yellow Bell [branch-*Zi*] pitch pipe. The three beginnings of the metal process having ended, it proceeds to the left and turns to the southern direction and the fire process.

'The pair stem-*Wu*/branch-*Zi* takes as its wife the adjacent pair stem-*Ji*/branch-*Chou*.'

Stem-*Ji*/branch-*Chou* is the Summoning Note [*zhi*–fire] of the Great Regulator [branch-*Chou*] pitch pipe.

'These pairs give birth to the pair stem-*Bing*/branch-*Shen*, which is the first third of the fire process.'

Stem-*Bing*/branch-*Shen* is the Summoning Note [*zhi*–fire] of the Tranquil Pattern [branch-*Shen*] pitch pipe.

'The pair stem-*Bing*/branch-*Shen* takes as its wife the adjacent pair stem-*Ding*/branch-*You*.'

Stem-*Ding*/branch-*You* is the Summoning Note [*zhi*–fire] of the Southern Regulator [branch-*You*] pitch pipe.

'These pairs give birth to the pair stem-*Jia*/branch-*Chen*, which is the last third of the fire process.'

Stem-*Jia*/branch-*Chen* is the Summoning Note [*zhi*–fire] of the Maiden Purity [branch-*Chen*] pitch pipe.

'The pair stem-*Jia*/branch-*Chen* takes as its wife the pair stem-*Yi*/branch-*Si*.'

Stem-*Yi*/branch-*Si* is the Summoning Note [*zhi*–fire] of the Median Regulator [branch-*Si*] pitch pipe.

'These pairs give birth to the pair stem-*Ren*/branch-*Zi*, which is the middle third of the wood process.'

Stem-*Ren*/branch-*Zi* is the Horn Note [*jue*–wood] of the Yellow Bell [branch-*Zi*] pitch pipe. The three beginnings of the fire process having ended, it proceeds to the left and turns to the eastern direction and wood process.

'In the manner just explained, the system continues moving to the left through to the pair stem-*Ding*/branch-*Si*, which is correlated with the Palace Note [*gong*–earth] of the Median Regulator [branch-*Si*] pitch pipe. Having concluded once, the Five Notes then start again from the pair stem-*Jia*/branch-*Wu*, which is the middle third of the metal process. The pair stem-*Jia*/branch-*Wu* then takes as its wife the pair stem-*Yi*/branch-*Wei* and then, shifting eight, gives birth to the pair stem-*Ren*/branch-*Yin*. The process thus continues in the same manner as the example above that began with the pair stem-*Jia*/branch-*Zi*, concluding in the latter case with the pair stem-*Gui*/branch-*Hai*.'

This means that the Luxuriant Guest [branch-*Wu*] pitch pipe takes as its wife the Forest Bell [branch-*Wei*] pitch pipe. Then, the Luxuriant Guest pitch pipe upwardly gives birth to the Great Budding [branch-*Yin*] pitch pipe.

'Branch-*Zi* through branch-*Si* are yang. Therefore, the Pitch Pipes Yellow Bell [branch-*Zi*] through Median Regulator [branch-*Si*] all "downwardly" give birth. Branch-*Wu* through branch-*Hai* are yin. Therefore, the Pitch Pipes Luxuriant Guest [branch-*Wu*] through Responsive Bell [branch-*Hai*] all "upwardly" give birth.'

The *Collected Writings on Measuring the Ocean with a Shell* (*Lihai ji*) says:

'The myriad things are able to be born only through the action of vital breath. Why is it, though, that this vital breath is metal? If metal has received vital breath, then "proceeding with the flow" is the form (lit. body) of the Five Processes and "proceeding against the flow" is the function of the Five Processes.

'The flowing progression that constitutes the form [lit. 'body' (*ti*)] of the Five Processes is this: metal gives birth to water, water gives birth to wood, wood gives birth to fire, and fire gives birth to earth. The winter solstice is the beginning from which the passage of time arises. From the winter solstice spring follows, from spring summer follows, from summer late summer follows, and from late summer it returns to fall. Turning back to its roots, returning to its origins, it is gathered in.

'The counter-flowing progression that constitutes the function (*yong*) of the Five Processes is this: metal comes from a mine [in the earth] and must undergo forging by fire before it can be crafted into a product. Only after it has thus been crafted into a product does it have the function of a living thing. Similarly, fire, if it were not for wood, could not be born. Fire must come into contact with wood in order to continue existing. Wood must rely on water for nourishment. Water must depend on earth to stop it and contain it. Thus where there is wood, there must first be water and where there is water, there must first be earth. This being the case, it follows that, in order to exist, all things that are correlated with the four cardinal processes must depend on the fixed position of earth.

'When Da Nao[92] created the stem-branch system [lit. stem-*Jia*/branch-*Zi*] and allocated the Five Processes as Received Notes, he knew that metal, being able to receive sound, could announce the vital breaths. The method, thus, states that, 'stem-*Jia* takes stem-*Yi* as its wife, shifts eight, and gives birth to a son. The son then gives birth to a grandson, after which the subsequent process continues on in its position.

'The first is called metal. Metal is the vital breath that dwells at the beginning. The pair stem-*Jia*/branch-*Zi* is the beginning of "receiving vital breath." Stem-*Jia* takes stem-*Yi* as its wife. Shifting eight, the pair stem-*Ren*/branch-*Shen*, is the son. Stem-*Ren* takes stem-*Gui* as its wife. Shifting eight, the pair stem-*Geng*/branch-*Chen*, is the grandson. Stem-*Geng* takes stem-*Xin* as its wife. Shifting eight, the pair stem-*Wu*/branch-*Zi*, takes over metal's position.

'The second is called fire. Stem-*Wu* continues as metal's successor. Stem-*Wu* takes stem-*Ji* as its wife. Shifting eight, the pair stem-*Bing*/branch-*Shen*, is the son. Stem-*Bing* takes stem-*Ding* as its wife. Shifting eight, the pair stem-*Jia*/branch-*Chen*, is the grandson. Stem-*Jia* takes stem-*Yi* as its wife. Shifting eight, the pair stem-*Ren*/branch-*Zi* takes over fire's position.

'The third is called wood. Stem-*Ren* continues as metal's successor. Stem-*Ren* takes stem-*Gui* as its wife. Shifting eight, the pair stem-*Geng*/branch-*Shen*, is the son. Stem-*Geng* takes stem-*Xin* as its wife. Shifting eight, the pair stem-*Wu*/branch-*Chen*, is the grandson. Stem-*Wu* takes stem-*Ji* as its wife. Shifting eight, the pair stem-*Bing*/branch-*Zi*, takes over wood's position.

'The fourth is called water. Stem-*Bing* continues as wood's successor. Stem-*Bing* takes stem-*Ding* as its wife. Shifting eight, the pair stem-*Jia*/branch-*Shen*, is the son. Stem-*Jia* takes stem-*Yi* as its wife. Shifting eight, the pair stem-*Ren*/branch-*Chen*, is the grandson. Stem-*Ren* takes stem-*Gui* as its wife. Shifting eight, the pair stem-*Geng*/branch-*Zi*, takes over water's position.

'The fifth is called earth. Stem-*Geng* continues as water's successor.[93] Stem-*Geng* takes stem-*Xin* as its wife. Shifting eight, the pair stem-*Wu*/branch-*Shen*, is the son. Stem-*Wu* takes stem-*Ji* as its wife. Shifting eight, the pair stem-*Bing*/branch-*Chen* is the grandson. Stem-*Bing* takes stem-*Ding* as its wife. Shifting eight, the pair stem-*Jia*/branch-*Zi* is again metal and takes over earth's position. The associations of the pairs stem-*Jia*/branch-*Wu* and stem-*Yi*/branch-*Wei* are assigned in the same manner as above.

'This is why there is a saying about the five branch-*Zi* pairs returning to stem-*Geng*. The Daoists commonly use this concept to assign numbers to the positions of the five directions. In the cycle of sixty stem-branch pairs, for each stem that is paired with the branch-*Zi*, one counts to stem-*Geng* to obtain the number.

'The pair stem-*Jia*/branch-*Zi* is metal. Counting from stem-*Jia*, there are seven places before stem-*Geng*. Consequently, western metal obtains the vital breath of the number seven. The pair stem-*Wu*/branch-*Zi* is fire. Counting from stem-*Wu*, there are three places before stem-*Geng*. Consequently, southern fire obtains the vital breath of the number three. The pair stem-*Ren*/branch-*Zi* is wood. Counting from stem-*Ren*, there are nine places before stem-*Geng*. Consequently, eastern wood obtains the vital breath of the number nine. The pair stem-*Bing*/branch-*Zi* is water. Counting from stem-*Bing*, there are five places before stem-*Geng*. Consequently, northern water obtains the vital breath of the number five. The pair stem-*Geng*/branch-*Zi* is earth. Counting from stem-*Geng*, itself, there is only one place. Consequently, the center obtains the vital breath of the number one.

This, then, is the meaning of the five branch-*Zi* stem-branch pairs returning to the stem-*Geng*.

'Thus understanding metal's prior reception of the vital breath, proceeding with the flow, one obtains the form [lit. body (*ti*)] of the Five Processes, while proceeding against the flow, one obtains the function of the Five Processes. This is what the sixty stem-*Jia*/branch-*Zi* Received Notes system employs to bring the myriad things to completion.'

The *Study of Calendrics* (*Xingli kaoyuan*) says:[94]

'In the "Great Plan" ("*Hong fan*") chapter of the *Book of Documents* (*Shang shu*), the processes are listed in this order: water–fire–wood–metal–earth. This sequence is based on idea that the Five Processes originate from vital breath and conclude with form (*xing*). In the "Monthly Ordinances" ("*Yue ling*") chapter of the *Book of Rites* (*Liji*), the processes are listed in this order: wood–fire–earth–metal–water. This sequence is based on the mutual production of the Five Processes throughout the cycle of the four seasons. In the "Plan of Yu the Great" ("*Da Yu mo*") chapter of the *Book of Documents* (*Shang shu*), the processes are listed in this order: water–fire–metal–wood–earth. This sequence is based on the mutual conquest of the Five Processes within the realm of the five materials. In the Received Notes system, the Five Processes are listed in this order: metal–fire–wood–water–earth. This is not "originating in vital breath and ending with form," nor does it derive from the orders of production or conquest. Among those who have offered explanations thus far, none appear to understand the origin of the Five Processes sequence that is used in the Received Notes system.'[95]

Careful examination suggests that this sequence is derived from the ideas depicted by the images of the trigrams of the *Book of Changes* (*Yijing*), i.e. the Former and Latter Heaven Arrangements of trigrams. Depicting each of these in diagrams below will clarify the matter.

The Received Notes Five Processes as They Correlate with the Former Heaven Chart

This section argues that the order of the trigrams in the Former Heaven arrangement produces the Received Notes' metal–fire–wood–water–earth sequence. The Former Heaven arrangement of trigrams follows a sequence from the most yang trigram to the most yin trigram. From trigram-*Qian* at the top-center (south) of the diagram, the order of the trigrams proceeds counterclockwise to trigram-*Zhen* in the bottom-left (northeast) and then a diametrical shift crosses to trigram-*Sun* at the top-right (southwest). The trigrams then proceed clockwise to trigram-*Kun* at the bottom-center (north). If one considers the Five-Processes correlates of the trigrams (trigram-*Qian*: metal, trigram-*Dui*: metal, trigram-*Li*: fire, trigram-*Zhen*: wood, trigram-*Sun*: wood, trigram-*Kan*: water, trigram-*Gen*: earth, trigram-*Kun*: earth), the order corresponds with that of the Received Notes, i.e. metal–fire–wood–water–earth.

The *Study of Calendrics (Xingli kaoyuan)*[96] says:

> 'In the Former Heaven Chart, trigram-*Qian* and trigram-*Dui* reside at the head and belong to the process of metal. Trigram-*Li*, which is taken to follow, belongs to the process of fire. Trigram-*Zhen* and trigram-*Sun*, following in turn, belong to the process of wood. Trigram-*Kan*, again following, belongs to the process of water. The correlations conclude with trigram-*Gen* and trigram-*Kun*, which belong to the process of earth.
>
> 'From the above we see that beginning with metal and ending with earth is implied by the concept of trigram-*Qian* beginning and trigram-*Kun* bringing to completion. The process metal derives from the hardness of heaven and the process earth (soil) derives from the softness of earth (the world). The process fire follows upon heaven and the process water follows upon earth. The process wood, then, employs the vital breath of living things to reside in the center. This explains how the Received Notes derive from the Former Heaven order of trigrams.'

Figure 22 The Received Notes Five Processes as they Correlate with the Former Heaven Chart

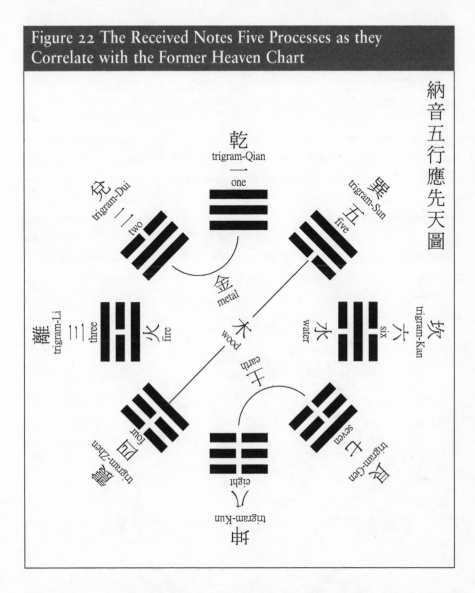

The Received Notes Five Processes as They Correlate with the Latter Heaven Chart

As with the last, this section traces the order of trigrams from the most yang trigram to least yang trigram and then from the least yin trigram to the most yin trigram. Since the Five-Processes correlates of the trigrams do not change, the correspondence here is the same as above. The only thing this section adds is the directional correlations of the trigrams. In the Latter Heaven arrangement, the metal trigrams are in the west (right), the fire trigram in the south (top), wood in the east (left), water in the north (bottom), and earth in the center (bottom left and top right).

The *Study of Calendrics* (*Xingli kaoyuan*) says:[97]

'The Latter Heaven Chart also places trigram-*Qian* and trigram-*Dui* at the head. It then rotates backwards (i.e. counterclockwise) from the west where the metal process of trigram-*Qian* and trigram-

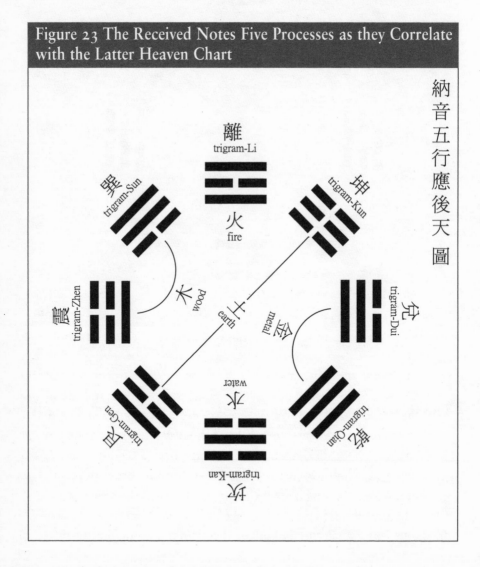

Figure 23 The Received Notes Five Processes as they Correlate with the Latter Heaven Chart

Dui flourishes. Through this rotation it next turns to the south where the fire process of trigram-*Li* flourishes. Again rotating, it moves to the east where the wood process of trigram-*Zhen* and trigram-*Sun* flourishes. Rotating again, it arrives at the north where the water process of trigram-*Kan* flourishes. The earth process flourishes in the final month of each of the four seasons. Therefore, the rotation concludes by returning to reside in trigram-*Gen* and trigram-*Kun*. This explains how the Received Notes derive from the Latter Heaven order of trigrams.'

The Diagram Depicting the Correlation between the Three Beginnings of the Received Notes Five Processes and the Musical Pipes' Shifting Eight and Mutually Giving Birth

The text of this section adds little to what has already been said in the above sections. The primary contribution of this section is the diagram that it presents.

The *Study of Calendrics* (*Xingli kaoyuan*) says:[98]

'This diagram takes the pairs stem-*Jia*/branch-*Zi* and stem-*Yi*/branch-*Chou* as the Upper Beginning of the metal process. It then takes the pairs stem-*Ren*/branch-*Shen* and stem-*Gui*/branch-*You* as the Middle Beginning of the metal process. Finally, it takes the pairs stem-*Geng*/branch-*Chen* and stem-*Xin*/branch-*Si* as the Lower Beginning of the metal process. These three "beginnings" thus having been completed, it transitions to the pairs stem-*Wu*/branch-*Zi* and stem-*Ji*/branch-*Chou*, which are taken as the Upper Beginning of the fire process. The pairs stem-*Bing*/branch-*Shen* and stem-*Ding*/branch-*You* next are taken as the Middle Beginning of the fire process. In turn the pairs stem-*Jia*/branch-*Chen* and stem-*Yi*/branch-*Si* are taken as the Lower Beginning of the fire process.

'From this point forward the chart follows its order of metal, fire, wood, water, and earth. At the same time it employs the method of the musical pipes, which holds that like takes like as a wife, moves eight positions, and then gives birth to a son. Thus the pro-

Figure 24 The Diagram Depicting the Correlation between the Three Beginnings of the Received Notes Five Processes and the Musical Pipes' Shifting Eight and Mutually Giving Birth

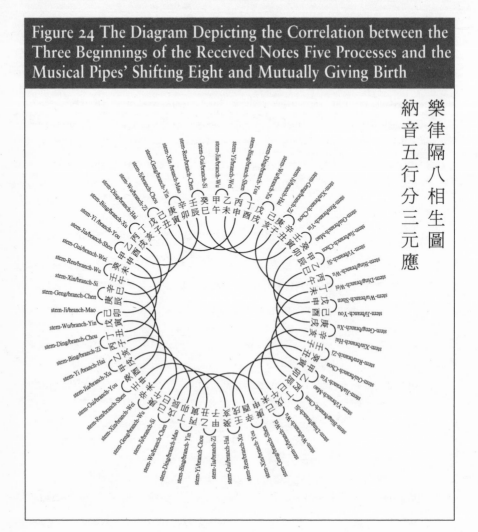

gression concludes with the stem-branch pair stem-*Ding*/branch-*Si*. This portion of the cycle is referred to as the Lesser Completion of the Received Notes.

'From that point, the process resumes with the pairs stem-*Jia*/branch-*Wu* and stem-*Yi*/branch-*Wei*, which are taken as the Upper Beginning of the metal process. It proceeds in exact accordance with the method described above and concludes with the stem-branch pair stem-*Ding*/branch-*Hai*. This second half of the process is thus referred to as the Greater Completion of the Received Notes.

Compilers' Note: The ten stems and the twelve branches are combined to make sixty stem-branch pairs. The Five Notes and the Twelve Pitch Pipes are also matched to produce sixty.

'The fact that both pairs stem-*Jia*/branch-*Zi* and stem-*Yi*/branch-*Chou* are correlated with the metal process is an example of how each takes one of its own kind in the same position as its wife. The fact that both pairs stem-*Yi*/branch-*Chou* and stem-*Ren*/branch-*Shen* are correlated with the metal process is an example of how they shift eight and give birth to a son.

'Each of the Five Processes has three beginnings after which it transfers power to the next process. This is similar to the way in which spring has its first, middle, and last month, and thereafter turns into summer.

'The pairs proceed from stem-*Jia*/branch-*Zi* to stem-*Ding*/branch-*Si*. Therein, the Three Beginnings of the Five Processes complete one cycle. This is similar to the way in which the three lines of the *Book of Changes* (*Yijing*) trigrams form the lesser completion. The pairs proceed from stem-*Jia*/branch-*Wu* to stem-*Ding*/branch-*Hai*. Therein, the Three Beginnings of the Five Processes complete another cycle. This is similar to the way in which the six lines of the *Book of Changes* (*Yijing*) hexagrams form the greater completion.

'The establishment of these methods is in complete accord with the Pitch Pipes.'

The Received Notes, the Stems, and the Branches Assume Numbers in Harmony with the Five Processes

This section explains the Received Notes system's Five-Processes correlations for the sixty stem-branch pairs in terms of the numerological associations of the stems and branches. Two numerological formulae are given for 'calculating' the correlates of the stem-branch pairs. Both involve the same assumption about the numerical values of the stems and branches. The values are assigned to diametrically opposed pairs of stems and branches. The first and fifth stems (stem-*Jia* and stem-*Ji*) and the first and sixth branches (branch-*Zi* and branch-*Wu*) correlate with the 'ultimate' yang number, i.e. nine. The remaining pairs assume numerical values in descending order, i.e. eight, seven, six, etc. Both of the formulae described in this section employ the principle of adding the values of the various stems and branches of two associated stem-branch pairs, e.g. stem-*Jia*/branch-*Zi* and stem-*Yi*/branch-*Chou*, paired because stem-*Jia* and stem-*Yi* are the yang and yin stems of the wood process. Both formulae also only consider the value of the digit in the ones place. The first formula, however, only considers the raw sum. The second formula, by contrast, posits that the sum must be subtracted from the magic number forty-nine; it then bases its conclusion on the value of the ones-place digit of the difference obtained.

The compilers argue that the second formula is more meaningful because the number pairs that it employs are consistent with the number pairs of the Luo River Diagram and Yellow River Chart. This indicates that the compilers believed it was important to establish a connection between the stems and branches and the numbers of the trigrams.

> Stem-*Jia*, stem-*Ji*, branch-*Zi*, and branch-*Wu* are correlated with the number nine. Stem-*Yi*, stem-*Geng*, branch-*Chou*, and branch-*Wei* are correlated with the number eight. Stem-*Bing*, stem-*Xin*, branch-*Yin*, and branch-*Shen* are correlated with the number seven. Stem-*Ding*, stem-*Ren*, branch-*Mao*, and branch-*You* are correlated with the number six. Stem-*Wu*, stem-*Gui*, branch-*Chen*, and branch-*Xu* are correlated with the number five. Branch-*Si* and branch-*Hai* are correlated with the number four.

The *Collected Writings on Measuring the Ocean with a Shell* (*Lihai ji*) says:

'Someone asked "What is the origin of the Former Heaven numbers?" The response was, "Numbers are at their extreme in nine. The associations of the stems and branches with numbers are derived by starting with nine and counting backwards. Therefore, stem-*Jia*, stem-*Ji*, branch-*Zi*, and branch-*Wu* are nine; stem-*Yi*, stem-*Geng*, branch-*Chou*, and branch-*Wei* are eight; stem-*Bing*, stem-*Xin*, branch-*Yin*, and branch-*Shen* are seven; stem-*Ding*, stem-*Ren*, branch-*Mao*, and branch-*You* are six; stem-*Wu*, stem-*Gui*, branch-*Chen*, and branch-*Xu* are five. The stems are thereby already exhausted, but branch-*Si* and branch-*Hai* remain. Therefore, branch-*Si* and branch-

Hai obtain the number four and the numerical correlations are thus concluded. This is why branch-*Hai* serves as the Gates of Heaven and branch-*Si* serves as the Doors of the Earth. The position of pure yang functions as the hinge that makes possible opening and closing. It is the pivot of the Five Processes.'"

The *Lucky Cassia Hall Diary*[99] (*Ruigui tang xialü*) says:

'The musical notes of metal, wood, water, fire, and earth can be used to explain the Received Notes of the sixty stem-*Jia*/branch-*Zi* pairs. One and six are the water process. Two and seven are the fire process. Three and eight are the wood process. Four and nine are the metal process. Five and ten are the earth process.

'Among the Five Processes, only metal and wood produce musical notes independently. Water, fire, and earth must interact with other processes in order to produce musical notes: water depends on earth; fire depends on water; and earth depends on fire. Thus, the metal note is four and nine, the wood note is three and eight, the water note is five and ten, the fire note is one and six, and the earth note is two and seven. This is an immutable concept.

'If what has just been said is true, then how is it that the stems and branches have the following numerical correlations: stem-*Jia*, stem-*Ji*, branch-*Zi*, branch-*Wu* (9); stem-*Yi*, stem-*Geng*, branch-*Chou*, branch-*Wei* (8); stem-*Bing*, stem-*Xin*, branch-*Yin*, branch-*Shen* (7); stem-*Ding*, stem-*Ren*, branch-*Mao*, branch-*You* (6); stem-*Wu*, stem-*Gui*, branch-*Chen*, branch-*Xu* (5); and, finally, branch-*Si*, branch-*Hai* (4)?

'The number of the pairs stem-*Jia*/branch-*Zi* and stem-*Yi*/branch-*Chou* is thirty-four. Four is the musical note of metal. Therefore, these pairs are called metal.

'The number of the pairs stem-*Wu*/branch-*Chen* and stem-*Ji*/branch-*Si* is twenty-three. Three is the musical note of wood. Therefore, these pairs are called wood.

'The number of the pairs stem-*Geng*/branch-*Wu* and stem-*Xin*/branch-*Wei* is thirty-two. Two is fire and since earth depends upon fire to produce a musical note, these pairs are called earth.

'The number of the pairs stem-*Jia*/branch-*Shen* and stem-*Yi*/branch-*You* is thirty. Ten is earth and since water depends upon earth to produce a musical note, these pairs are called water.

'The number of the pairs stem-*Wu*/branch-*Zi* and stem-*Ji*/branch-*Chou* is thirty-one. One is water and since fire depends upon water to produce a musical note, these pairs are called fire.

'Among the sixty stem-*Jia*/branch-*Zi* pairs, none fail to follow this pattern. This, then, is the origin of the Received Notes.'

The *Study of Calendrics (Xingli kaoyuan)* says:[100]

'This is the system that Yang Xiong described in his *Book of the Great Mystery (Taixuan jing)*.[101] The system assigns numbers to the sounds of the Pitch Pipes. To determine the process that is correlated with two sexagenary stem-branch pairs, one must sum the values of the stems and branches of both pairs. If the number in the singles place of the resulting sum is four or nine, then the pairs are metal. If the number is one or six, then the pairs are fire. If it is three or eight, then the pairs are wood. If it is five or ten, then the pairs are water. If it is two or seven, then the pairs are earth.

'Since stem-*Jia* and branch-*Zi* each have a value of nine, their sum is eighteen. Since stem-*Yi* and branch-*Chou* each have a value of eight, their sum is sixteen. Eighteen plus sixteen equals thirty-four. [The number in the singles place of this sum is four and four is metal.] Therefore, the pairs stem-*Jia*/branch-*Zi* and stem-*Yi*/branch-*Chou* are metal.

'The value of stem-*Ren* is six and the value of branch-*Shen* is seven; six plus seven equals thirteen. The value of stem-*Gui* is five and the value of branch-*You* is six; five plus six equals eleven. Thirteen plus eleven equals twenty-four. Therefore, these two stem-branch pairs are also metal.

'If one uses this method to determine the Five-Processes correlations of the remaining stem-branch pairs, one will see that none deviate from the model. However, the Five-Processes correlations of the number pairs one and six, two and seven, etc., as set forth here, differ from the numbers of the Yellow River Chart.'

The following compilers' note refers to fifty as 'number of great abundance.' This attribution is mentioned in the 'Appended Verbalizations'('*Xici*'), which is one of the ten 'wings' or appendices of the *Book of Changes* (*Yijing*). A commentary on that passage attributed to the Han scholar Jing Fang explains that the number fifty is derived by adding the numbers of the Heavenly Stems (10), Earthly Branches (12), and lunar lodges (28). The compilers, however, do not explain why only the number forty-nine is used, rather than fifty.

'**Compilers' note:**[102] The number of great abundance (*dayan*) is fifty, but the number employed is forty-nine. First one sums the values of the stems and branches of two sexagenary pairs. Then one subtracts the sum from the number forty-nine. Values in the tens place are not considered. If the number remaining in the ones place is one or six, it corresponds to water. If the number is two or seven, it corresponds to fire. If it is three or eight, it corresponds to wood. If it is four or nine, it corresponds to metal. If it is five or ten, it corresponds to earth. Next, one identifies the process that is produced by the process just identified. The process produced is the Received Notes system's Five-Processes correlate for the two stem-branch pairs in question. The numbers of this system are in perfect accord with the numbers of the Yellow River Chart. The system also bears resemblances to the method of divining with milfoil stalks, which uses the remainder to determine odd or even. Since the method currently being described uses the number remaining in the ones place to determine the Five-Processes affiliation, the two methods employ compatible principles.

'An example of the this system is as follows: stem-*Jia* and branch-*Zi* are nine. Stem-*Yi* and branch-*Chou* are eight. Their sum is thirty-four. Forty-nine minus thirty-four equals fifteen. The ten in the tens place is not used. This leaves five, which is affiliated with earth. Earth gives birth to metal. Therefore, the Five-Processes correlate of the pairs stem-*Jia*/branch-*Zi* and stem-*Yi*/branch-*Chou* is metal.

'The pairs stem-*Bing*/branch-*Yin* and stem-*Ding*/branch-*Mao* produce a combined value of twenty-six. Forty-nine minus twenty-six equals twenty-three. The twenty in the tens place is not used. This leaves three. Three is associated with the process wood. Wood gives birth to fire. Therefore, the pairs stem-*Bing*/branch-*Yin* and stem-*Ding*/branch-*Mao* are affiliated with fire.

'The pairs stem-*Wu*/branch-*Chen* and stem-*Ji*/branch-*Si* produce a combined value of twenty-three. Forty-nine minus twenty-three equals twenty-six. The twenty in the tens place is not used. This leaves six. Six is associated with the process water. Water gives birth to wood. Therefore, the pairs stem-*Wu*/branch-*Chen* and stem-*Ji*/branch-*Si* are affiliated with wood.

'The pairs stem-*Geng*/branch-*Wu* and stem-*Xin*/branch-*Wei* produce a combined value of thirty-two. Forty-nine minus thirty-two equals seventeen. The ten in the tens place is not used. This leaves seven. Seven is associated with fire. Fire gives birth to earth. Therefore, the pairs stem-*Geng*/branch-*Wu* and stem-*Xin*/branch-*Wei* are affiliated with earth.'[103]

The remaining pairs are calculated in this same manner.

Compilers' Note: The *Book of the Great Mystery* (*Taixuan jing*) Yang Xiong says:[104]

'The number of branch-*Zi* and branch-*Wu* is nine. The number of branch-*Chou* and branch-*Wei* is eight. The number of branch-*Yin* and branch-*Shen* is seven. The number of branch-*Mao* and branch-*You* is six. The number of branch-*Chen* and branch-*Xu* is five. The number of branch-*Si* and branch-*Hai* is four.

'Therefore, the Regulator Pipes (*Lü*) produce a combined value of forty-two. [These being the yang/odd-numbered pipes, the sum of the values of branch-*Zi* (9), plus branch-*Yin* (7), plus branch-*Chen* (5), plus branch-*Wu* (9), plus branch-*Shen* (7), plus branch-*Xu* (5) equals forty-two.] The Spine Pipes (*Lü*) produce a combined value of thirty-six. [These being the yin/even-numbered pipes, the sum of the values of branch-*Chou* (8), plus branch-*Mao* (6), plus branch-*Si* (4), plus branch-*Wei* (8), plus branch-*You* (6), plus branch-*Hai* (4) equals thirty-six.] The sum of the combined values of both sets of pipes (i.e. seventy-eight) may constitute a returning or it may not.[105] Therein, the number of the Yellow Bell pipe (branch-*Zi*) is established. The Yellow Bell pipe is regarded as the standard because it gives birth to all the other pipes.'

The *Book of the Great Mystery* (*Taixuan jing*) goes on to say:

'The number of stem-*Jia* and stem-*Ji* is nine. The number of stem-*Yi* and stem-*Geng* is eight. The number of stem-*Bing* and stem-*Xin* is seven. The number of stem-*Ding* and stem-*Ren* is six. The number of stem-*Wu* and stem-*Gui* is five.[106]

'The sounds [i.e. the Five Notes] are born from the sun [i.e. 10 days/Heavenly Stems]. The [twelve] pipes are born from the zodiacal signs [i.e. moon/12 months/Earthly Branches]. The sounds resonate emotionally with matter. The pipes harmonize with the sounds. As the sounds and pipes advance together, the eight notes are born.'[107]

People have venerated these numbers since great antiquity. They are called the numbers of the Former Heaven. If one examines the rationale behind these numbers, rarely will one find a coherent explanation of why stem-*Jia*, stem-*Ji*, branch-*Zi*, and branch-*Wu* are nine or of why stem-*Yi*, stem-*Geng*, branch-*Chou*, and branch-*Wei* are eight.

Compilers' Note: Branch-*Zi* and branch-*Wu* are the branches that trigram-*Qian* and trigram-*Zhen* receive. Branch-*Chou* and branch-*Wei* are the branches that trigram-*Kun* and trigram-*Sun* receive. Branch-*Yin* and branch-*Shen* are the branches that trigram-*Kan* receives. Branch-*Mao* and branch-*You* are the branches that trigram-*Li* receives. Branch-*Chen* and branch-*Xu* are the branches that trigram-*Gen* receives. Branch-*Si* and branch-*Hai* are the branches that trigram-*Dui* receives.

Since the yang numbers are at their extreme in the number nine and the yin numbers are at their extreme in the number eight, trigram-*Qian* and trigram-*Kun*, respectively, obtain these two numbers. Trigram-*Zhen* and trigram-*Sun*, as the eldest offspring, are governed by the father and mother.[108] The remaining trigrams and numbers, according to their birth order proceed downwardly from here. This is the order of the two great ones and the six children, male and female, elder and junior. Naturally ordered in this way, the system does not become chaotic. This is a concrete truth and is not something that man can simply force.

The order of ten days (i.e. the stems) also follows the numbers of elder and younger in the transformation of the vital breaths. Not one of them varies in even the slightest degree from this standard. Consider as an example the earth process. The stems stem-*Jia* and stem-*Ji* are earth. Even though earthen ash may fall upon the surface of a pond and dissipate as in a void, that earth matter never actually ceases to exist. Since it is the eldest of the Five Processes it takes the number nine.

Next [to earth] is metal. Although metal may be smelted in fire and some of its vital breath be exhausted in the smoke, the metal matter nevertheless always remains. Therefore, it is considered the king of the myriad things. Since stem-*Yi* and stem-*Geng* are metal, they follow stem-*Jia* and stem-*Ji*.

Next [to metal] is water. Although the sun, wind, and fire may evaporate water, there is never a time when water is completely exhausted. Although not as hard as metal, its suppleness allows water to exist for a long time. In this, nothing is water's equal. Since stem-*Bing* and stem-*Xin* are water, they follow stem-*Yi* and stem-*Geng*.

Next [to water] is wood. In any given year, wood's periods of growth and decline are fixed. Since stem-*Ding* and stem-*Ren* are wood, they follow stem-*Bing* and stem-*Xin*.

Next to [wood] is fire. In the span of one day and one night, fire's phases of illuminating and going dim have fixed periods. Since stem-*Wu* and stem-*Gui* are fire, they follow stem-*Ding* and stem-*Ren*.

In addition to what has already been discussed, there are also the following truths: the earth stems stem-*Jia* and stem-*Ji* give birth to the metal stem-*Yi* and stem-*Geng*. The metal stem-*Yi* and stem-*Geng* give birth to the water stems stem-*Bing* and stem-*Xin*. The water stems stem-*Bing* and stem-*Xin* give birth to the wood stem-*Ding* and stem-*Ren*. The wood stem-*Ding* and stem-*Ren* give birth to the fire stem-*Wu* and stem-*Gui*. In piling up one upon one another in layers, the stem and the process that come first form the base upon which the following stem and process establish themselves.

This discussion begs the question of why the numbers ten, one, two, and three do not appear in these reckonings. Numbers end in nine and thus the number ten is really just a case of the number one. As for one, two, and three, they are the great numbers that represent heaven, earth, and Man. Thus, they are not fixed to one specific day (Heavenly Stem) or zodiacal sign (Earthly Branch). Moreover, in discussing these numbers, one, two, and three are already subsumed when one refers to nine, eight, seven, and six.[109] Thus the Yellow Bell pitch pipe is eighty-one and the twelve zodiac signs only procure seventy-eight, but Yang Xiong claims that the number of the Yellow Bell pipe is nonetheless established in seventy-eight. This is most likely because he factored in the three vacant numbers (i.e. one, two, and three) that would complete the total of eighty-one.

The Five Processes and the Five Musical Notes

This section discusses two issues: the associations of the five musical notes with the sexagenary stem-branch pairs and the pairs' 'poetic names.' The compilers explain the musical-note associations by quoting a long passage written by the famous Song dynasty Confucian scholar, Zhu Xi (1130–1200 CE). The explanation provided by Zhu Xi adds little to what has been said above, aside from his point about the Five-Processes correlate of the Received Notes being the process produced by the process of the musical note in question. The five traditional Chinese musical notes were associated with the Five Processes as follows: Palace Note (*gong*) – earth, Exchange Note (*shang*) – metal, Horn Note (*jue*) – wood, Summoning Note (*zhi*) – fire, and Feather Note (*yü*) – water.

The explanations of the 'poetic' names of the Received Notes were penned by an early-Ming dynasty (late-fourteenth century) scholar named Táo Zòngyí. These explanations draw heavily on the twelve-stage life-cycle principle. The reasoning is, however, highly erratic. At times, the author bases his justifications on the Five-Processes correlate of the branch, at other times on that of the stem, and at still other times on that of a related trigram. Clearly, the Received Notes' Five-Processes correlates and their poetic names do not derive systematically from the stems or branches of the sexagenary pairs, but the author felt a need to demonstrate that they do. It is noteworthy that the compilers of the Treatise could not locate another better-known or older reference to these poetic names, which suggests that the system was neither very old nor of great significance.

Zhu Xi said:[110]

'The musical sounds are earth, metal, wood, fire, and water. In the

161

Great Plan, these are water, fire, wood, metal, and earth. The Received Notes system takes each of the sixty stem-branch pairs and matches it with one of the five musical notes. The process to which the musical note gives birth serves as the musical note that the stem-branch pair receives.

'In the first series, the Palace Note (*gong*), Exchange Note (*shang*), Horn Note (*jue*), Summoning Note (*zhi*), and Feather Note (*yü*) receive stem-*Jia*, stem-*Bing*, stem-*Wu*, stem-*Geng*, and stem-*Ren* as each stem is paired with the branch-*Zi*. The five adjacent pairs that have branch-*Chou* follow the affiliations of the branch-*Zi* pairs. Thus the Palace Note (*gong*) obtains the pair stem-*Jia*/branch-*Zi*, the Exchange Note (*shang*) obtains stem-*Bing*/branch-*Zi*, the Horn Note (*jue*) obtains stem-*Wu*/branch-*Zi*, the Summoning Note (*zhi*) obtains stem-*Geng*/branch-*Zi*, and the Feather Note (*yü*) obtains stem-*Ren*/branch-*Zi*. The Palace Note (*gong*) is earth. Earth gives birth to metal. Therefore, the stem-branch pairs stem-*Jia*/branch-*Zi* and stem-*Yi*/branch-*Chou* receive the note of metal. The Exchange Note (*shang*) is metal. Metal gives birth to water. Therefore, the stem-branch pairs stem-*Bing*/branch-*Zi* and stem-*Ding*/branch-*Chou* receive the note of water. The Horn Note (*jue*) is wood. Wood gives birth to fire. Therefore, the pairs stem-*Wu*/branch-*Zi* and stem-*Ji*/branch-*Chou* receive the note of fire. The Summoning Note (*zhi*) is fire. Fire gives birth to earth. Therefore, the pairs stem-*Geng*/branch-*Zi* and stem-*Xin*/branch-*Chou* receive the note of earth. The Feather Note (*yü*) is water. Water gives birth to wood. Therefore, the pairs stem-*Ren*/branch-*Zi* and stem-*Gui*/branch-*Chou* receive the note of wood.

'In the second series, the Exchange Note (*shang*), Horn Note (*jue*), Summoning Note (*zhi*), Feather Note (*yü*), and Palace Note (*gong*) receive stem-*Jia*, stem-*Bing*, stem-*Wu*, stem-*Geng*, and stem-*Ren* as each stem is paired with the branch-*Yin*. The five adjacent pairs that have branch-*Mao* follow the affiliations of the branch-*Yin* pairs. Thus, since the metal Exchange Note (*shang*) obtains them, the pairs stem-*Jia*/branch-*Yin* and stem-*Yi*/branch-*Mao* receive the note of water. Since the wood Horn Note (*jue*) obtains them, the pairs stem-*Bing*/branch-*Yin* and stem-*Ding*/branch-*Mao* receive the note of fire. Since the fire Summoning Note (*zhi*) obtains them, the pairs stem-*Wu*/branch-

Yin and stem-*Ji*/branch-*Mao* receive the note of earth. Since the water Feather Note (*yü*) obtains them, the pairs stem-*Geng*/branch-*Yin* and stem-*Xin*/branch-*Mao* receive the note of wood. Since the earth Palace Note (*gong*) obtains them, the pairs stem-*Ren*/branch-*Yin* and stem-*Gui*/branch-*Mao* receive the note of metal.

'In the third series, the Horn Note (*jue*), Summoning Note (*zhi*), Feather Note (*yü*), Palace Note (*gong*), and Exchange Note (*shang*) receive stem-*Jia*, stem-*Bing*, stem-*Wu*, stem-*Geng*, and stem-*Ren* as each stem is paired with the branch-*Chen*. The five adjacent pairs that have branch-*Si* follow the affiliations of the branch-*Chen* pairs. Thus, since the wood Horn Note (*jue*) obtains them, the pairs stem-*Jia*/branch-*Chen* and stem-*Yi*/branch-*Si* receive the note of fire. Since the fire Summoning Note (*zhi*) obtains them, the pairs stem-*Bing*/branch-*Chen* and stem-*Ding*/branch-*Si* receive the note of earth. Since the water Feather Note (*yü*) obtains them, the pairs stem-*Wu*/branch-*Chen* and stem-*Ji*/branch-*Si* receive the note of wood. Since the earth Palace Note (*gong*) obtains them, the pairs stem-*Geng*/branch-*Chen* and stem-*Xin*/branch-*Si* receive the note of metal. Since the metal Exchange Note (*shang*) obtains them, the pairs stem-*Ren*/branch-*Chen* and stem-*Gui*/branch-*Si* receive the note of water.

'In the fourth series, the Palace Note (*gong*), Exchange Note (*shang*), Horn Note (*jue*), Summoning Note (*zhi*), and Feather Note (*yü*) – in the same order here as in the first series – receive stem-*Jia*, stem-*Bing*, stem-*Wu*, stem-*Geng*, and stem-*Ren* as each stem is paired with branch-*Wu*. The five adjacent pairs that have branch-*Wei* follow the affiliations of branch-*Wu* pairs. Thus, since the earth Palace Note (*gong*) obtains them, the pairs stem-*Jia*/branch-*Wu* and stem-*Yi*/branch-*Wei* receive the note of metal. Since the metal Exchange Note (*shang*) obtains them, the pairs stem-*Bing*/branch-*Wu* and stem-*Ding*/branch-*Wei* receive the note of water. Since the wood Horn Note (*jue*) obtains them, the pairs stem-*Wu*/branch-*Wu* and stem-*Ji*/branch-*Wei* receive the note of fire. Since the fire Summoning Note (*zhi*) obtains them, the pairs stem-*Geng*/branch-*Wu* and stem-*Xin*/branch-*Wei* receive the note of earth. Since the water Feather Note (*yü*) obtains them, the pairs stem-*Ren*/branch-*Wu* and stem-*Gui*/branch-*Wei* receive the note of wood.

'In the fifth series, the Exchange Note (*shang*), Horn Note (*jue*), Summoning Note (*zhi*), Feather Note (*yü*), and Palace Note (*gong*) – in the same order here as in the second series – receive stem-*Jia*, stem-*Bing*, stem-*Wu*, stem-*Geng*, and stem-*Ren* as each stem is paired with the branch-*Shen*. The five adjacent pairs that have branch-*You* follow the affiliations of the branch-*Shen* pairs. Thus, since the metal Exchange Note (*shang*) obtains them, the pairs stem-*Jia*/branch-*Shen* and stem-*Yi*/branch-*You* receive the note of water. Since the wood Horn Note (*jue*) obtains them, the pairs stem-*Bing*/branch-*Shen* and stem-*Ding*/branch-*You* receive the note of fire. Since the fire Summoning Note (*zhi*) obtains them, the pairs stem-*Wu*/branch-*Shen* and stem-*Ji*/branch-*You* receive the note of earth. Since the water Feather Note (*yü*) obtains them, the pairs stem-*Geng*/branch-*Shen* and stem-*Xin*/branch-*You* receive the note of wood. Since the earth Palace Note (*gong*) obtains them, the pairs stem-*Ren*/branch-*Shen* and stem-*Gui*/branch-*You* receive the note of metal.

'In the sixth series, the Horn Note (*jue*), Summoning Note (*zhi*), Feather Note (*yü*), Palace Note (*gong*), and Exchange Note (*shang*) – in the same order here as in the third series – receive stem-*Jia*, stem-*Bing*, stem-*Wu*, stem-*Geng*, and stem-*Ren* as each stem is paired with the branch-*Xu*. The five adjacent pairs that have branch-*Hai* follow the affiliations of the branch-*Xu* pairs. Thus, since the wood Horn Note (*jue*) obtains them, the pairs stem-*Jia*/branch-*Xu* and stem-*Yi*/branch-*Hai* receive the note of fire. Since the fire Summoning Note (*zhi*) obtains them, the pairs stem-*Bing*/branch-*Xu* and stem-*Ding*/branch-*Hai* receive the note of earth. Since the water Feather Note (*yü*) obtains them, the pairs stem-*Wu*/branch-*Xu* and stem-*Ji*/branch-*Hai* receive the note of wood. Since the earth Palace Note (*gong*) obtains them, the pairs stem-*Geng*/branch-*Xu* and stem-*Xin*/branch-*Hai* receive the note of metal. Since the metal Exchange Note (*shang*) obtains them, the pairs stem-*Ren*/branch-*Xu* and stem-*Gui*/branch-*Hai* receive the note of water.

'With this, the six stem-*Jia* are finished and the Received Notes system achieves its greater completion. Since yang is born from the branch-*Zi*, the pairs from stem-*Jia*/branch-*Zi* through stem-*Gui*/branch-*Si* are yang. Since yin is born from branch-*Wu*, the pairs from stem-*Wu*/branch-*Zi* through stem-*Gui*/branch-*Hai* are yin. Therefore, after thirty pairs, the series begins again with the Palace Note (*gong*). The Palace Note (*gong*) corresponds to the lord, the Exchange Note (*shang*) to his ministers, and the Horn Note (*jue*) to the people. Since these three all correspond to the way of man, they can serve to begin the series. By contrast, the Summoning Note (*zhi*) corresponds to affairs and the Feather Note (*yü*) to objects and as such these latter two notes correspond to that which man employs. Therefore, neither of them can serve as the head of the series. This is why the series begins again with the Palace Note (*gong*) after the three stem-*Jia* have finished. The stems correspond to heaven, the branches to the earth, and the musical notes to Man. Therein the Five Processes of the three forms of matter are completely contained.'[111]

Tào Zóngy[112] said:

'The pairs stem-*Jia*/branch-*Zi* and stem-*Yi*/branch-*Chou* are called "Metal in the Sea" because branch-*Zi* belongs to the water process, functions as a lake, and serves as the place in which the water process flourishes. Moreover, metal dies in branch-*Zi* and is buried in branch-*Chou*. Therefore, since water is flourishing while metal is dying and being buried, these pairs are called "Metal in the Sea."

'The pairs stem-*Bing*/branch-*Yin* and stem-*Ding*/branch-*Mao* are called "Fire in the Oven" because branch-*Yin* represents three yang and branch-*Mao* represents four yang. Therein, the fire process obtains its own ground. It also obtains the wood from branch-*Yin* and branch-*Mao* that gives birth to fire. Since at this time heaven and the earth light the fire in the oven and the myriad things begin to be born, these pairs are called "Fire in the Oven."

'The pairs stem-*Wu*/branch-*Chen* and stem-*Ji*/branch-*Si* are called "Wood of the Great Forest" because branch-*Chen* represents the primordial wilderness and branch-*Si* represents six yang. In [the month of] six yang branches of trees are stout and their leaves are verdant. Together then, the symbols of these branches produce an image of a verdant tree in a primordial wilderness. Therefore, these pairs are called "Wood of the Great Forest."

'The pairs stem-*Geng*/branch-*Wu* and stem-*Xin*/branch-*Wei* are called "Earth on the Roadside" because the [dead] wood process inherent in branch-*Wei* gives birth to the flourishing of the fire process in the position of branch-*Wu*. When the fire process flourishes, earth is burnt before it is able to gestate things and is thus like the earth that stands at the side of a road. Therefore, these pairs are called "Earth on the Roadside."

'The pairs stem-*Ren*/branch-*Shen* and stem-*Gui*/branch-*You* are called "Metal in the Sword-Tip" because branch-*Shen* and branch-*You* are the correct positions of the metal process. Metal approaches official appointment in branch-*Shen* and imperially flourishes in branch-*You*. Thus, when metal is born and flourishes, it becomes hard and there is nothing harder than the tip of a sword. Therefore, these pairs are called "Metal in the Sword-Tip."

'The pairs stem-*Jia*/branch-*Xu* and stem-*Yi*/branch-*Hai* are called "Fire on the Mountaintop" because branch-*Xu* and branch-*Hai* serve as the Gates of Heaven. When it shines upon the Gates of Heaven, the light of fire has reached the highest heights. Therefore, these pairs are called "Fire on the Mountaintop."

'The pairs stem-*Bing*/branch-*Zi* and stem-*Ding*/branch-*Chou* are called "Water at the Bottom of the Stream" because the water process flourishes in branch-*Zi* and declines in branch-*Chou*. When water flourishes and then declines, it is not able to become a great river. Therefore, these pairs are called "Water at the Bottom of the Stream."

'The pairs stem-*Wu*/branch-*Yin* and stem-*Ji*/branch-*Mao* are called "Earth in the Top of the Ramparts" because stem-*Wu* and stem-*Ji* belong to the earth process. At the same time, branch-*Yin* corresponds to trigram-*Gen*, which is known as the mountain trigram. These three correspondences suggest earth piling up to form a mountain.[113] Therefore, these pairs are called "Earth in the Top of the Ramparts."

'The pairs stem-*Geng*/branch-*Chen* and stem-*Xin*/branch-*Si* are called "Metal in Pig Iron"[114] because the metal process is nurtured in branch-*Chen* and is born in branch-*Si*. When its form and substance are only initially formed, metal is as yet unable to be advantageously employed. Therefore, these pairs are called 'Metal in Pig Iron.'

'The pairs stem-*Ren*/branch-*Wu* and stem-*Gui*/branch-*Wei* are called "Wood of Poplars and Willows" because the wood process dies in branch-*Wu* and is buried in branch-*Wei*. When it is dying and being buried, even though it is receiving the water of stem-*Ren* and stem-*Gui* that could give it life, wood will nevertheless still be weak and soft. Therefore, these pairs are called "Wood of Poplars and Willows."

'The pairs stem-*Jia*/branch-*Shen* and stem-*Yi*/branch-*You* are called "Water of Wells and Springs" because the metal process approaches official appointment in branch-*Shen* and imperially flourishes in branch-*You*. When metal is thus born and flourishes, the water process is thereby able to be born. At the time of its birth, water's strength is not yet great. Therefore, these pairs are called "Water of Wells and Springs."

'The pairs stem-*Bing*/branch-*Xu* and stem-*Ding*/branch-*Hai* are called "Earth of Rooftops" because stem-*Bing* and stem-*Ding* belong to the fire process and branch-*Xu* and branch-*Hai* are the Gates of Heaven. If there is blazing above, then earth is not below. Thus it is born. Therefore, these pairs are called "Earth of Rooftops."

'The pairs stem-*Wu*/branch-*Zi* and stem-*Ji*/branch-*Chou* are called "Fire of Thunderclaps" because branch-*Chou* belongs to the earth process and branch-*Zi* belongs to the water process.[115] Thus, for these two pairs the water process is in its appropriate position with respect to branches. Nonetheless, the received note of the pairs is that of fire. This clearly suggests that the case of fire within water could be none other than the divine dragon.[116] Therefore, these pairs are called "Fire of Thunderclaps."

'The pairs stem-*Geng*/branch-*Yin* and stem-*Xin*/branch-*Mao* are called "Wood of Cedars and Pines" because the wood process approaches official appointment in branch-*Yin* and imperially flourishes in branch-*Mao*. When wood flourishes, it cannot be called soft or weak. Therefore, these pairs are called "Wood of Cedars and Pines."

'The pairs stem-*Ren*/branch-*Chen* and stem-*Gui*/branch-*Si* are called "Water of Long-Flowing [Rivers]" because branch-*Chen* is the storehouse (i.e. burial place)[117] of the water process and branch-*Si* is the place where the metal process is born. When metal is born, the nature of the water process already exists. Thus, where the storehouse of water encounters the place where metal (i.e. water's mother) is born, the wellspring will never be exhausted. Therefore, these pairs are called "Water of Long-Flowing Rivers."

'The pairs stem-*Jia*/branch-*Wu* and stem-*Yi*/branch-*Wei* are called "Metal of Sand and Stones" because the fire process flourishes in branch-*Wu* and where fire flourishes metal is defeated. Furthermore, the fire process declines in branch-*Wei* and where fire declines, metal dons cap and sash. Since it goes through the rite of passage of donning cap and sash after having just been defeated, the metal process is thought not yet to have arisen fully. Therefore, these pairs are called "Metal of Sand and Stones."

'The pairs stem-*Bing*/branch-*Shen* and stem-*Ding*/branch-*You* are called "Fire on the Foot of the Mountain" because branch-*Shen* functions as the Doors of the Earth and branch-*You* acts as the Gates of the Sun Entry. When the sun comes to this point in time, its light is buried. Therefore, these pairs are called "Fire on the Foot of the Mountain."

'The pairs stem-*Wu*/branch-*Xu* and stem-*Ji*/branch-*Hai* are called "Wood of the Flatlands" because branch-*Xu* represents the primordial wilderness and branch-*Hai* is the place where the wood process is born. When wood is born in the primordial wilderness, then it will certainly not amount to only one root and one stem. Therefore, these pairs are called "Wood of the Flatlands."

'The pairs stem-*Geng*/branch-*Zi* and stem-*Xin*/branch-*Chou* are called "Earth of the Top of a Wall" because although branch-*Chou* is the proper position in which the earth process should resides, branch-*Zi* is the place where the water process is born. When earth encounters much water, it will turn to mud [such as that which is used to build walls]. Therefore, these pairs are called "Earth of the Top of a Wall."

'The pairs stem-*Ren*/branch-*Yin* and stem-*Gui*/branch-*Mao* are called "Metal of a Gilt Screen" because branch-*Yin* and branch-*Mao* are where the wood process flourishes. When wood flourishes, metal is emaciated. Furthermore, since it terminates in branch-*Yin* and is conceived in branch-*Mao*, metal in the place of those branches is without strength. Therefore, these pairs are called "Metal of a Gilt Screen."

'The pairs stem-*Jia*/branch-*Chen* and stem-*Yi*/branch-*Si* are called "Fire of the Overturned Lamp" because branch-*Chen* represents the midday mealtime while branch-*Si* is midday. When the sun approaches the middle of the sky, it is brilliant; it is the force of yang shining upon the world. Therefore, these pairs are called "Fire of the Overturned Lamp."

'The pairs stem-*Bing*/branch-*Wu* and stem-*Ding*/branch-*Wei* are called "Water of the Celestial River" because stem-*Bing* and stem-*Ding* belong to fire and branch-*Wu* is the place where the fire process flourishes, but the received note of the pairs is of the water process. Water thus proceeding out from fire could be nothing other than the river of the Milky Way. Therefore, these pairs are called "Water of the Celestial River."

'The pairs stem-*Wu*/branch-*Shen* and stem-*Ji*/branch-*You* are called "Earth of the Great Courier Station"[118] because branch-*Shen* is correlated with trigram-*Kun*, which is the earth, and branch-*You* is correlated with trigram-*Dui*, which is the marsh. Thus, the earth process of stem-*Wu* and stem-*Ji* is added upon trigram-*Kun* and the marsh. This could be none other than earth that is unfounded and shifting.[119] Therefore, these pairs are called "Earth of the Great Courier Station."

'The pairs stem-*Geng*/branch-*Xu* and stem-*Xin*/branch-*Hai* are called "Metal of Hairpins and Bracelets" because the metal process declines in branch-*Xu* and becomes ill in branch-*Hai*. When the metal process declines and becomes ill, it is truly weak. Therefore, these pairs are called "Metal of Hairpins and Bracelets."

'The pairs stem-*Ren*/branch-*Zi* and stem-*Gui*/branch-*Chou* are called "Wood of Mulberry Trees" because branch-*Zi* belongs to water and branch-*Chou* belongs to metal.[120] Thus, water first gives birth to wood, after which metal fells it; this is like the fate of the mulberry tree. Therefore, these pairs are called "Wood of Mulberry Trees."

'The pairs stem-*Jia*/branch-*Yin* and stem-*Yi*/branch-*Mao* are called "Water of Great Streams" because branch-*Yin* represents an angle in the northeast and branch-*Mao* represents due east. Flowing in the direction of due east is the nature of water. Following this, the water of all rivers, streams, lakes, and ponds flow together. Therefore, these pairs are called "Water of Great Streams."

'The pairs stem-*Bing*/branch-*Chen* and stem-*Ding*/branch-*Si* are called "Earth of Fine River-Sand" because the earth process is stored (buried) in branch-*Chen* and terminates in branch-*Si* while the fire of stem-*Bing* and stem-*Ding* undergoes the ritual donning of sash and cap in branch-*Chen* and approaches official appointment in branch-*Si*. Thus, when the earth process is being stored away and terminated, the simultaneous flourishing of the fire process revives earth. Therefore, these pairs are called "Earth of Fine River-Sand."

'The pairs stem-*Wu*/branch-*Wu* and stem-*Ji*/branch-*Wei* are called "Fire of Heaven Above" because branch-*Wu* is the place where fire flourishes and the wood process that is inherent in branch-*Wei*[121] provides fuel to replenish any depletion of that fire. Thus, it is the nature of fire to burn upwardly and in this case it encounters above the place [of the wood process] that gives birth to fire.[122] Therefore, these pairs are called "Fire of Heaven Above."

'The pairs stem-*Geng*/branch-*Shen* and stem-*Xin*/branch-*You* are called "Wood of Pomegranate Trees" because branch-*Shen* represents the seventh month and branch-*You* represents the eighth month, in which times wood terminates. Nevertheless, at this time the pomegranate alone continues to bear fruit. Therefore, these pairs are called "Wood of Pomegranate Trees."

'The pairs stem-*Ren*/branch-*Xu* and stem-*Gui*/branch-*Hai* are called "Water of the Great Sea" because the water process undergoes ritual capping and donning of sash in branch-*Xu* and approaches official appointment in branch-*Hai*. Thus, when it dons cap and sash and approaches official appointment, the water process is extremely strong. Furthermore, branch-*Hai* is none other than the correlate of the Great Yangtze River. Therefore, these pairs are called "Water of the Great Sea."'

The Received Stem-*Jia*

This and the remaining three sections of this part of the Treatise deal with the Received Stem-*Jia* system. This system correlates the Ten Heavenly Stems with the eight trigrams. It was traditionally believed to have been the creation of the Han scholar and student of the *Book of Changes* (*Yijing*) Jing Fang (79–37 BCE). A description of the system appears in a book attributed to him, the *Jingshi yizhuan*.[123] However, that text is not generally considered to be authentic, being ascribed by some scholars to the Song dynasty (960–1279 CE).[124] The Qing compilers of the current work cite the Ming dynasty *Collected Writings on Measuring the Ocean with a Shell* (*Lihai ji*). Thus, even if the text of the *Jingshi yizhuan* cannot be accepted as a product of the first century BCE, it still constitutes the earliest documentary evidence of the Received Stem-*Jia* system.

The Received Stem-*Jia* system is based upon the sequential order of the Latter Heaven arrangement of trigrams. Remember that the Former Heaven arrangement regards as yang the four trigrams in which the bottom line is solid/yang; the four trigrams in which the bottom line is broken/yin are considered yin. In the Latter Heaven arrangement, however, trigram-*Qian* (all yang lines) is considered the father and trigram-*Kun* (all yin lines) is considered mother. Of the remaining six trigrams, those with only one yang line are considered the sons and those with only one yin line are considered the daughters. The position of that one yang or yin line determines the birth order of the trigrams: bottom line constitutes eldest, middle line is middle child, and top line is youngest. The Received Stem-*Jia* pairs the yang (i.e. odd-numbered) stems with the Latter Heaven's male trigrams and pairs the yin stems with the female trigrams.

Trigram-*Qian* represents the beginning and end of yang. Therefore, trigram-*Qian* receives the first and last yang stems, i.e. stem-*Jia* and stem-*Ren*. Similarly, trigram-*Kun* represents the beginning and end of yin. Therefore, trigram-*Kun* receives the first and last yin stems, i.e. stem-*Yi* and stem-*Gui*. Trigram-*Zhen* is the eldest son because it contains only one yang line in the bottom position. Therefore, trigram-*Zhen* receives the second highest yang stem, i.e. the seventh, stem-*Geng*. Trigram-*Sun*, with only one yin line located in the bottom position, is the eldest daughter. Trigram-*Sun*, therefore, receives the second highest yin stem, i.e. the eighth, stem-*Xin*. Trigram-*Kan* is the middle son because it contains only one yang line located in the middle position; it, therefore, receives the third highest yang stem, i.e. the fifth, stem-*Wu*. Trigram-*Li* is the middle daughter because it contains only one yin line located in the middle position; it, therefore, receives the third highest yin stem, i.e. the sixth, stem-*Ji*. Trigram-*Gen* is the youngest son because it contains only one yang line located in the top position; it, therefore, receives the fourth highest yang stem, i.e. the third, stem-*Bing*. Trigram-*Dui* is the youngest daughter because it contains only one yin line located in the top position; it, therefore, receives the fourth highest yin stem, i.e. the fourth, stem-*Ding*.

The text also briefly refers to the pairings of Earthly Branches with stems and trigrams. This convention makes it possible to equate one sexagenary stem-branch pair with each line of a hexagram. Among the eight primary hexagrams (each of the eight trigrams doubled), there are only forty-eight lines (8 hexagrams times 6 lines). Therefore, twelve of the sexagenary pairs (60 - 48=12) are not linked with a hexagram line. In being doubled to form the primary hexagrams, the six 'children' trigrams each correlate with exactly one stem. For hexagram-*Qian* and hexagram-*Kun*, the lower and upper trigrams correlate with different stems. The lower trigram-*Qian* correlates with stem-*Jia*, and the upper trigram-*Qian* correlates with stem-*Ren*. The lower trigram-*Kun* correlates with stem-*Yi*, and the upper trigram-*Kun* correlates with stem-*Gui*.

The six lines of the male hexagrams correlate with the six yang Earthly Branches and the lines of the female hexagrams correlate with the yin branches. The branches are matched with the hexagram lines from bottom to top. The male hexagram lines take branches in order, the female hexagram lines take branches in reverse order. The bottom line of hexagram-*Qian* begins from branch-*Zi* (1st), followed by branch-*Yin* (3rd), followed by branch-*Chen* (5th), etc. The bottom line of hexagram-*Kun* begins from branch-*Wei* (8th), followed by branch-*Si* (6th), followed by branch-*Mao* (4th), etc. The bottom lines of the remaining hexagrams follow the order of the first six branches, i.e. branch-*Zi*, branch-*Chou*, branch-*Yin*, branch-*Mao*, branch-*Chen*, and branch-*Si*. These are assigned to the children hexagrams according to birth order, male followed by female. Thus the first male son, hexagram-*Zhen*, begins with branch-*Zi* as the bottom line. The first daughter, hexagram-*Sun*, begins with branch-*Chou* as the bottom line.

The *Collected Writings on Measuring the Ocean with a Shell* (*Lihai ji*) says:

'The Received Stem-*Jia* system can be explained as follows: the yang numbers begin in stem-*Jia*, which is the number one, and end in the stem-*Ren*, which is the number nine. Thus returning to trigram-*Qian*, they constitute the flowing order of the numbers of the *Book of Changes* (*Yijing*). The yin numbers begin in the stem-*Yi*, which is the number two, and end in the stem-*Gui*, which is the number ten. Thus returning to trigram-*Kun*, they constitute the counter-flowing order of the numbers of the *Book of Changes* (*Yijing*).

'Trigram-*Qian*, upon its first seeking, obtains a son, which is trigram-*Zhen*. Trigram-*Kun*, upon its first seeking, obtains a daughter, which is trigram-*Sun*. Thus, stem-*Geng* enters trigram-*Zhen* and stem-*Xin* enters trigram-*Sun*.

'Trigram-*Qian*, upon its second seeking, again obtains a son, which is trigram-*Kan*. Trigram-*Kun*, upon its second seeking, again obtains a daughter, which is trigram-*Li*. Thus, stem-*Wu* follows trigram-*Kan* and stem-*Ji* follows trigram-*Li*.

'Trigram-*Qian*, upon its third seeking, again obtains a son, which is trigram-*Gen*. Trigram-*Kun*, upon its third seeking, again obtains a daughter, which is trigram-*Dui*. Thus, stem-*Bing* follows upon trigram-*Gen* and stem-*Ding* follows upon trigram-*Dui*.

'Yang is born in the north and matures in the south. Therefore, trigram-*Qian* begins with the stem-branch pair stem-*Jia*/branch-*Zi* and takes as its end the stem-branch pair stem-*Ren*/branch-*Wu*. Yin is born in the south and matures in the north. Therefore, trigram-*Kun* begins with the stem-branch pair stem-*Yi*/branch-*Wei* and takes as its end the stem-branch pair stem-*Gui*/branch-*Chou*.

'Trigram-*Zhen* and trigram-*Sun* are the first offspring. Therefore, stem-*Geng* and stem-*Xin* begin in branch-*Zi* and branch-*Chou*. Trigram-*Kan* and trigram-*Li* are the second offspring. Therefore, stem-*Wu* and stem-*Ji* begin in branch-*Yin* and branch-*Mao*. Trigram-*Gen* and trigram-*Dui* are the third offspring. Therefore, stem-*Bing* and stem-*Ding* begin in branch-*Chen* and branch-*Si*.

In another passage it explains:

'Trigram-*Qian* and trigram-*Kun*, respectively, are the proper positions of the two vital breaths, while trigram-*Kan* and trigram-*Li* serve as the positions in which the two vital breaths transition. Since the proper positions completely contain both beginning and end, stem-*Jia* and stem-*Ren* return to trigram-*Qian* and stem-*Yi* and stem-*Gui* return to trigram-*Kun*. Since the transitional positions stand in the center, stem-*Wu* returns to trigram-*Kan* and stem-*Ji* returns to trigram-*Li*. Since trigram-*Zhen* and trigram-*Sun* are the start of receiving vital breaths, stem-*Geng* and stem-*Xin* return to trigram-*Zhen* and trigram-*Sun*. Since trigram-*Gen* and trigram-*Dui* are the ends of coming to life and transforming, stem-*Bing* and stem-*Ding* return to trigram-*Gen* and trigram-*Dui*.

'Since trigram-*Qian* and trigram-*Kun* stand at the extreme positions of yin and yang, branch-*Zi* and branch-*Wu* accompany stem-*Jia* and stem-*Ren* and branch-*Chou* and branch-*Wei* accompany stem-*Yi* and stem-*Gui*. This symbolizes the way that father and mother respectively control the inside and outside of the home. Since trigram-*Zhen* and trigram-*Sun* are the eldest son and daughter, the first born, branch-*Zi* and branch-*Chou* are taken to accompany stem-*Geng* and stem-*Xin*. Since trigram-*Kan* and trigram-*Li* are the middle son and daughter, the second born, branch-*Yin* and branch-*Mao* are taken to accompany stem-*Wu* and stem-*Ji*. Since trigram-*Gen* and trigram-*Dui* are the youngest son and daughter, the third born, branch-*Chen* and branch-*Si* are taken to accompany stem-*Bing* and stem-*Ding*.

'The term "receive" in the name of the Received Stem-*Jia* system means "to take in." This refers to the taking of the six stem-*Jia* into the midst of the eight trigrams. Since the method of the *Book of Changes* (*Yijing*) proceeds backwards, the numbers in this system are always counted backwards.'

The Columnar Chart of the Received Stem-*Jia*

In light of the above discussion, the text and diagram of this section are self-explanatory. Essentially, in ordering the hexagrams and stems, this diagram places father and mother at the top and places sons under father and daughters under mother. The ordering of sons and daughters proceeds from eldest at the bottom to youngest at the top, just as the lines of trigrams proceed from bottom

Figure 25 The Columnar Chart of the Received Stem-*Jia*

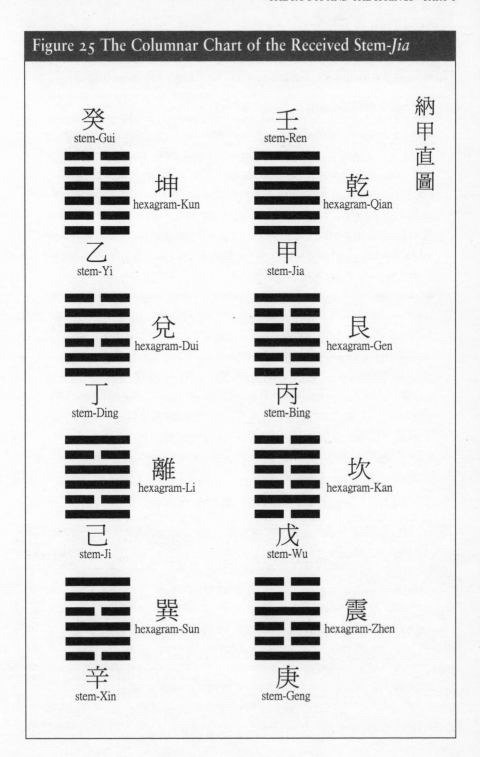

納甲直圖

癸
stem-Gui

hexagram-Kun 坤

乙
stem-Yi

兌 hexagram-Dui

丁
stem-Ding

離 hexagram-Li

己
stem-Ji

巽 hexagram-Sun

辛
stem-Xin

壬
stem-Ren

乾 hexagram-Qian

甲
stem-Jia

艮 hexagram-Gen

丙
stem-Bing

坎 hexagram-Kan

戊
stem-Wu

震 hexagram-Zhen

庚
stem-Geng

to top. Viewing from top down, we thus see father, youngest son, middle son, and eldest son. This arrangement makes it possible to list the Heavenly Stems in order, reading from left to right and from top to bottom.

The *Study of Calendrics* (*Xingli kaoyuan*) says:[125]

'Saying that trigram-*Qian* and trigram-*Kun* encompass beginning and end means that trigram-*Qian* receives stem-*Jia* and stem-*Ren* and trigram-*Kun* receives stem-*Yi* and stem-*Gui*. The manner in which the remaining six trigrams are arrayed from the bottom upwards is in accord with the way that the component lines of trigrams are also traced from the bottom upwards. Arising from the bottom in accord with yin-yang affiliations, trigram-*Zhen* receives the stem-*Geng* below the yang trigram-*Qian* and trigram-*Sun* receives the stem-*Xin* below the yin trigram-*Kun*. Trigram-*Kan* and trigram-*Li* are at the transitional point of yin and yang in the middle and thus trigram-*Kan* receives the yang stem-*Wu* and trigram-*Li* receives the yin stem-*Ji*. Trigram-*Gen* and trigram-*Dui* are at the extreme low position of yin and yang, so that trigram-*Gen* receives the yang stem-*Bing* and trigram-*Dui* receives the yin stem-*Ding*. Stem-*Jia*, stem-*Bing*, stem-*Wu*, stem-*Geng*, and stem-*Ren* are the yang stems and each receives a yang trigram. The stems stem-*Yi*, stem-*Ding*, stem-*Ji*, stem-*Xin*, and stem-*Gui* are the yin stems and each receives a yin trigram.'

The Circular Chart of the Received Stem-*Jia*

This chart displays six of the eight trigrams around a circle with trigram-*Kan* and trigram-*Li* in the middle. The chart's explanatory text says that the outlying trigrams represent the phases of the moon and that trigram-*Kan* and trigram-*Li*, which correlate with the central earth of stem-*Wu* and stem-*Ji*, represent the original body of the sun and moon. In terms of the graphic composition of the trigrams, this arrangement resembles the diagram of the twelve months receiving hexagrams: trigram-*Kun*, as pure yin stands at the bottom/north; thereafter, the lines become progressively yang, from bottom to top as one examines the trigrams clockwise, with trigram-*Qian*, as pure yang standing at the top/south. Thereafter, the trigrams become progressively yin, starting from the bottom line and moving up. This arrangement divides the moon's phases into six parts rather than into four quarters, as is customary in the West. Consequently, each of a trigram's lines represents one third of the moon's surface.

To understand the directional associations, one must keep in mind that at the time of a full moon, the moon rises in the east at about sundown, reaches the zenith of the sky at midnight, and sets in the west at about sunrise. A new moon, by contrast rises at about sunrise, reaches the zenith at noon, and sets at around sunset. If one observes the position of the moon at sunset each day as the moon waxes, it will first appear in the west, then in the zenith (south), and finally in the east as the moon approaches fullness. If one changes the time of observation to sunrise as the moon wanes, it will again first appear in the west, then in the zenith (south) and finally in the east. Thus, by changing the time of observation, the trigram/stem/directional associations correspond with the respective phases of the moon.

The *Study of Calendrics* (*Xingli kaoyuan*) says:[126]

'This construct correlates six of the trigrams with the phases of the moon. As representations of the original physical body of the sun and the moon, trigram-*Kan* and trigram-*Li* are placed in the center of the diagram and not used.

'Trigram-*Zhen* is directly associated with the moon's "Birth of Light"(i.e. waxing crescent) phase because the trigram contains one yang [line at the bottom, which is thus conceived as light] being born. Furthermore, during the Birth of Light Phase, the moon faces the direction of the stem-*Geng* (i.e. west) at dusk.

'Trigram-*Dui* is directly associated with the moon's "Upper Crescent" (i.e. waxing gibbous) phase because the trigram contains two yang [lines] that are gradually rising. Furthermore, during the Upper Crescent Phase, the moon faces the direction of the stem-*Ding* (i.e. south – zenith) at dusk.

'Trigram-*Qian* is directly associated with the moon's "Fully Facing" (i.e. full moon) phase because the trigram contains three yang [lines] that are fully ascended. Furthermore, during the Fully Facing Phase, the moon faces the direction of the stem-*Jia* (i.e. east) at dusk.

'Trigram-*Sun* is directly associated with the moon's "Birth of Darkness"(i.e. waning gibbous) phase because the trigram

Figure 26 The Circular Chart of the Received Stem-*Jia*

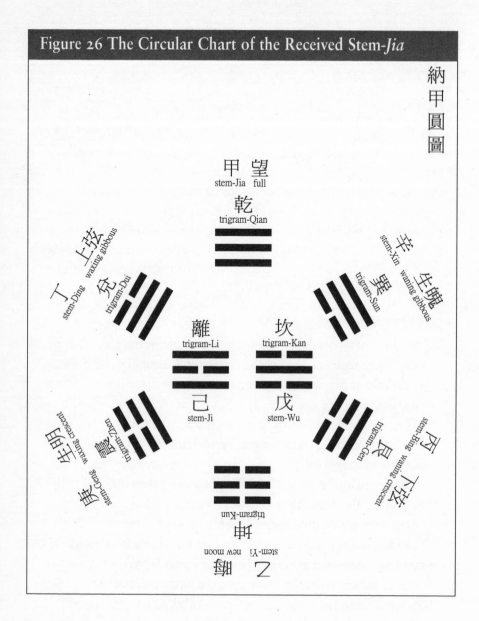

contains one yin [line] beginning to be born. Furthermore, during the Birth of Darkness Phase, the moon faces the direction of the stem-*Xin* (i.e. west) at dawn.

'Trigram-*Gen* is directly associated with the moon's "Lower Crescent" (i.e. waning crescent) phase because the trigram contains two yin [lines] that are gradually rising. Furthermore, during the

Lower Crescent Phase, the moon faces the direction of the stem-*Bing* (i.e. south – zenith) at dawn.

'Trigram-*Kun* is directly associated with the moon's "Complete Obscurity" (i.e. new moon) phase because the trigram contains three yin [lines] that are fully ascended. Furthermore, during the Complete Obscurity Phase, the moon faces the direction of the stem-*Yi* (i.e. east) at dawn.

'All of the correlations just described correspond perfectly with the system of the Received Notes.'

The Chart of the Received Stem-*Jia* Receiving the Twelve Branches

The *Study of Calendrics* (*Xingli kaoyuan*) says:[127]

'This construct pairs the six lines of the twin-trigram hexagrams with six [of the twelve branches, i.e.] zodiacal signs.

'The lines of the inner (i.e. lower) trigram of hexagram-*Qian*, which are correlated with stem-*Jia*, receive branch-*Zi*, branch-*Yin*, and branch-*Chen*. Thus, the first nine (i.e. yang line) is correlated with the pair stem-*Jia*/branch-*Zi*, the second nine with the pair stem-*Jia*/branch-*Yin*, and the third nine with the pair stem-*Jia*/branch-*Chen*. The lines of the outer (i.e. upper) trigram of hexagram-*Qian*, which are correlated with stem-*Ren*, receive branch-*Wu*, branch-*Shen*, and branch-*Xu*. Thus, the fourth nine is correlated with the pair stem-*Ren*/branch-*Wu*, the fifth nine with the pair stem-*Ren*/branch-*Shen*, and the uppermost nine with the pair stem-*Ren*/ branch-*Xu*.

'The lines of the inner trigram of hexagram-*Kun*, which are correlated with stem-*Yi*, receive branch-*Wei*, branch-*Si*, and branch-*Mao*. Thus, the first six (i.e. yin line) is correlated with the pair stem-*Yi*/branch-*Wei*, the second six with the pair stem-*Yi*/branch-*Si*, and the third six with the pair stem-*Yi*/branch-*Mao*. The lines of the outer trigram of hexagram-*Kun*, which are correlated with the stem-*Gui*, receive the branch-*Chou*, branch-*Hai*, and branch-*You*. Thus, the fourth six is correlated with the pair stem-*Gui*/branch-*Chou*, the fifth six with the pair stem-*Gui*/branch-*Hai*, and the uppermost six with the pair stem-*Gui*/branch-*You*.

179

'Since hexagram-*Qian* and hexagram-*Kun* each receive two stems, the lines of the inner and outer trigrams are delimited separately. Hexagram-*Zhen*, however, only receives stem-*Geng*. Thus, in the latter case, the first nine is correlated with the pair stem-*Geng*/branch-*Zi*. The second six is correlated with the pair stem-*Geng*/branch-*Yin*. The third six is correlated with the pair stem-*Geng*/branch-*Chen*. The fourth nine is correlated with the pair stem-*Geng*/branch-*Wu*. The fifth six is correlated with the pair stem-*Geng*/branch-*Shen*. The uppermost six is correlated with the pair stem-*Geng*/branch-*Xu*.

'Hexagram-*Sun* only receives the one stem-*Xin*. Therefore, the first six is the pair stem-*Xin*/branch-*Chou*. The second nine is stem-*Xin*/branch-*Hai*. The third nine is stem-*Xin*/branch-*You*. The fourth six is stem-*Xin*/branch-*Wei*. The fifth nine is stem-*Xin*/branch-*Si*. The uppermost nine is stem-*Xin*/branch-*Mao*.

'The lines of the remaining four hexagrams, hexagram-*Kan*, hexagram-*Li*, hexagram-*Gen*, and hexagram-*Dui*, are matched with stem-branch pairs in the same manner as was just described for hexagram-*Zhen* and hexagram-*Sun*.'

The *Study of Calendrics* (*Xingli kaoyuan*) goes on to say:

'The Received Stem-*Jia* system is of unknown origin. There are similarities between the Former Heaven Chart and the manner in which the Received Stem-*Jia* pairs the stems and trigrams with the waxing and waning of yin and yang during the moon's phases.

'In his *Kinship of the Three* (*Cantong qi*), Wei Boyang[128] sets forth this explanation:

"As the third day sets forth briskly, trigram-*Zhen* and stem-*Geng* take in the direction west.

"On the eighth day, trigram-*Dui* takes in the stem-*Ding* and the Upper Crescent is like [the straight line of a] cord.

"The fifteenth day is the physical body of trigram-*Qian*; the moon waxes full; the stem is stem-*Jia*; the direction is east; seven [days added to the] eighth – the way is already finished.

"Bending low and with decreasing light, on the sixteenth day it rotates and proceeds to control trigram-*Sun* and stem-*Xin*.

"Upon seeing level light, trigram-*Gen* aligns with stem-*Bing* in the direction south. This is the Lower Crescent phase of the moon and it occurs on the twenty-third day.

"Trigram-*Kun* and stem-*Yi* on the thirtieth day correlate with the northeast. It is bereft of its companions and the period is completely exhausted.

"The ending and beginning months mutually cleanse one another and the beginning month continues the physical body of the ending month. The dragon is once again given birth. Stem-*Ren* and stem-*Gui* accompany stem-*Jia* and stem-*Yi* because trigram-*Qian* and trigram-*Kun* encompass both beginning and end."

'Zhu Xi regarded this as the tradition of the Former Heaven. The various Confucians after Confucius himself forgot this teaching and it was transmitted secretly from generation to generation in a heterodox tradition where it is known as the Art of the Cinnabar Furnace.

Compilers' Note:[129] The Former Heaven and Received Stem-*Jia* systems are not in complete accord because the former contains the full set of eight trigrams, while the latter excludes trigram-*Kan* and trigram-*Li* because it regards them as the two 'functions.' This explanation is based on a passage from the 'Shuo gua' section of the *Book of Changes* (*Yijing*), which says that 'heaven (trigram-*Qian*) and earth (trigram-*Kun*) fix their positions. The mountain (i.e. highlands – trigram-*Gen*) and the marsh (i.e. lowlands – trigram-*Dui*) communicate their vital breaths to each other. Thunder (trigram-*Zhen*) and wind (trigram-*Sun*) mutually press against each other.' This is based upon the order of the trigrams wherein their lines transform

Figure 27 The Chart of the Received Stem-*Jia* Receiving the Twelve Branches

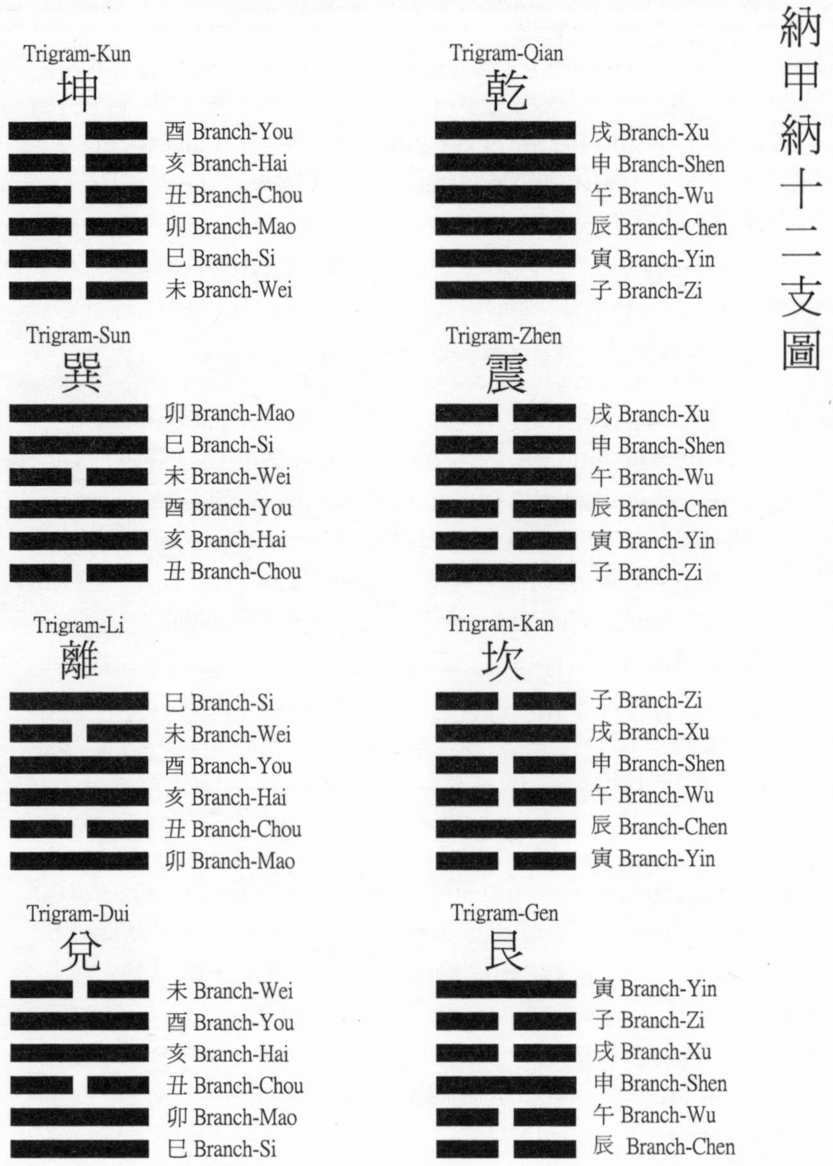

Trigram-Kun

坤

酉 Branch-You
亥 Branch-Hai
丑 Branch-Chou
卯 Branch-Mao
巳 Branch-Si
未 Branch-Wei

Trigram-Qian

乾

戌 Branch-Xu
申 Branch-Shen
午 Branch-Wu
辰 Branch-Chen
寅 Branch-Yin
子 Branch-Zi

Trigram-Sun

巽

卯 Branch-Mao
巳 Branch-Si
未 Branch-Wei
酉 Branch-You
亥 Branch-Hai
丑 Branch-Chou

Trigram-Zhen

震

戌 Branch-Xu
申 Branch-Shen
午 Branch-Wu
辰 Branch-Chen
寅 Branch-Yin
子 Branch-Zi

Trigram-Li

離

巳 Branch-Si
未 Branch-Wei
酉 Branch-You
亥 Branch-Hai
丑 Branch-Chou
卯 Branch-Mao

Trigram-Kan

坎

子 Branch-Zi
戌 Branch-Xu
申 Branch-Shen
午 Branch-Wu
辰 Branch-Chen
寅 Branch-Yin

Trigram-Dui

兌

未 Branch-Wei
酉 Branch-You
亥 Branch-Hai
丑 Branch-Chou
卯 Branch-Mao
巳 Branch-Si

Trigram-Gen

艮

寅 Branch-Yin
子 Branch-Zi
戌 Branch-Xu
申 Branch-Shen
午 Branch-Wu
辰 Branch-Chen

納甲納十二支圖

progressively from three yang and three yin to one yang and one yin.[130] After this, the 'Shuo gua' goes on to say that, 'Water (trigram-*Kan*) and Fire (trigram-*Li*) do not issue forth one from the other.' This explanation suggests that the first six trigrams mentioned mutually recreate their opposites, while water and fire serve as the 'function,' or 'application.' Thus, it can be seen that in ancient times this explanation already existed.

'In pairing the lines of the hexagrams with the six zodiacal signs (i.e. branches), the yang all proceed with the flow, while the yin all rotate against the flow. The elders, seniors, middling ones, and lesser of yin and yang each differ by one position. Only hexagram-*Zhen* is the same as hexagram-*Qian* because, as hexagram-*Zhen* is the eldest son, it continues the physical body of the father.

'Hexagram-*Kun* rises not from branch-*Chou*, but from branch-*Wei*. This is in keeping with the Luo River Diagram, in which the partnered numbers each arise from the position of branch-*Wei*. In the Latter Heaven Chart trigram-*Kun* resides in the southwest (branch-*Wei* direction). Among the musical pipes, the Forest Bell (branch-*Wei*) pipe, as the correlate of the earth, in exerting its control, responds to the vital breath of the month with branch-*Wei* (i.e. the sixth lunar month). All of these tenets accord with each other. Thus, among the teachings of the various numerological schools, only this Received Stem-*Jia* method provides the greatest range of appropriate correlations. This is the teaching that is now known as the Fiery Pearl Forest Hexagram Prognostication method.'

CHAPTER TWO

The Roots and the Springs
– Part 2

The latter half of the Treatise describes the relationship between spatial positions and cosmological forces (yin yang/Five Processes) and categories (trigrams, Heavenly Stems, Earthly Branches, etc). The theories set forth in this portion of the book constitute the conceptual framework of Chinese geomancy or *feng shui*. While the astrologically-focused first part of the Treatise was concerned with relating yin-yang and five forces theories to celestial time cycles, the following chapters seek to tie the same theories to terrestrial space divisions. Writings by the early patriarchs of *feng shui* suggest that they held in contempt people who studied only astrology while ignoring the art of positioning. From the perspective of *feng shui* practitioners, astrology provided only half of the information required to fathom the workings of the cosmos. To calculate accurately whether a proposed action was cosmically appropriate, they believed it was also necessary to incorporate variables gathered from one's position and orientation on the earth.

The second half of the Treatise assumes that the reader possesses a basic understanding of *feng shui*. As with Chinese astrology, *feng shui* is primarily based on yin-yang and Five Processes theory. Since these theories have already been described in the previous half of the introduction, the second half is correspondingly shorter. However, because these chapters assume a high level of familiarity with *feng shui*, a few introductory comments below will help the reader to understand more clearly the issues discussed in part two. Since the general theory of *feng shui* has already been discussed in the translator's introduction, the following explanation will only deal with the basic technical vocabulary of the art.

The term *feng shui* itself literally means 'wind' and 'water.' As a mantic art, *feng shui* seeks to determine how people should situate themselves and organize their constructed environment in order to derive maximum benefit from the ebb and flow of cosmic forces within the natural environment. The art acquired its name because wind and water were considered the most dynamic and transformational natural forces that affect the vital breath of an environment. In the words of the art's founding father, Guo Pu, 'When affected by wind, vital breath disperses; upon encountering water, vital breath stops.' Since *feng shui* aims to manipulate the flow of vital breath in the environment, wind and water are consequently of great importance. Aside from wind and water, however, the art also addresses the influence of land formations, flora and fauna, human constructions, directional orientation, seasonal rhythms, and celestial constellations.

According to Chinese tradition, there were, at one point, two distinct schools of *feng shui* but over the course of history the two have become more or less fused. It is becoming conventional to refer to these two schools in English as the landform school and the compass school, although each is also known by various other names. The names suggest the major difference between the two 'traditions.' To broadly generalize, the landform school was said to concern itself primarily with the physical contours of the environment and features of the landscape. Its practitioners intuited the relationship between environmental features and cosmic forces and then interpreted how the features interacted according to the general laws of yin and yang and the Five Processes. The compass school was named for its emphasis on the use of the *luopan* or Chinese geomancer's compass. Practitioners of the compass school determined the auspices of an environment mainly by examining the interaction between directional positions and calendrical/astral forces, all of which found representations in the various concentric rings on the surface of this school's quintessential tool. The advocates of each tradition criticized proponents of the other for what they had failed to consider – the landform school attacked the compass school for ignoring land features and the compass school accused the landform school of overlooking the macrocosmic influences of heaven and time.

Although there is documentary evidence that *feng shui* practitioners did indeed criticize one another's methods on the grounds mentioned above, it appears that too much emphasis has been placed on the differences between the two schools both by pre-modern Chinese writers and by modern scholars of *feng shui* in China and the West. An investigation of the classical canon of *feng shui* reveals that the original authors and subsequent commentators consistently warn against the dangers of considering only landforms while ignoring temporal-astrological influences, and vice versa. Many modern books on *feng shui* claim that the landform school developed first because its earliest manual, written in the third–fourth century CE, predates the works of the compass school. However, it is commonly accepted that the *luopan* or *feng shui* compass was an evolutionary development of the *shi* or cosmograph, which was in use at least by the third century BCE. The traditional history of these schools argues that each developed independently but that the two were synthesized during the late imperial period. It seems much more reasonable to assume that the two 'schools' really only represent methodological differences of emphasis within a tradition whose pedigree dates from before the imperial era. Whichever version of *feng shui* history one chooses to accept, the relevance of these two schools to the present discussion is simply that the Treatise deals primarily with issues that one would tend to associate with the compass school.

Certain basic *feng shui* concepts are common to both schools. Not surprisingly, these foundational concepts are also the ideas that the authors of the Treatise do not explain for the reader. These include the following: mountain (*shan*), orientation (*xiang*), dragon (*long*), vein (*mai*), lair (*xue*), water (*shui*), sand (*sha*), vital breath (*qi*) and killing force (*sha* not to be confused with sand). It is a generally accepted principle of *feng shui* that one should seek to locate one's residence, either a home or a grave, facing to the south with a mountain to the rear and a body of water to the front. In the Chinese mythic tradition, the dragon is considered to be the most powerful of creatures and is believed to be able to change its physical form at will. Since Five Processes theory associates it with the direction east and the process wood, the dragon is a symbol of vitality. At the same time, the dragon is closely connected to water and is believed to elevate itself from bodies of water as mist and ascend to the heavens as clouds from which the rains fall. Within the earth, mountains are considered to be the physical manifestations of the dragon's body. Therefore, the presence of a mountain within an environment indicates the potential for all of the beneficial powers of the dragon. In practice, an actual mountain is not always present. In such an environment, other features, such as a stand of trees, a tall building, or a slight rise in the landscape might represent the presence of a dragon.

In order to benefit from the presence of a dragon, one must orient one's residence properly with respect to the mountain. *Feng shui* principle holds that entities that face the self are benevolent while those that turn their 'backs' on oneself are baleful. This is why it is considered beneficial to face the vitality of yang in the south and to turn one's back to the destructive force of yin in the north. When a mountain is also positioned to the north facing south then the powerful dragon faces the self and turns its back to repel the destructive influences of the north. To be precise, it is actually ideal for the dragon to lie somewhat west of due north and for the body of water to lie somewhat east of south. This refinement recalls traditional cosmology. According to myth, the cataclysmic act that threw the cosmic order awry caused the archetypal mountains, Kunlun, to rise up in the northwest and caused floodwaters to pool in the southeast. As we shall see, this also reflects the arrangement of the imperial palace in the circumpolar constellations in which the emperor's star sits in the northwest facing southeast. Although this axial orientation is ideal in principle, in practice the contours of the landscape might dictate any orientation on the compass.

Once a *feng shui* expert has identified the dragon, he looks for a vein within the dragon's body. A dragon's vein within the earth correlates with the meridians along which vital breath circulates throughout the human body according to the theory of traditional Chinese medicine. By being near a dragon's vein it is believed that the occupant of the home or grave will absorb the living/yang vital breath of the dragon. It is also believed that, just as with human meridians, the dragon's vital breath tends to pool at certain points as it flows throughout the dragon's body. These pooling points correlate with the acupuncture points that Chinese doctors manipulate in order to normalize the flow of vital breath within the human body. After the *feng shui* expert locates the dragon's vein, he seeks a point in which vital breath pools, but does not coagulate. This point then represents the ideal location for the lair, which is to say the ideal position in which to build a home or bury a relation. Although one might assume that 'lair' would refer to the residence of the dragon, in fact, it is a point on the dragon's body. *Feng shui* texts explain that the term is used because a lair is a place where an animal goes to rest and recuperate its energies. The belief is that animals intuitively sense the presence of vital breath and choose to reside where it is strong. Humans lack this instinct and thus must study *feng shui* in order to find appropriate lairs.

Water and sand represent the second half of the orientation equation.

Once the dragon's head has been located and situated relatively to the rear and after a lair has been pinpointed, the *feng shui* master must determine which way the residence should face. The vital breath of an environment is believed to flow downwards like water. Indeed water is considered a conduit of vital breath. In terms of yin-yang theory, a mountain is considered yang in form because it is hard and elevated, but is yin in function because it does not move. Water by contrast is considered yin in form because it is soft and low-lying, but is yang in function because it flows. Therefore, in order to ideally balance the yin and yang elements of the mountain, it is considered important to have a source of water that passes in front of the residence. Ideally that water should flow in a direction opposite the lay of the mountain. If the mountain range originates in the east and enters the living environment in the north, then a river should ideally flow from the west to the south. The rate of flow must be neither too fast nor too slow. As with a dragon's vein, it is best if the river curves and pools in front of the residence before flowing out of view. Confluences of water are considered good, while a stream that divides into branches is thought to dissipate vital breath. As mentioned above, water was believed to stop the flow of vital breath, as opposed to wind which disperses vital breath. As the theory developed, it came to be believed that a pool of water slows and retains, while rapidly and lineally flowing water disperses vital breath.

Second in importance to water, sand refers both to the actual soil of a location and to the (ideally) relatively low-lying foreground of a site. The importance of sand in the equation naturally increases when water is not present. Most discussions of sand tend to focus on its potentially dangerous manifestations. Where natural bodies of water are absent, there is a danger that the vital breath of the dragon will be weak and stagnant. In such circumstances, *feng shui* analysts take great caution to ensure that the land that features in front of the dragon and the lair do not obstruct the egress of what is already considered to be a weak flow of vital breath. Thus, without water in an environment *feng shui* practitioners seek to disperse sand in the foreground in order to regulate the flow of vital breath within the landscape.

The discussion thus far has focused on the landscape features that should ideally be present in a potential residential or burial site but *feng shui* places an equal stress on avoiding negative influences known as killing force. Killing force is to some extent the opposite of vital breath. In this respect it is sometimes characterized as yin vital breath as opposed to yang vital breath. Again the use of vital in this translation is rather awkward when one thinks of this as a deadly force. While yang is the force of birth and maturity, yin is the force of dying and burial. In fact, homes of the living are known as yang houses (*yang zhai*) and graves are known as yin houses (*yin zhai*). One might assume, therefore, that residential sites would require yang vital breath and burial sites would require yin vital breath but this is not the case. The reason for this is that the objective in burying one's ancestors is to preserve the vital breath that inhabits their human remains. For both the living and the dead it is yang vital breath that preserves and vitalizes.

Killing force manifests itself in both of the major areas of *feng shui*, that is in both landscape features as well as in compass positions and stellar conjunctions. A mountain with a sharp ridge that resembles a knife and points directly towards a residence is a killing force. A river or road that runs rapidly and directly towards a site or that turns at sharp angles is a killing force. In these cases, sharp straight lines represent the killing force of yin vital breath. Among the conjunctions of heavenly bodies and directions, the worst killing force is the Great Year (*tai sui*). Any site that is located facing directly towards the position occupied by the Great Year star in a given year is incomparably inauspicious.

Equipped with this rudimentary understanding of *feng shui*, we now turn our attention to the main concepts addressed in part two of the Treatise. The central concern of this half of the Treatise is the set of twenty-four 'mountains' or compass positions. Simply stated, the twenty-four mountains represent a division of the compass face into twenty-four equal divisions. The Twelve Earthly Branches occupy the points of the compass that correspond with the hours of a clock face, with the first branch, branch-*Zi*, at 12 o'clock. The positions between each hour are represented by the four inter-cardinal trigrams from the Latter Heaven trigram arrangement and eight of the Heavenly Stems, excluding stems five and six, i.e. stem-*Wu* and stem-*Ji*. The latter stems are omitted because they correspond with earth and the center and so have no connection with the circumferential positions. Only half of the trigrams are used because the other four correspond to the cardinal positions already held by branch-*Zi*, branch-*Mao*, branch-*Wu*, and branch-*You*. In practice, the four branches just mentioned are sometimes replaced by the four cardinal Latter Heaven trigrams. Pairs of the eight Heavenly Stems flank the four cardinal positions of the branches according to the stems' normal Five-Processes correlations. Thus as water correlates, stem-*Ren* precedes and stem-*Gui* follows branch-*Zi*. As wood correlates, stem-*Jia* precedes and stem-*Yi* follows branch-*Mao*. As fire correlates, stem-*Bing* precedes and stem-*Ding* follows branch-*Wu*. As metal correlates, stem-*Geng* precedes and stem-*Xin* follows branch-*You*.

The first half of Part Two explains four different schemes that are used to correlate the twenty-four mountains with the Five Processes. The first three schemes correspond to the three major ring divisions of the *feng shui* compass, i.e. Standard Needle/Earth Plate, Middle Needle/Man (Inner Heaven) Plate, and Sewing Needle/(Outer) Heaven Plate. The fourth of the Five Processes schemes is known as the Great Plan Five Processes. After describing its correlations, the compilers explain how the Great Plan scheme is used to determine the auspices of a mountain (direction) with reference to the sexagenary correlate of the year and month. The second half of Part Two describes the Lesser and Greater Roaming Year Trigram Transformations. The Roaming Year schemes assign trigram correlates to directions and determines the auspices of a position with reference to eight possible transformations of a base trigram. The mountains of the four remaining branches and eight stems are correlated with the trigrams according to the Triune Harmonies and Received Stem-*Jia* systems. The methods by which these various systems were applied will be described in the relevant commentary to each section.

In light of the previous discussion of landform and compass *feng shui* techniques, the contents of the second half of the Treatise seem to lean heavily toward the compass school tradition. However, it is important to keep in mind the overall objective of the Treatise. As the imperial introduction explains, the function of the Treatise was to harmonize heaven's times and distinguish earth's directions. Consequently, the Treatise seeks to treat only general and universal principles. It was not intended to function as an astrologer's or *feng shui* reader's sole guide. Instead the Treatise sought to identify the unifying principles that generally governed the practice of these two predictive arts. In practical application, the mantic expert would always need to consider either the eight characters of the individual contemplating a course of action or the actual landscape features of a potential building site. In many cases the expert would consider both sets of specifics. Therefore, the absence of information about landform interpretation should not be taken to suggest that Emperor Qianlong was partial to the compass school of *feng shui*. Furthermore, the imperial application of the treatise was to guide the selection of orientations for less permanent constructions than palaces and tombs. The orientation materials of the Treatise were intended to enable ritual specialists to advise the emperor on how to orient important ritual activities. For more permanent ventures, the specific advice of a *feng shui* expert would always be required.

As with the first part of the Treatise, we see in Part Two a concern with reducing all formulae to their basic grounding in yin-yang and Five Processes theory. Indeed, throughout the remainder of the Treatise, the compilers regularly dismiss traditional practices that they believed deviated from these basic theories. This serves to highlight the importance and indeed the primacy of yin-yang, Five Processes theory in traditional Chinese cosmological thought. These theories provided the common denominator regardless of which *feng shui* tradition was favored and regardless of which mantic art was being considered – be it *feng shui*, astrology, palm reading, etc. In fact, as we have seen, these same correlative theories pervaded every traditional art in China from medicine to martial arts to governance and cooking. Thus, whether or not one accepts the claims of Chinese astrologers and geomancers, without understanding these theories it is extremely difficult to gain insight into traditional Chinese culture.

The Twenty-Four Directional Positions

This set of twenty-four corresponds almost perfectly with the stem/branch/weft cord indications of the Dipper during the twenty-four solar nodes described in the *Huainanzi* (Major, pp.88–9). The only difference is that the present set substitutes the four corner trigrams for the *Huainanzi*'s four weft cords. Major indicates that the Huang-Lao authors of the *Huainanzi* employed sets of eight, such as the eight winds, but did not use the trigrams because the latter were then the exclusive possession of the Confucians. He further argues that the Eastern Han *Huainanzi* commentator, Gao You, was the first to supply the trigram correlates for the groups of eight in the *Huainanzi*.

> The twenty-four directional positions[131] consist of a combination of four trigrams, eight Heavenly Stems, and Twelve Earthly Branches. The yin-yang school refers to this grouping as the twenty-four mountains. When one mentions a 'mountain,' the concept of 'orientation' is already implied therein. For example, a branch-*Zi* mountain (due north), of necessity, has a branch-*Wu* (due south) orientation. A branch-*Wu* mountain has a branch-*Zi* orientation. A stem-*Ren* mountain has a stem-*Bing* orientation. A stem-*Bing* mountain has a stem-*Ren* orientation.

Of the eight trigrams (as they appear in the latter heaven arrangement), only those of the four corners are used. The four trigrams of the cardinal directions are not used. This is because the trigrams of the cardinal directions appear in the exact same positions as the four branches; branch-*Zi*, branch-*Wu*, branch-*Mao*, and branch-*You*. Therefore, those trigrams are not used, but instead the branches are used. Using the branches is equivalent to using the trigrams.

Since the eight trigrams determine the four cardinal directions, the eight stems are taken to support the cardinal points. Stem-*Jia* and stem-*Yi* support the two sides of trigram-*Zhen* [i.e. the branch-*Mao* mountain or 3 o'clock]. Stem-*Bing* and stem-*Ding* support the two sides of trigram-*Li* [i.e. the branch-*Wu* mountain or 6 o'clock]. Stem-*Geng* and stem-*Xin* support the two sides of trigram-*Dui* [i.e. the branch-*You* mountain or 9 o'clock]. Stem-*Ren* and stem-*Gui* support the two sides of trigram-*Kan* [i.e. the branch-*Zi* mountain or 12 o'clock].

Eight branches are taken to support the four corners. Branch-*Xu* and branch-*Hai* support the two sides of trigram-*Qian*. Branch-*Chou* and branch-*Yin* support the two sides of trigram-*Gen*. Branch-*Chen* and branch-*Si* support the two sides of trigram-*Sun*. Branch-*Wei* and branch-*Shen* support the two sides of trigram-*Kun*.

Together, the four binding cords (trigrams), the eight stems, and the twelve branches equal twenty-four. Heavenly stem-*Wu* and stem-*Ji* are not used in the set of twenty-four because they are the correlates of the central earth process and therefore lack a fixed position (with relation to the other four directions).

In relating the twenty-four mountains with the eight trigrams, each trigram manages three mountains. Thus, the three mountains designated by branch-*Xu*, trigram-*Qian*, and branch-*Hai* all belong to trigram-*Qian*. The mountains designated by stem-*Ren*, branch-*Zi*, and stem-*Gui* belong to trigram-*Kan*. The mountains designated by branch-*Chou*, trigram-*Gen*, and branch-*Yin* belong to trigram-*Gen*. The mountains designated by stem-*Jia*, branch-*Mao*, and stem-*Yi* belong to trigram-*Zhen*. The mountains designated by branch-*Chen*, trigram-*Sun*, and branch-*Si* belong to trigram-*Sun*. The mountains designated by stem-*Bing*, branch-*Wu*, and stem-*Ding* belong to tri-

Figure 28 The Twenty-Four Directional Positions

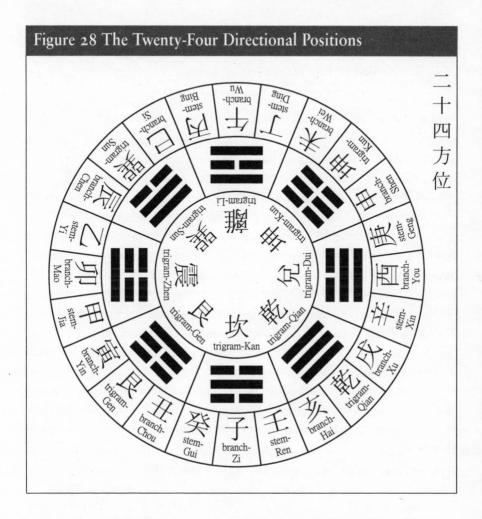

gram-*Li*. The mountains designated by branch-*Wei*, trigram-*Kun*, and branch-*Shen* belong to trigram-*Kun*. The mountains designated by stem-*Geng*, branch-*You*, and stem-*Xin* belong to trigram-*Dui*. These groupings are called the 'eight palaces.'

The various schools have different ways of correlating the twenty-four mountains with the Five Processes. Each of those conventions has a unique meaning.

The Standard Five Processes

The following three sections describe three 'needles' of the geomancer's compass (*luopan*). These needles are used to determine the Five Processes correlations of the twenty-four mountains. In the Standard Needle, the stems and branches assume their normal correlations, with the branch-*Chou*, branch-*Chen*, branch-*Wei*, and branch-*Xu* relating to earth. The trigrams also assume their standard correlations: trigram-*Qian* – metal, trigram-*Kun* and trigram-*Gen* – earth, and trigram-*Sun* – wood. In the central and Sewing Needle systems, the branches determine the correlations of the stems/trigrams directly adjacent to the given branch. Stephen Skinner in *The Living Earth Manual of Feng-Shui*, argues that Joseph Needham was incorrect in assuming that the sewing and Central Needles were developed to account for differences in declinations. Skinner argues that the two rings were devised sheerly for geomantic purposes (Skinner, pp.88–101).

According to *feng shui* principles, the standard Five Processes of the Standard Needle determine the Five Processes correlations of points in space. This is to be understood in contrast with the Central and Sewing Needle Five Processes, which have temporal applications. The latter are used to determine the Five Processes correlation of various vital breaths that flow into and out from the site being examined. The Standard Needle is used before the other needles to assess the static nature of a given direction. Thus, the compilers explain that the Standard Needle is used to determine orientations (*xiang*). Once the *feng shui* master has identified the mountain (*shan*) that dominates a site, he employs the Standard Needle to determine where the spatial axis of the house should be. The other two needles are subsequently used to assess the dynamic flows of vital breaths that are perceived to be acting on the static positions.

> The mountains correlated with branch-*Hai*, stem-*Ren*, branch-*Zi*, and stem-*Gui* belong to the water process. The mountains correlated with branch-*Yin*, stem-*Jia*, branch-*Mao*, stem-*Yi*, and trigram-*Sun* belong to the wood process. The mountains correlated with branch-*Si*, stem-*Bing*, branch-*Wu*, and stem-*Ding* belong to the fire process. The mountains correlated with branch-*Shen*, stem-*Geng*, branch-*You*, stem-*Xin*, and trigram-*Qian* belong to the metal process. The mountains correlated with branch-*Chen*, branch-

Figure 29 The Standard Five Processes

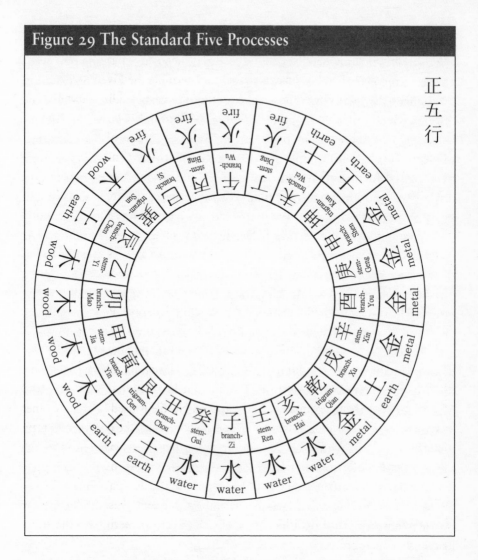

Wei, branch-*Xu*, branch-*Chou*, trigram-*Kun*, and trigram-*Gen* belong to the earth process.

The above presents the correlation of the eight trigrams and the stems and branches with the Five Processes. This arrangement is referred to as the 'standard Five Processes' (of the twenty-four mountains) because it was followed historically by the development of other systems such as the 'Double Mountains' and 'Great Plan' expounded by various schools.

The Central Needle, Double Mountain Five Processes

The compilers indicate here, and again later in the Treatise, that *feng shui* practitioners employ the Central Needle to seek out or reach for a dragon (*ge long*) – a common *feng shui* term. The dragon vein is to be understood as the channel through which active, living, yang vital breath approaches a site. This refers to the *feng shui* practice of selecting an appropriate time for connecting a residence to a dragon vein that the *feng shui* master has identified. For a site that is to be occupied for the first time, 'connecting' simply means moving into a residence or interring remains in a tomb at an appropriate time. It is also possible by other means to connect a site that is already occupied to a dragon vein.

In contrast with the Standard Needle, which indicates the static Five Processes correlation of a direction in space, the Central Needle has a dynamic, temporal application. This is also indicated by the fact that the Central Needle employs the Double Mountain Triune Harmonies Five Processes system. The system is 'double' because the twenty-four mountains are grouped into twelve pairs, each containing an earthly branch. The Triune Harmonies Five Processes correlation of the branch determines the correlation of the mountain with which that branch is paired. Consequently, the earth process doesn't appear in the Central Needle system. Only the four cardinal processes of the four directions and four seasons are used.

On the *feng shui* compass, the mountains of the Central Needle are uniquely associated with a set of twenty-four constellations or asterisms, to be precise. These asterisms are mostly located near the North Pole – the center of the stellar axis – rather than along the belt of the ecliptic or equator – as are the 28 lunar lodges. By referring to these astral associations, the *feng shui* master is able to correlate the positions of a site with the circumpolar region of the heavens. The four most important of these are the Celestial Emperor (*tianhuang*, branch-*Hai*), the Celestial Market (*tianshi*, trigram-*Gen*), the Greater Subtlety (*taiwei*, stem-*Bing*), and the Lesser Subtlety (*shaowei*, branch-*You*). Although only the last of these is located in a cardinal direction, the four star groups symbolize the four cardinal directions. The most ideal *feng shui* site would therefore find the Celestial Emperor behind, the Celestial Market to the left, Greater Subtlety to the front, and Lesser Subtlety to the right.

The Qing dynasty *feng shui* specialist Ye Tai argues that the Central Needle was created by Yang Yunsong and that the Sewing Needle was created by Lai Wenjun in the book *Dispelling Fog with the Compass Collection* (*Luojing zhinan bowu ji*).[132]

That which is displayed in the outer ring of the diagram is the 'Standard Needle' – those being the standard positions of the twenty-four mountains. That which is displayed in the inner ring is the Central Needle. The position of the mountain correlated with branch-*Zi* in the Central Needle is in between the positions of the mountains correlated with stem-*Ren* and branch-*Zi* of the Standard Needle. As such, the Central Needle precedes the Standard Needle by one half of one position.

This system is 'double' because of the two mountains (thus joined). The system is also related to the Triune Harmonies because of the Five-Processes correlations of the Double Mountains. *Feng*

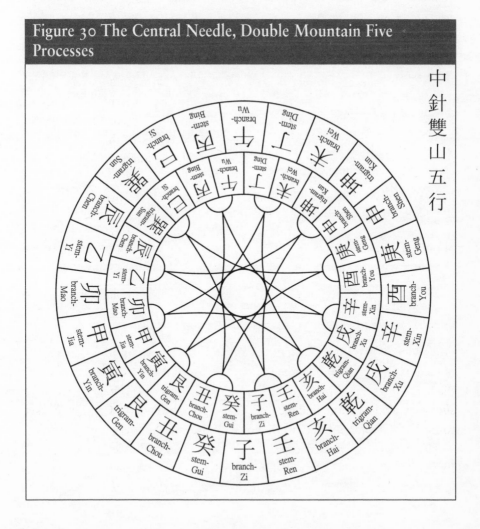

Figure 30 The Central Needle, Double Mountain Five Processes

shui masters (lit. geographers – i.e. geomancers) use this system when attempting to identify the [hidden] dragon [in the landscape] because the dragon is the vein of arrivals. Thus by anticipating the dragon's approach (i.e. shifting the twenty-four positions back half a unit, as a marksman leads a moving target), the master never fails to find the vein.

The Sewing Needle, Triune Harmonies Five Processes

The Sewing Needle is used in connection with sand and water. It indicates the vital breath that exits from the point towards which a site is oriented (*xiang*). As with the Central Needle, the Sewing Needle gives the *feng shui* master information about the influence of time on a direction – not about the physical matter of a direction. However, the Central Needle indicates vital breath that approaches from the dragon vein (*long mai*, where the dragon is the mountain – *shan*) behind the site, while the Sewing Needle indicates vital breath that departs through sand and water (i.e. orientation – *xiang*) in front of the site.

The positions of the twenty-four mountains in the Central Needle are shifted one half of one position counterclockwise from the positions of the Standard Needle. Those of the Sewing Needle are shifted one half of one position clockwise from the positions of the Standard Needle. Consequently, the mountains of the central and Sewing Needles differ by exactly one position.

On the *feng shui* compass, the variance of the Sewing Needle from the Standard Needle serves to put the twenty-four mountains into proper alignment with the twenty-four 'seasonal nodes.' Just like the twenty-four directional mountains, the seasonal nodes are correlated to 8 stems, 12 branches, and 4 trigrams. However, while the branch-*Wu* mountain designates the area 7.5 degrees east and west of due south, the correlated seasonal node, summer solstice, does not indicate the period 7.5 days before and after the summer solstice. The summer solstice node indicates the period of roughly fifteen days commencing from the solstice. Therefore, in factoring the time element into the design of the *feng shui* compass, the creator of the Sewing Needle shifted the twenty-four mountain positions 7.5 degrees clockwise so that the area of branch-*Wu* on the Sewing Needle would correspond perfectly with the time period of the summer solstice seasonal node.

The outer ring of the diagram is the Standard Needle. The inner ring is the Sewing Needle. The position of the mountain designated by branch-*Zi* on the Sewing Needle ring stands halfway between the positions of the mountains designated by branch-*Zi* and stem-*Gui* on the Standard Needle ring. This is one half of one position after the Standard Needle. The paired mountains receive the Five Processes Triune Harmonies correlations. The Sewing Needle positions differ from the Central Needle positions by exactly one position.

Figure 31 The Sewing Needle, Triune Harmonies Five Processes

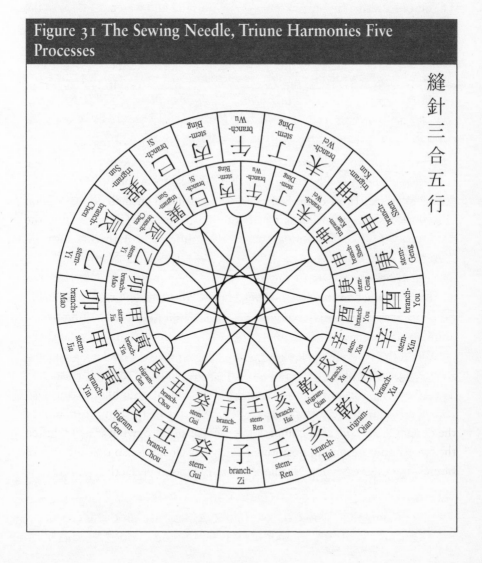

Feng shui masters employ the Sewing Needle system when they are attempting to dispel sand and gather water because sand and water are the roads of departures. Thus, by aiming behind them, the master never fails to obtain them.

Compilers' Note: The Double Mountain Five Processes are the same as the Triune Harmonies Five Processes. The twelve branches take the three life stages of birth, flourishing, and burial as their Triune Harmony offices and the four trigrams and eight stems are all one position in front of exactly one branch.

Compilers' Note: This system is called the Double Mountain Five Processes because each branch, together with its immediately preceding trigram or stem, assumes the Five Processes correlation of each branch as designated by the Triune Harmonies system. Thus, trigram-*Kun*, branch-*Shen*, stem-*Ren*, branch-*Zi*, stem-*Yi*, and branch-*Chen* harmonize as the water office; the six mountains all belong to the water process.

Trigram-*Qian*, branch-*Hai*, stem-*Jia*, branch-*Mao*, stem-*Ding*, and branch-*Wei* harmonize as the wood office; the six mountains all belong to the wood process.

Trigram-*Gen*, branch-*Yin*, stem-*Bing*, branch-*Wu*, stem-*Xin*, and branch-*Xu* harmonize as the fire office; the six mountains all belong to the fire process.

Trigram-*Sun*, branch-*Si*, stem-*Geng*, branch-*You*, stem-*Gui*, and branch-*Chou* harmonize as the metal office; the six mountains all belong to the metal process.

When the geomancer's texts speak of the standard Five Processes, they refer to the physical matter of the Five Processes. When they speak of the Double Mountain Five Processes, they refer to the vital breath of the Five Processes. Therefore, in seeking out the birth and flourishing of the dragon's vital breath, they use the Double Mountains and do not use the standard Five Processes.

Feng shui masters (*dili jia*) employ three needles. One is called the standard needle, which consists of the standard positions of the twenty-four mountains and is used to determine orientations. Another is called the Central Needle; the branch-*Zi* position of the Central Needle is located in the center of the standard needle's stem-*Ren* and branch-*Zi* positions; this Central Needle is used to locate the dragon. The third needle is called the Sewing Needle; the branch-*Zi* position of the Sewing Needle is located on the seam (in Chinese, this is the same character as that for sewing) of the Standard Needle's branch-*Zi* and stem-*Gui* positions; the Sewing Needle is used to dispel sand and gather water. Thus, the Central Needle and the Sewing Needle differ by one position. When discussing the Central Needle, one speaks of the Double Mountain Five Processes. When discussing the Sewing Needle, one speaks of the Triune Harmonies Five Processes. In actuality, the Central and Sewing Needles both employ the Double Mountain method (for determining their Five-Processes correlations).

The Great Plan Five Processes

This is perhaps the most complex and confusing section of the Treatise. The text presents an explanation of yet another system of Five-Processes correlations for the twenty-four mountains of the *feng shui* compass. For all their confidence in asserting the logic of their own explanation, the compilers do not appear to have been able to trace the origin of this system or offer a satisfying description of how the correlations derive. Of the twelve branches, only six obtain standard correlations (the four cardinal ones plus branch-*Chou* and branch-*Wei* as earth). Of the eight stems, only one follows its normal correlation (stem-*Bing* as fire). Of the four trigrams, only trigram-*Qian* and trigram-*Kun* retain their regular correlations. The explanations of the remaining correlations are neither consistent nor convincing. In concluding, the compilers revert to cosmological principles based on astronomy.

Although it doesn't appear that the history of this system was very carefully preserved, it remains a very important principle of the *feng shui* art. The primary application of these correlations is to the system of years and months conquering mountains, explained two sections below. This connection, however, can only be understood after examining the Buried Dragon and its transformed revolutions in the immediately following section. Briefly stated, this construct posits that fluctuations of cosmic forces create conflicts between certain times and directions. To avoid misfortune, one must ensure that the Five-Processes correlation of a time's sexagenary pair does not conflict with the Great Plan Five Processes correlation of the orientation.

The eight mountains designated by stem-*Jia*, branch-*Yin*, branch-*Chen*, trigram-*Sun*, branch-*Xu*, trigram-*Kan*, stem-*Xin*, and branch-*Shen* belong to the water process.

The four mountains designated by trigram-*Li*, stem-*Ren*, stem-*Bing*, and stem-*Yi* belong to the fire process.

The three mountains designated by trigram-*Zhen*, trigram-*Gen*, and branch-*Si* belong to the wood process.

The four mountains designated by trigram-*Qian*, branch-*Hai*, trigram-*Dui*, and stem-*Ding* belong to the metal process.

The five mountains designated by branch-*Chou*, stem-*Gui*, trigram-*Kun*, stem-*Geng*, and branch-*Wei* belong to the earth process.

The *Great Compendium of Geo-principles* (*Dili dacheng*) says:

'The Great Plan Five-Processes were derived by tracing back and identifying the original vital breaths of the standard Five Processes. The Five Processes Correlations of branch-*Zi*, branch-*Wu*, branch-*Mao*, and branch-*You* in the Great Plan scheme do not differ from the standard correlations because those branches occupy the standard positions of the Five Processes.

'Branch-*Mao* is wood. Wood, of necessity, depends on water. Therefore, stem-*Jia* (which immediately precedes branch-*Mao*) changes to water.

'Branch-*You* belongs to metal. Metal, of necessity, depends on earth. Therefore, stem-*Geng* changes to earth.

'Branch-*Wu* is fire. Fire does not require wood to be born, but is born from the rays of the sun. Therefore, stem-*Bing* is the fire of the sun.

'Branch-*Zi* is water. Water does not depend on metal to be born, but, on the contrary, is rooted in fire. If water (the winter process) were not to obtain fire, then winter's cold would result in freezing and death. Therefore, stem-*Ren* is the fire within water.

'Branch-*Mao* is wood. When wood flourishes, it takes pleasure in giving birth to fire. Therefore, stem-*Yi* is fire.

'Branch-*You* is metal. When metal flourishes, it takes pleasure in giving birth to water. Therefore, stem-*Xin* is water.

'Branch-*Wu* is fire. When fire flourishes, it takes pleasure in smelting metal. Therefore, stem-*Ding* is metal.

'Branch-*Zi* is water. When water flourishes but is without earth, the water will be dissipated. Therefore, stem-*Gui* is earth.

'With regards to the twelve positions just described, in each case, the eight stems are taken to support the vital breath of the four cardinal directions. Among the correlations thus set forth, the cases for fire and water differ from those for metal and wood. This is because metal and wood function in accordance with their outward forms. Consequently, they employ principle and transform straightforwardly. By contrast, water and fire function in accordance with their inner spirits. Consequently, they employ mystery and are hidden circuitously.

'The four birthplaces[133] are the beginning vital breaths of the four cardinal directions. Since water's beginning was originally in metal, branch-*Hai* is metal. Since wood's beginning was originally in water, branch-*Yin* is water. Since fire's beginning was originally in wood, branch-*Si* is wood. However, although [one would assume that] metal's beginning was originally in earth, branch-*Shen* does not transform to earth, but instead transforms to water. This is because dry earth cannot give birth to metal. Only after it obtains water can earth give birth to metal. Therefore, in fact, water is the beginning vital breath of metal. This is why the Daoists seek to obtain metal from within water. Therefore, branch-*Shen* is water.

'The four burials[134] are the returning vital breaths of the four cardinal directions. In being born, the myriad things face above. When returning, they face below. The things that are below are water and earth. Fire's returning to earth is manifested as ashes. Being absorbed into and drying up, is the way that water returns to earth. Therefore, branch-*Chou* and branch-*Wei* are earth. Since it originally came out of earth, metal cannot again return to earth. In the same way, since it originally came out of earth, wood cannot again return to earth. Therefore, the two both return to water. Upon entering water, metal sinks. Wood, upon entering water, rots. Therefore, branch-*Chen* and branch-*Xu* are water.

'The four binding cords (i.e. the mountains designated by trigrams) are the intersections of the four directions. Trigram-*Qian* originally gave birth to the metal of northern water. Trigram-*Kun* originally gave birth to the earth of western metal. Since these two trigrams are the elders, they do not transform (i.e. they remain correlated with metal and earth respectively). Trigram-*Gen* resides in the intersection of water and wood. Trigram-*Gen* receives and employs water to give birth to wood. Earth (which is the process normally associated with trigram-*Gen*), by contrast, cannot give birth to wood. Therefore, in keeping with this principle, trigram-*Gen* transforms to wood. Trigram-*Sun* resides in the intersection of wood and fire. Wood can certainly give birth to fire. Fire, however, is actually rooted in water. The yang line in the center of trigram-*Kan* is the root of fire. The yin line in

Figure 32 The Great Plan Five Processes

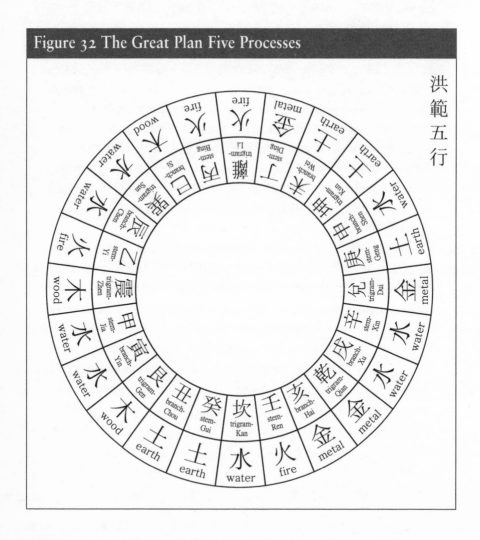

the center of trigram-*Li* is the root of water. Thus water and fire mutually serve as one another's roots. Therefore, trigram-*Sun* transforms to water in order that it may serve as the root of fire.'

The *Regulations Governing Gods and Demons (Shensha qili)* says:

'In his commentary on the 'Mountain School Five Processes' chapter of Guo Pu's[135] classic, the Jin dynasty (265–420 CE) scholar Zhao Zai did not employ the standard Five Processes but rather used the Great Plan Five Processes. From this evidence, it can be seen that the history of this Great Plan Five Processes tradition is quite old. Some claim that the system was developed by the Tang dynasty Chan (Zen) Buddhist master Yi Xing, but this is not true. It is a pity that, although such gentlemen as Guo Pu and Zhao Zai employed the Great Plan Five Processes arrangement, they never explained the meaning of the system.

'Toward the end of the Yuan dynasty, a certain unnamed master first made reference to the theory of the Purple-White, Root-Source, Conjoined-Mountains Great Plan. This theory holds that the Luo River Diagram's positions generate and bring to completion odd and even[136] numbers, establish the Five Processes, and differentiate fortunate and unfortunate. This was still only a preliminary, and not yet a full, explanation. Thus, it remained something which people could not explain. Eventually, the scholar Wan Minying of the Chu River region presented a lucid explanation of the Yellow River Chart and the Five Processes when he edited the *Complete Compendium on the Three Fates (Sanming tonghui)*. In that work, Wan Minying said:[137]

> "When, of old, Fu Xi governed the world, he used the Yellow River Chart to create the eight trigrams. By means of this he explained the names of trigram-*Qian*, trigram-*Kun*, trigram-*Kan*, trigram-*Li*, trigram-*Zhen*, trigram-*Sun*, trigram-*Gen*, and trigram-*Dui* as well as the symbolic images of heaven, earth, sun, moon, wind, thunder, mountain, and marsh. The '*Xici*,' or 'linked expressions,' section of the *Book of Changes* says,

'Heaven and earth fix positions. Mountain and marsh communicate the vital breath. Thunder and wind press upon and cover one another. Fire and water do not issue forth one from the other. These are the mutual interactions of the Eight Trigrams.' In this way, the eight trigrams assume their order. The twenty-four positions similarly proceed within the realm of the trigrams.

"It is also possible to use data pertaining to the forces of yin and yang to analyze this. Consider the transformations of the eight trigrams. Stem-*Jia* originally belongs to the wood process and receives trigram-*Qian* as its associated trigram. Trigram-*Qian* and trigram-*Kun* oppose one another.[138] If one takes the top and bottom lines of trigram-*Kun* and uses them to replace the top and bottom lines of trigram-*Qian*, trigram-*Kan* is thereby produced. Since it follows the transformation of trigram-*Kan*, stem-*Jia* is therefore associated with the water process.

Stem-*Yi* originally belongs to the wood process and receives trigram-*Kun* as its associated trigram. Trigram-*Kun* and trigram-*Qian* oppose one another. If one takes the top and bottom lines of trigram-*Qian* and uses them to replace the top and bottom lines of trigram-*Kun*, trigram-*Li* is thereby produced. Since it takes the transformation of trigram-*Li*, stem-*Yi* therefore belongs to the fire process.

"Stem-*Bing* originally belongs to the fire process and receives trigram-*Gen* as its associated trigram. Trigram-*Gen* and trigram-*Dui* oppose one another. If one takes the bottom line of trigram-*Dui* and uses it to replace the bottom line of trigram-*Gen*, trigram-*Li* is thereby produced. Since it takes the transformation of trigram-*Li*, stem-*Bing* therefore belongs to the fire process.

"Stem-*Ding* originally belongs to the fire process and receives trigram-*Dui* as its associated trigram. Trigram-*Dui* and trigram-*Gen* oppose one another. If one takes the top line of trigram-*Gen* and uses it to replace the top line of trigram-*Dui*, trigram-*Qian* is thereby produced. Since it takes the transformation of trigram-*Qian*, stem-*Ding* therefore belongs to the metal process.

"Stem-*Geng* originally belongs to the metal process and receives trigram-*Zhen* as its associated trigram. Trigram-*Zhen* and trigram-*Sun* oppose one another. If one takes the bottom line of trigram-*Sun* and uses it to replace the bottom line of trigram-*Zhen*, trigram-*Kun* is thereby produced. Since it takes the transformation of trigram-*Kun*, stem-*Geng* therefore belongs to the earth process.

"Stem-*Xin* originally belongs to the metal process and receives trigram-*Sun* as its associated trigram. Trigram-*Sun* and trigram-*Zhen* oppose one another. If one takes the top line of trigram-*Zhen* and uses it to replace the top line of trigram-*Sun*, trigram-*Kan* is thereby produced. Since it takes the transformation of trigram-*Kan*, stem-*Xin* therefore belongs to the water process.

"Stem-*Ren* originally belongs to the water process and receives trigram-*Li* as its associated trigram. Trigram-*Li* and trigram-*Kan* oppose one another. If one takes the middle line of trigram-*Kan* and uses it to replace the middle line of trigram-*Li*, trigram-*Qian* is thereby produced. Since it takes the transformation of trigram-*Qian*, the stem-*Ren* should initially belong to the metal process. However, stem-*Ren* receives the fire of trigram-*Li*. When fire tempers metal, the metal melts. Melting, metal cannot return to stand on its own. Therefore, stem-*Ren* must continue to rely upon the support of the fire of trigram-*Li* and is thus associated with the fire process.

"Stem-*Gui* originally belongs to the water process and receives trigram-*Kan* as its associated trigram. Trigram-*Kan* and trigram-*Li* oppose one another. If one takes the middle line of trigram-*Li* and uses it to replace the middle line of trigram-*Kan*, trigram-*Kun* is thereby produced. Since it takes the transformation of trigram-*Kun*, stem-*Gui* therefore belongs to the earth process.

These are the transformations of the trigrams associated with the eight Heavenly Stems. Although the interchanging of the component lines differs from one case to another, there is a meaning behind each instance. For example, the way in which the two upper and lower lines of trigram-*Qian* and trigram-*Kun* are exchanged derives its meaning from the images of hexagram-*Pi* (#11 trigram-*Qian* below, trigram-*Kun* above) and hexagram-*Tai* (#12 trigram-*Kun* below, trigram-*Qian* above). Therefore, it is said that, 'Heaven and earth fix positions.'

"Trigram-*Zhen* and trigram-*Gen* exchange their top lines with trigram-*Sun* and trigram-*Dui*. Trigram-*Sun* and trigram-*Dui* exchange their bottom lines with trigram-*Zhen* and trigram-*Gen*. These exchanges derive their meanings from the images of hexagram-*Xian* (#31 trigram-*Gen* below, trigram-*Dui* above) and hexagram-*Heng* (#32 trigram-*Sun* below, trigram-*Zhen* above) as well as hexagram-*Sun* (#41 trigram-*Dui* below, trigram-*Gen* above) and hexagram-*Yi* (#42 trigram-*Zhen* below, trigram-*Sun* above). Therefore, it is said that, 'Thunder and wind press upon and cover one another. Mountain and marsh communicate the vital breath.'

"Trigram-*Kan* and trigram-*Li* exchange their middle lines with trigram-*Qian* and trigram-*Kun*. Trigram-*Qian* and trigram-*Kun* exchange their middle lines with trigram-*Kan* and trigram-*Li*. These exchanges derive their meanings from the images of hexagram-*Jiji* (#63 trigram-*Li* below, trigram-*Kan* above) and hexagram-*Weiji* (#64 trigram-*Kan* below, trigram-*Li* above). Therefore, it is said that, 'Fire and Water do not issue forth one from the other.'

"As for the Five-Processes correlations that pertain to the eight trigrams, although the permutation or absence of permutation differs from one case to another, there is also a meaning behind each instance. Trigram-*Qian* and trigram-*Kun* are originally correlated with metal and earth respectively and this does not change. This is because trigram-*Qian* and trigram-*Kun* are the ancestors of yin and yang. They are the father and mother of the other trigrams. They retire to a place of rest. Because they are old and indomitable, they do not transform.

"Trigram-*Kan*, trigram-*Li*, trigram-*Zhen*, and trigram-*Dui*, being positioned in the four cardinal directions of metal, wood, water, and fire, do not transform.[139] Branch-*Zi*, branch-*Wu*, branch-*Mao*, and branch-*You* reside in the four flourishing positions. From those locations they announce the commands of the four seasons and the vital breaths thereby move through their changes. Therefore, these trigrams and branches do not undergo a transformation of their Five-Processes correlations.

"Trigram-*Gen* and trigram-*Sun*, in contrast with the trigrams just described, do transform. Trigram-*Gen*, correlated with earth, stands in a transitional position on the boundary between trigram-*Kan* and trigram-*Zhen* in the northeast; it resides in between the declining life stage of branch-*Chou* and the sickening life stage of branch-*Yin*.[140] Thus, since trigram-*Gen* would wish to transform its stand, it is natural that in becoming a mountain, it would transform to wood.

"Trigram-*Sun*, correlated with wood, stands in a transitional position on the boundary between trigram-*Zhen* and trigram-*Li* in the southeast; it resides in between the declining life stage of branch-*Chen* and the sickening life stage of branch-*Si*.[141] Thus, not being able to stand on its own, trigram-*Sun* returns to water.

Branch-*Chen* is the burial place [of the water process]. Therefore, trigram-*Sun* and branch-*Chen* are both water.

"Branch-*Hai* originally belongs to water. Since metal gives birth to water, metal in this instance replaces water. Therefore, branch-*Hai* belongs to metal. Branch-*Yin* originally belongs to wood. Since water gives birth to wood, water in this instance replaces wood. Therefore, branch-*Yin* belongs to water. Branch-*Si* originally belongs to fire. Since wood gives birth to the declining of trigram-*Zhen*, it replaces trigram-*Zhen* and is able to stand. Therefore, branch-*Si* belongs to wood. Branch-*Shen* originally belongs to metal. Water is capable of giving birth. The metal of branch-*Shen* assists with water's power. Therefore, branch-*Shen* belongs to water.

"Branch-*Chen*, branch-*Xu*, branch-*Chou*, and branch-*Wei* are the gods of the five earths of the five directions. Divided among the four seasons, they are the master potters of creation, the matter of the great year. Originally they could not transform. Since earth is required to give birth to wood, wood lends assistance to earth. The process that took one half of the earth by force is water. Water moves, while earth is still. Branch-*Chen* and branch-*Xu* are the mobility of yang. Therefore, they belong to water. Branch-*Chou* and branch-*Wei* are the stillness of yin. Therefore, they belong to earth.

"The principles that govern the transformation of the vital breaths of the Five Processes proceed from the great to the minute. Therefore, heaven and earth meet and the myriad things begin to move. Above and below meet and the work of virtue is accomplished. Man and woman meet and a determined will is made whole. Therefore, from time immemorial there has never been an instance in which something was able to be accomplished without the proper meeting together. In declining and substituting, there has yet to be an instance in which something was able to be transformed without being replaced. Thus, the Great Plan system of Five Processes is the superior Five Processes.

"With regards to human fate, when one encounters the Heavenly Stems stem-*Jia*, stem-*Yi*, [stem-*Bing*,] stem-*Ding*,[142] stem-*Geng*, stem-*Xin*, stem-*Ren*, and stem-*Gui* residing in the territories of trigram-*Qian*, trigram-*Gen*, trigram-*Sun*, and trigram-*Kun*, the transformations must also be considered. When discussing this in connection with the transformations of vital breaths of the ten stems, the sixty Received Notes, and the Received Stem-*Jia* systems, it is not sufficient to merely consider only the theory of the Yellow River Chart standard Five Processes.'"

In his work entitled *Dispelling Doubts* (*Quyi shuo*), Chu Yong explained that:

'Since ancient times people have made use of the so called "Great Five-Processes." This system had already been defended in Guo Pu's First Classic, where it was described as the Mountain School's Five Processes. However, since that time all commentators have said that they do not understand the rationale behind the system, which is to say that they knew of no reliable explanation for it. If this is the case, then how is it that from antiquity until the present everyone has made reference to the system and none have cast any doubts upon it. Considering this carefully one observes that an explanation cannot be found in connection with the numbers of the Complete Record of the Great Monad. Similarly, the numbers of the August Extreme Former Heaven and Middle Heaven offer no explanatory powers. Furthermore, the explanation of the six vital breaths and five movements within the transformations and conjunctions of the Latter Heaven are of no help. It is only upon examining the lines of the trigrams that one is able to identify a suitable explanation. This discovery is set forth immediately below:

Trigram-*Qian* receives stem-*Ren* and stem-*Jia*.

Trigram-*Qian* is Heaven. Heaven first gives birth to water.

Water:

Branch-*Xu* – stem-*Ren* and branch-*Xu*, water.

Branch-*Zi* – trigram-*Kan* is one of the cardinal trigrams.

Branch-*Yin* – stem-*Jia* and branch-*Yin*, water.

Stem-*Jia* – stem-*Jia* belongs to branch-*Yin*; trigram-*Qian* receives stem-*Jia*.

Branch-*Chen* – stem-*Ren* and branch-*Chen*, water.

Trigram-*Sun* – stem-*Ren* and branch-*Chen*, water; trigram-*Sun* belongs to branch-*Chen*.

Branch-*Shen* – stem-*Jia* and branch-*Shen*, water.

Stem-*Xin* – stem-*Yi* and branch-*You*, water; stem-*Xin* belongs to branch-*You*.

Branch-*Xu* belongs to trigram-*Qian*. Making one complete revolution clockwise through the twenty-four mountains from branch-*Xu*, one arrives at stem-*Xin*, which is the extreme. Trigram-*Qian* as the ultimate of yang, transforms into trigram-*Kun*. Therefore, the stem-*Xin* receives stem-*Yi*.

Trigram-*Kun* receives stem-*Yi* and stem-*Gui*.

Trigram-*Kun* serves as the Lord of Fire.

Fire:

Branch-*Wu* – trigram-*Li* is one of the cardinal trigrams.

Stem-*Bing* – stem-*Yi* and branch-*Si*, fire; stem-*Bing* belongs to branch-*Si*.

Stem-*Yi* – trigram-*Kun* receives stem-*Jia*.

Stem-*Ren* – stem-*Yi* and branch-*Hai*, fire; stem-*Ren* belongs to branch-*Hai*.

Trigram-*Kun* employs stem-*Yi*, but does not get to the point of employing stem-*Gui*. Therefore, of the six sexagenary pairs containing stem-*Gui*, none transform to fire. Stem-*Gui* instead transforms to wood.

Wood:

Branch-*Mao* – trigram-*Zhen* is one of the cardinal trigrams.

Trigram-*Gen* – stem-*Gui* and branch-*Chou*, wood.

Branch-*Wei* – stem-*Gui* and branch-*Wei*, wood.

Branch-*Si* – stem-*Ji* and branch-*Si*, wood.

Metal:

Branch-*You* – trigram-*Dui* is one of the cardinal trigrams.

Trigram-*Qian* – stem-*Geng* and branch-*Xu*, metal; trigram-*Qian* belongs to branch-*Xu*.

Branch-*Hai* – stem-*Xin* and branch-*Hai*, metal.

Stem-*Ding* – trigram-*Dui* receives stem-*Jia*.

Earth:

Trigram-*Kun* – cardinal trigram of the original palace.

Branch-*Chou* – stem-*Xin* and branch-*Chou*, earth.

Stem-*Gui* – stem-*Geng* and branch-*Zi*, earth; stem-*Gui* belongs to branch-*Zi*.

Stem-*Geng* – stem-*Wu* and branch-*Shen*, earth; stem-*Geng* belongs to branch-*Shen*.

Wood receives the transformation of trigram-*Kun*, concluding with the yin earth of stem-*Ji*.

Earth receives the transformation of trigram-*Qian*, concluding with the yang earth of stem-*Wu*.

Trigram-*Qian*, employing stem-*Ren* and stem-*Jia*,[143] gives birth to water. As for trigram-*Kun*, stem-*Yi* gives birth to fire and stem-*Gui* gives birth to wood. Each controls the eight positions. Trigram-*Qian* and trigram-*Kun* use those that are arrayed at their feet to inherit their position. They take as the eldest son and eldest daughter stem-*Geng* and stem-*Xin*, which in their turn transmute metal and earth and thereby fix the five vital breaths. Thus, in an alternating fashion, the work of creating and transforming is complete.

Originally, having used the form and numbers of trigram lines to examine it, the sixty stem-*Jia*/branch-*Zi* first obtained regularity. The initial structure through which its method was established did not run counter to the regulations. Once the forms and the numbers had been combined, the system was clarified. Therefore, it does not change what I have said.'[144]

'The great Five Processes proceed forth from trigram-*Qian* and trigram-*Kun*. The twelve positions proceed forth from the six branch-*Zi*. Furthermore, the twelve positions together with the six branch-*Zi* are sufficient to represent the numbers of trigram-*Qian* and trigram-*Kun*. The number of the orders of trigram-*Qian* and trigram-*Kun* is 360. Since the numbers of the orders of the six branch-*Zi* are also 360 in number, they are sufficient to represent the orders of trigram-*Qian* and trigram-*Kun*.

Only Guo Jungchún (i.e. Guo Pu) claimed that the branch-*Wei* originally belongs to wood, with the result that the processes metal, earth, and wood each obtained four positions in the twenty-four mountain scheme. Thus the 'Mountain School Five Processes' chapter [of his original classic] says, 'The stem-*Gui*, the branch-*Chou*, trigram-*Kun*, and the stem-*Geng* are called "Agriculture." Trigram-*Gen*, trigram-*Zhen*, the branch-*Si*, and the branch-*Wei* are "Crooked and Straight."'[145] It is now generally accepted that, within the system of twenty-four positions, the branch-*Wei* belongs to the earth process. Alas! there must be some rational basis for the fact that wood possesses three positions, metal four, and earth five.

Thus, it can be accepted that the number one is the progenitor of all other numbers and as such it subsumes or governs all eight positions. Even so, this raises the question of why it is that fire does not possess two or seven positions, but rather possesses four. Between these two points of view, it is unclear which is correct. Among those gentlemen who established the principles of this specialized discipline there are those who point to the fact that aside from his famous treatise containing the chapter named 'Mountain School Five Processes,' Guo Pu also penned the *Book of Burial* (*Zang shu*) which offers another perspective on the question. In discussing the water and earth mountains designated by trigram-*Kan* and trigram-*Kun*, he explains that 'Venerable earth augments the birth stage of the branch-*Shen*.' At another point, in discussing the mountain designated by trigram-*Gen*, he says, 'Venerable earth augments the branch-*Hai*. Is that not the birth stage of the wood process?' In discussing the mountain designated by trigram-*Sun*, he says, 'Venerable earth augments the branch-*Shen*, the birth stage of the water process.' These are all statements from the work of Guo Pu himself and as such they evidence his use of the great Five Processes system.

Medical texts employ a system of left-side blockages and right-side obstructions to describe the single system of vital breath circulation throughout the body. One inhalation circulates throughout the bones, the tendons, and the hair follicles. If it does not pass through, then an illness arises. Sicknesses caused by left-side blockages do not reach the right side. Sicknesses caused by right-side obstructions do not reach the left side. If the five organs and six viscera are all part of a unitary system, then where is there a boundary that could prevent sicknesses of the left from reaching the right or sicknesses of the right from reaching the left? Although there is only one each of the four other organs, the kidneys number two. The one on the left, serving as the kidney, is the essence of the organ; the one on the right, serving as the fate, is the vital breath of the organ. Because the spirit relies upon vital breath in order to sustain itself (lit. to stand), the kidneys are called the Gates of the Spirit (or Divine Gate). They accompany the water of the stem-*Ren* and the branch-*Zi*. Thus, when a person's essence is corrupted, a left-side blockage will develop. When a person's vital breath is corrupted, a right-side obstruction will arise. Since each of the two kidneys governs its own realm, the diseases caused by one or the other also have a specific side of the body that they affect.

The stem-branch pair stem-*Ren*/branch-*Zi* represents one position. The branch-*Zi* belongs to water, while the stem-*Ren* belongs to fire.

The left kidney accompanies the branch-*Zi*. The right kidney accompanies the stem-*Ren*. The branch-*Zi* and water serve as the essence. The stem-*Ren* and fire serve as the spirit.[146]

The five organs resemble the Five Processes. The six viscera resemble the six spirits. Stem-*Jia* and stem-*Yi* accompany the Green Dragon. Stem-*Bing* and stem-*Ding* accompany the Red Bird. Stem-*Geng* and stem-*Xin* accompany the White Tiger. Stem-*Ren* and stem-*Gui* accompany the Black Warrior. Stem-*Wu*, then, accompanies the Angular Arranger (Gouzhen),[147] while the stem-*Ji* accompanies the Teng Snake.

Since the water trigram-*Kan* receives stem-*Wu* and the fire trigram-*Li* receives stem-*Ji*, there are Five Processes but six spirits and there are five organs but six viscera. From this discussion, it is evident that the explanation concerning stem-*Ren*'s fire and branch-*Zi*'s water has a bearing on the twenty-four positions.

Compilers' Note: Although the explanation expounded in the *Great Compendium of Geo-Principles* (*Dili dacheng*) may have been venerated for generations, it relies on forced logic and as such is not sufficient to wipe out the doubts in people's minds. The *Regulations Governing Gods and Demons* (*Shensha qili*) theory, which holds that the positions of the eight stems follow the transformations of the trigrams, seems at first glance to be reasonable. However, on further examination, the latter argument also proves flawed because it requires that stem-*Ren* not follow the metal process. In doing so, the argument appears to arbitrarily alter its line of reasoning. Furthermore, the way in which it substitutes the lines is an artificial substitution. Upon closer inspection, it becomes clear that the substitutions are not rational or natural and in fact there is no reason why other substitutions than those mentioned could not be made. As for the other theories discussed above, they are little more than alternate versions of what was propounded in the *Great Compendium of Geo-Principles* (*Dili dacheng*).

As for Chu Yong's *Dispelling Doubts* (*Quyi shuo*), it bases its explanation on the Received Stem-*Jia* and Received Notes systems and is therefore far superior to the theories expounded in the other two texts. The explanation proceeds logically from the roots to the tips of the branches. However, one statement it makes about stem-*Gui* belonging to the wood process is without basis.

Compilers' Note: To bury is to conceal in the earth. The vital breath of earth depends upon water for its birth and death. Therefore, the discussions of the standard Five Processes only have reference to the two processes of water and earth. All references to the metal, fire, and wood mountains are only speaking about the apparent forms and are thus not real. This is why they are not used.

The following is an explanation of the Great Plan Five Processes. Water resides in eight positions and earth resides in five. The processes of water and earth alone occupy so many positions. Trigram-*Kan* is water, trigram-*Li* is fire, trigram-*Dui* is metal, trigram-*Zhen* is wood, trigram-*Qian* is metal, and trigram-*Kun* is earth. These are the positions that the *Regulations Governing Gods and Demons (Shensha qili)* claims do not transform. However, the remainder follows the actual Five Processes associated with their directional positions on the basis of abstruse but primordial meaning. Therefore, those could also be said to not transform.

Trigram-*Gen* links branch-*Chou* and branch-*Yin*. Its direction is the beginning vital breath of the wood process. Therefore, trigram-*Gen* is wood. Trigram-*Sun* links branch-*Chen* and branch-*Si*. Its direction is the tail end of the water process. Therefore, trigram-*Sun* is water. Be these as they may, the direction of trigram-*Gen* is originally earth and the direction of trigram-*Sun* is originally wood. Therefore, branch-*Chou* is earth and the branch-*Si* is wood.

Trigram-*Zhen* links stem-*Jia* and stem-*Yi*. Trigram-*Dui* links stem-*Geng* and stem-*Xin*. These are the complete offices of wood and metal, respectively.

Trigram-*Zhen* serves as wood in the sense that wood serves as a process. Its nourishment is always water and the vital breath to which it gives birth is always that of fire. Therefore, it begins in water and ends in fire. Its beginning must derive from the Lake (another name for trigram-*Dui*) of rain and dew. In ending, it inevitably burns itself in fire. Therefore, the stem-*Jia* is water and the stem-*Yi* is fire. Water is that which trigram-*Zhen* takes to act as the dragon. Fire is that which trigram-*Zhen* takes to act as lightning.

Trigram-*Dui* serves as metal in the sense that metal serves as a process. It is the product of water and earth. When water and earth remain together for a sufficiently lengthy period of time, they produce stone. Stone, in its turn, gives birth to metal. When metal is born, a well-spring issues forth. Therefore, it begins in earth and ends in water. Its beginning must be earth. Its ending must be water. Therefore, stem-*Geng* serves as earth and stem-*Xin* serves as water. Its earth is that which trigram-*Dui* takes to act as the hard and crude. Its water is that which trigram-*Dui* takes to act as the Lake.

Trigram-*Kan* links stem-*Ren* and stem-*Gui*. Trigram-*Li* links stem-*Bing* and stem-*Ding*. These are the complete offices of water and fire, respectively.

Trigram-*Kan* serves as water. Among the beasts of the four directions, the direction north claims two; the turtle acts as water and the snake acts as fire. Now, stem-*Ren* is received by trigram-*Li*. Water can be analogized to the water that lies within earth. If it is separated from earth, then it loses its nature. Stem-*Gui* is the water within earth. Therefore, stem-*Ren* serves as fire and stem-*Gui* serves as earth.

Trigram-*Li* serves as fire. Fire can bring metal to completion. Without fire, metal would in the end remain buried in earth. Thus, stem-*Ding* is taken to be the concubine of stem-*Geng* and trigram-*Dui* receives stem-*Ding*. Stem-*Bing* is the sun. Among the eight stems, only stem-*Bing* is suitable enough to be spoken of in the same context as trigram-*Qian* and trigram-*Kun*. Therefore, stem-*Bing* serves as fire and stem-*Ding* serves as metal.

The sun and the moon are in the same category as trigram-*Qian* and trigram-*Kun*. When specifically referring to the sun, stem-*Xin* for its part serves as the moon. The moon serves as water. Thus, stem-*Xin*, without a doubt, is water.

As for the reasoning behind branch-*Yin*'s association with water, it is based on the fact that earth does not completely fill the southeast. The area ranging from the ferry of Splitting Wood (*Ximu*) to trigram-*Sun*'s Doors of Earth is where water accumulates. It is the place that acts as the tail and spinal column. No one knows when it will be drained. Thus, branch-*Yin*, stem-*Jia*, branch-*Chen*, and trigram-*Sun* are all water.

As for the reasoning behind branch-*Hai*'s association with metal, it is based on the fact that heaven does not completely fill the north-west. The area ranging from the mound of the [sage emperor] Shao Hao to branch-*Hai*'s Gates of Heaven is where mountains cluster. Mountains are stone and stone is metal. Thus, trigram-*Dui*, trigram-*Qian*, and branch-*Hai* are all metal.

Metal accumulates in the northwest while water fills the southeast. The ocean is that which all waters venerate and the river is their origin. This is why, in offering sacrifices to waters, one begins with the river and later addresses the ocean. The source of the river proceeds from the position of branch-*Xu* and the Kun Lun mountains. Thus, branch-*Xu* serves as water.

In speaking of the terrestrial Han River, the astronomical office chapter of the *Shiji* says that the river was originally referred to simply as 'water.' The Yellow River Chart attempts to incorporate terrestrial images and says that the essence of the Yellow River is the celestial Han River, i.e. the Milky Way. The astronomical treatise of the *History of the Tang Dynasty* says, 'The Northern Dipper, from trigram-*Qian* looking forward to trigram-*Sun*, constitutes Heaven's Major Regulating Cord. The Cloud River (Milky Way), from trigram-*Kun* looking back-wards to trigram-*Gen*, constitutes Earth's Minor Regulating Cord.'

This being as it is, branch-*Yin* and branch-*Shen* are the respective begin-ning and ending of water. Thus branch-*Yin* serves as water and branch-*Shen* also serves as water. Examining into and setting forth the principles behind these, it becomes evident that they all adhere to mys-terious and primordial concepts; they are genuinely existing principles and are not instances of arbitrary, man-made transformations.

The Buried Dragon and its Transformed Revolution

This section discusses the relationship between the Five-Processes correlates of directions and times. With reference to the twenty-four directions/mountains, this section uses the Great Plan system of Five-Processes correlations. For times, it employs the Received Notes system of Five-Processes correlations. The system posits that an important change of fortune occurs for each mountain on the month in which its process is buried (according to the Triune Harmonies system, but here the earth mountains are considered to be buried with the water process in branch-*Chen*). The relationship between the Received Note process of the year (time) and that of the mountain's burial month (space) determines whether the space-time dynamic will be good, bad, or neutral.

As an example, the three wood mountains represented by trigram-*Zhen*, trigram-*Gen*, and branch-*Si* are subject to an important transformation of fortune each year during the sixth or branch-*Wei* month since the wood process is buried in branch-*Wei*. In a stem-*Jia*/branch-*Zi* year the sixth month is stem-*Xin*/branch-*Wei*. The Received Note process of stem-*Xin*/branch-*Wei* is earth which is to say that the buried revolution of the three wood mountains during this year is earth. The Received Note process of the year, i.e. stem-*Jia*/branch-*Zi*, is metal. Earth produces metal. Therefore, the relationship between the wood mountains and the *Jia-Zi* year is positive.

The *Complete Compendium of Almanacs (Tongshu daquan)* says:

'The Great Plan Five Processes of the twenty-four mountains constitute the original revolutions. For any given year count the stem-branch pairs from the branch-*Zi* month of the preceding year (i.e. the month of the winter solstice) to the month containing the branch in which the mountain is buried. The Received Note processes of the burial stem-branch pairs constitute the transformed revolutions.[148] It is considered fortunate if the Received Note of the Great Year (Taisui) and the Received Note of the buried revolution mutually produce one another. It is even more fortunate if the Received Note of the buried revolution conquers[149] the Received Note of the Great Year (Taisui). The only unfortunate situation occurs when the Received Note of the year, month, day, or hour conquers the Received Note of the buried revolution.

'Water is the standard revolution of the eight mountains designated by stem-*Jia*, branch-*Yin*, branch-*Chen*, trigram-*Sun*, branch-*Xu*, trigram-*Kan*, stem-*Xin*, and branch-*Shen*. Earth is the standard revolution of the five mountains designated by branch-*Chou*, stem-*Gui*, trigram-*Kun*, stem-*Geng*, and branch-*Wei*. The processes water and earth reach the burial stage in branch-*Chen*.

'In stem-*Jia* and stem-*Ji* years, the stem-branch pair is stem-*Wu*/branch-*Chen*, i.e. the wood transformed revolution; be wary of employing a metal year, month, day, or hour.

'In stem-*Yi* and stem-*Geng* years, the stem-branch pair is stem-*Geng*/branch-*Chen* and the metal revolution; be wary of employing a fire year, month, day, or hour.

In stem-*Bing* and stem-*Xin* years, the stem-branch pair is stem-*Ren*/branch-*Chen* and the water revolution; be wary of employing an earth year, month, day, or hour.

In stem-*Ding* and stem-*Ren* years, the stem-branch pair is stem-*Jia*/branch-*Chen* and the fire revolution; be wary of employing a water year, month, day, or hour.

'In stem-*Wu* and stem-*Gui* years, the stem-branch pair is stem-*Bing*/branch-*Chen* and the earth revolution; be wary of employing a wood year, month, day, or hour.

'Fire is the standard revolution of the four mountains designated by trigram-*Li*, stem-*Ren*, stem-*Bing*, and stem-*Yi*. The process fire reaches the burial stage in branch-*Xu*.

'In stem-*Jia* and stem-*Ji* years, the stem-branch pair is stem-*Jia*/branch-*Xu* and the fire revolution; be wary of employing a water year, month, day, or hour.

'In stem-*Yi* and stem-*Geng* years, the stem-branch pair is stem-*Bing*/branch-*Xu* and the earth revolution; be wary of employing a wood year, month, day, or hour.

'In stem-*Bing* and stem-*Xin* years, the stem-branch pair is stem-*Wu*/branch-*Xu* and the wood revolution; be wary of employing a metal year, month, day, or hour.

'In stem-*Ding* and stem-*Ren* years, the stem-branch pair is stem-*Geng*/branch-*Xu* and the metal revolution; be wary of employing a fire year, month, day, or hour.

'In stem-*Wu* and stem-*Gui* years, the stem-branch pair is stem-*Ren*/branch-*Xu* and the water revolution; be wary of employing an earth year, month, day, or hour.

'Wood is the standard revolution of the three mountains designated by trigram-*Zhen*, trigram-*Gen*, and branch-*Si*. The process wood reaches the burial stage in branch-*Wei*.

'In stem-*Jia* and stem-*Ji* years, the stem-branch pair is stem-*Xin*/branch-

Wei and the earth revolution; be wary of employing a wood year, month, day, or hour.

'In stem-*Yi* and stem-*Geng* years, the stem-branch pair is stem-*Gui*/branch-*Wei* and the wood revolution; be wary of employing a metal year, month, day, or hour.

'In stem-*Bing* and stem-*Xin* years, the stem-branch pair is stem-*Yi*/branch-*Wei* and the metal revolution; be wary of employing a fire year, month, day, or hour.

In stem-*Ding* and stem-*Ren* years, the stem-branch pair is stem-*Ding*/branch-*Wei* and the water revolution; be wary of employing an earth year, month, day, or hour.

'In stem-*Wu* and stem-*Gui* years, the stem-branch pair is stem-*Ji*/branch-*Wei* and the fire revolution; be wary of employing a water year, month, day, or hour.

'Metal is the standard revolution of the four mountains designated by trigram-*Qian*, branch-*Hai*, trigram-*Dui*, and stem-*Ding*. The process metal reaches the burial stage in branch-*Chou*.

'In stem-*Jia* and stem-*Ji* years, the stem-branch pair is stem-*Yi*/branch-*Chou* and the metal revolution; be wary of employing a fire year, month, day, or hour. After the winter solstice, the stem-branch pair is stem-*Ding*/branch-*Chou* and the water revolution; be wary of employing an earth year, month, day, or hour.

'In stem-*Yi* and stem-*Geng* years, the stem-branch pair is stem-*Ding*/branch-*Chou* and the water revolution; be wary of employing an earth year, month, day, or hour. After the winter solstice, the stem-branch pair is stem-*Ji*/branch-*Chou* and the fire revolution; be wary of employing a water year, month, day, or hour.

'In stem-*Bing* and stem-*Xin* years, the stem-branch pair is stem-*Ji*/branch-*Chou* and the fire revolution; be wary of employing a water year, month, day, or hour. After the winter solstice, the stem-branch pair is stem-*Xin*/branch-*Chou* and the earth revolution; be wary of employing a wood year, month, day, or hour.

'In stem-*Ding* and stem-*Ren* years, the stem-branch pair is stem-*Xin*/branch-*Chou* and the earth revolution; be wary of employing a wood year, month, day, or hour. After the winter solstice, the stem-

Figure 33 The Buried Dragon and its Transformed Revolution

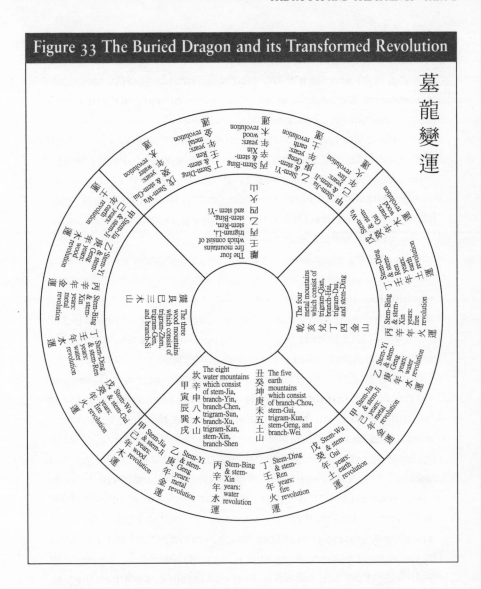

branch pair is stem-*Gui*/branch-*Chou* and the wood revolution; be wary of employing a metal year, month, day, or hour.

'In stem-*Wu* and stem-*Gui* years, the stem-branch pair is stem-*Gui*/branch-*Chou* and the wood revolution; be wary of employing a metal year, month, day, or hour. After the winter solstice, the stem-branch pair is stem-*Yi*/branch-*Chou* and the metal revolution; be wary of employing a fire year, month, day, or hour.'

Compilers' Note: The Buried Dragon is the burial/stored stage of the Great Plan Five Processes correlate of whatever mountain may be in question. The transformed revolution is the Received Note of the burial/storage position that is under discussion. It transforms in accordance with the revolution of the year. 'Using the primordially hidden five branch-*Zi*' is similar to the concept of how the seven governors (i.e. sun, moon, and five visible planets) are calculated commencing from the winter solstice. The previous year's winter solstice belongs to the current year and the current year's winter solstice belongs to the following year. The revolutions of heaven and earth all begin from branch-*Zi*. Thus, the primordially hidden five branch-*Zi* begins with the branch-*Zi* month and ends with the branch-*Hai* month. The four seasons are thus united in one year. After the winter solstice, in the branch-*Chou*, or second, lunar month, the lord of the year will not yet have changed, but the buried revolution will already have altered. Branch-*Chou* is the burial place of the metal process. Therefore, the buried revolution of the metal mountains changes again after the winter solstice.

Take as an example the mountain designated by the stem-*Jia*. Its standard revolution belongs to the water process. The water process is buried in branch-*Chen*. In stem-*Jia* and stem-*Ji* years, the primordially hidden five branch-*Zi* start from the stem-branch pair stem-*Jia*/branch-*Zi*. Counting forwards from there, one obtains for the branch-*Chen* the stem-branch pair stem-*Wu*/branch-*Chen*. The Received Note of the pair stem-*Wu*/branch-*Chen* belongs to the wood process. Therefore, this is the wood revolution.

The mountain designated by trigram-*Qian* belongs to the metal process. The metal process is buried in branch-*Chou*. In stem-*Jia* and stem-*Ji* years, the primordially hidden five branch-*Zi* again start from the pair stem-*Jia*/branch-*Zi*. Counting forwards from there, one obtains for the branch-*Chou* the pair stem-*Yi*/branch-*Chou*. The Received Note of the pair stem-*Yi*/branch-*Chou* belongs to the metal process. Therefore, this is the metal revolution. After the winter solstice, the year belongs to the category of stem-*Yi* and stem-*Geng* years. Employing the primordially hidden five branch-*Zi* of stem-*Yi* and stem-*Geng* years, one starts counting forward from the pair stem-*Bing*/branch-*Zi*. Counting forward from there, one obtains for the branch-*Chou* the pair stem-*Ding*/branch-*Chou*. Alternatively, one can use the primordially hidden five branch-*Zi* for the stem-*Jia* and stem-*Ji* year and count forward from the pair stem-*Jia*/branch-*Zi* through to the pair stem-*Yi*/branch-*Hai* and beyond to the branch-*Chou* again and one will still obtain the pair stem-*Ding*/branch-*Chou*. The Received Note of the pair stem-*Ding*/branch-*Chou* belongs to the water process. Therefore, this is the water process. The remainder is extrapolated according to this formula.

The Year or Month Conquers the Mountain School

The *Complete Compendium of Almanacs* (*Tongshu daquan*) says:

'With respect to the Transformed Revolutions of the Buried Dragons that pertain to the twenty-four mountains in a given year, if the process indicated by the revolution of a given mountain is conquered by the process indicated by the Received Note of the year or month's stem-branch pair, then it is said that the year or the month conquers that mountain. This convention is only discussed in connection with newly built domestic residences or newly established graves. It is not considered in connection with rebuilding or refurbishing work that does not move the ground foundation nor does it apply to additions made to an existing gravesite.

'Take for example the year with the stem-branch pair stem-*Jia*/branch-*Zi*. The Received Note of this pair belongs to the metal process. In such a year, the buried revolution of the water and earth mountains has the stem-branch pair stem-*Wu*/branch-*Chen*, which belongs to the wood process. In this case, the buried revolution of wood is conquered by the metal Received Note of the year. Therefore, this year conquers the eight water mountains designated by the stem-*Jia*, the branch-*Yin*, the branch-*Chen*, trigram-*Sun*, the branch-*Xu*, trigram-*Kan*, the stem-*Xin*, and the branch-*Shen*. The year also conquers the five earth mountains designated by the branch-*Chou*, the stem-*Gui*, trigram-*Kun*, the stem-*Geng*, and the branch-*Wei*.

'In the year designated by the stem-branch pair stem-*Jia*/branch-*Zi*, the Received note of the months with the stem-branch designations stem-

Bing/branch-*Yin* (1st lunar month), stem-*Ding*/branch-*Mao* (2nd lunar month), stem-*Jia*/branch-*Xu* (9th lunar month), and stem-*Yi*/branch-*Hai* (10th lunar month) all belong to the fire process. In this year, the buried revolutions of the metal mountains have the stem-branch pair stem-*Yi*/branch-*Chou*, which belongs to metal. Since the metal buried revolution of these metal mountains is conquered by the fire Received Note of the said months, it is said that the first (i.e. stem-*Bing*/branch-*Yin*), the second (*Ding*/branch-*Mao*), the ninth (*Jia*/branch-*Xu*), and the tenth (*Yi*/branch-*Hai*) months conquer the four metal mountains designated by trigram-*Qian*, the branch-*Hai*, trigram-*Dui*, and the stem-*Ding*.

'The Received Note of the months with the stem-branch designations stem-*Wu*/branch-*Chen* (3rd lunar month) and stem-*Ji*/branch-*Si* (4th lunar month) belongs to wood. In this year, the stem-branch designation of the buried revolution of the wood mountains is stem-*Xin*/branch-*Wei*, which belongs to the earth process. Thus, the wood Received Note of the 3rd and 4th lunar months conquers the earth buried revolution of the three wood mountains designated by trigram-*Zhen*, trigram-*Gen*, and the branch-*Si*.

'The Received Note of the months with the stem-branch designations stem-*Geng*/branch-*Wu* (5th lunar month) and stem-*Xin*/branch-*Wei* (6th lunar month) belongs to earth. In this year none of the twenty-four mountains exhibit the water process revolution, water being the process that is conquered by earth. Therefore, these months do not conquer any mountains.

'The received note of the months with the stem-branch designations stem-*Ren*/branch-*Shen* (7th lunar month) and stem-*Gui*/branch-*You* (8th lunar month) belongs to metal. Since this is the same as the Received Note of the year, these months also conquer the water and earth mountains.

'The Received Note of the months with the stem-branch designations stem-*Bing*/branch-*Zi* (11th lunar month) and stem-*Ding*/branch-*Chou* (12th lunar month) belongs to water. In this year, the stem-branch designation of the buried revolution of the fire mountains is stem-*Jia*/branch-*Xu*, which belongs to the fire process. Thus, the water Received Note of the 11th and 12th lunar months conquers the fire buried revolution of the four fire mountains designated by trigram-*Li*, the stem-*Ren*, the stem-*Bing*, and the stem-*Yi*.

'Another example is the year designated by the stem-branch pair stem-*Ren*/branch-*Shen*. The Received Note of this pair, like that of the year stem-*Jia*/branch-*Zi*, is metal. However, during the stem-*Ren*/branch-*Shen* year, none of the twenty-four mountains manifest the wood revolution. It is only after the winter solstice that the buried revolution of the metal mountains produces the stem-branch pair stem-*Gui*/branch-*Chou*, the Received Note of which is wood. Thus, the stem-*Ren*/branch-*Shen* year does not conquer any of the twenty-four mountains until, after the winter solstice, the year conquers the four metal mountains designated by trigram-*Qian*, the branch-*Hai*, trigram-*Dui*, and the stem-*Ding*.

'The "Days or Hours Conquering the Mountains" School follows the same methodology. The school that derives the mountain from the year or month, employs the primordially hidden five branch-*Zi* of the year and calculates to the Received Note of one of the four burial branches of branch-*Chou*, branch-*Chen*, branch-*Wei*, and branch-*Xu*. This determines if the Received Note of the stem-branch pair is conquered by the Received Note of the year or month. The grave is the grave of whatever mountain is under discussion. Thus, they arrive at the conclusion about whether the year or month conquers a given mountain. Within the transformed revolution of the Buried Dragon system, they calculate the misfortunate nature from the mountain, while the year or month conquers the Mountain School calculates from the year or month to determine which mountain is conquered. They both derive the same conclusion from different angles but are based on the same principle.[150]

The Correlation between the Twenty-Four Directional Positions and the Twenty-Four Seasonal Nodes

The Beginning of Spring (node) corresponds with trigram-*Gen*.[151]

The Rain Water (node) corresponds with the branch-*Yin*.

The Awakening of Insects (node) corresponds with the stem-*Jia*.

The Spring Equinox (node) corresponds with trigram-*Zhen*.

The Clear Bright (*qingming*) (node) corresponds with the stem-*Yi*.

The Rain of the Grains (node) corresponds with the branch-*Chen*.

The Beginning of Summer (node) corresponds with trigram-*Sun*.

The Lesser Fullness (node) corresponds with the branch-*Si*.

The Grain in Ear (node) corresponds with the stem-*Bing*.

The Summer Solstice (node) corresponds with trigram-*Li*.

The Lesser Heat (node) corresponds with the stem-*Ding*.

The Greater Heat (node) corresponds with the branch-*Wei*.

The Beginning of Autumn (node) corresponds with trigram-*Kun*.

Figure 34 The Correlation between the Twenty-Four Directional Positions and the Twenty-Four Seasonal Nodes

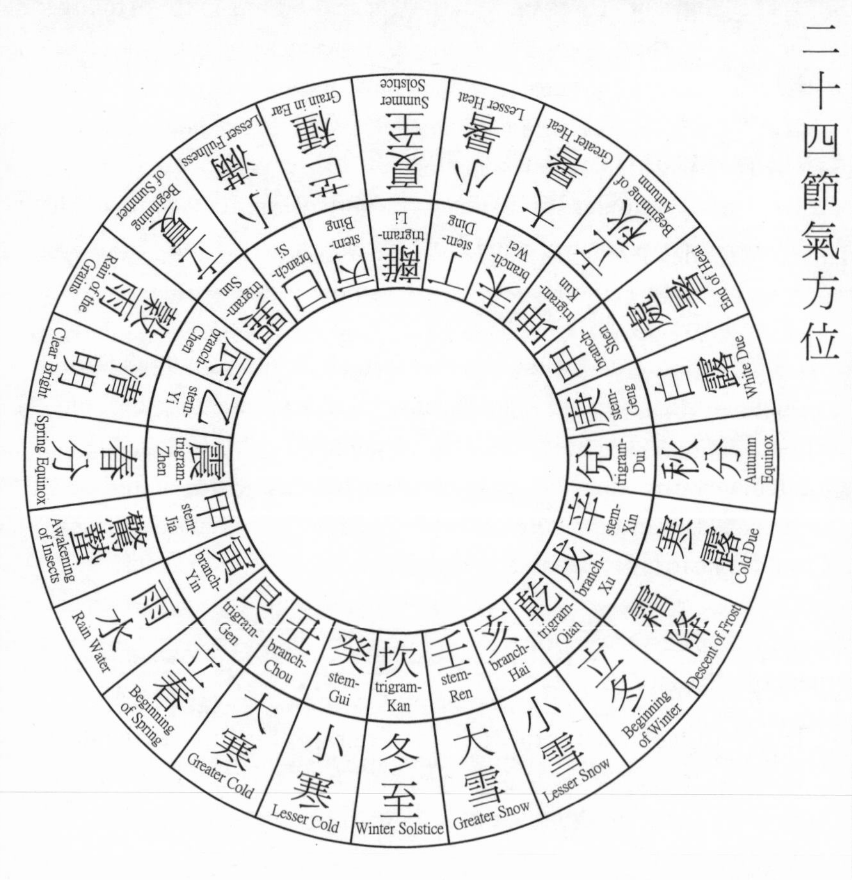

The End of Heat (node) corresponds with the branch-*Shen*.

The White Due (node) corresponds with the stem-*Geng*.

The Autumn Equinox (node) corresponds with trigram-*Dui*.

The Cold Due (node) corresponds with the stem-*Xin*.

The Descent of Frost (node) corresponds with the branch-*Xu*.

The Beginning of Winter (node) corresponds with trigram-*Qian*.

The Lesser Snow (node) corresponds with the branch-*Hai*.

The Greater Snow (node) corresponds with the stem-*Ren*.

The Winter Solstice (node) corresponds with trigram-*Kan*.

The Lesser Cold (node) corresponds with the stem-*Gui*.

The Greater Cold (node) corresponds with the branch-*Chou*.

The four seasonal beginning nodes, the two equinox nodes, and the two solstice nodes directly correspond to the eight trigrams. These correspondences are the inspiration behind the system of the Mysterious Gates of the Eight Nodes and the Nine Offices.

The Eight Trigram's Received Stem-*Jia* and Triune Harmony Associations

This section describes the relationship between each of the twenty-four mountains and the eight trigrams. Each trigram is associated with one of the eight Heavenly Stem mountains as dictated by the Received Stem-*Jia* system. In addition, the trigrams occupying the cardinal positions govern three branches according to the Triune Harmonies system. As a result, the cardinal position trigrams each govern three branch mountains and one stem mountain, while the inter-cardinal trigrams govern only their own trigram mountain and one stem mountain. This system is applied to the Lesser Roaming Year Trigram Transformations described in the next section. That system assigns rotating Five Processes associations to each of the eight trigrams, which are subsequently applied to each of the twenty-four mountains through the use of this system of associations.

Trigram-*Qian* receives the stem-*Jia*. Trigram-*Kan* receives the stem-*Gui*, the branch-*Shen*, and the branch-*Chen*. Trigram-*Gen* receives the stem-*Bing*. Trigram-*Zhen* receives the stem-*Geng*, the branch-*Hai*, and the branch-*Wei*. Trigram-*Sun* receives the stem-*Xin*.

Trigram-*Li* receives the stem-*Ren*, the branch-*Yin*, and the branch-*Xu*. Trigram-*Kun* receives the stem-*Yi*. Trigram-*Dui* receives the stem-*Ding*, the branch-*Si*, and the branch-*Chou*.

Trigram-*Kan* and trigram-*Li* do not receive stem-*Wu* and stem-*Ji* because the twenty-four mountains do not contain stem-*Wu* or stem-*Ji*. Therefore, instead of receiving the stem-*Ji*, trigram-*Li* receives trigram-*Qian*'s stem-*Ren*. Similarly, instead of receiving stem-*Wu*, trigram-*Kan* receives trigram-*Kun*'s stem-*Gui*. The origin of this method is unknown.

Compilers' Note: The '*Qimeng fulun*' or 'Premier Appendix' says:

'The form of fire is yin. However, the function of fire is yang and heaven uses fire. Therefore, the central line of trigram-*Qian* (heaven) is replaced with the central line of trigram-*Kun* (earth) to produce trigram-*Li* (fire).

'The form of water is yang. However, the function of water is yin and earth uses water. Therefore, the central line of trigram-*Kun* (earth) is replaced with the central line of trigram-*Qian* (heaven) to produce trigram-*Kan* (water).'

This clearly demonstrates that trigram-*Kan* and trigram-*Li* receiving stem-*Wu* and stem-*Ji* is a tradition of the Former Heaven, while trigram-*Li* receiving stem-*Ren* and trigram-*Kan* receiving stem-*Gui* is a usage of the Latter Heaven.

The four cardinal trigrams each receive two of eight branches. These two branches together with the branch originally associated with the position of the trigram constitute the Triune Harmony offices.[152]

The geomancers' 'mountain seat,' 'nine stars,' 'pure yin,' and 'pure yang' conventions are all derived from this concept.

The Lesser Roaming Year Trigram Transformations

The Lesser and Greater Roaming Year trigram transformations form the subject matter of the remainder of the Treatise. The two systems correlate the trigrams of the eight directions with trigrams associated with different years. The term 'Roaming Year' refers to the fact that one of the eight trigrams is believed to govern the general fortune of any given year. The stem-branch pair

Figure 35 The Triune Harmonies of the Eight Trigrams' Received Stem-*Jia*

that designates the year determines which of the eight trigrams governs that year. The trigram designation of a year is believed to have a unique relationship with each of the trigrams associated with the eight directions. Both the Greater and Lesser Roaming Year trigram transformation systems employ the Latter Heaven arrangement for correlating trigrams with directions. To determine the nature of the relationship between the year and a direction, one looks at which lines of the annual trigram must be altered, if any, in order to 'transform' it into the trigram of the direction in question. The annual trigram will always be identical to one of the eight directional trigrams, which is considered the base trigram.

The first transformation technique is termed 'Lesser' because it was originally only used for funerary *feng shui*. Because burial sites are considered yin, which is inferior to yang, this transformation technique is referred to as 'Lesser.' The Greater Roaming Year trigram transformation system was used primarily for yang residences, or homes of the living, and is therefore called 'Greater.' One must not conclude from this that residential *feng shui* is considered more important than funerary *feng shui* in China. In fact, quite the opposite is true. Thus, 'Greater' and 'Lesser' here refer only to the yin or yang nature of the site to which these techniques are applied.

Beginning from the base trigram there are seven possibile ways to alter its constituent lines to produce all of the seven other trigrams. If we employ the Lesser Roaming Year transformation order and use trigram-*Kun* ☷ as the base, the possibilities are: (1) top line *Gen* ☶; (2) top line and middle line *Sun* ☴; (3) top line, middle line, and bottom line *Qian* ☰; (4) top line and bottom line *Li* ☲; (5) bottom line *Zhen* ☳; (6) middle line and bottom line *Dui* ☱; and (7) middle line *Kan* ☵. If we consider these line changes from each trigram to the one following, we see that the pattern is top, middle, bottom, middle, top, middle, bottom, i.e. from *Kun* **to** *Gen* the top line changes; from *Gen* to *Sun* the middle line changes; from *Sun* to *Qian* the bottom line changes, etc.

From at least the Tang dynasty, these seven alterations came to be associated with the seven stars of the Big Dipper which, as we saw earlier, has always been regarded as a very important grouping of stars in Chinese astrology. The Roaming Year systems refer to the trigrams produced by these line transformations using the esoteric Daoist names of the Dipper's stars rather than their standard astronomical names. Those names are, in order: (1) Voracious Wolf (Corrupted); (2) Giant Gates; (3) Prosperous Existence (Wealth); (4) Lettered Composition (Civil); (5) Incorruptible (Virtuous); (6) Martial Composition; and (7) Destroyed Army (Defeat). The name 'Servants' is used to designate the base trigram. Considered by themselves, these names seem somewhat arbitrary, but when they are arranged in their order as if around an open court, an interesting pattern appears, (above right).

Traditionally in China the left-hand side, which lay to the east of the south-facing emperor was considered the position of honor because east signified growth, life and development (yang). By contrast, the west was associated with military activity, autumn, and death (yin). Since Confucian government favored the civil over the military, civil officials always stood to the east or left of the emperor. In the table we see that each item stands across

West	Virtuous	East
Martial		Civil
Defeat		Wealth
Servants		Gates
	Corrupted	

from its conceptual opposite. Not too much should be made of this pattern, however, since the connotations of these names do not actually play out in the divinatory interpretations of the stars.

Both systems of trigram transformations rely on complementary groups of four trigrams to determine whether the relationship between year and direction is positive or negative. The 'Lesser' Roaming Year trigram transformations divide the trigrams into two groups of four on the basis of their numerical yin or yang nature. This is determined by the Luo River Diagram numbers as paired with the Former Heaven arrangement of trigrams. In that arrangement trigrams *qian*, *kun*, *kan*, and *li* are paired with odd numbers and are therefore considered yang trigrams. Conversely, the yin trigrams are *Zhen*, *Gen*, *Dui*, and *Sun*. According to the Lesser Roaming Year trigram transformations, if one starts from a yin base trigram, then the four yang trigrams will be considered lucky, whereas the yin trigrams are lucky when a yang trigram is used as the base.

The Greater Roaming Year trigram transformation system differs in that it bases its groups of four on the sets of greater yin/yang and lesser yin/yang. According to the Former Heaven arrangement of trigrams, those trigrams in which the bottom two lines are both yang ⚌ are considered greater yang. Those in which the two bottom lines are yin ⚏ are considered greater yin. Thus trigrams *Qian* ☰ and *Dui* ☱ are greater yang, while *Kun* ☷ and *Gen* ☶ are greater yin. These four greater yin and yang trigrams constitute one complementary group known as the 'western four positions.' The four lesser yin and yang trigrams – *Li* ☲, *Zhen* ☳, *Sun* ☴, and *Kan* ☵ – are grouped together as the 'eastern four positions.' In contrast to the Lesser Roaming Year system, the Greater Roaming Year trigram transformation system asserts that if one starts from a western trigram base, then the four western positions will be lucky while the four eastern positions will be unlucky and vice versa.

Because the two Roaming Year systems use different sets of four, they also assign star names to the trigram transformation stages in different ways. Both systems agree that the annual base trigram and the corresponding directional trigram are regarded as the 'Servants,' position. This does not correspond to an actual star in the Big Dipper, which has only seven stars. Both systems also agree on the designations for the three stars 'Corrupted,' 'Civil,' and 'Defeat.' These stars are said to apply to the following three transformations from the base trigram: top line, top & bottom line, and middle line. With regard to the remaining transformation stages and star names, the two systems are in disagreement. The comparison is best considered in the form of a table. (overleaf)

Although they attribute star names to trigram transformations differently, both systems agree that the three stars 'Corrupted,' 'Gates,' and 'Martial' form a group known as the Three Luckies. The Qing dynasty compilers highlight a great deal of confusion surrounding which fourth transformation the Greater and Lesser systems regarded as lucky, if any. Generally speaking, the Lesser Roaming Year system regards 'Virtuous' as the fourth lucky star, while the Greater Roaming Year assigns this status to the base trigram, i.e. 'Servants.' These attributions are based on the two groups of four trigrams described above.

Because the Lesser Roaming Year trigram transformation system is used to identify burial sites, it places primary emphasis on beneficial orientation vis-à-vis the external environment. Therefore, the base trigram resonates positively with the group of four trigrams that complement itself. In other words, if the base trigram is numerically yang (odd), then the four yin trigram positions will be considered lucky. In selecting burial sites, *feng shui* experts have considerably more geographical freedom than they do with residences. Chinese normally bury their dead in scattered plots among the hills and fields, not in concentrated cemeteries as in the West. Consequently, when looking for a burial site, the *feng shui* specialist roams far and wide to find a location that is properly aligned with the surrounding landscape features. In matching the external features to the internal grave the key consideration is that the other (external) be the complementary opposite of the self (internal), i.e. yang should face yin and vice versa.

An example will help to clarify this. The compilers of the Treatise discuss later in the text a system known as mountain and the zodiac. This system holds

Comparison of Names Affiliated with the Stars of the Big Dipper and Roaming Year Line Transformations

Esoteric name/ Standard name/ Ursa Majoris	Lesser line changes/ Auspices/ Alternate name	Greater line changes/ Auspices/ Alternate name
1. Corrupted	Top	Top
Celestial pivot	Lucky	Lucky
UMa α	Birth of breath	Birth of breath
2. Gates	Top, mid	Mid, bot
Celestial gear	Lucky	Lucky
UMa β	Celestial healing	Celestial healing
3. Wealth	Top, mid, bot	Bot
Celestial cog	Unlucky	Unlucky
UMa γ	End of body	Calamity & harm
4. Civil	Top, bot	Top, bot
Celestial post	Unlucky	Unlucky
UMa δ	Roaming soul	Six killers
5. Virtuous	Bot	Top, mid
Celestial beam	Unlucky	Unlucky
UMa ε	Five ghosts	Five ghosts
6. Martial	Mid, bot	Top, mid, bot
Opening yang	Lucky	Lucky
UMa ζ	Joy & virtue	Extended year
7. Defeat	Middle	Middle
Wavering light	Unlucky	Unlucky
UMa η	End of body	End of fate
8. Servants	None	None
	Unlucky	Lucky

that the trigram that stands opposite from the branch of the year is to be considered the base trigram. In the year *Jia-Zi* the trigram-*Li* ☲ will serve as base because branch-*Zi* correlates with trigram-*Kan* ☵ and stands opposite trigram-*Li*. If one follows the Lesser Roaming Year trigram transformations with trigram-*Li* as the base, then the three lucky trigrams will be *Zhen* ☳ as 'Corrupted,' *Dui* as 'Gates,' and *Sun* ☴ as 'Martial.' Trigram-*Li* is numerically yang and thus it is fortunate for this poition to face the numerically yin positions of *Zhen*, *Dui*, and *Sun*. This system further divides the eight trigrams among the twenty-four mountains and so the Three Harmonies branches and Received Stem-*Jia* stems follow their associated trigrams. Trigram-*Zhen* receives the stem-*Geng* and the branches *Wei* and *Hai*. Therefore, those mountains are also identified as the 'Corrupted' star and are thus lucky orientations.

The Greater Roaming Year trigram transformations are applied to residential *feng shui*. In this case, the primary emphasis is on harmonizing the internal elements of the residence with one another. A major reason for this is practical. Although the *feng shui* master is free to search the wilds for a suitable burial site, the location of a home is normally determined by practical considerations. Especially in towns and cities, families rarely have the freedom to choose a location for a house at will. Given these constraints, the *feng shui* expert shifts emphasis to the arrangement of what lies within the home. Furthermore, where a burial site serves only one function and one individual, residences are normally occupied by several individuals and contain various rooms that serve different functions. Naturally in this case the goal of *feng shui* treatment stresses the harmonizing of these various individuals and room functions.

Because residential *feng shui* emphasizes internal harmonizing, the Greater Roaming Year trigram transformation system requires that like be grouped with like. In applying this system to *feng shui* treatments, the specialist considers the year in which the house was built, the year of birth of the head of household, or the position occupied by the main door of the house. Consider for example a residence in which the head of household was born in a year governed by the trigram-*Qian* ☰, which is a greater yang trigram. Following the Greater Roaming Year line transformations, the three remaining greater yang trigrams will obtain the three lucky positions, i.e. *Dui* ☱ 'Corrupted,' *Gen* ☶ 'Gates,' and *Kun* ☷ 'Martial.' These three positions, together with *Qian* as the base trigram, or 'Servants,' are none other than the four western positions. In this case these four positions constitute the lucky parts of the home.

In the *Qingnang jing* or *Green Satchel Classic*,[153] the Lesser Roaming Year transformations are referred to as the nine luminaries.[154] This system is also called 'transmuting the trigrams.' The set of transmutations that start from trigram-*Qian* are the Father Heaven trigrams, while those that start from trigram-*Kun* are the Mother Earth trigrams. All of the transmutations are alterations that proceed forth from the trigrams as fixed by heaven. The geomancers' 'pure yin,' 'pure yang,' 'three luckies,' 'six elegants,' 'eight nobles,' and 'twelve lucky dragons' conventions all originated from this system. However, later generations borrowed the tradition and used it in determining the outcome of engagements of young men and women. Therefore, it is called the 'Roaming Year.' Since there is another technique pertaining to residences of living people that is also known as the 'Roaming Year trigram transformations,' the present example is known as the 'Lesser Roaming Year.'

The method orders its nine elements as follows: the Voracious Wolf, the Giant Gates, the Prosperous Existence, the Lettered Composition, the Incorruptible, the Martial Composition, the Destroyed Army, the Aide of the Left, and the Assistant of the Right.

When the nine elements are spoken of in connection with the eight trigrams, the Aide of the Left and the Assistant of the Right together constitute one palace.

When the nine elements are spoken of in connection with the nine palaces,[155] the Voracious Wolf is the number 1, the color white, and belongs to the water process; the Giant Gates is the number 2, the color black, and belongs to the earth process; the Prosperous Existence is the number 3 and the color emerald; the Lettered Composition is the number 4, the color green, and belongs to the wood process; the Incorruptible is the number 5, the color yellow, and belongs to the earth process; the Martial Composition is the number 6 and the color white; the Destroyed Army is the number 7, the color red, and belongs to the metal process; the Aide of the Left is the number 8, the color white, and belongs to the earth process; and the Assistant of the Right is the number nine, the color purple, and belongs to the fire process.

When the nine elements are spoken of in connection with the five stars, the Voracious Wolf is the 'Birth of Vital Breath' and belongs to the wood star (Jupiter); the Giant Gates is the 'Heavenly Physician'; the Prosperous Existence is the 'Termination of the Body' and belongs to the earth star (Saturn); the Lettered Composition is the 'Roaming Soul' and belongs to the water star (Mercury); the Incorruptible is the 'Five Ghosts' and belongs to the fire star (Mars); the Martial Composition is the 'Blessing and Virtue'; the Destroyed Army is the 'Termination of the Fate' and belongs to the metal star (Venus); the Aide and the Assistant follow the original palace in lacking a focused belonging.

Because it begins its computations from the perspective of dragons, the Geomancy School considers the Voracious Wolf, the Giant Gates, the Martial Composition, and the Incorruptible to be fortunate, whereas it regards the Prosperous Existence, the Lettered Composition, the Destroyed Army, and the Aide and the Assistant to be unfortunate. Because it begins its computations from the perspective of orientations, the Selection School, by contrast, regards the Voracious Wolf, the Giant Gates, the Martial Composition, and the Lettered Composition to be fortunate, whereas it regards the Prosperous Existence, the Incorruptible, the Destroyed Army, and the Aide and the Assistant to be unfortunate. They derive these differing conclusions on the basis of different trigrams. Examples of all of these are set forth in detail below.

The Heaven-Fixed Trigrams

The Heaven-Fixed Trigram arrangement places in a horizontal line on the bottom the four yang trigrams of the Latter Heaven, i.e. trigram-*Qian*, trigram-*Gen*, trigram-*Kan*, and trigram-*Zhen*. It places in a horizontal line on the top the four yin trigrams of the Latter Heaven, i.e. trigram-*Li*, trigram-*Sun*, trigram-*Kun*, and trigram-*Dui*. According to the production ordering of the Former Heaven, trigram-*Qian* and trigram-*Dui* are paired,[156] as are trigram-*Li* and trigram-*Zhen*, trigram-*Sun* and trigram-*Kan*, and trigram-*Gen* and trigram-*Kun*. To effect the transmutations, one begins from one

Figure 36 The Heaven-Fixed Trigrams

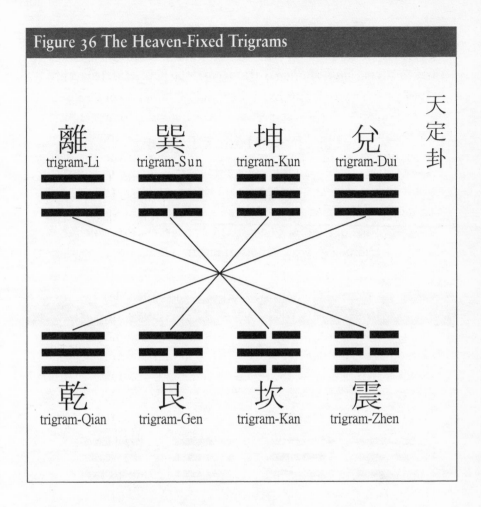

palace (i.e. trigram) and proceeds to its partner and moves in order from one trigram above to another trigram below. If one begins with one of the central trigrams, then one will conclude with a central trigram. If one begins with a peripheral trigram, then one will conclude with a peripheral trigram.

Compilers' Note: The Heaven-Fixed Trigram arrangement merely takes the transformation of the upper line of the initial trigram as an appropriate transmutation. If one examines into the matter, it becomes clear that trigram-*Qian* and trigram-*Zhen* can reside in the center and trigram-*Gen* and trigram-*Kan* on the periphery. Also, the yang trigrams can reside above and the yin trigrams below. Such alternate versions of the diagram would not affect the system. The *Great Compendium of Geo-Principles* (*Dili dacheng*) contains three other alternate versions of these. Thus, the given arrangement is not necessarily fixed in form.

The Heaven Father Trigrams

The Heaven Father Trigrams begin their transmutations from trigram-*Qian* (i.e. heaven). The transmutations alternate from upper, to middle, to lower, back to middle, and again to upper. Transforming the upper line of trigram-*Qian* produces trigram-*Dui*, which thus acts as the Voracious Wolf. Transforming the middle line of trigram-

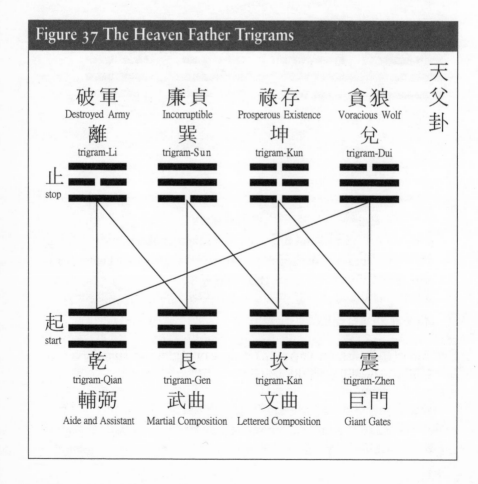

Figure 37 The Heaven Father Trigrams

Dui produces trigram-*Zhen*, which acts as the Giant Gates. Transforming the lower line of trigram-*Zhen* produces trigram-*Kun*, which acts as the Prosperous Existence. Transforming the middle line of trigram-*Kun* produces trigram-*Kan*, which acts as the Lettered Composition. Transforming the upper line of trigram-*Kan* produces trigram-*Sun*, which acts as the Incorruptible. Transforming the middle line of trigram-*Sun* produces trigram-*Gen*, which acts as the Martial Composition. Transforming the lower line of trigram-*Gen* produces trigram-*Li*, which acts as the Destroyed Army. Transforming the middle line of trigram-*Li* produces once again trigram-*Qian*, which acts as the Aide and Assistant. This is an instance of beginning from the periphery and concluding with the periphery.

The Earth Mother Trigrams

The Earth Mother Trigrams begin their transmutations from trigram-*Kun* (i.e. earth). Transforming the upper line of trigram-*Kun* produces trigram-*Gen*, which thus acts as the Voracious Wolf. Transforming the middle line of trigram-*Gen* produces trigram-*Sun*, which acts as the Giant Gates. Transforming the lower line of trigram-*Sun* produces trigram-*Qian*, which acts as the Prosperous Existence. Transforming the middle line of trigram-*Qian* produces trigram-*Li*, which acts as the Lettered Composition. Transforming the upper line of trigram-*Li* produces trigram-*Zhen*, which acts as the Incorruptible. Transforming the middle line of trigram-*Zhen* produces trigram-*Dui*, which acts as the Martial Composition. Transforming the lower line of trigram-*Dui* produces trigram-*Kan*, which acts as the Destroyed Army. Transforming the middle line of trigram-*Kan* produces once again trigram-*Kun*, which acts as the Aide and Assistant. This is an instance of beginning from the center and concluding with the center.

Compilers' Note: The *Qingnang jing* or *Green Satchel Classic*'s diagram of the great primordial and terminal changes takes trigram-*Kun* as the original palace and says of it by means of explanation,

Figure 38 The Earth Mother Trigrams

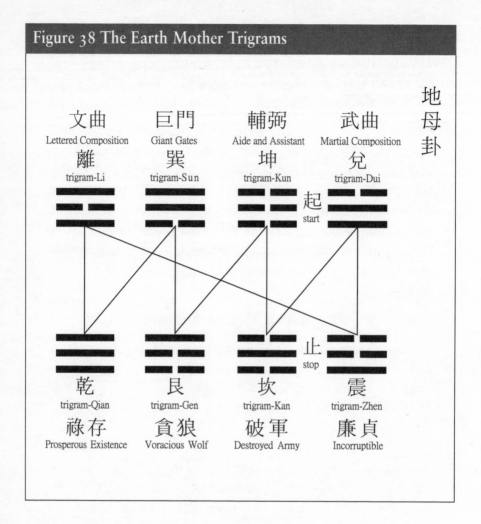

'Trigram-*Kun* is the Earth Mother. The "three luckies," "six elegants," etc., of the various mountains are all determined by this trigram.' An exemplary verse on the subject says:

'The classic says, "In order to properly determine the coming force of the three luckies, one need only take the Earth Mother trigram as the determinant. From this one can calculate the twelve yin dragons that the various mountains uphold, which are trigram-*Gen*, stem-*Bing*, trigram-*Sun*, stem-*Xin*, trigram-*Dui*, stem-*Ding*, branch-*Si*, branch-*Chou*, trigram-*Zhen*, stem-*Geng*, branch-*Hai*, and branch-*Wei*."'

Qiu Gongsong[157] said:

> 'How is it that among the three kinds of great trigrams the primordial mother stands as the parent of the year? One oral tradition states, "With regards to the three luckies, one need only properly seek the coming force." For the practitioners of the Orientation School it is necessary to transform the lines of the ghost.'

If one examines the commentaries on this, they state:

> 'Trigram-*Kun* serves as the Earth Mother and is that which the various mountains support. In seeking out the dragon, trigram-*Kun* regulates the three luckies. Following this statement, later generations developed the idiom about the geomancers tending to give primary valuation to the yin.'

Compilers' Note: In describing the system, the *Qingnang jing* or *Green Satchel Classic* refers to all eight of the palaces as the Earth Mother Three Luckies. A commentary to the work says, 'Concerning the three lucky approaching mountains, the most lucky situation occurs when there is a yang mountain with yin descending or a yin mountain with yang descending. Second to this is when there is a yang mountain with yang descending and yin water looking on or when there is a yin mountain with yin descending and yang water looking on.' Therefore, the mountains are not all yin. The ranking regards the aspect of water accompanying as lucky. Thus the so called Earth Mother Trigram takes trigram-*Kun* as a concrete example.

If, for example, trigram-*Kun* is the original dragon, then trigram-*Gen* serves as the Voracious Wolf, trigram-*Sun* serves as the Giant Gates, and trigram-*Dui* serves as the Martial Composition. Thus, trigram-*Gen*, trigram-*Sun*, and trigram-*Dui* act as the three luckies. Trigram-*Gen* receives stem-*Bing*, trigram-*Sun* receives stem-*Xin*, and trigram-*Dui* receives stem-*Ding*. Therefore, stem-*Bing*, stem-*Xin*, and stem-*Ding* together with the three luckies constitute the six elegants.

Furthermore, if one removes the middle line from trigram-*Gen*, trigram-*Sun*, trigram-*Zhen*, and trigram-*Dui* and considers only the remaining upper and lower lines, then one will see that for each of these trigrams there remains one yin line accompanying one yang line. This is said to be an instance of a number nine line (i.e. yang, unbroken) existing in harmony with a number six line (i.e. yin, broken). Although trigram-*Zhen*, in acting as the Incorruptible, is inauspicious, because of its accompanying (of lines), it is lucky. Trigram-*Zhen* receives the stem-*Geng*. Thus taking trigram-*Zhen* and the stem-*Geng* together with the three luckies and six elegents, the eight nobles are produced.

In addition, the Triune Harmonies of trigram-*Dui* are the branch-*Si* and branch-*Chou*. The Triune Harmonies of trigram-*Zhen* are branch-*Hai* and branch-*Wei*. Thus, taking branch-*Si*, branch-*Chou*, branch-*Hai*, and branch-*Wei* together with the eight nobles, the twelve luckies. In this way, the mountains are all determined by the Mother Earth trigrams. Thus, the eight palaces all possess the nine luminaries. The Father Heaven trigrams obtain the Heaven-Fixed trigrams' pairing of trigram-*Qian* and trigram-*Dui* on the one hand and trigram-*Sun* and trigram-*Kan* on the other. The Mother Earth trigrams obtain the Heaven-Fixed trigrams' pairing of trigram-*Li* and trigram-*Zhen* on the one hand and trigram-*Gen* and trigram-*Kun* on the other. Therein, the functions of the six offspring are completely present. The method of transmuting the trigrams upholds the Father Heaven and Mother Earth as examples for ordering the twelve lucky mountains and in doing so, it is particularly prone to using the Mother Earth as an example. This was what Qiu Gongsòng was referring to when he said that one must subsequently proceed to transmute the eight mountains.

The Trigram Transmutations of Trigram-*Dui* Palace

Transforming the upper line of trigram-*Dui* produces trigram-*Qian*, which thus acts as the Voracious Wolf. Transforming the middle line of trigram-*Qian* produces trigram-*Li*, which acts as the Giant Gates. Transforming the lower line of trigram-*Li* produces trigram-*Gen*, which acts as the Prosperous Existence. Transforming the middle line of trigram-*Gen* produces trigram-*Sun*, which acts as the Lettered Composition. Transforming the upper line of trigram-*Sun* produces trigram-*Kan*, which acts as the Incorruptible. Transforming

Figure 39 The Trigram Transmutations of Trigram-*Dui* Palace

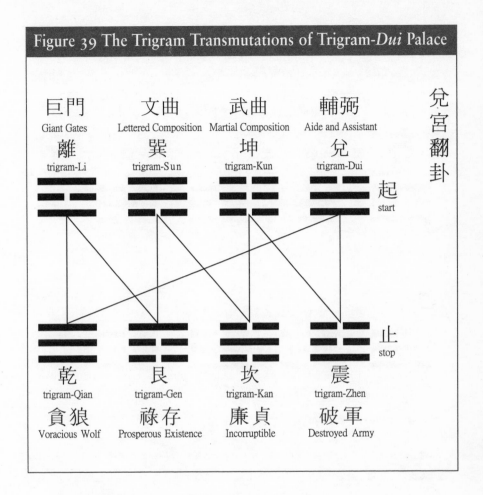

the middle line of trigram-*Kan* produces trigram-*Kun*, which acts as the Martial Composition. Transforming the lower line of trigram-*Kun* produces trigram-*Zhen*, which acts as the Destroyed Army. Transforming the middle line of trigram-*Zhen* produces once again trigram-*Dui*, which acts as the Aide and Assistant.

The Trigram Transmutations of Trigram-*Sun* Palace

Transforming the upper line of trigram-*Sun* produces trigram-*Kan*, which thus acts as the Voracious Wolf. Transforming the middle line of trigram-*Kan* produces trigram-*Kun*, which acts as the Giant Gates. Transforming the lower line of trigram-*Kun* produces trigram-*Zhen*,

Figure 40 The Trigram Transmutations of Trigram-*Sun* Palace

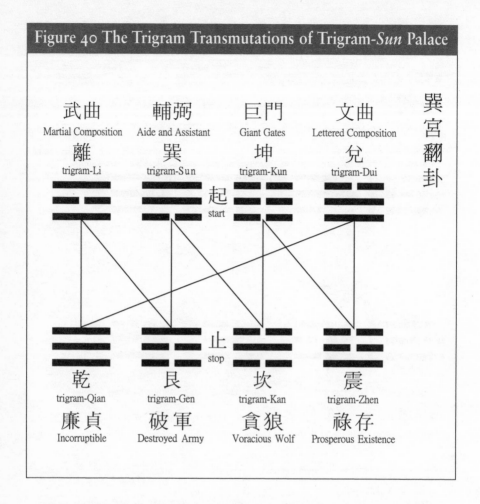

which acts as the Prosperous Existence. Transforming the middle line of trigram-*Zhen* produces trigram-*Dui*, which acts as the Lettered Composition. Transforming the upper line of trigram-*Dui* produces trigram-*Qian*, which acts as the Incorruptible. Transforming the middle line of trigram-*Qian* produces trigram-*Li*, which acts as the Martial Composition. Transforming the lower line of trigram-*Li* produces trigram-*Gen*, which acts as the Destroyed Army. Transforming the middle line of trigram-*Gen* produces once again trigram-*Sun*, which acts as the Aide and Assistant.

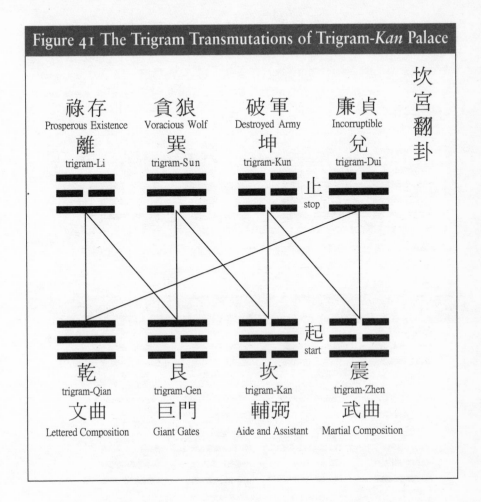

Figure 41 The Trigram Transmutations of Trigram-*Kan* Palace

The Trigram Transmutations of Trigram-*Kan* Palace

Transforming the upper line of trigram-*Kan* produces trigram-*Sun*, which thus acts as the Voracious Wolf. Transforming the middle line of trigram-*Sun* produces trigram-*Gen*, which acts as the Giant Gates. Transforming the lower line of trigram-*Gen* produces trigram-*Li*, which acts as the Prosperous Existence. Transforming the middle line of trigram-*Li* produces trigram-*Qian*, which acts as the Lettered Composition. Transforming the upper line of trigram-*Qian* produces trigram-*Dui*, which acts as the Incorruptible. Transforming the middle line of trigram-*Dui* produces trigram-*Zhen*, which acts as the Martial Composition. Transforming the lower line of trigram-*Zhen* produces trigram-*Kun*, which acts as the Destroyed Army. Transforming the middle line of trigram-*Kun* produces once again trigram-*Kan*, which acts as the Aide and Assistant.

The above three trigrams all follow the example of the Father Heaven trigrams.

The Trigram Transmutations of Trigram-*Gen* Palace

Transforming the upper line of trigram-*Gen* produces trigram-*Kun*, which thus acts as the Voracious Wolf. Transforming the middle line of trigram-*Kun* produces trigram-*Kan*, which acts as the Giant Gates. Transforming the lower line of trigram-*Kan* produces trigram-*Dui*, which acts as the Prosperous Existence. Transforming the middle

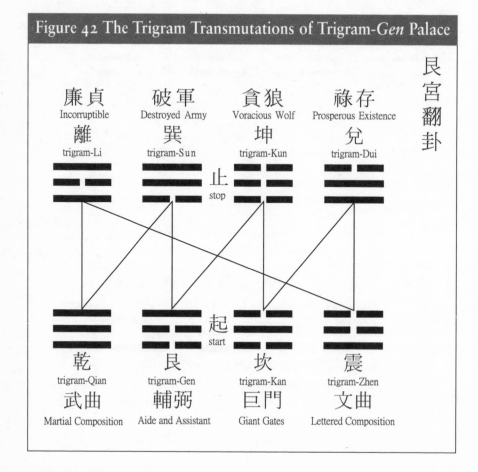

Figure 42 The Trigram Transmutations of Trigram-*Gen* Palace

line of trigram-*Dui* produces trigram-*Zhen*, which acts as the Lettered Composition. Transforming the upper line of trigram-*Zhen* produces trigram-*Li*, which acts as the Incorruptible. Transforming the middle line of trigram-*Li* produces trigram-*Qian*, which acts as the Martial Composition. Transforming the lower line of trigram-*Qian* produces trigram-*Sun*, which acts as the Destroyed Army. Transforming the middle line of trigram-*Sun* produces once again trigram-*Gen*, which acts as the Aide and Assistant.

The Trigram Transmutations of Trigram-*Zhen* Palace

Transforming the upper line of trigram-*Zhen* produces trigram-*Li*, which thus acts as the Voracious Wolf. Transforming the middle line

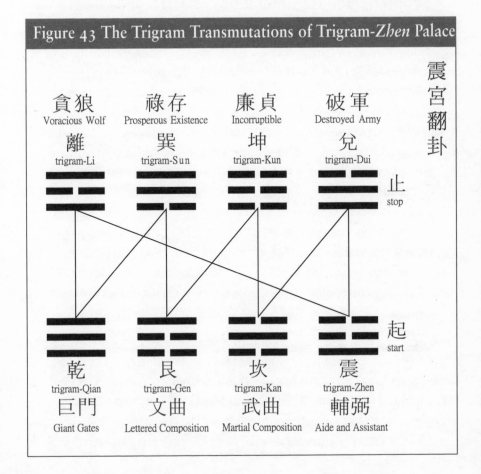

Figure 43 The Trigram Transmutations of Trigram-*Zhen* Palace

of trigram-*Li* produces trigram-*Qian*, which acts as the Giant Gates. Transforming the lower line of trigram-*Qian* produces trigram-*Sun*, which acts as the Prosperous Existence. Transforming the middle line of trigram-*Sun* produces trigram-*Gen*, which acts as the Lettered Composition. Transforming the upper line of trigram-*Gen* produces trigram-*Kun*, which acts as the Incorruptible. Transforming the middle line of trigram-*Kun* produces trigram-*Kan*, which acts as the Martial Composition. Transforming the lower line of trigram-*Kan* produces trigram-*Dui*, which acts as the Destroyed Army. Transforming the middle line of trigram-*Dui* produces once again trigram-*Zhen*, which acts as the Aide and Assistant.

The Trigram Transmutations of Trigram-*Li* Palace

Transforming the upper line of trigram-*Li* produces trigram-*Zhen*, which thus acts as the Voracious Wolf. Transforming the middle line of trigram-*Zhen* produces trigram-*Dui*, which acts as the Giant Gates. Transforming the lower line of trigram-*Dui* produces trigram-*Kan*, which acts as the Prosperous Existence. Transforming the middle line of trigram-*Kan* produces trigram-*Kun*, which acts as the Lettered Composition. Transforming the upper line of trigram-*Kun* produces trigram-*Gen*, which acts as the Incorruptible. Transforming the middle line of trigram-*Gen* produces trigram-*Sun*, which acts as the Martial Composition. Transforming the lower line of trigram-*Sun* produces trigram-*Qian*, which acts as the Destroyed Army. Transforming the middle line of trigram-*Qian* produces once again trigram-*Li*, which acts as the Aide and Assistant.

The above three trigrams all follow the example of the Earth Mother trigrams.

Compilers' Note: The method of transmuting the trigrams always follows this pattern: transforming (i.e. changing a yang line to yin or a yin line to yang) the upper line of a trigram produces the 'Birth of Vital Breath,' the 'Voracious Wolf.' Transforming the upper two lines (i.e. upper and middle) of a trigram produces the 'Heavenly Physician,' the 'Giant Gates.' Transforming the lower line of a trigram produces

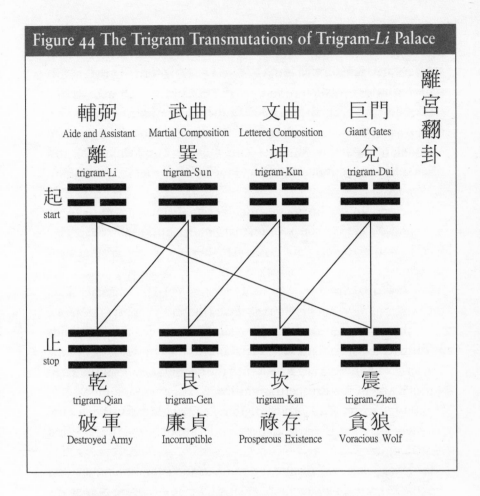

Figure 44 The Trigram Transmutations of Trigram-*Li* Palace

the 'Five Ghosts,' the 'Incorruptible.' Transforming the lower two lines of a trigram produces the 'Blessing and Virtue,' the 'Martial Composition.' Transforming the upper and lower lines of a trigram produces the 'Roaming Soul,' the 'Lettered Composition.' Transforming the middle line of a trigram produces the 'Termination of the Fate,' the 'Destroyed Army.' Transforming all three lines of a trigram produces the 'Termination of the Body,' the 'Prosperous Existence.' Not transforming any of the three lines produces the 'Prostrate Position,' the 'Aide and the Assistant.'

In the transformations of the one upper, the two upper, the one lower, and the two lower lines, each of the four yang trigrams[158] – trigram-*Qian*, trigram-*Kun*, trigram-*Kan*, and trigram-*Li* – is inevitably

251

transformed into one of the four yin trigrams – trigram-*Zhen*, trigram-*Gen*, trigram-*Dui*, and trigram-*Sun*. The four yin trigrams are by the same means transformed into the four yang trigrams. Thus it is that the three luckies are derived with reference to the concept of the seated mountain.[159] This is the meaning of the Geomancy School's saying that 'A yang dragon sits on a yin mountain and stands in a yang orientation; a yin dragon sits on a yang mountain and stands in a yin orientation.' Mountains and Orientations thus differ in terms of yin and yang.

Therefore, those who discuss orientations say that they raise up the Voracious Wolf from the position that stands opposite[160] to the 'Five Ghosts' of the original palace. As such, they refer to the arrangement that transposes the original palace with the 'Five Ghost' palace as the 'Five Ghost' trigrams. For example, if trigram-*Qian* is the original palace, then trigram-*Sun* functions as the 'Five Ghosts.' Then, if in turn one takes trigram-*Sun* as the original palace, then the palace that stands as the partner of trigram-*Sun* is trigram-*Kan*, from which arises the Voracious Wolf. Trigram-*Kun* is then the Giant Gates, trigram-*Zhen* is the Prosperous Existence, trigram-*Dui* is the Lettered Composition, trigram-*Qian* is the Five Ghosts, trigram-*Li* is the Martial Composition, trigram-*Gen* is the Destroyed Army, and trigram-*Sun* is the Aide and Assistant.

If, after having exchanged trigram-*Qian* and trigram-*Sun*, one still regards trigram-*Qian* as the original palace and trigram-*Sun* as the Five Ghosts, then the trigrams that were obtained as the three luckies [of trigram-*Sun*] – trigram-*Kan*, trigram-*Kun*, and trigram-*Li* – also together with trigram-*Qian* as the original palace constitute the 'pure yang.' Moreover, the transformation of the trigrams, moving from one above to one below, takes as its order: Aide (#8), Destroyed (#7), Martial (#6),[161] Incorrupt (#5), Voracious (#1), Giant (#2), Prosperous (#3), and Lettered (#4). In this way, the good and bad fortune deriving from the transformations of a trigram are always determined by the way in which yin and yang are distinguished. Thus, it is not necessary for one to shy away from this on the pretense that it derives from some mysterious concept.

Another explanation states that the order of the trigrams is rational.

This explanation says the following: When the upper line of each of the trigrams in the Former Heaven arrangement are transformed, the respective yin or yang that is generated by the image of each trigram mutually accompanies, generates, and stands together with its appropriate partner. Thus, the vital breaths that are of a kind mutually obtain one another. Therefore, the trigram that is produced by transforming the upper line of the original trigram is referred to as the 'Birth of Vital Breath.'

When the two upper lines of each trigram are transformed, the trigram that is produced is the fitting odd or even partner of the original trigram's appearance. The trigram produced and the original trigram mutually constrain but do not mutually harm one another. This is like the supplementing of insufficiencies and the repair of damages. Therefore, the trigram produced by transforming the upper two lines is known as the 'Heavenly Physician.'

When the lower line of each trigram is transformed, the yang goes to exchange places with the yin and the yin goes to exchange places with the yang. 'Going to' is equivalent to 'bending low' and that which is bent low is the ghost. In the ordering of the trigrams, there is always a complete separation by five positions. Therefore, the trigram produced by transforming the lower line is known as the 'Five Ghosts.'

When the lower two lines of each trigram are transformed, the old and the young mutually sympathize with one another, the yin and yang interchange, the intentions mutually obtain one another, and the vital breaths mutually produce one another. Therefore, the trigram produced by transforming the lower two lines is known as the 'Blessing and Virtue.'

When the uppermost and lowest lines of each trigram are transformed, the yang appearance changes its position and is exchanged with the yin. The yin appearance also changes its position and is exchanged with the yang. In this case, neither yin nor yang, and neither odd nor even mutually accompany one another. Therefore, the trigram produced by transforming the uppermost and lowest lines is known as the 'Roaming Soul.'

When the middle line of each trigram is transformed, the yang appearance changes its position and returns to yang. The yin appearance also changes its position and returns to yin. The vital breaths return to their origins and are conquered. Therefore, the trigram produced by transforming the middle line is known as the 'Termination of the Fate.'

When the three lines of each trigram are all transformed, this is the position of the opposite facing trigram in the Former Heaven arrangement. No part of the resulting trigram is continuous with any part of the original trigram. Therefore, the trigram produced by transforming all three lines is known as the 'Termination of the Body.'

When none of the three lines of each trigram are transformed, then the trigram obtains its original palace. Therefore, the trigram remaining when none of the lines are transformed is known as the 'Prostrate Position.' It is also called the 'Prostrate Moan.'

Among the trigram images of the eight palaces, the upper line upholding the generation trigram is the original palace, the 'Prostrate Position.' The first generation trigram is the 'Five Ghosts.' The second generation trigram is the 'Blessing and Virtue.' The third generation trigram is the 'Termination of the Body.' The fourth generation trigram is the 'Heavenly Physician.' The fifth generation trigram is the 'Birth of the Vital Breath.' The roaming soul trigram is the 'Roaming Soul.' The returning soul trigram is the 'Termination of the Fate.'

Taking trigram-*Qian* as an example, the following results. When trigram-*Qian* meets trigram-*Qian*, trigram-*Qian* is double-stacked. This is the upper line upholding the generations trigram, it is the 'Prostrate Moan.'

The meeting of trigram-*Qian* and trigram-*Sun* forms either hexagram-*Gòu* (#44 trigram-*Sun* – wind below, trigram-*Qian* – heaven above) or hexagram-*Xiaochu* (#9 trigram-*Qian* – heaven below, trigram-*Sun* – wind above). These are both first generation hexagrams; they are the 'Five Ghosts.'

The meeting of trigram-*Qian* and trigram-*Gen* forms either hexagram-*Dun* (#33 trigram-*Gen* – mountain below, trigram-*Qian* – heaven above) or hexagram-*Dachu* (#26 trigram-*Qian* – heaven below, trigram-*Gen* – mountain above). These are both second generation hexagrams; they are the 'Blessing and Virtue.'

The meeting of trigram-*Qian* and trigram-*Kun* forms either hexagram-*Tai* (#11 trigram-*Qian* – heaven below, trigram-*Kun* – earth above) or hexagram-*Pi* (#12 trigram-*Kun* – earth below, trigram-*Qian* – heaven above). These are both third generation hexagrams; they are the 'Termination of the Body.'

The meeting of trigram-*Qian* and trigram-*Zhen* forms either hexagram-*Wuwang* (#25 trigram-*Zhen* – thunder below, trigram-*Qian* – heaven above) or hexagram-*Dazhuang* (#34 trigram-*Qian* – heaven below, trigram-*Zhen* – thunder above). These are both fourth generation hexagrams; they are the 'Heavenly Physician.'

The meeting of trigram-*Qian* and trigram-*Dui* forms either hexagram-*Lü* (#10 trigram-*Dui* – lake below, trigram-*Qian* – heaven above) or hexagram-*Guai* (#43 trigram-*Qian* – heaven below, trigram-*Dui* – lake above). These are both fifth generation hexagrams; they are the 'Birth of Vital Breath.'

The meeting of trigram-*Qian* and trigram-*Kan* forms either hexagram-*Xu* (#5 trigram-*Qian* – heaven below, trigram-*Kan* – water above) or hexagram-*Song* (#6 trigram-*Kan* – water below, trigram-*Qian* – heaven above). These are both roaming soul hexagrams; they are the 'Roaming Soul.'

The meeting of trigram-*Qian* and trigram-*Li* forms either hexagram-*Tongren* (#13 trigram-*Li* – fire below, trigram-*Qian* – heaven above) or hexagram-*Dayou* (#14 trigram-*Qian* – heaven below, trigram-*Li* – fire above). These are both returning soul hexagrams; they are the 'Termination of the Fate.'

The remaining instances all follow the foregoing pattern.

Compilers' Note: This explanation based on the Former Heaven arrangement of the trigrams is very clever. However, with regards to the trigram images of the eight palaces, only the 'Termination of the Body,' the 'Roaming Soul,' and the 'Termination of the Fate' have meanings that are congruous with the transformations of the trigrams. The remainder is without foundation. This is being cited here specially as a reminder. The order of the diagram is presented below.

The Greater Roaming Year Trigram Transformations

The Greater Roaming Year trigram transformations are used by practitioners of the Residence Pairing School to determine an appropriate match between the head of household and the year in which construction or repairs of a residence are to be made [yang here referring to living peoples' residences]. Therefore, it is called 'Roaming Year.' Because the Geomancy School [which deals with yin residences, i.e. burial sites] also employs a Roaming Year system of transforming trigrams, the present system is called 'Greater.' Lesser is yin and Greater is yang. The present system is also derived by transmuting and transforming the Heaven-Fixed trigrams. It takes as its order the following: 'Voracious Wolf,' 'Incorruptible,' 'Martial Composition,' 'Lettered Composition,' 'Prosperous Existence,' 'Giant Gates,' 'Destroyed Army,' and 'Aide and Assistant.'

If one takes trigram-*Qian* as an example, then trigram-*Qian* serves as the original palace. Transforming the upper line of trigram-*Qian* produces trigram-*Dui*, which thus serves as the 'Voracious Wolf.' Transforming the middle line of trigram-*Dui* produces trigram-*Zhen*, which serves as the 'Five Ghosts' (i.e. the 'Incorruptible'). Transforming the lower line of trigram-*Zhen* produces trigram-*Kun*, which serves as the 'Martial Composition.' Transforming the middle line of trigram-*Kun* produces trigram-*Kan*, which serves as the 'Lettered Composition.' Transforming the upper line of trigram-*Kan* produces trigram-*Sun*, which serves as the 'Prosperous Existence.' Transforming the middle line of trigram-*Sun* produces trigram-*Gen*, which serves as the 'Giant Gates.' Transforming the lower line of trigram-*Gen* produces trigram-*Li*, which serves as the 'Destroyed Army.' Transforming the middle line of trigram-*Li* produces once again trigram-*Qian*, which serves as the 'Aide and Assistant.'

The 'Voracious Wolf' of this series is the same as that of the Lesser Year cycle, and thus both are the 'Birth of Vital Breath.' The Greater Year's 'Incorruptible' is the 'Giant Gates (Heavenly Physician)' of the Lesser Year series. However, for the Greater Year, the 'Incorruptible' is the 'Five Ghosts.' The Greater Year's 'Martial Composition' is the 'Termination of the Body (Prosperous Existence)' of the Lesser Year series. However, for the Greater Year series, this is called the 'Extension of the Year.' The Greater Year's 'Lettered Composition' is the same as the Lesser Year's (i.e. being the fourth transformation, it changes the uppermost and lowest lines of the original – in the lesser year this produces 'Lettered Composition/Roaming Soul'). In the Greater Year series, it is called the 'Six Killers.' The Greater Year's 'Prosperous Existence' is the Lesser Year's 'Five Ghosts (the 'Incorruptible').' In the Greater Year series, it is known as the 'Calamity and Harm.' The Greater Year's 'Giant Gates' is the Lesser Year's 'Blessing and Virtue (the 'Martial Composition').' In the Greater Year series, however, it bears the name 'Heavenly Physician.' The Greater Year's 'Destroyed Army (i.e. the 'Termination of the Fate')' and 'Aide and Assistant (i.e. the 'Prostrate Position')' are the same as their correlates in the Lesser Year series.

The method used for Yang Residences[162] regards trigram-*Qian* and trigram-*Dui* as the elder yang trigrams. It regards trigram-*Gen* and trigram-*Kun* as the elder yin trigrams. It regards trigram-*Li* and trigram-*Zhen* as the younger yin trigrams. It regards trigram-*Sun* and trigram-*Kan* as the younger yang trigrams. Two elders mutually paired are the four western residences. Two youngers mutually paired are the four eastern residences. East accompanying east and west accompanying west is lucky. East accompanying west and west accompanying east is unlucky. It is for this reason that the lucky and unlucky natures of the Greater and Lesser Year trigram transformations have some similarities and some differences.

Both methods of transmuting the trigrams regard the transformation of the upper line of the original trigram as the (lucky) 'Beginning of the Vital Breath'; 'Voracious Wolf.' The transformation of the two lower lines (6th transformation) of the original trigram is the Greater Year's (lucky) 'Heavenly Physician'; 'Giant Gates' (the Lesser Year's 'Martial Composition' 'Blessing and Virtue'). The transformation of all three lines forms the Greater Year's 'Extension of the Year' the 'Martial Composition' (the Lesser Year's 'unlucky'

'Termination of the Body' the 'Prosperous Existence'). The non-changing of all three lines is the Greater Year's 'Prostrate Position' the 'Aide and Assistant' (the Lesser Year has the same).

When the upper line changes, then trigram-*Qian* and trigram-*Dui* mutually transform into the other (i.e. the two elder yang exchange forms); trigram-*Gen* and trigram-*Kun* mutually transform into the other (i.e. the two elder yin); trigram-*Li* and trigram-*Zhen* (i.e. the two younger yin) mutually transform into the other; and trigram-*Sun* and trigram-*Kan* (i.e. the two younger yang) mutually transform into the other.

When the three lines all change, then trigram-*Qian* and trigram-*Kun* (i.e. elders yang and yin) transform into each other; trigram-*Dui* and trigram-*Gen* (i.e. second elders yang and yin) transform into each other; trigram-*Li* and trigram-*Kan* (i.e. youngers yin and yang) transform into each other; trigram-*Zhen* and trigram-*Sun* (i.e. second youngers yin and yang) transform into each other.

When none of the lines transform, then each obtains its original palace. In each of the above three scenarios, elders accompany elders and youngers accompany youngers. Therefore, they are considered to be fortunate. In the other transformations, youngers accompany elders and elders accompany youngers. Therefore, the rest are unfortunate.

In the chart of the eight palace trigrams, the upper line upholds the generation trigram is the 'Prostrate Position'; the first generation trigram is the 'Calamity and Harm'; the second generation trigram is the 'Heavenly Physician'; the third generation trigram is the 'Extension of the Year'; the fourth generation trigram is the 'Five Ghosts'; the fifth generation trigram is the 'Birth of Vital Breath'; the roaming soul generation trigram is the 'Six Killers'; the returning soul generation trigram is the 'Termination of the Fate.' These have similarities and differences when compared with the Lesser Roaming Year as depicted in the images presented below.

The Diagram of the Transformation of the Upper Line

The Lesser Roaming Year – the Birth of Vital Breath – Lucky

The Greater Roaming Year – the Birth of Vital Breath – Lucky

Transforming the upper line of trigram-*Qian* produces trigram-*Dui*.
Transforming the upper line of trigram-*Dui* produces trigram-*Qian*.
Transforming the upper line of trigram-*Li* produces trigram-*Zhen*.
Transforming the upper line of trigram-*Zhen* produces trigram-*Li*.
Transforming the upper line of trigram-*Sun* produces trigram-*Kan*.
Transforming the upper line of trigram-*Kan* produces trigram-*Sun*.
Transforming the upper line of trigram-*Gen* produces trigram-*Kun*.

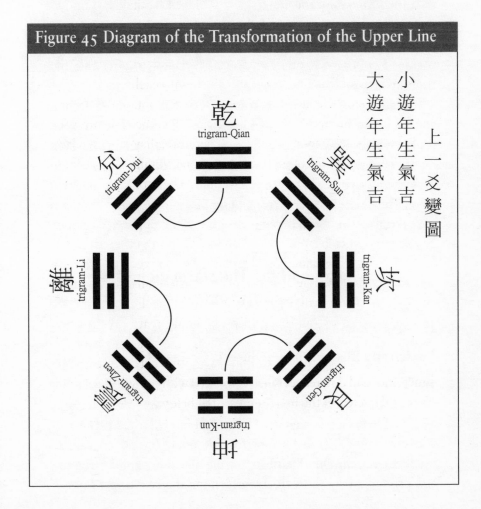

Figure 45 Diagram of the Transformation of the Upper Line

Transforming the upper line of trigram-*Kun* produces trigram-*Gen*.

Trigram-*Qian* and trigram-*Dui* are produced by greater yang. Trigram-*Li* and trigram-*Zhen* are produced by lesser yin. Trigram-*Sun* and trigram-*Kan* are produced by lesser yang. Trigram-*Gen* and trigram-*Kun* are produced by greater yin.

The natural order of the Former Heaven production of the trigrams is as follows. The two metal trigrams, trigram-*Qian* and trigram-*Dui*, stand together. The wood and fire trigrams, trigram-*Zhen* and trigram-*Li*, mutually produce one another. The water and wood trigrams, trigram-*Kan* and trigram-*Sun*, mutually produce one another. The two earth trigrams, trigram-*Gen* and trigram-*Kun*, stand together.

However, according to the Latter Heaven, trigram-*Qian* is yang and trigram-*Dui* is yin; trigram-*Zhen* is yang and trigram-*Li* is yin; trigram-*Kan* is yang and trigram-*Sun* is yin; trigram-*Gen* is yang and trigram-*Kun* is yin.

Trigram-*Qian*, trigram-*Kun*, trigram-*Kan*, and trigram-*Li* accompany the odd numbers of the Luo River Diagram. Trigram-*Dui*, trigram-*Zhen*, trigram-*Gen*, and trigram-*Sun* accompany the even numbers of the Luo River Diagram. In all of these pairings, yang accompanies yin and therefore, this chart is the luckiest arrangement. The Lesser Roaming Year and the Greater Roaming Year each regard this as the 'Birth of Vital Breath.'

The Diagram of the Transformation of the Upper Two Lines

The Lesser Roaming Year – the Heavenly Physician – Lucky

The Greater Roaming Year – the Five Ghosts – Unlucky

Transforming the two upper lines of trigram-*Qian* produces trigram-*Zhen*. Transforming the two upper lines of trigram-*Zhen* produces trigram-*Qian*. Transforming the two upper lines of trigram-*Dui* produces trigram-*Li*. Transforming the two upper lines of trigram-*Li* produces trigram-*Dui*. Transforming the two upper lines of trigram-*Sun* produces trigram-*Kun*. Transforming the two upper lines of trigram-*Kun* produces trigram-*Sun*. Transforming the two upper lines of trigram-*Kan* produces trigram-*Gen*. Transforming the two upper lines of trigram-*Gen* produces trigram-*Kan*.

The metal of trigram-*Qian* conquers the wood of trigram-*Zhen*. The fire of trigram-*Li* conquers the metal of trigram-*Dui*. These are all produced by the form of yang. The wood of trigram-*Sun* conquers the earth of trigram-*Kun*. The earth of trigram-*Gen* conquers the water of trigram-*Kan*. These are all produced by the form of yin.

The Luo River Diagram also takes the mutual accompanying of yin and yang to have the sense of mutually constraining and not mutu-

Figure 46 Diagram of the Transformation of the Upper Two Lines

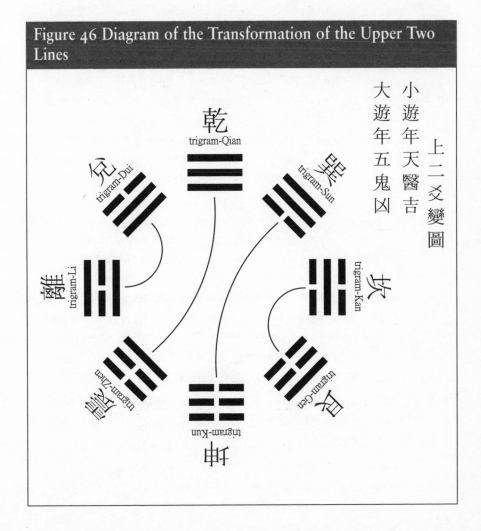

ally harming. Therefore, the Lesser Roaming Year regards this as the 'Heavenly Physician.' The Greater Roaming Year, however, on the reasoning that elder and younger should not be paired together regards this as unlucky. It takes the mutual conquest to imply a ghost and therefore calls this arrangement the 'Five Ghosts.' Each system has a rational explanation behind their respective claims.

The Diagram of the Transformation of the Lower Line

The Lesser Roaming Year – the Five Ghosts – Unlucky

The Greater Roaming Year – the Calamity and Harm – Unlucky

Transforming the lower line of trigram-*Qian* produces trigram-*Sun*. Transforming the lower line of trigram-*Sun* produces trigram-*Qian*. Transforming the lower line of trigram-*Dui* produces trigram-*Kan*. Transforming the lower line of trigram-*Kan* produces trigram-*Dui*. Transforming the lower line of trigram-*Li* produces trigram-*Gen*. Transforming the lower line of trigram-*Gen* produces trigram-*Li*. Transforming the lower line of trigram-*Zhen* produces trigram-*Kun*. Transforming the lower line of trigram-*Kun* produces trigram-*Zhen*.

Since the four yang trigrams, trigram-*Qian*, trigram-*Dui*, trigram-*Li*, and trigram-*Zhen*, go to exchange positions with the four yin trigrams, trigram-*Sun*, trigram-*Kan*, trigram-*Gen*, and trigram-*Kun*, and vice versa, and since the elders are inappropriately paired with the youngers, the Lesser Roaming Year regards this as a case of bending low. They thus regard this as a ghost. Furthermore, since in the Former Heaven ordering of the trigrams, this constitutes a separation of five positions (i.e. this is the 5th transformation), the Lesser Roaming Year considers this the 'Five Ghosts.' The Greater Roaming Year considers this to be a ghost because of the mutual conquest situation and regards the scenario as the 'Calamity and Harm.' Both systems regard this scenario as unlucky.

Figure 47 Diagram of the Transformation of the Lower Line

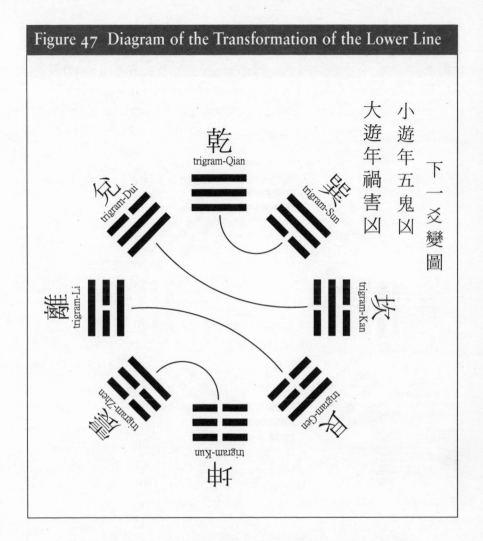

The Diagram of the Transformation of the Lower Two Lines

The Lesser Roaming Year – the Blessing and Virtue – Lucky

The Greater Roaming Year – the Heavenly Physician – Lucky

Transforming the lower two lines of trigram-*Qian* produces trigram-*Gen*. Transforming the lower two lines of trigram-*Gen* produces trigram-*Qian*. Transforming the lower two lines of trigram-*Dui* produces trigram-*Kun*. Transforming the lower two lines of trigram-*Kun*

Figure 48 Diagram of the Transformation of the Lower Two Lines

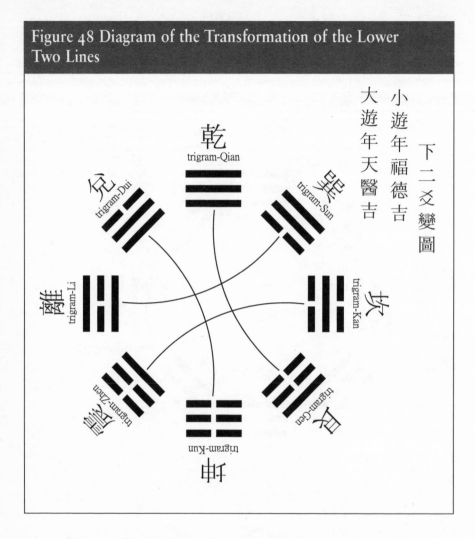

produces trigram-*Dui*. Transforming the lower two lines of trigram-*Li* produces trigram-*Sun*. Transforming the lower two lines of trigram-*Sun* produces trigram-*Li*. Transforming the lower two lines of trigram-*Zhen* produces trigram-*Kan*. Transforming the lower two lines of trigram-*Kan* produces trigram-*Zhen*.

The earth process of trigram-*Gen* produces the metal process of trigram-*Qian*. The earth process of trigram-*Kun* produces the metal process of trigram-*Dui*. These two pairings constitute matches of the two pairs of elders. The wood process of trigram-*Sun* produces the fire process of trigram-*Li*. The water[163] process of trigram-*Kan* produces the wood process of trigram-*Zhen*. The latter two pairings constitute matches of the two pairs of youngers.

Discussions involving the eight trigrams refer to the pairing of yang with yang and yin with yin as a 'blessing.'[164] Discussions surrounding the nine palaces refer to the pairing of yang with yang and yin with yin as a 'virtue.' Therefore, the Lesser Roaming Year system refers to this transformation of the lower two lines as the 'Blessing and Virtue.' The Greater Roaming Year regards as lucky the complete transformation of all three lines of a trigram because such a complete transformation perfectly pairs the trigrams as eldest with eldest, senior with senior, middle with middle, and youngest with youngest. However, the Greater Roaming Year does not refer to that three line transformation as 'Blessing and Virtue,' but instead as the 'Extension of the Year.' Consequently, the Greater Roaming Year regards the present transformation of the two lower lines as the 'Heavenly Physician.'

The Diagram of the Transformation of the Uppermost Line and the Lowest Line

The Lesser Roaming Year – the Roaming Soul – Unlucky

The Greater Roaming Year – the Six Killers – Unlucky

Transforming the uppermost line and the lowest line of trigram-*Qian* produces trigram-*Kan*. Transforming the uppermost line and the lowest line of trigram-*Kan* produces trigram-*Qian*. Transforming the uppermost line and the lowest line of trigram-*Dui* produces trigram-*Sun*. Transforming the uppermost line and the lowest line of trigram-*Sun* produces trigram-*Dui*. Transforming the uppermost line and the lowest line of trigram-*Li* produces trigram-*Kun*. Transforming the uppermost line and the lowest line of trigram-*Kun* produces trigram-*Li*. Transforming the uppermost line and the lowest line of trigram-*Zhen* produces trigram-*Gen*. Transforming the uppermost line and the lowest line of trigram-*Gen* produces trigram-*Zhen*.

In this transformation of uppermost line and the lowest line, the two forms (i.e. yin and yang) and the four images (i.e. eldest, senior,

Figure 49 Diagram of the Transformation of the Uppermost Line and the Lowest Line

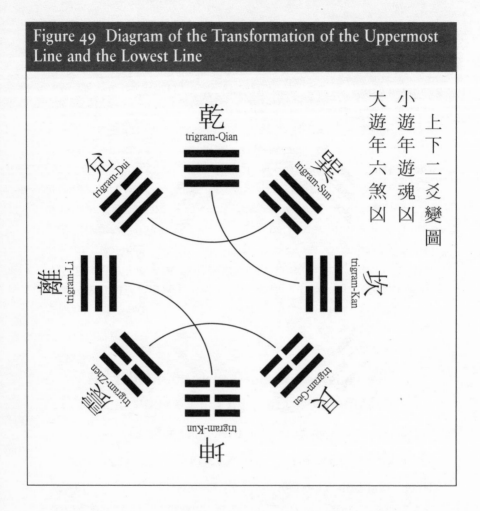

middle, youngest) mutually change and transform.[165] As such, the elders and youngers and yin and yang of the eight trigrams and nine palaces all proceed out but fail to pair up with their fitting partners. Therefore, the Lesser Roaming Year regards this transformation of the uppermost line and the lowest line as the 'Roaming Soul.' The Greater Roaming Year regards this as the 6th transformation from the original palace. Therefore, the Greater Roaming Year refers to this as the 'Six Killers.'

Both the Lesser Roaming Year and the Greater Roaming Year regard as unlucky this transformation of the uppermost line and the lowest line of the original trigram.

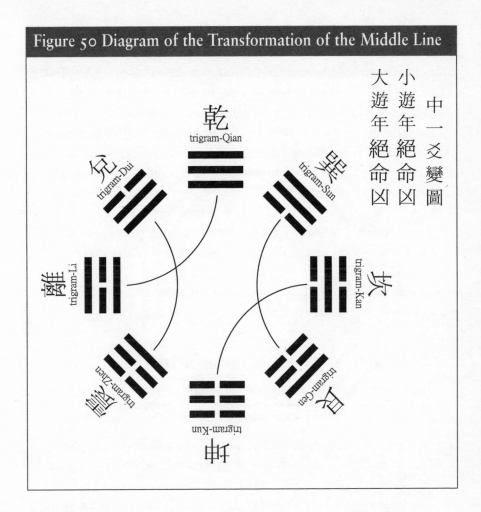

Figure 50 Diagram of the Transformation of the Middle Line

The Diagram of the Transformation of the Middle Line

The Lesser Roaming Year – the Termination of the Fate – Unlucky

The Greater Roaming Year – the Termination of the Fate – Unlucky

Transforming the middle line of trigram-*Qian* produces trigram-*Li*. Transforming the middle line of trigram-*Li* produces trigram-*Qian*. Transforming the middle line of trigram-*Dui* produces trigram-*Zhen*. Transforming the middle line of trigram-*Zhen* produces trigram-*Dui*. Transforming the middle line of trigram-*Sun* produces trigram-*Gen*. Transforming the middle line of trigram-*Gen* produces trigram-*Sun*. Transforming the middle line of trigram-*Kan* produces trigram-*Kun*. Transforming the line of trigram-*Kun* produces trigram-*Kan*.

The fire process of trigram-*Li* conquers the metal process of trigram-*Qian*. The metal process of trigram-*Dui* conquers the wood process of trigram-*Zhen*. The wood process of trigram-*Sun* conquers the earth process of trigram-*Gen*. The earth process of trigram-*Kun* conquers the water process of trigram-*Kan*. This transformation causes the odd to be inappropriately paired with even and causes the young to be inappropriately paired with the old. Furthermore, for both the Lesser and Greater Roaming Year, this transformation has the trigram returning to its roots. The change is the perfect opposite of the 'Birth of Vital Breath.' Both systems also regard this as the seventh and final transformation. Therefore, it is considered the unluckiest image. The Lesser and Greater Roaming Year both regard this as the 'Termination of the Fate.'

The Diagram of the Transformation of All Three Lines

The Lesser Roaming Year – the Termination of the Body – Unlucky

The Greater Roaming Year – the Extension of the Year – Lucky

Transforming all three lines of trigram-*Qian* produces trigram-*Kun*.
Transforming all three lines of trigram-*Kun* produces trigram-*Qian*.
Transforming all three lines of trigram-*Dui* produces trigram-*Gen*.
Transforming all three lines of trigram-*Gen* produces trigram-*Dui*.
Transforming all three lines of trigram-*Kan* produces trigram-*Li*.
Transforming all three lines of trigram-*Li* produces trigram-*Kan*.
Transforming all three lines of trigram-*Zhen* produces trigram-*Sun*.
Transforming all three lines of trigram-*Sun* produces trigram-*Zhen*.

Trigram-*Qian*, trigram-*Kun*, trigram-*Kan*, and trigram-*Li* are paired with the odd numbers in the Luo River Diagram. Trigram-*Dui*, trigram-*Gen*, trigram-*Zhen*, and trigram-*Sun* are paired with the even numbers in the Luo River Diagram. Also, the pairs of numbers 1 and 9, 3 and 7, 2 and 8, and 4 and 6, when added together each produce the number 10. The Geo-Principle School regards a solitary yin and a solitary yang as unlucky. Therefore, the Lesser Roaming

Figure 51 Diagram of the Transformation of All Three Lines

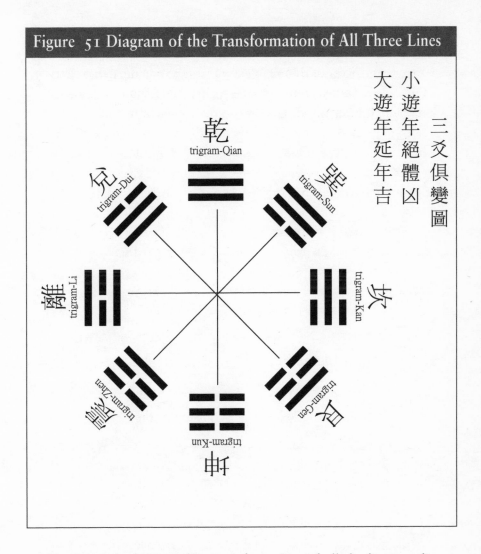

Year regards the complete transformation of all the lines as the 'Termination of the Body.'

Trigram-*Qian* is the father and trigram-*Kun* is the mother. Trigram-*Zhen* is the senior son and trigram-*Sun* is the senior daughter. Trigram-*Kan* is the middle son and trigram-*Li* is the middle daughter. Trigram-*Gen* is the youngest son and trigram-*Dui* is the youngest daughter. The Residence Siting School regards the proper pairing of yin and yang as lucky. Therefore, the Greater Roaming Year regards this as meaning that each trigram obtains its complementary partner. As such, they consider this transformation as the 'Extension of the Year.'

One school regards the complete transformation of all three lines as unlucky and one considers it as lucky. Each derives its conclusion from the way in which they use the systems.

Notes

1. Major (1993), p.37.

2. Regulating the calendar was listed as one of the nine parts of the *Great Plan of Yu*, an extremely important text for the Confucian school and by extension the state. The text is estimated to date from around 400 BCE. See Legge (1991a), pp.327–8.

3. The concept of 'timeliness' or 'acting at the proper time' is implicit in the very first statement of the *Analects (Lunyu)*, the book is said to record the teachings of Confucius and is one of the most important texts of the Confucian canon. 'Having studied, to then repeatedly apply what you have learned – is this not a source of pleasure?' (*xue er shi xi zhi bu yi le hu*) translated by Ames and Rosemont (1998), p.71. This can be interpolated to mean, 'Having studied [etiquette], to put that knowledge into practice at the appropriate times – is this not a source of pleasure?' Regardless of whether one accepts this interpolation, the idea is confirmed at other points in the *Analects* that behaviors are not absolutely right or wrong but must be evaluated relative to circumstances. Confucius praises those who demonstrate moral behavior, but praises more highly those who know when it is appropriate to act out moral principles and when it is better to refrain from action. On this see Lau (1979) pp.31–2.

4. Dong Zhongshu states that wood is the beginning and water the end of the Five Processes' sequence. Chan (1963), p.279, argues that this fixes the five in a lineal order and claims that this contrasts with the Yin Yang school, which tended to conceive of the five as cyclical.

However, Dong's original, which Chan translates, clearly states that the 'relationships' among the five begin with wood producing fire and conclude with water producing wood, which is to say that the sequence is closed and cyclical.

5. Graham, p.326.

6. I have considerably altered Legge's translation, which I took as the base for my own. The *Shoo King*, translated by Legge, pp.325–6. Considering the flavors, seawater left to soak down will leave salt. Things burnt up tend to taste bitter. Vegetative matter (wood) gathered from the forests (wood again, since earth stakes its claim to cultivated vegetable matter), like fruit, if left to the processing effects of time will ferment and become sour. Why metal produces a spicy hot flavor is unclear. Earth produces the grains and other cultivated plants which the early Chinese probably associated with sweetness.

7. Smith (1991), p.59.

8. The interpretation just described also suggests that there was from the earliest times a tendency to associate the Five Processes with the concept of polar opposites, though they are not yet termed as yin and yang in the *Hong fan*. This is important because it has long been held that Zou Yan (305–240 BCE) was the first person to link the two correlative groups of yin/yang and Five Processes.

9. The *Ch'un Ts'ew*, with the *Tso Chuen*, translated by Legge, p.819. This reference clearly documents a portion of the conquest cycle but not the entirety. Nonetheless, it does document its existence. See Chan (1963), p.250.

10. Major (1993), p.187 also suggests that wood may have been thought to conquer earth by virtue of plants growing on soil and rending the soil with their roots.

11. The Cambridge History of China, vol. 1, pp.737–9.

12. Graham (1989), p.341.

13. Graham (1989), p.326.

14. Eliade (1958), 73ff.

15. In fact, some argue that the production sequence was derived from the conquest sequence. However, the conclusion of this debate does

not bear upon the present discussion.

16. Graham (1989), p.346.

17. Major (1993), p.186.

18. The 720 different possible day/hour stem branch combinations each combine with exactly 180 different year/month stem branch combinations to make 129,600 possible combinations of stem branch pairs for year/month/day/hour.

19. With the exception of the *jian chu* system, the nine palaces, and certain calendar-based formulae, these then form the elemental building blocks of the system of gods and demons: i.e. yin and yang, the Five Processes, the stems, the branches, the sexagenary cycle, and the eight trigrams. The 28 Lodges, as the compilers say, are unimportant.

20. By using a year of only 354 days, and not 365, the Chinese calendar caused the new moon to shift gradually over time. This, together with the insertion of intercalary months, compensated for the fact that the Jovian cycle is only 11.88 years and not actually 12 years or 30 degrees per year.

21. The *Shoo King*, translated by James Legge, p.18 from the 'Book of Tang' in the 'Canon of Yao.' The part about 'whereupon the people split (*xi*), accord (*yin*), kill (*yi*), and store (*yu*)' actually occurs in four different passages in the original text.

22. This line is a quote from the *Canon of Shun* in The *Shoo King*, translated by James Legge, p.49.

23. The characters *xieji* in the title are clearly a reference to a passage from the *Hong fan* in which they appear in connection with the fourth of the nine divisional plan. The passage instructs to '*xie yong wu ji*' or harmoniously employ the five periods – which are *sui* (year), *yue* (month), *ri* (day), *xingchen* (stars/zodiacs), and *lishu* (calendar calculations). see Legge, The *Shoo King*, pp.324 and 327–8.

24. i.e. the numerical and Five-Processes correlations inherent in the Yellow River Chart and the Luo River Diagram.

25. This line appears in Shao Yong's *Huangji jingshi shu* in *Siku shushulei congshu*, vol. 1, p.803-1065 (13:27a). Although the remainder of the paragraph is consistent with statements made in other sec-

tions of the *Huangji jingshi shu*, they do not directly follow the quote cited. It may appear in the text or some other work by Shao.

26. This sentence in *Huangji jingshi shu* in *Siku shushulei congshu*, vol. 1, p.803-1066 (13:28b, column 5). As with the above note, the remainder of the paragraph is consistent with statements made in other sections of the *Huangji jingshi shu*, they do not directly follow the quote cited.

27. The term is literally the *shujia*, meaning 'skill' or 'art' school, and is short for *shushujia*, or 'art of numbers school' as in the name of the series in which the current text is collected.

28. Li, p.5 (1:5a) contains a discussion with the same title, which attributes the quote to the *Tonglan wangmu*.

29. Major (1993), p.121, has *Ming'e*.

30. For the 28 Lunar Lodges, see Nivison, pp.203–18. Nivison explains that the lodges were originally designed as a primitive system for tracking the sun by extrapolating from the moon's nightly position in equatorial asterisms. The positions of the asterisms moved over time due to gradual shifting of the equator caused by the declension of the earth's axis. He posits that there were originally 27 lodges of 13 *du* and one of 14 *du*. Later revisions, after the invention of the 24 *jieqi* system, increased the size of some lodges to 15 or 16 degrees. The main point here is that these lodges no longer have any correlation to movement of the moon.

31. The main executor of the inscription in stone of the classics (175–183 CE) during the reign of Han Emperor Lingdi. See Cambridge History of China Vol. 1, p.340.

32. This quote also appears in Li, p.5 (1:6b).

33. This text is interesting in that it appears to be one of the earliest prototypes of the twenty-four mountains, because it brings together the eight winds (correlates of the eight trigrams), eight of the Ten Heavenly Stems (all but stem *Wu* and stem *Ji*, which correspond to earth) and the Twelve Earthly Branches. To produce the twenty-four mountains from this, all that is needed is to substitute the trigrams for the winds, remove the four trigrams that are reduplicated by the

branches of the cardinal directions, and then to sandwich the cardinal branches between pairs of the stems corresponding to those directions. The order and names of the lodges differ at points from the normal order. The directions correspond with modern usage.

34. In his commentary to Yang Xiong's *Taixuan jing* (*Siku shushulei congshu*, vol. 1, pp.803–92 (9:8b-9a)), Fan Wang explicitly correlates the eight winds with the eight trigrams in the following manner: trigram *Kan* and Vast Darkness (*Guangmo*) wind; trigram *Gen* and Ordering (*Tiao*) wind; trigram *Zhen* and Brilliant Abundance (*Mingshu*) wind; trigram *Sun* and Clear Brilliance (*Qingming*) wind; trigram *Li* and Midday Sunlight (*Jing*) wind; trigram *Dui* and Gate of Heaven (*Changhe*) wind; trigram *Kun* and Cool (*Liang*) wind (the respective orders of *Changhefeng* and *Liangfeng* are reversed here in Fan Wang's comment – *Liangfeng* should come first); and trigram *Qian* and Not Circling (*Buzhou*) wind.

35. The relative order of *Xing* (normally #25) and *Zhang* (normally #26) is reversed in this version. Since this is proceeding through the lodges in reverse numerical order, one would expect to see *Zhang* (Extension) first, followed by *Xing* (here *Qi Xing* – Seven Stars).

36. As the lodge following *Zhang* and *Xing*, one would expect this to be *Liu* (willow). However, the lodges from this point onwards differ from the standard names and order. The exception is that *Can* (triad) bears the correct name, but is out of order judging simply by the number of lodges interceding.

37. The graph of *jing* shows a sun over the character for *jing* meaning capital. The latter character means 'high' and so *jing* means the sun at its high point and the brightness of that peak sun.

38. The character *wu* also indicates the crossing of longitudinal and latitudinal, its graph deriving from the character for 10. The original graph was a picture of a pestle.

39. The graph of stem-*Bing* alone was a picture of a base, but the character was also used to mean fire/bright, with the later distinction being depicted by adding the character for fire to the left of stem-*Bing*.

40. The original graph of stem-*Ding* was of a nail, with the metal

character being added later to distinguish that meaning. Ding also means stout.

41. Apparently deriving from the wolf's methodical assessing of and subsequent tearing up of its prey.

42. The graph of *duo* is a picture of a hand snatching a bird that is already spreading its wings to fly.

43. The English idiomatic use of heavy breathing, like that of one in distress, is a loose translation. The Chinese has the term 'forest,' implying crowded like the trees of a forest.

44. The character *duo* translated as 'apprehend' here is the same as that translated as 'pull in,' mentioned in note 42 above. The context implies two variations in translation, in this case because of the association with legal punishment, while the former implied that the earth at fall harvest time recovers into its belly that which it gestated and gave birth to in spring.

45. The character is originally the name of a river (*zhuo*) which, being muddy, later came to be used as an adjective meaning 'murky, muddled,' etc. My translation is thus loose.

46. The graph of *liu* depicts 'accomplished' – interestingly enough for the order here, this 'accomplished' is the character '*you*' of the Twelve Earthly Branches, with which this lodge is affiliated – over a field, indicating agricultural chores are completed and can be ceased. The two-character explanation, *jiliu*, simply means to stay in one place for a long time.

47. The character *you* was the original form of the character for alcohol (*jiu*). Apparently, due to the time required to ferment alcohol, *you* is associated with a long period of time. The character is also related to the *liu* (stay, remain) used as the name of the lodge in this series as well as the *liu* (willow) which is normally one of the lodges in this relative position. The author appears to be trying to link the graph of the lodge with the earthly branch semantically and graphically.

48. Here the 28 Lodges resume their normal order and names.

49. This entire section is borrowed from the Li, p.7 (1:9a-12a).

50. Li, p.8 (1:11b-12a).

51. Shao Yong, p.1078 says, 'Since heaven is muddled above, it cannot be measured. Therefore, one examines the number of the dipper to prognosticate heaven. That which the dipper establishes is the movement of heaven. When the bowl indicates the branch-*Zi*, the handle indicates the branch-*Yin*. The stars take the branch-*Yin* as daylight. The dipper has seven stars. Therefore, the daylight does not have more than seven *fen*.'

52. *Xieji bianfang shu* p.811-521 (13:50b).

53. Li, p.22 (1:40b-42b, column 3).

54. At this point Li, p.23 (1:41a), presents another example, which for some reason the *Xieji bianfang shu* opts not to quote.

55. Li, p.83 (5:8a).

56. Li, p.5 (1:5a-5b). The *Xieji bianfang shu* editors have made some minor changes to the *Xingli kaoyuan* passage, but these are only minor. Therefore, I place the entire passage in block text.

57. Legge (1991a), p.325. See Legge's notes on *wuxing*.

58. Legge (1991a), p.56. The translation here is mine, not Legge's. Actually, I would prefer to translate, 'Only by means of water, fire, metal, wood, and earth can the grains be cultivated.' However, this translation would not imply any significance to the order of presentation. It could be interpreted as meaning that fire burns off the wood to clear and fertilize the earth (which wood also ploughs), water feeds the grain as it grows and metal reaps the grain (metal could also be for felling trees before burning).

59. This entire section is borrowed from Li, p.12 (1:19a).

60. That is birth, ritual bathing, donning cap and sash, approaching official position, imperial flourishing, decline, sickness, death, burial, conclusion, conception, and development.

61. Li, p.13 (1:22b-23a).

62. Li, p.14 (1:23b-24a).

63. At this point, the *Xingli kaoyuan* says, 'The preceding is common to all explanations from past to present. The Star Fate School (*xingming jia*)...' Li, p.14 (1:24a, column 1).

64. At this point, the *Xingli kaoyuan* also says, 'Why is it that they (i.e. the two systems of correlating the Earthly Branches with the Five Processes) differ? It is most likely because the Star Fate School pairs the twelve palaces (*gong*) with the top, bottom, and four directions..." Li, p.14 (1:24a, column 3).

65. Li, p.14 (1:24a) continues on to state, 'As for the Five Processes of the Received Notes, there is also the explanation that produces the pairing according to the principle of the sixty days' moving eight and mutually producing. There is also "the stems and branches taking up numbers, mutually pairing, and separately receiving the five musical notes." For a detailed discussion of this, see the following section.' The importance of these concluding sections is that they highlight the possible connection between the unusual ordering of the Five Processes in the Received Notes system and the Five Planets or Star Fate School's arrangement.

66. This statement is very similar to one found in Shao Yong, p.1079, which states, 'The stars are the excess of the sun. The zodiacal signs are the excess of the moon.' This interesting quote goes on to say, 'Heaven is odd and earth is even. This is why in prognosticating the heavens, one only examines the stars and in prognosticating the earth, one only examines mountains and water... Heaven has five *chen*. The sun, moon, stars, and *chen* together with heaven form five. Earth has Five Processes. Metal, wood, water, and fire together with earth form five. The wood of the Five Processes is of the class of the myriad things. The metal of the Five Processes comes out of stone. Therefore, water, fire, earth, and stone do not include metal and wood because metal and wood are born from the midst of these four.'

67. This statement refers to the fact that the process metal is born in the earthly branch *Si*.

68. It is important to note that this term, in Chinese – *san he*, and the term discussed in the following section, *liu he* or six harmonies appear to be similar in construction but are clearly understood very differently. The original terms each consist of two characters, the first of which is a number, three and six respectively, and the second character in both cases is the same, i.e. harmony. That is where the similarities end. The second term, *liu he* or six harmonies, is rather straightforward to translate. The explanation demonstrates that it implies six pairs of Earthly

Branches, in which each member of the pair harmonizes with its partner. By contrast, the first term, *san he*, which would initially seem to imply 'three harmonies,' actually refers to either four (Five Processes minus earth) or five (all Five Processes) sets of harmonies, each of which is comprised of three Earthly Branches (thus, my translation as triune).

69. Li, p.24 (1:43b-44a).

70. Scribal error: 'flourishes' is only used in this instance where the others all read 'reaches maturity.'

71. See Major (1993), p.124 and commentary on p.126.

72. The term six harmonies (*liu he*) here is the same pair of characters as that which Major in his translation of the *Huainanzi* renders as the 'Six Coordinates,' see Major (1993), p.262. However, the present set differs drastically from that of the *Huainanzi*. In the *Huainanzi*, the *liu he* are six diagonals drawn across the circle of the Twelve Earthly Branches laid out like a clock, i.e. 12 with 6, 1 with 7, etc. In the *Xieji bianfang shu* they are latitudinal lines, i.e. 12 to 1, 2 to 11, 3 to 10, etc. In this latter version, they provide an explanation for the odd Five Processes' correlates of the branches discussed in connection with the Five Planets School above.

73. Li, p.24 (1:44b).

74. Actually, the quote is not exact. In the sentence that describes the Establishment and Compliances' revolving and rotating, Li, p.24 (1:44b), actually says, 'the Lunar Establishment, following the path of heaven, turns to the left and the Lunar Compliance, following the movement of the sun, turns to the right...'

75. See Li, p.44 (3:12a-12b).

76. Both hidden Tigers and Rats are documented in the commentary to the *Jingshi yizhuan* by Lu Ji (187-219 CE) in *Jing Fang*, p.441.

77. Li, p.24 (1:43b). The text quoted here is the same, but prior to this the *Xingli kaoyuan* also contains a quote of a poetic *gejue*.

78. Li, p.23 (1:42b-43a). The quote is on 43a, but it is preceded by another poetic *gejue* that is not quoted here.

79. See *Huainanzi*, Major (1993), pp.26, 32, and 45.

80. Li, p.24 (1:44a).

81. The *Xingli kaoyuan* goes on to say, 'Since 1, 3, 5, 7, & 9 are odd and 2, 4, 6, 8, & 10 are even, stem-*Jia*, stem-*Bing*, stem-*Wu*, stem-*Geng*, and stem-*Ren* belong to the class of yang and stem-*Yi*, stem-*Ding*, stem-*Ji*, stem-*Xin*, and stem-*Gui* belong to the class of yin.' The *Xieji bianfang shu* doesn't indicate that the quote has ended and goes on with further statements that it seems to be attributing to the *Xingli kaoyuan*.

82. Two illegible characters appear here.

83. In other words, in stem *Jia* and stem *Ji* years, the ninth and tenth months, which correspond to the Gates of Heaven, have the stem branch pairs stem *Jia*/branch *Xu* and stem *Yi*/branch *Hai*, respectively, while the Doors of the Earth, or the third and fourth months, as explained above, are stem *Wu*/branch *Chen* and stem *Ji*/branch *Si*.

84. The character *mo* used here is not normally used in connection with the life cycle stages, but by itself normally means the end.

85. The stem *Geng*, yang metal, normally flourishes in branch *You*, declines in branch *Xu*, sickens in branch *Hai*, dies in branch *Zi*, is buried in branch *Chou*, and terminates in branch *Yin*.

86. The stem *Wu*, yang earth, is normally buried in branch *Xu*, terminates in branch *Hai*, and is conceived in branch *Zi*.

87. The stem *Ji*, yin earth, normally approaches official appointment in branch *Wu*, flourishes in the branch *Si*, and declines in the branch *Chen*.

88. According to normal reckoning, water (yang stem *Ren*) reaches the burial stage in the branch *Chen* and reaches the termination stage in branch *Si*.

89. I have translated *xianyuan* as 'very mysterious,' based on the context. No one seems to agree on the meaning. It first occurred in the *Huangyi* poem in the *Daya* section of the *Shijing*, Legge (1991c) p.453. Legge, reviewing the opinions of various commentators, explains that it is variously interpreted as meaning 'good,' 'distinguishing low hills from tall ones,' or simply as a meaningless place name. It is generally understood to mean both 'distinguishing' and 'good.' Why the author uses such a controversially understood term

here is unclear. Moreover, his usage does not seem to gel with either of the main interpretations.

90. I have adopted John S Major's translations of the names of the Twelve Pitch Pipes. Major (1993) p.109.

91. The stems stem-*Jia* and stem-*Yi* are paired because they are both correlated with the process wood. The ten stems are affiliated with the Five Processes in pairs – stem-*Jia* (yang) & stem-*Yi* (yin) wood, stem-*Bing* (yang) & stem-*Ding* (yin) fire, stem-*Wu* (yang) & stem-*Ji* (yin) earth, stem-*Geng* (yang) & stem-*Xin* (yin) metal, and stem-*Ren* (yang) & stem-*Gui* (yin) water.

92. This was the mythical minister to the Yellow Emperor who first created the stem-*Jia*/branch-*Zi* and paired the stems and branches to name the days.

93. This sentence is missing but it would complete the perfect parallelism of these paragraphs.

94. Li, p.14 (1:24b), column 4. The beginning of the section from the *Xingli kaoyuan* quoted here is missing. It states that this section is quoted from the *Tonglan wangmu* compiled by Zhu Xi during the Song dynasty.

95. The exact quoting of the *Xingli kaoyuan* ends here, but the remaining paragraph of this section is largely a paraphrase of the corresponding section from the *Xingli kaoyuan*.

96. Li, p.15 (1:25b). Though the editors of the *Xieji bianfang shu* do not mention it, this entire section, from title to conclusion is a direct quote from the *Xingli kaoyuan*.

97. Li, p.15 (1:26a). Again the editors of the *Xieji bianfang shu* do not mention it, but this entire section, from title to conclusion is a direct quote from the *Xingli kaoyuan*.

98. Li, p.16 (1:27a-28b). Again the editors of the *Xieji bianfang shu* do not mention it, but this entire section, from title to conclusion is a direct quote from the *Kao yuan*.

99. Literally, 'Notes recorded during leisure hours in the Hall of the Propitious Cassia.' This text is believed to have been written during the Song dynasty (960–1279 CE) but the author is not known.

100. Li, p.16 (1:28b).

101. Yang Xiong (53 BCE –18 CE) author of the *Taixuan jing*, which creates a system of trigrams with three possible lines. See Chan, pp.289–291; Smith (1991), pp.29–33, 120; Twitchett, pp.774–7.

102. This 'Compilers' Note:' is from the *Xingli kaoyuan* authors, not from the authors of the *Xieji bianfang shu*.

103. The *Xingli kaoyuan* actually goes on to describe each of the derivations.

104. See Yang Xiong, p.87 (8:12a-12b); Nylan, p.359.

105. The Jin dynasty (265–420 CE) commentator, Fan Wang says, 'The combined value of both sets of Pipes is 78. The number 8 is correlated with the branch-*Chou* and branch-*Wei*...' as in other reckonings, the number in the ones place, i.e. 8, is the only significant number; the branch-*Chou* and branch-*Wei* and the number 8 represent a Spine Pipe (*Lü*). 'The so-called "returning" thus refers to the obtaining of a Spine Pipe (*Lü*) and not a Regulator Pipe (*Lü*). Thus, it may be regarded as a returning (vis-à-vis the Spine Pipe – *Lü*) and it may also not be regarded as a returning (vis-à-vis the Regulator Pipe – *Lü*).'

106. Fan Wang explains that the numbers of the stems are derived from the branches. The yang stem and its yin stem partner take the number of the yang branch with which the yang stem is correlated. Thus, stem *Jia* is correlated with branch *Zi*, so stem *Jia* and stem *Ji* take 9 as their number.

107. Fan Wang's commentary suggests that the 'sounds,' or *sheng*, refer to the five musical notes, or *yin* ('note,' not yin/yang), which in turn are correlated with the Ten Heavenly Stems. This would explain why they are said to be born from the sun. Thus the Twelve Pipes are correlated with the Twelve Earthly Branches and the twelve zodiac signs. He also suggests that the eight notes, *yin*, here refer to eight types of sounds produced by eight types of materials from which musical instruments are fashioned, i.e. metal, stone, silk, bamboo, gourd (*pao*), earth, leather, and wood.

108. Or 'inherit the mantle from the father and mother.'

109. Presumably because each of the members of the latter set are multiples of the former. This passage appears in the *Taixuan jing*, Michael

Nylan, p.359 and Yang Xiong, p.87, (8:12a).

110. This entire quote of Zhu Xi and the accompanying chart are taken directly from the *Xingli kaoyuan*, Li, p.18 (1:32b-36a). Again the editors of the *Xieji bianfang shu* do not mention this.

111. The remainder of this section is not from the *Xingli kaoyuan*.

112. An author who lived toward the end of the Yuan and beginning of the Ming dynasty (mid-fourteenth century CE).

113. Ramparts – city walls – in China were constructed from the earliest times by pounding earth to form the structure.

114. This is a free translation. The term used is a form of tin-lead alloy used to produce other forms of metal. In any case, the concept is that of embryonic metal and for this, I feel pig iron is the most colloquial English rendering.

115. The ensuing explanation makes no reference to branch-*Chou*'s earthiness, but only emphasizes the paradox of fire in water. Therefore, it seems that this should only refer to branch-*Zi* and branch-*Chou*'s water affiliations.

116. A yang/fire creature that brings yin/water in the form of rain.

117. The term here is storehouse, but this is the equivalent of the place of burial according to the Triune Harmonies – birthplace, place of flourishing, and burial place.

118. The term for 'courier station' is also the name of a constellation. Thus this could refer to that astral figure, as does the Celestial River of the last two pairs.

119. Apparently the idea is that there are three earth elements piled upon the marsh, which would make the assemblage poorly founded. The connection with a courier station would ostensibly be that the station is a transient place, but this is admittedly a long stretch.

120. This is presumably a reference to the convention that places the burial of metal in the branch-*Chou*. This is an odd argument to make, however, because one would assume that metal is weak in branch-*Chou*, whereas here the author seems to be pressing the fact that metal conquers wood.

121. This must refer to the burial place, or storehouse, of wood in the branch-*Wei*.

122. Presumably because the pair stem-*Ji*/branch-*Wei* immediately follows stem-*Wu*/branch-*Wu*, the branch-*Wei* is considered to be 'above' branch-*Wu*.

123. Jing Fang, p.466.

124. Twitchett, p.692, n. 102. Smith (1991), p.28 and 56 accepts that the system may have originated with Jing Fang.

125. Li, p.20 (1:36b-37a).

126. Li, p.21 (1:37b-38a).

127. Li, p.21 (1:38a-40a) – the entire section here is from the *Xingli kaoyuan*.

128. The quote of the *Xingli kaoyuan* is not precise here in that the *Xieji bianfang shu* editors have supplied the name of the *Cantong qi*'s author where the *Xingli kaoyuan* simply refers to it as a Daoist text. The book is said to contain 'much discussion of the importance of trigram *Kan* and trigram *Li*, the processes of water and fire, the directional animals dragon and tiger, and the metals lead and mercury. The teachings of the book are what later generations have called the ancestor of the Furnace of Fire method. The book's name, which means 'harmoniously unified three' is meant to suggest that it unites the three schools of the *Yijing*, *Huang-Lao*, and Furnace of Fire in a subtle harmony with the Great Way. Zhu Xi wrote a commentary to the *Cantong qi* entitled *Cantong qi kaoyi*. See Smith (1991), p.27, Ho (1985) p.176, and Kaltenmark (1969) pp.129–30. Also Cleary (1986), Introduction, p.x.

129. This 'Compilers' Note' is directly quoted from the *Xingli kaoyuan*.

130. Trigram-*Kan* and trigram-*Li* are the only ones in which two yin lines are separated by one yang line or two yang lines are separated by one yin line.

131. The group of 24 directions is strongly hinted at by the *Huainanzi*'s section on solar nodes; see Major (1993), pp.88–9. At the latest by the Tang dynasty (618–907 CE), they were known as the 'twenty-four

mountains.' See Yang Yunsong, p.89.

132. Skinner (1982) p.92.

133. That is branch *Hai*, branch *Yin*, branch *Si*, and branch *Shen*, which correspond to the birth aspect of the Triune Harmonies' birth, flourishing, and burial stages. This section is strange in that it makes reference to the Triune Harmonies but uses the standard branch/Five-Processes correlations rather than those appropriate to the Triune Harmonies system.

134. Branch-*Chou*, branch-*Chen*, branch-*Wei*, and branch-*Xu*, which correspond to the burial aspect of the Triune Harmonies' birth, flourishing, and burial stages.

135. Jin dynasty (265–420 CE) author (276–324 CE).

136. Read *yu* ('couple') as *yu* ('even' as opposed to 'odd').

137. Wan Minying, p.60–62 (2:1a-4a)

138. This and the following references to trigram oppositions assume the Former Heaven arrangement of trigrams.

139. The order in which the four trigrams are listed does not correspond with the order in which the processes are listed.

140. This statement is confusing because branch-*Chou* and branch-*Yin* only represent the respective 'declining' and 'sickening' life stages for the yang heavenly stem-*Ren*, which is correlated with water. Trigram-*Gen* is correlated with earth. The stem-*Bing* receives trigram-*Gen* and the stem-*Bing* is fire. In the passage here, it describes how trigram-*Gen* transforms to wood. Thus, there are applicable earth, fire, and even wood correlations but no connection to yang/water/stem-*Ren*. Consequently, it is not clear why the author refers to branch-*Chou* and branch-*Yin* as representing the declining and sickening stages.

141. Branch-*Chen* and branch-*Si* are the declining and sickening stages for the yang stem-*Jia*, which is wood.

142. Stem-*Bing* is missing from this list. Stem-*Wu* and stem-*Ji* should be absent as the earth stems, but stem-*Bing* should be present.

143. Read the branch-*Shen* as the stem-*Jia*, on the logic that the trigram-*Qian* receives the stems stem-*Jia* and stem-*Ren* and

the trigram-*Kun* receives stem-*Yi* and stem-*Gui*. The characters for branch-*Shen* and stem-*Jia* are similar.

144. The translation here is highly tentative. By 'forms,' I believe the author meant the lines of the trigrams and by 'numbers,' I believe he meant the numbers of the *Luo* or Yellow River charts.

145. This 'crooked and straight' is a reference to the description of the nature of the wood process in the *Hong Fan* or Great Plan, as is the reference to the earth processes as 'agriculture.'

146. It would seem that the term 'spirit' here should be 'vital breath' to preserve the parallel, but there was a point made about the spirit relying on vital breath; also *jing* and *shen* make a nice pair.

147. This translation derives from Major (1993), p.119.

148. The original passage is as unclear as the translation I have rendered. The passage deals with three concepts, namely, the standard revolution of the twenty-four mountains (dragons), the burial place of the dragons, and the transformed revolution.

The standard revolution is the Five-Processes correlate that is assigned to a given mountain according to the *Hong fan* 24 directional positions system. Dragon is another name for a mountain.

The burial place of the mountain/dragon is the branch that acts as the burial stage of the mountain/dragon's associated process according to the Triune Harmonies system. Thus, water is buried in the branch-*Chen*, wood in the branch-*Wei*, fire in the branch-*Xu*, and metal in the branch-*Chou*. For some reason, the system under discussion asserts that the burial branch of the earth process is the same as that of the water process, namely the branch-*Chen*, rather than equating its burial branch with that of fire, i.e. the branch-*Xu*, as the Triune Harmonies system normally does.

The transformed revolution is the Received Note Five-Processes correlate of the stem-branch pair that acts as the burial place of the mountain in question. Obtaining a stem-branch pair for the burial branch requires reference to the months of the year. This system assumes that a year is defined as the period between two winter solstices. The winter solstice occurs in the eleventh lunar month of each year, which is the branch-*Zi* month. Thus the branch-*Chou*, or twelfth month of one year is assigned to the next year under this reckoning. Consequently, the stem-branch pair for a given burial branch is the stem-branch pair of the month that bears the appropriate branch within the said year.

149. The character, which I read here as *ke*, is an alternate version.

150. The authors suggest that the previous section starts with a mountain (space) and derives the lucky or unlucky nature of year, month, day, and hour (time) from it; by contrast, the present section starts with the year/month or day/hour (time) and derives the lucky or unlucky nature of the various mountains (space). In other words, both sections say the same thing.

151. All of the solar nodes together with their stem and branch correlates presented here are to be found in the *Huainanzi* with the exception of the fact that the four seasonal beginnings nodes lack stem-branch correlates. See Major (1993), pp.88–9. The text correlates the dipper handle and stem-branches with directions.

152. Thus, for example, trigram-*Kan*, which in the twenty-four mountains is equivalent to branch-*Zi*, receives the branch-*Chen* and branch-*Shen*. Branch-*Shen*, branch-*Zi*, and branch-*Chen* are the triune harmony office of water.

153. The *Siku quanshu* contains a copy of the *Qingnang aoyu* of Yang Yunsong, which contains only 450 or so characters. Stephen Skinner (p.95) refers to another similarly named text, which he attributes to Yang Yunsong as well, entitled *Jiutian xuannü qingnang haijiao jing*. The two versions are clearly different.

154. The Qing editors claim that the locus classicus of the nine stars is Yang Yunsong's *Hanlong jing* or *Jolt the Dragon Classic*. The passage of the text that mentions the nine appears on Yang Yunsong p.41. See also Smith (1991), p.144.

155. This system of colors and numbers associated with the nine palaces is attributed by the editors to the Han dynasty Confucian Zhang Heng (78–139 CE); in the *Xieji bianfang shu*, Yunlu, p.382.

156. This must mean stand next to one another as neighbors rather than facing one another across the circle, as one would normally expect with the word *dui* that is used here.

157. Not identified.

158. It is not clear on what this reckoning of yin and yang is based, other possibly than that in the Former Heaven arrangement, trigram-*Qian*, trigram-*Kun*, trigram-*Kan*, and trigram-*Li* are all the cardinal points (S, N, W, E), while trigram-*Zhen*, trigram-*Gen*, trigram-*Dui*, and trigram-*Sun* are in NE, NW, SE and SW. The transformations of 1 or 2 upper and 1 or 2 lower would be those that produce the Voracious Wolf, Giant Gates, Incorruptible, and Martial Composition, respectively. And this is exactly what the editors earlier said are the lucky palaces for the Geo-Principle school (*dili jia*).

159. This is opposed to the standing orientation and goes back to the point made earlier about the Geo-Principle school (*dili jia*) using the dragon, whereas the Selection school (*xuanze jia*) uses orientation.

160. This is the crux. They judge not by standing position, but rather by what it faces.

161. Emendation – I have switched the positions of *wuqu* and *lianzhen*.

162. That is for living people as opposed to yin residences for the dead.

163. The text actually writes 'earth,' which must have been an error.

164. There is another textual error here because the word in quotes in both this and the following sentence is the term 'virtue.' In order to justify the selection of the name 'blessing and virtue' for this scenario, one of them should read 'blessing.'

165. That is, in a heterogeneous and not homogenous fashion – the ideal being like with like. Thus, assuming that trigram-*Qian*, trigram-*Dui*, trigram-*Li*, and trigram-*Zhen* are yang, each of these pair with a yin trigram-*Kan*, trigram-*Sun*, trigram-*Kun*, and trigram-*Gen* respectively. Also trigram-*Qian* eldest yang with trigram-*Kan* middle yin, trigram-*Dui* youngest yang with trigram-*Sun* senior yin; trigram-*Li* middle yang with trigram-*Kun* eldest yin; and trigram-*Zhen* senior yang with trigram-*Gen* youngest yin. In this, the age rankings derive from the Latter Heaven while the yin and yang affiliations are according to the Former Heaven.

Glossary of Chinese Terms, Titles of Works Cited, and Names of Individuals

bagua (八卦) – the 'eight trigrams.' These are the basic building blocks of the *Yijing* or *Book of Changes*. They are, in the Former Heaven sequence: trigram-*Qian* (☰乾), trigram-*Sun* (☴巽), trigram-*Kan* (☵坎), trigram-*Gen* (☶艮), trigram-*Kun* (☷坤), trigram-*Zhen* (☳震), trigram-*Li* (☲離), and trigram-*Dui* (☱兌). The Latter Heaven sequence orders them as follows: trigram-*Zhen* (☳震), trigram-*Sun* (☴巽), trigram-*Li* (☲離), trigram-*Kun* (☷坤), trigram-*Dui* (☱兌), trigram-*Qian* (☰乾), trigram-*Kan* (☵坎), and trigram-*Gen* (☶艮).

Baihu tongyi (白虎通義 *Recensions from the White Tiger Observatory*) – a recension of the five classics commissioned by the Han Emperor Zhangdi (r.75–88 CE) and edited by the author of the *History of the Han Dynasty*, Ban Gu (班固 32–92 CE). The book was so named because work on it was carried out in the White Tiger Observatory, which was a part of the emperor's northern palace.

Ban Gu (班固 32–92 CE) – see *Baihu tongyi*.

Cai Yong (蔡邕 133–192 CE) – was the main executor of the inscription in stone of the classics (175–183 CE) during the reign of Han Lingdi (168–189 CE). He is cited in the current work for his book the *Duduan*.

Cantong qi (參同契 *The Kinship of the Three*) – a Daoist text written in 142 CE by Wei Boyang (fl.147–167). It contains much discussion of the importance of trigram-*Kan* and trigram-*Li*, the processes of water and fire, the directional animals, i.e. dragon and tiger, and the metals lead and mercury. The teachings of the book are what later generations have called the ancestor of the Furnace of Fire method. The book's name, which means 'harmoniously unified three' is meant to suggest that it unites the three schools of the *Yijing*, Huang-Lao, and Furnace of Fire in a subtle harmony with the Great Way. Zhu Xi wrote a commentary to the *Cantong qi* entitled *Cantong qi kaoyi*.'

Cao Zhengui (曹振圭 or 曹震奎) – author of the *Lishi mingyuan* (曆事明原 dates unknown) which is cited as a common source for the *Xieji bianfang shu* (i.e. the present treatise) and the *Xingli kaoyuan*.

chidao (赤道 the red way) – the equator or celestial equator.

Chunqiu yundou shu (春秋運斗樞) – the '*Pivot of the Dipper*' an aprocraphal *chanwei* (讖緯 'prognostication and weft') text of the Han dynasty (221 BCE –220 CE) containing an often cited passage on the stars of the Big Dipper.

Chunqiu Zuozhuan (春秋左傳) – the Zuo commentary on the *Spring and Autumn Annals* attributed to Zuo Qiuming (左丘明). (circa 4th cent. BCE). For a translation see Legge (1991b) in bibliography.

Da Nao (大撓 occasionally 大橈) – Minister to the mythical Yellow Emperor (Huangdi). Da Nao is credited with creating the stems and branches and using the sexagenary cycle to name the days.

Dili dacheng or (地理大成) – the *Great Compendium of Geo-principles*, possibly that of Ye Tai although many works share this title.

dizhi (地支) – the Earthly Branches. A set of twelve Chinese characters associated with the twelve zodiacal spaces, or segments of the celestial sphere in which the sun and moon appear to converge over the course of a year. The names of the branches are *zi* (子), *chou* (丑), *yin* (寅), *mao* (卯), *chen* (辰), *si* (巳), *wu* (午), *wei* (未), *shen* (申), *you* (酉), *xu* (戌), and *hai* (亥). The sun appears to progress through the branches' zodiacal spaces in reverse order, i.e. *hai, xu, you*, etc. The branches are also used to define twelve different directional positions on the face of the earth, with *zi* corresponding to north, *mao* to east, *wu* to south, and *you* to west. Anciently, at midnight on the first day of each month, the handle of the Big Dipper appears to point to each of these directional positions. Thus, the order of the branch sequence is defined by the order in which the Dipper's handle points to the twelve directional positions on the earth, i.e. *zi, chou, yin*, etc. In actuality, at present the Dipper handle indicates the direction north at midnight sometime near the beginning of November, which corresponds roughly with the tenth or branch-*hai* Chinese lunar month. The names of the twelve branches are used to designate uniquely the twelve (approximate) years that it takes for the planet Jupiter to orbit the sun, the twelve months of the year, and the twelve two-hour periods of the day. Each of the branches is also associated with one of the twelve animal signs, which are at times used instead of the names of the branches. Although alternate associations do exist (e.g. Triune Harmonies) the Five-Processes correlations of the branches are usually regarded as follows: *zi* (water), *chou* (water/earth), *yin* (wood), *mao* (wood), *chen* (wood/earth), *si* (fire), *wu* (fire), *wei* (fire/earth), *shen* (metal), *you* (metal), *xu* (metal/earth), and *hai* (water). The odd-numbered branches (*zi* being #1) are considered to be yang and the even (*hai* being #12) to be yin. The Ten Heavenly Stems combine with the Twelve Earthly Branches to form the sexagenary stem-branch cycle.

Duduan (獨斷) – the '*Independent Conclusions*' by the Later Han dynasty author Cai Yong.

dunjia jia (遁甲家) – the 'Hidden stem-*Jia* school' which focuses on 'tracing back the yin (as opposed to yang) hidden in the six stem-branch pairs that contain the stem-*Jia*. See the *chu* commentary to the 'Fangshu zhuan' or 'Biography of the magicians' in the *Houhan shu* or *History of the Latter Han Dynasty*. See the entry under *Qimen dunjia*.

ershiba xiu (二十八宿) – the 28 Lunar Lodges. A group of constellations formerly used to trace the movements of the sun by observing the location of the moon in the night sky over the roughly 28 days of the lunar month.

Erya (爾雅) – 'Approaching Correctness' is the earliest Chinese version of a dictionary and since the Song dynasty it has been considered one of the 'thirteen classics.' Confucian scholars compiled the text during the Later Han dynasty (25–220 CE) from materials as early as the third century BCE.

There is a *zhu* commentary by the Jin dynasty (265–420 CE) *feng shui* founder Guo Pu and a *shu* commentary by the Song dynasty Xing Bing (932–1010 CE).

Guo Pu (郭璞 276–324 CE) – sometimes regarded as the founder of *feng shui*; author of the *Zang shu* or *Book of Burial*.

Hong fan (洪範) – the 'Great Plan' is the name of a section of the *Shangshu* or *Book of Documents* purportedly promulgated by King Wu upon his founding of the Zhou dynasty (c.1045 BCE). Actually, it was revealed to King Wu by his minister Qi Zi. Graham argues that the text was written no later than approximately 400 BCE. The greatest importance of this work to the present text is the fact that the *Hong fan* orders the Five Processes as water, fire, wood, metal, and earth. It is also argued that the *Hong fan* was derived from the Luo River Diagram discovered by the sage emperor Yu on the back of a tortoise.

Huainanzi (淮南子) – or '*Master of Huainan*' is a syncretic philosophical work of the Former Han dynasty, which was probably compiled in the mid-second century BCE. Its cosmological chapters contain the earliest documented occurrences of many of the theories summarized in the current treatise. For a complete English language translation of those cosmological chapters, see Major (1993).

huangdao (黃道) – the 'yellow way' is the Chinese term for the the ecliptic. Also written in classical Chinese as *guang dao* 'the bright way' or *zhong dao* 'the middle way.'

Huangdi suwen (黃帝素問 properly 黃帝內徑素問) – the '*Plain Inquiry of the Yellow Emperor*' is generally regarded as the first Chinese classic on traditional medicine. It records conversations between the Yellow Emperor and one of his ministers, the famous doctor Qi Bo. Although the book is not as old as it claims, it does contain materials transmitted from the Zhou (1045–256 BCE) and Qin (221–206 BCE) dynasties and is not later than the Han dynasty (206 BCE–220 CE). There are a great number of commentaries on the text, the earliest being that of the Tang dynasty author Wang Bing completed in 762 CE. It was also edited by Shen Gua (1031–1095 CE). The *Suwen* is cited in the current work as the source for the Received Notes or *na yin* system.

Huangji jingshi shu (皇極經世書) – the '*Supreme Principles Governing the World*' the magnum opus of the Neo-Confucian philosopher Shao Yong.

As in other works of this school, the author examines the principles of things in the universe in order to understand their relevance to man. The major difference, however, is that Shao Yong in this work pays special attention to the numerical principles inherent in things and dedicates a great deal of effort to studying the significance of these numbers. Thus, his work greatly influenced the numerological schools which in turn shaped both Chinese astrology and *feng shui*.

Jing Fang (京房 79–37 BCE) – Han *Yijing* scholar commonly believed to have been the creator of the Received Stem-*Jia* system (*na jia*) that correlates the Ten Heavenly Stems with the eight trigrams. A description of the system appears in a book attributed to Jing, the *Jingshi yizhuan* (*Siku shushulei congshu*, vol. 6, p.808-466). However, modern scholarship suggests that the *Jingshi yizhuan* is not authentic, but was written during the Song dynasty; see Twitchett, et.al. (1986), p.692, n.102. Smith (1991), pp.28 & 56, accepts that the system may have originated with Jing Fang.

jiuqi (九尥) – the 'nine leaders' are first mentioned in the Odes of Chu (楚辭 compiled first century BCE). A commentary on that reference by Hong Xingzu (洪興祖 1070–1135 CE) explains that these consist of the seven stars of the Big Dipper, a star near the sixth star of the Dipper (i.e. near Ursa Major), and another star at the end of the Dipper's handle.

jiuyao (九曜) – the 'nine luminaries' are the nine planets of Indian astronomy, namely: the sun (日曜 or 太陽), the moon (月曜 or 太陰), Mars (火曜 or 熒惑 'dazzling deceiver'), Mercury (水曜 or 辰星 'morning star'), Jupiter (木曜 or 歲星 'year star'), Venus (金曜 or 太白星 'great white star'), Saturn (土曜 or 鎮星 'subduing star'), Rahu (羅睺 or 黃旛星 'yellow streamer star'), and Ketu (計都 or 豹尾星 'leopard tail star'). They are also called the nine upholders (九執). A passage in the calendar treatise of the *History of the Tang Dynasty* says on the sixth year of the Kaiyuan reign period (718 CE) an ethnically Indian court official named Gautama was summoned to create the 'Nine Upholders Calendar,' i.e. an Indian calendar. The *Qingnang jing* or *Green Satchel Classic* refers to the Lesser Roaming Year trigram transformations as the *jiuyao* or 'nine luminaries.' This identifies the nine luminaries with the nine palaces (九宮). Smith (p.144) points out that the nine stars of the Dipper are different from the nine palaces of the eight trigrams. There are, therefore, three important groups of nine luminaries: the nine heavenly bodies of

Indian astronomy, the nine directional palaces associated with the eight trigrams, and the nine stars of the Big Dipper.

Lai Wenjun (賴文俊 also Lai Buyi 賴布衣) – Song dynasty *feng shui* master and author of the famous *feng shui* manual *Cuiguan pian* (催官篇). He is credited with inventing the Sewing Needle ring of the *feng shui* compass.

Li Guangdi (李光地 1642–1718 CE) – chief compiler of the *Xingli kaoyuan* and the Neo-Confucian text *Xingli jingyi* or *Essentials of Neo-Confucianism* in 1717 CE.

Lihai ji (蠡海集) – a book compiled by the Ming dynasty (1368–1644 CE) scholar Wang Kui (王逵) in two fascicles. The text is sometimes incorrectly attributed to the Song dynasty. Wang Kui's learning is said to derive from the scholarship of Shao Yong.

Liji (禮記) – the '*Book of Rites*' one of the Confucian classics which takes as its subject ritual propriety. The treatise primarily refers to the *Yueling* or Monthly Ordinances chapter of that book, which itself dates at least to the mid-second century BCE. See Legge (1885).

Li li (歷例) – the '*Period Regulations*' not identified, but as it is quoted in the *Xingli kaoyuan*, it must be from the seventeenth century CE or earlier.

Lishi mingyuan (曆事明原) by Cao Zhengui. A text of unknown date but frequently cited in the *Xingli kaoyuan* and the present treatise. See Cao Zhengui.

liuren (六壬) – the 'method of the six stem-*Ren*.' Out of the sexagenary cycle of sixty stem-branch pairs there are six pairs that contain the stem-*Ren*. The Qing dynasty compilers of the treatise and other works on numerology explain that the 'six stem-*Ren*' is a system of prognostication, which, together with Tai Yi (太乙) and Dunjia (遁甲) constitute what are popularly known as the 'three systems.' This system focuses on the stem-*Ren* due to an argument that the Five Processes all originate in the water process. It employs the number six because the number one of heaven gives birth to water while the number six of earth completes water. The method has its origins in the *Yijing*, which has sixty-four sections. It is also based on the twelve zones of divided fields in the heavens, called the Heaven Plate; as well as the twelve zones of directional positions on the earth, called the Earth Plate. The Heaven Plate rotates along with the hours, while the Earth Plate remains in a fixed position. When the branch-*Zi* on the Heaven Plate is aligned with the branch-*Zi* on the Earth Plate, the arrangement is known as the 'Prone Cry' (伏吟); when the branch-*Zi* on the Heaven Plate is aligned with branch-*Wu* on the Earth Plate, the arrangement is known as the 'Supine Cry' (反吟). The Six stem-*Ren* method is based on the position of the sun. For example, in the first month, the sun is located in the zodiacal zone of the branch-*Hai*. On the first month and during branch-*Wu* two-hour period, the branch-*Hai* of the Heaven Plate will therefore be aligned with branch-*Wu* of the Earth Plate. One can then determine the good or bad luck pertaining to a time by considering the upward or downward conquest of the Five Processes implied by the conjunctions of the branches of the Heaven Plate and the Earth Plate together with the stem-branch pair of the day in question. The source of this method is extremely ancient. It is said that the Mysterious Woman of the Nine Heavens employed it to help Huangdi defeat Chi You. The 'Jingjie zhi' of the *Sui shu*, the 'Yiwen zhi' of the *Tang shu*, and the 'Yiwen zhi' of the *Song shu* all contain references to books about the Six stem-*Ren*. The Six stem-*Ren* techniques currently employed by fortune tellers all derive from the *Liuren daquan* or *Complete Compendium of the Six stem-Ren* compiled during the Ming dynasty.

liushi huajia (六十花甲) – 'the sexagenary stem-branch cycle' or the set of sixty unique pairs composed of one of the Ten Heavenly Stems and one of the Twelve Earthly Branches; traditionally believed to have been created by the Yellow Emperor's minister Da Nao. The nature of the pairing dictates that odd stems are only paired with odd branches and that even stems are only paired with even branches. Consequently, the five odd stems each join in pairs with the six odd branches to form thirty pairs. The same is true of the even stems and branches. Since Chinese regard odd numbers as being of the class of yang and even numbers as being of the class of yin, the pairs are always either yin or yang. However, the Five-Processes correlations of the sixty pairs are determined by the complex method known as the *na Jia* or Received *Jia*. The pairing occurs as follows, where 's' stands for stem, 'b' stands for branch, and the number in parentheses stands for the number of the pair in the series: (1) 1s&1b, (2) 2s&2b... (10) 10s&10b; (11) 1s&11b; (12) 2s&12b; (13) 3s&1b. The series continues in this manner through the pair (60) 10s&12b, after which it returns to (1) 1s&1b. The pairs of the sexagenary cycle were used to designate days even before the Han dynasty. See Twitchett, et.al. (1986), p.687; and Smith (1991), pp.15 & 291, note 10, who indicates that they date from the Shang dynasty (before eleventh century BCE). The cycle was permanently fixed to the cycle of years in the year 4 CE.

luohou (羅睺) – the Chinese transliteration of the Sanskrit 'Rahu,' which is the personification of the moon's ascending or north node. The plane of the moon's orbit around the earth is tilted with respect to the ecliptic or apparent plane of the sun through the stars. Thus, the two planes intersect at two points. When crossing to north of the ecliptic the moon is considered to be ascendant. A node that coincides with a full or new moon causes lunar and solar eclipses, respectively. Indian astronomers regarded the nodes as invisible heavenly bodies. The ascendant node was personified as Rahu and the descendant as Ketu. In the Indian cosmogony, as the gods and demons were churning the sea of milk, amrita or the elixir of life was produced. One demon stole a drink of this but was spotted by the sun and moon and the transgression reported. Consequently, the god Visnu severed the demon's head. Having already consumed the elixir, however, the creature was now immortal. His head became Rahu and his body Ketu. To take revenge for their whistle-blowing, Rahu is occasionally allowed to devour his accusors, causing eclipses, but because Rahu has only a head the sun and moon escape from his throat. In the European astronomical conception, the north node is known as *caput dragonis* (dragon's head) and the descending node as *cauda draconis* (dragon's tail). In India and China also the nodes are depicted as the head and body or tail of a dragonlike creature. Rahu's depiction in China was eventually identified with the disembodied mythical *taotie* (饕餮).

Luojing zhinan bowu ji (羅經指南撥霧集) – the *Dispelling Fog with the Compass Collection* by the Qing dynasty *feng shui* specialist Ye Tai.

Lüshu (律書) – the 'Regulation book' of the *Record of the Historian (Shiji)* early first century BCE.

najia (納甲) – a system that pairs the Ten Heavenly Stems with the eight trigrams. The system is sometimes attributed to the Han dynasty scholar Jing Fang (79–37 BCE). See *Jingshi yizhuan* (2:2a) in *Siku shushulei congshu*, vol. 6, p.808-466.

nayin (納音) – the 'Received Notes' is a complex numerological system used to pair one of the Five Processes with each of the sixty pairs of stems and branches.

qimen dunjia (奇門遁甲) – the 'strange gates of the hidden stem-*Jia*' is one of the earliest documented numerological mentods in China. Although the earliest surviving work describing its complex methodology dates to the Ming dynasty, the system is clearly documented during the Han dynasty. Together with the Taiyi and 'six stem-*Ren*' it is one of the three main systems of traditional Chinese numerology. Often used to select auspicious times and directions by military tactitions, it is reputed to have been one of the most effective methods employed by the renowned general Zhuge Liang (181–234 CE). Its invention is traditionally ascribed to one of the Yellow Emperor's ministers, Feng Hou (風后).

Qimeng fulun (啟蒙附論) – an *Appendix on the Premier* by Li Guangdi 1715 CE which expands upon the *Yixue qumeng* (易學啟蒙 or *A Premier on Studying the Changes* circa 1186 CE) by Zhu Xi.

Qingnang jing (青囊經) – late-ninth century CE, the *Green Satchel Classic* attributed to the Tang dynasty *feng shui* master Yang Yunsong (楊筠松); also known as the *Qingnang aoyu* (青囊奧語) or *Esoteric Pronouncements on the Green Satchel*.

Quyi shuo (祛疑說) – *Dispelling Doubts* by Chu Yong (儲泳 1065–1101 CE).

Ruigui tang xialü (瑞桂堂暇錄) – the '*Lucky Cassia Hall Diary*;' author unknown; mid-twelfth century CE.

Sanming tonghui (三命通會) – the *Complete Compendium on the Three Fates* by Wan Minying (萬民英) *jinshi* 1550 CE. This work has been considered one of the most authoritative books on Chinses fate calculation techniques since the Ming dynasty.

sanshi (三式 also 三世) – the 'three styles' or 'three systems' of traditional Chinese numerology. Two different lists are given: one consists of *leigong* (雷公), *taiyi* (太乙), and the 'six stem-*Ren*;' another gives the 'hidden stem-*Jia*,' *taiyi*, and the 'six stem-*Ren*.'

Shao Yong (邵雍 1011–1077 CE) – One of the 'Five Confucian Masters of the Early Song.' Shao presaged Wang Yangming's idealism and, consequently, Zhu Xi did not recognize Shao's contribution to Neo-Confucianism – Zhu Xi having been the founder of the rationalistic school. Shao Yong's focus was on observing principle through the medium of numbers in things (natural phenomenon). Other Neo-Confucians criticized Shao for not addressing the issues of humanity and righteousness. Shao developed a theory of historical cycles of 129,600 years as described in his *Huangji jingshi shu*, from which the compilers of this treatise borrow heavily.

Shen Gua (沈括 1031–1095 CE) – Song dynasty, scientist, director of the Imperial Bureau of Astronomy, and commentator on the *Huangdi suwen*. He was reputed to have broad knowledge in the fields of letters, astronomy/astrology, geology/geomancy, calendar science, medicine, and prognostication.

Shensha qili (神煞起例) – the *Regulations Governing Gods and Demons*; dates unknown.

Shenshu jing (神樞經) – the '*Classic of the Divine Pivot*' not identified, but as it is quoted in the *Xingli kaoyuan*, it must date from the seventeenth century CE or earlier.

shier gong (十二宮) – the 'twelve palaces' the Chinese equivalent of the twelve western zodiacal constellations. The Twenty-Eight Lunar Lodges are divided among these twelve, with the four cardinal palaces encompassing three lodges each and the other eight palaces encompassing two lodges each. The palace named Xingji, or 'star period,' was considered the starting point of the heavenly bodies' movements. During the Zhou dynasty, the winter solstice occurred in the Xingji Palace, but this gradually shifted later, so that the winter solstice now occurs somewhere between the Lunar Lodges Dou, 'ladle' and Wei, 'tail.' (*Dictionary of Astronomy and Astronautics*, p.9).

shier xingci (十二星次) – the twelve 'rest stops' or 'inns' the Chinese equivalent of the twelve western zodiacal signs of the ecliptic – meaning the slowly shifting area of the sky in which the sun and moon appear to converge, rather than the unmoving constellations in front of which they appear to converge. Juzi (娵訾) is the branch-*Hai* and the zodiacal sign Pisces or the current zodiacal constellation Aquarius. Jianglou (降婁) is the branch-*Xu* and the zodiacal sign Aries or the current zodiacal constellation Pisces. Daliang (大梁) is the branch-*You* and the zodiacal sign Taurus or the current zodiacal constellation Aries. Shichen (實沈) is the branch-*Shen* and the zodiacal sign Gemini or the current zodiacal constellation Taurus. Quanshou (鶉首) is the branch-*Wei* and the zodiacal sign Cancer or the current zodiacal constellation Gemini. Quanhuo (鶉火) is branch-*Wu* and the zodiacal sign Leo or the current zodiacal constellation Cancer. Quanwei (鶉尾) is the branch-*Si* and the zodiacal sign Virgo or the current zodiacal constellation Leo. Shouxing (壽星) is the branch-*Chen* and the zodiacal sign Libra or the current zodiacal constellation Virgo. Dahuo (大火) is the branch-*Mao* and the zodiacal sign Scorpio or the current zodiacal constellation Libra. Ximu (析木) is the branch-*Yin* and the zodiacal sign Sagittarius or the current zodiacal constellation Scorpio. Xingji (星紀) is the branch-*Chou* and the zodiacal sign Capricorn or the current zodiacal constellation Sagittarius. Xuanxiao (玄枵) is the branch-*Zi* and the zodiacal sign Aquarius or the current zodiacal constellation Capricorn; see Tang Shan (1967), p.204.

Shiji (史記) – *Record of the Historian* by Sima Qian (司馬遷); China's earliest history; late-second century /early-first century BCE.

Shuogua zhuan (說卦傳) – the 'Explanation of the Trigrams' wing of the Book of Changes (*Yijing*). According to traditional reckoning this was considered the eighth of the ten wings, or commentaries on the Book of Changes (*Yijing*).

Sima Qian (司馬遷 145–90 BCE) – author of the *Shiji*.

Taixuan jing (太玄經) – the *Book of the Great Mystery* by Yang Xiong. The *Mystery* creates a system of graphs similar to the *Yijing* trigrams. In the case of the *Taixuan jing* each graph consists of four stacked lines and there are three possible forms for each of those lines. These graphs, called tetragrams, number eighty-one in total, which was considered a spiritually significant figure in China. Unlike the *Yijing* which was formed by centuries of accretion and commentary, the *Taixuan jing* is the work of one author and was completed in 2 CE. The Qing dynasty compilers of this treatise regarded Yang's references to cosmological forces in this work as authoritative. See Nylan (1994) in bibliography.

taiyi shu (太乙數) – the 'great one number' is one of the 'three systems' of traditional Chinese numerology. The Qing dynasty commentators on the numerological collection point out that Taiyi was one of the seven numerological schools listed in the the *Record of the Historian*. The *History of the Han Dynasty* says that the Yin Yang School possessed a book in thirty-two chapters named the *Taiyi yinyang*. The '*taiyi*' of that title was simply an alternate written form of the '*taiyi*' under discussion. Thus, this system of numerology must have existed before the Han dynasty. In the *Yiwei Qianzuodu* Zheng Xuan (鄭玄 127–200 CE) discusses 'Taiyi Traversing the Nine Palaces' method and interprets Taiyi as the god of the northern zodiacal zone). The *Taiyi jinjingshi jing* written by the Tang dynasty author Wang Ximing is based on the former work.

Tao Zongyi (陶宗儀 1329–1417 CE) – Ming dynasty scholar, author and calligrapher. He is credited with assigning the poetic descriptions of the stem/branch pairs' Five Processes associations.

tiangan (天干) – the Heavenly Stems. A set of ten Chinese characters normally conceived of as constituting a linear sequence. Their names are *jia* (甲), *yi* (乙), *bing* (丙), *ding* (丁), *wu* (戊), *ji* (己), *geng* (庚), *xin* (辛), *ren* (壬), and *gui* (癸). From very early times, these ten stems were used as designations for days and the complete set constituted the traditional ten-day Chinese 'week.' There were thus three weeks in a traditional Chinese lunar month, but, much as with the Western week, a month did not necessarily begin at the beginning of a ten-day week. The Five Processes and yin-yang correlations of the stems are as follows: *jia* (yang wood), *yi* (yin wood), *bing* (yang fire), *ding* (yin fire), *wu* (yang earth), *ji* (yin earth), *geng* (yang metal), *xin* (yin metal), *ren* (yang water), and *gui* (yin water). The Heavenly Stems were combined with the set of Twelve Earthly Branches to form the sexagenary stem-branch cycle.

Tongshu daquan (通書大全) – the *Complete Compendium of Almanacs*, date unknown.

Wang Bing (王冰 fl. mid-eighth century CE) – Tang dynasty scholar and minor court official most famous for his commentary on the *Huangdi suwen*. Wang Bing espoused Daoist practices.

Wei Boyang (魏伯陽 fl.147–167 CE) – Han dynasty practitioner of Daoist inner alchemy techniques who wrote the famous *Cantong qi* and the *Wuxing xianglei*.

wuxing (五行) – the 'Five Processes' or elemental cosmological forces. In the syncretic cosmological system which became orthodox during the Later Han dynasty (25–220 CE), the Five Processes were integrated with the complementary opposites *yang* and *yin* to provide a general theory of the universe. The full development of the Five Processes theory is attributed to the Confucian philosopher Dong Zhongshu (董仲舒 179–104 BCE). The individual processes in their generative/depleting order are: *mu* (木 wood), *huo* (火 fire), *tu* (土 earth), *jin* (金 metal), and *shui* (水 water). The conquering/controlling cycle orders them as: *mu* (木 wood), *tu* (土 earth), *shui* (水 water), *huo* (火 fire), and *jin* (金 metal).

Xici zhuan (繫辭) – the 'Appended Verbalizations' which comprise the fifth and sixth 'wings' or commentaries on the Book of Changes (*Yijing*). These date to the third century BCE.

Xieji bianfang shu (協紀辨方書 or 欽定協紀辨方書) – the '*Imperially Authorized Treatise on Harmonizing Times and Distinguishing Directions*' i.e. the present treatise; compiled by Yunlu (允祿1695–1767 CE), Mei Juecheng (梅毅成 1681–1763 CE), and He Guozong (何國宗 d.1766 CE). See Yunlu (1741) in bibliography.

xingli (星曆) – the 'astral calendar' being one of the most important tools employed by Chinese astrologers and *feng shui* experts. The mythical origins of this branch of Chinese knowledge are often explained by reference to a passage from the calendrical section of the *Record of the Historian* (*Shiji*), which says, 'The Yellow Emperor investigated and fixed the astral calendar.' A commentary on this passage further explains, 'To assess the sun, moon, and stars, the Yellow Emperor employed, respectively, Xi and He, Chang Yi, and Yu. He ordered Ling Guan to create the Pitch Pipes, Da Nao to make the sexagenary cycle, and Li Shou to perform mathematical calculations. Finally, he had Rong Cheng synthesize these six arts and from them to harmonize the calendar.' These all being among the emperor's most renowned officials, we see how important calendrical regulation was to ancient Chinese governance.

Xingli kaoyuan (星歷考原) – the '*Study of Calendrics*' commissioned by the Qing Emperor Kangxi in 1682 CE and completed in 1713 CE. The present treatise was meant to correct the mistakes of, expand upon, and replace the *Xingli kaoyuan*. See Li Guangdi (1713) in bibliography.

xingsha (星煞) – the term literally means stars and killing forces, but is also used as an abbreviation for the term *tianxing disha* (天星地煞) or celestial stars and terrestrial demons. In the latter case the term indicates all of the good and evil forces that form the subject matter of *feng shui* and Chinese astrology. As such the term indicates good and bad stars (times) as well as good and bad earthly positions.

xuanze jia (選擇家) – the 'selection school' also commonly known as the 'day selection' school. During the Qing dynasty this school was grouped together with the 'hidden stem-*Jia*' and the 'six stem-*Ren*' schools under the general category of 'Yin Yang School.' Unlike the other two schools mentioned here, the selection school was not defined by a specific numerological technique, nor did it have a definitive written text and thus it is difficult to identify.

Xuanze tongshu (選擇通書) – the *Almanac for Selections* printed in 1683 CE; a work commissioned by the Qing Emperor Kangxi to aid officials in the Board of Rituals with the task of selecting auspicious days.

yang (陽) – the celestial/male element in the complementary pair of opposites, yin and yang, which comprise the most basic cosmological forces in Chinese philosophy.

Yang Xiong (揚雄 53 BCE–18 CE) – author of the *Taixuan jing*; see that entry.

Yang Yunsong (楊筠松 ninth century CE) – renowned *feng shui* master and author of the *Qingnang aoyu*; see that entry.

Ye Tai (葉泰 also 葉九升先生) – Qing dynasty author of the *Luojing zhinan bowu ji.*

Yijing (易經) – the *Book of Changes* also known as the *Changes of the Zhou* (*Zhou yi*). A book of oracles with appended philosophical commentaries which had an enormous influence not only on Confucian, but also Daoist and Chinese Buddhist thought.

Yixing (一行禪師 683–727 CE) – a famous Buddhist monk of the Tang dynasty who worked for the court to develop a new calendar based on Indian astronomical methods.

yin (陰) – the terrestrial/female element in the complementary pair of opposites, yin and yang, which comprise the most basic cosmological forces in Chinese philosophy.

younian biangua (遊年變卦) – the 'roaming year trigram transformations,' the 'Lesser Roaming Year' transformations are named in this order: *tanlang* (貪狼 the 'Voracious Wolf'); *jumen* (巨門 the 'Giant Gates'); *lucun* (祿存 the 'Prosperous Existence'); *wenqu* (文曲 the 'Lettered Composition'); *lianzhen* (廉貞 the 'Incorruptible'); *wuqu* (武曲 the 'Martial Composition'); *pojun* (破軍 the 'Destroyed Army'); *zuofu* (左輔 the 'Aide of the Left'); and *youbi* (右弼 the 'Assistant of the Right'). The order of the 'Greater Roaming Year' transformations is: *tanlang* (貪狼 the 'Voracious Wolf'); *lianzhen* (廉貞 the 'Incorruptible'); *wuqu* (武曲the 'Martial Composition'); *wenqu* (文曲 the 'Lettered Composition'); *lucun* (祿存 the 'Prosperous Existence'); *jumen* (巨門 the 'Giant Gates'); *pojun*

(破軍 the 'Destroyed Army'); and *fubi* (輔弼 the 'Aide and Assistant').

Yueling (月令) – the 'Monthly Ordinances' chapter of the *Book of Rites*, see *Liji*.

Zang shu (藏書) – the *Book of Burial* attributed to Guo Pu; the first treatise on the art of *yinzhai feng shui* or *feng shui* for burials.

Zhao Zai (趙載) – Jin dynasty commentator on Guo Pu's *Book of Burial* (*Zang shu*).

Zheng Xuan (鄭玄 127–200 CE) – a student of the famous Later Han Confucian scholar and commentator Ma Rong, Zheng was himself a prolific commentator on the classics and presaged Neo-Confucianism with his frequent speculations on metaphysical matters. He is cited in the present treatise for his comments on the *Yueling* chapter of the *Liji*.

Zhou li (周禮) – the *Rites of the Zhou* is a text on ritual dating from the third or second centuries BCE. A commentary on the original by Zheng Xuan (127–200 CE) is quoted by the Qing dynasty compilers of the treatise.

Zhouyi cantong qi – see *Cantong qi*

Zhu Xi (朱熹 1130–1200 CE) – the most important of the Song dynasty Neo-Confucian philosophers. His *Yixue qumeng* (*A Premier on Studying the Changes* circa 1186 CE) is quoted at the opening of this treatise. A commentary on that text, the *Qimeng fulun* (*Appendix on the Premier*) by Li Guangdi completed in 1715 CE is quoted by the compilers of the treatise.

Zuozhuan – see *Chunqiu*

Bibliography

Ames, Roger T and Henry Rosemont, Jr. (trans.) (1998). *The Analects of Confucius: a Philosophical Translation*. New York: Ballantine.

Ban Gu 班固 (1781). *Baihu tongyi* 白虎通義. *Siku quanshu* 四庫全書, folio 860 册, section *zi* no.10子部 十, miscellaneous schools no.2 雜家類二, miscellaneous examinations category 雜考之屬. Shanghai: Shanghai guji chuban she.

Cai Yong 蔡邕 (1781). *Duduan* 獨斷. *Siku quanshu* 四庫全書, folio 860 册, section *zi* no.10子部 十, miscellaneous schools no.2 雜家類二, miscellaneous examinations category 雜考之屬. Shanghai: Shanghai guji chuban she.

Chan, Wing-Tsit (1963). *A Source Book in Chinese Philosophy*. Princeton: Princeton University Press.

Chen Xuguo 陳戌國 (ed.) (1990). *Zhouyi* 周易 in *Sishu wujing* 四書五經 vol.1. Changsha: Yuelu shushe.

Chu Yong 儲泳. *Quyi shuo* 祛疑說. *Siku quanshu* 四庫全書, folio 865 册, section *zi* no.10子部 十, miscellaneous schools no.3 雜家類三, miscellaneous explanations category 雜說之屬. Shanghai: Shanghai guji chuban she.

Cleary, Thomas (trans.) (2001). *The Inner Teachings of Taoism by Chang Po-tuan (Zhang Boduan)*. Boston & London: Shambhala.

————(trans.) (1987). *The Buddhist I Ching (with commentary by Chih-hsu Ou-i)*. Boston & London: Shambhala.

Eliade, Mircea (1958). *The Sacred and the Profane*. Translated by Willard R Trask. San Diego, New York & London: Harcourt Brace Jovanovich.

Guo Pu 郭璞 (1781). *Zang shu* 藏書. *Siku quanshu* 四庫全書, folio 808 册, section *zi* no.7 子部七, numerological works no.3 術數類三, residential geomancy/funerary geomancy category 相宅相墓之屬. Shanghai: Shanghai guji chuban she.

Graham, A. C. (1989). *Disputers of the Tao*: *Philosophical Argument in Ancient China*. La Salle, Illinois: Open Court.

Ho, Peng Yoke (1985). *Li, Qi, and Shu*: *An Introduction to Science and Civilization in China*. Hong Kong: Hong Kong University Press.

Jing Fang 京房 (1781). *Jingshi yizhuan* 京氏易傳. *Siku quanshu* 四庫全書, folio 808 册, section *zi* no.7 子部七, numerological works no.4 術數類四, prognostication category 占卜之屬. Shanghai: Shanghai guji chuban she.

Kaltenmark, Max (1969). *Lao Tzu and Taoism*. Translated by Roger Greaves. Stanford, California: Stanford University Press.

Lai Wenjun 賴文俊 (1781). *Cuiguan pian* 催官篇. *Siku quanshu* 四庫全書, folio 808 册, section *zi* no.7 子部七, numerological works no.3 術數類三, residential geomancy/funerary geomancy category 相宅相墓之屬. Shanghai: Shanghai guji chuban she.

Lau, D C (trans.) (1979). *Confucius*: *the Analects*. London: Penguin.

Legge, James (trans.) (1885). *Li Chi* 禮記. In the Sacred Books of the East series, vols.27&28. Oxford: Clarendon.

———— (trans.) (1991a). *The Shoo King or Book of Historical Documents* 尚書. Taipei: SMC Publishing.

————(trans.) (1991b). *The Ch'un Ts'ew with the Tso Chuen* 春秋左傳. Taipei: SMC Publishing.

————(trans.) (1991c). *The She King* 詩經. Taipei: SMC Publishing.

Li Guangdi 李光地 (ed.) (1713). *Yuding Xingli kaoyuan* 御定星歷考原. *Siku quanshu* 四庫全書, folio 811 册, section *zi* no.7 子部七, numerological works no.6 術數類六, yin yang/five processes category 陰陽五行之屬. Shanghai: Shanghai guji chuban she.

Major, John S (trans.) (1993). *Heaven and Earth in Early Han Thought*: *Chapters Three, Four, and Five of the Huainanzi*. Albany: State University of New York Press.

Nivison, David S (1986). 'The Origin of the Chinese Lunar Lodge System.' Paper no.15 in *World Archaeoastronomy – Selected Papers from the 2nd Oxford International Conference on Archaeoastronomy Held at Merida, Yucatan, Mexico 13–17 January 1986*. Edited by A F Aveni. Cambridge: Cambridge University Press.

Nylan, Michael (trans.) (1994). *The Elemental Changes: The Ancient Chinese Companion to the I Ching (the Tai Hsuan Ching of Master Yang Hsiung)*. Albany: State University of New York Press.

Qinding Xieji bianfang shu 欽定協紀辨方書. See Yunlu (1741).

Shao Yong 邵雍 (1781). *Huangji jingshi shu* 皇極經世書. *Siku quanshu* 四庫全書, folio 808 冊, section *zi* no.7 子部七, numerological works no.1 術數類一, numerology category 數學之屬. Shanghai: Shanghai guji chuban she.

Sima Qian 司馬遷 (1997). *Shiji* 史記. Shanghai: Shanghai guji chuban she.

Skinner, Stephen (1982). *The Living Earth Manual of Feng-Shui: Chinese Geomancy*. Singapore: Graham Brash.

Smith, Richard J (1991). *Fortune-Tellers and Philosophers: Divination in Traditional Chinese Society*. Boulder: Westview Press.

————(1992). *Chinese Almanacs*. Hong Kong: Oxford University Press.

Tang Shan 唐山 (1967). *Tianwen xue taikong hangkong xue cidian* 天文學太空航空學辭典. Taibei: Guangwen shuju.

Twitchett, Denis; John K Fairbank and Michael Loewe (eds.) (1986). *The Cambridge History of China, Volume I: the Ch'in and Han Empires, 221 B.C. – A.D. 220*. Cambridge: University of Cambridge Press.

Wan Minying 萬民英 (circa 1550). *Sanming tonghui* 三命通會. *Siku quanshu* 四庫全書, folio 810 冊, section *zi* no.7 子部七, numerological works no.5 術數類五, fate books/prognostication books category 命書相書之屬. Shanghai: Shanghai guji chuban she.

Wang Kui 王逵 (1781). *Lihai ji* 蠡海集. *Siku quanshu* 四庫全書, folio 866 冊, section *zi* no.10子部 十, miscellaneous schools no.3 雜家類三, miscellaneous explanations category 雜說之屬. Shanghai: Shanghai guji chuban she.

Wilhelm, Richard (trans.) (1961). *I Ching, or Book of Changes* 易經. Translated by Cary F Baynes. Princeton: Princeton University Press.

Wilkins, W J (2003). Hindu Gods and Goddesses. Mineola, New York: Dover.

Xieji bianfang shu 欽定協紀辨方書. See Yunlu (1741).

Xingli kaoyuan 御定星歷考原. See Li Guangdi (1713).

Yang Xiong 揚雄 (1781). *Taixuan jing* 太玄經. *Siku quanshu* 四庫全書, folio 808 冊, section *zi* no.7 子部七, numerological works no.1 術數類一, numerology category 數學之屬. Shanghai: Shanghai guji chuban she.

Yang Yunsong (ninth cent.). *Qingnang aoyu* 青囊奧語 and *Hanlong jing* 撼龍經. *Siku quanshu* 四庫全書, folio 808 册, section *zi* no.7 子部七, numerological works no.3 術數類三, residential geomancy/funerary geomancy category 相宅相墓之屬. Shanghai: Shanghai guji chuban she.

Yijing 易經. For original Chinese text, see Chen Xuguo; for English translation see Wilhelm.

Yuding Xingli kaoyuan 御定星歷考原. See Li Guangdi (1713).

Yunlu 允祿, Mei Juecheng 梅𣏌成, He Guozong 何國宗 (eds.) (1741). *Qinding Xieji bianfang shu* 欽定協紀辨方書. *Siku quanshu* 四庫全書, folio 811 册, section *zi* no.7 子部七, numerological works no.6 術數類六, yin yang/five processes category 陰陽五行之屬. Shanghai: Shanghai guji chuban she.

Index